Professional Office Procedures is dedicated to my husband, Bill. His assistance, support, encouragement, dedication, and perseverance have made this fourth edition possible.

In addition, *Professional Office Procedures* is dedicated in memory of my mother, Libby, who believed in and encouraged this project.

Thank you for all of your help.

Professional Office Procedures

FOURT

Susan H. Cooperman
Montgomery College

Upper Saddle River, New Jersey 07458

Library of Congress Cataloging-in-Publication Data

Cooperman, Susan H., 1949-
Professional office procedures / Susan H. Cooperman. — 4th ed.
p. cm.
Includes index.
ISBN 0-13-118383-4
1. Office practice—Vocational guidance. I. Title.

HF5547.5.C66 2006
651'.023'73—dc22

2004061774

Director of Production and Manufacturing: Bruce Johnson
Editorial Assistant: Cyrenne Bolt de Freitas
Marketing Manager: Leigh Ann Sims
Managing Editor—Production: Mary Carnis
Manufacturing Buyer: Ilene Sanford
Production Liaison: Denise Brown
Full-Service Production and Composition: Ginny Schumacher/Carlisle Publishers Services
Design Director: Cheryl Asherman
Senior Design Coordinator/Cover Design: Christopher Weigand
Cover Printer: Phoenix Color
Printer/Binder: Command Web

Photo Credits: Photos used courtesy of William Cooperman: Figures 1-1, 1-2, 1-6, 1-7, 3-1, 3-2, 3-4, 3-5, 3-11, 3-12, 4-1, 4-5, 4-12, 5-1, 5-2, 5-3, 5-4, 5-5, 5-6, 5-7, 5-8, 5-9, 5-10, 6-1, 6-2, 6-3, 6-4, 6-7, 6-12, 6-13, 6-14, 7-3, 7-4, 7-5, 8-1, 8-2, 9-1, 10-1, 10-2, 10-3, 10-4, 10-5, 10-6, 10-8, 10-9, 11-6, 11-7, 12-2, 13-1; United States Postal Service: Figure 4-9; DHL Worldwide Express: Figure 4-10.

Pearson Education Ltd.
Pearson Education Singapore Pte, Ltd.
Pearson Education Canada, Ltd.
Pearson Education—Japan
Pearson Education Australia Pty. Limited
Pearson Education North Asia Ltd.
Pearson Educación de Mexico, S.A. de C.V.
Pearson Education Malaysia Pte. Ltd.

10 9 8 7 6 5 4 3 2 1
ISBN 0-13-118383-4

CONTENTS

PREFACE TO THE FOURTH EDITION

THE CHANGING OFFICE ENVIRONMENT

Professional Office Procedures will assist, inform, and train people for office careers. The present-day workplace has changed from the traditional suite of offices often found in large organizations to include many nontraditional sites, such as a room in a person's house converted into a home office, an at-home desk, or even the kitchen table. Mobile office workers rely on a notebook or handheld computer and a cell phone to conduct their business from a car, hotel room, airport, coffee shop, and so on. Regardless of the size of the organization, the type of business, or the location of the workplace, all employees from entry-level to management need to know office procedures, so they can function effectively in today's workplace.

The information contained in this book will be useful to students entering the world of business for the first time, as well as those workers currently employed in business-related vocations. This material will also be useful to individuals returning to work after a period of time at home attending to family responsibilities, and to persons who have made a career change. To survive in the current employment market, workers must have the skills to perform a wide variety of job functions. Office employees will find many practical procedures in this book to enhance their skills and assist in their career advancement.

THINK, WORK, AND PERFORM BY DOING

The purpose of the text is to train people to think, to work under stressful and difficult situations, and to perform office duties in a professional manner. The focus of the book is to prepare students for the *realistic* problems and situations they will encounter in a state-of-the-art office environment. Instead of just reading about a topic, students are directed to practice the skills and discuss the professional office procedures presented in this book. Each chapter contains a series of activities which allow the student to implement the material covered. For example, when discussing business travel, students are given projects requiring them to call or use the Internet to obtain information about airline schedules and prices; when planning a meeting, they must contact local restaurants and inquire about luncheon costs.

Shown below are sample activities from Chapters 1 and 10.

- Write a job description for the position you hope to obtain when you leave school. You may use the Internet for research for this activity.
- Visit two offices and prepare a written report describing the office layout, use of color, use of plants, sunlight, and placement of equipment. Be prepared to give an oral summary of your report to the class.

AN EMPHASIS ON HUMAN RELATIONS

Special emphasis is given in the book to the development of positive human relations skills. Being able to work as a cooperative member of a team, getting along well with co-workers and managers, and dealing with difficult clients are all vital to a successful career. Each chapter contains a Human Relations Skills Development section and a Situations section. In these sections, the student is encouraged to analyze problem situations that occur in the workplace and develop appropriate solutions. The problems are typical situations that occur in an office and often do not have right or wrong answers.

The following is a sample Human Relations activity:

Functioning as a Member of a Team

Working as a member of a team requires that all members be able to work together even though they have different viewpoints. Learning to respect the thoughts of others and to listen to the views of others encourages a good working relationship. Completing your part of a project by the due date is a team requirement. One member of the team who does not complete an assignment on time may hamper the progress of other members of the team.

- What would you do if a member of your team did not complete an assigned project on time?
- What would you do if a member of your team took credit for an idea that you developed?
- What would you do if two members of your team had an argument and refused to work on a project?
- What would you do if a member of your team always needed extra help to complete projects?

New Technology Innovations and Updates in This Edition

This fourth edition of *Professional Office Procedures* has been updated to reflect the technology-driven innovations in today's office environment. In addition to completely revising the sections on computers and telecommunications, this *fourth edition* integrates computers, the Internet, and other office technologies into every aspect of basic office procedures that are essential to success in the business world. Each chapter contains information, activities, and projects which direct the student to use the Internet for information and research.

Professional Office Procedures, fourth edition, discusses such important topics as seeking employment, oral and written communications, working with a supervisor, office security, business etiquette, time management, meeting planning, office design, making presentations, stress management, and telecommunications.

New updates include the following:

All chapters contain new marginal Hints, which call out the most relevant tips, hints, and definitions, to the students.

Chapter 1—The Successful Employee

The chapter updates the impact technology has on the office employee and includes expanded discussions of computerized calendars and telecommuting.

Chapter 2—The Written Word

The use of email has been moved to this chapter and updated. The section on preparing reports has been expanded with additional information on doing Internet research.

Chapter 3—Workplace Telecommunications

This chapter has been completely revised, with information on relevant Internet sites added throughout the chapter. New topics covered include VoIP (Voice over IP—Internet Protocol) telephones, digital voice recorders, and the use of wireless telecommunications. The discussions of audio and video teleconferencing, cell phones, satellite telephones, and paging equipment have also been updated or expanded.

Chapter 4—Processing the Mail

The discussions of mail and package delivery available from the United States Postal Service and private carriers have been updated and expanded. A new chart clearly displays the class of mail and special services available from the USPS. Appropriate Internet sites are provided for each organization or service discussed. The use of fax machines has been moved to the chapter.

Chapter 5—Computers in the Office

This chapter has been completely updated to reflect current technologies, including new sections on Flash Memory, Wireless Technology, Firewall Software, and Instant Messaging. A section provides an overview of computer software commonly used in the office, including software for word processing, desktop publishing, database management, spreadsheets, presentation software, clip art and drawing, computer-assisted-design, scanning, project management, Internet browsers, web development, anti-virus, firewall, email, and instant messaging.

Chapter 6—Information and Records Management: Filing

The use of technology in records management has been strengthened.

Chapter 7—Meetings and Conferences

The use of technology in the planning for meetings has been expanded, including new sections on meetings conducted over the Internet.

Chapter 8—Business Travel

The chapter has been completely updated to reflect current travel practices with an emphasis on airline travel, including new sections on current security procedures and the use of electronic tickets. The use of the Internet is stressed in all aspects of travel planning and sample Internet sites are provided for each service discussed. A new section discusses mobile communications and other technologies available so a traveler can access the Internet or remain in contact with the office.

Chapter 9—Terminology of Business and E-Commerce

The chapter stresses the impact of the Internet on the emergence of e-commerce and e-government, and it includes numerous sample web sites to assist students.

Chapter 10—The Office Environment and Design

Sections have been expanded to include discussions of security issues, including personal safety as well as file and computer security.

Chapter 11—Seeking Employment

The chapter has been updated and expanded to stress the use of the Internet in seeking employment. Sample employment related web sites are provided as additional resource material.

Chapter 12—Career Advancement

Expanded sections on management and supervisory skills, which help students advance from entry-level positions to supervisory positions, is provided throughout the chapter. Information is included on obtaining MS Office Specialist and IAAP certification.

Chapter 13—Tips of the Trade

Updates to the last chapter, Tips of the Trade, include office attire, humor in the workplace, company policy on personal use, charitable activities, business lunches, accessing personal information, sharing ideas, buddy system, business acronyms, stress management, business etiquette, and working with foreign cultures.

Variety of End of Chapter Activities Provide Reinforcement

Each chapter includes the following seven assignment areas: Chapter Review, Activities, Projects, Human Relations Skill Development, Situations, Punctuation Review, and CD Assignments. In addition, following Chapter 13 is a new Software Application unit.

- The Chapter Review reinforces the topics discussed in each chapter with questions from the chapter.
- The Activities reinforce the topics discussed. Many activities require personal analysis and research skills. The student is often instructed to talk with someone in their chosen field to learn firsthand their experiences.
- Each chapter has two Projects which require the student to use word processing software to keyboard typical office projects such as memos, letters, flyers, and so on. The student is encouraged to think and revise the documents as needed.
- The Human Relations Skill Development contains two activities which provide problems encountered in the workplace and asks the student to respond with an appropriate solution.
- The Situations provide several short workplace situations and asks the students to solve the problems. This activity strengthens the student's ability to function in a difficult workplace.
- The Punctuation Review contains 15 sentences for the student to punctuate. This activity reviews punctuation skills. A review of punctuation rules is found in the Appendix.
- The CD Assignments contain additional activities where the student must think, analyze, research, keyboard, and respond to typical office projects. Many of the activities require the student to use the Internet.
- The Software Application Unit provides jobs using word processing, spreadsheet, and database software, which are all frequently used in the workplace.

Text Support

Instructor's Resource materials are available online at *www.prenhall.com*. These materials include supplementary punctuation reviews and supplementary situations. Answers are provided for the Chapter Review, Activities, Projects, Human Relations Skills Development, Situations, Punctuation Review, CD Assignments, and Software Application Unit. In addition, a PowerPoint presentation can be downloaded from the instructor web site and is available for each chapter.

A free student Companion Website is available at *www.prenhall.com/cooperman*.

Acknowledgments

Special thanks to the reviewers of this text: Nelda Shelton of Tarrant County College, TX and Joyce Woodmansee of College of the Canyons, CA.

The Successful Employee

1

Objectives

After studying this chapter, you should be able to

1. List the personal traits of an office employee.
2. Understand how to improve listening skills.
3. List the duties of an office employee.
4. Understand concept of time management.
5. Understand how to schedule appointments.
6. Understand an organization chart.
7. Become an effective team player.
8. Apply leadership skills.
9. Understand brainstorming.
10. Understand alternative work schedules.

THE OFFICE EMPLOYEE

Technology in the Office

Today's office employee works in an environment shaped by technology. The modern workplace is centered on the use of computers, the Internet, and a variety of electronic equipment that were unavailable only a few years ago. The use of these technologies has modified and redesigned the nature of most office work.

The widespread use of technology has created an upheaval in the employees' duties and responsibilities and has transformed the worklife of the office staff. The basic office tasks of placing and answering telephone calls, keyboarding documents, greeting clients, arranging meetings, filing, and performing numerous other jobs are no longer solely the responsibility of the administrative assistant.

Today these office-sustaining duties are performed by all workers, regardless of their degree of responsibility, from an individual in an entry-level position to an employee at the management level. Therefore, knowledge of essential office procedures, which includes Internet skills, cannot be limited to a secretary, an administrative assistant, or an administrative aide. Employees at all levels must be technically skilled and socially competent. Knowing only the technical aspects of a job is insufficient; soft skills, such as how to work with others, are also important. In addition to being able to discuss and articulate office-related issues, employees must function as members of an office community which values cordial and effective social interaction.

> **HINT**
>
> Technology has revolutionized the traditional office and has transformed it into a computer-based administrative center, an "at-home office," or a traveling workplace.

As technology has changed, so has the appearance of the office. Almost anywhere you and your notebook computer and telephone go can become your office. The office has evolved from the traditional desk to a "car office," a "kitchen table office," a "hotel room office," even a "notebook computer while traveling office." The workplace is now a global technology driven environment where you will work with a diverse team of professionals.

In this book, *Professional Office Procedures,* you will learn more than just the basic office skills which are the foundation of all business-related jobs. Since you will work in a technologically driven workplace, office technology is stressed in every chapter and activity. In addition, the soft skills, the ability to work well with co-workers, supervisors, and clients, are emphasized throughout your learning experience. Your mastery of these three elements—office skills, the use of office technology, and the soft skills—will enable you to become a successful employee and advance in your profession.

Titles and Responsibilities

Many titles can be used to describe persons who work in an office. Some of these titles are administrative assistant, administrative aide, personal assistant, coordinator, office manager, office worker, executive assistant, and clerk. In the past, the term *secretary* described the office support staff individual with responsibility for shorthand and typing. As office jobs have become more complex, the responsibilities of the office support staff have also increased. Today's administrative assistant makes decisions, plans job tasks, and accepts responsibility in addition to performing many other job duties. For the purposes of this book, these titles will be used interchangeably to refer to office employees with a variety of skill levels.

The person who supervises the office employee can be identified by any of the following titles: manager, supervisor, executive, boss, principal, or office manager. These titles will be used interchangeably in this book.

Working as an office employee offers a wide range of job opportunities. For a person with skills, there are entry-level and advanced positions in accounting, merchandising, education, government, medicine, social services, law, technology, research, journalism, insurance, and many other fields. An entry-level position may eventually evolve into a professional or management position or to a new career in a related profession. An office

FIGURE 1-1 The office receptionist.

employee position can be an open door to the future with advancement to a higher-level position. With good skills and a professional attitude, you will be able to find a rewarding career.

Characteristics of an Excellent Office Employee

Your Abilities

As an office employee, you are hired for your ability to assist your supervisor. The greatest ability you have, and the one most often overlooked, is simply your ability to think. An employee who does not think, solve problems, or show initiative requires frequent supervision by the manager. Usually the employee who does not assist in solving office problems becomes part of the problem.

As a competent office employee, you should use initiative and accept responsibility. You were hired to assist in solving problems and to develop new and better ways to complete your work. Be sure you always meet deadlines and do not make excuses. Plan to complete projects early, in case there are last-minute problems. In summary, your goal should be to develop a reputation for dependability and reliability.

Working together with your supervisor is a major component of the office routine, so do not be afraid of your supervisor. It is difficult to work in an environment where fear is your constant companion. Fear is a psychological feeling that many employees will experience sometime during their career. Fear can inhibit your decision-making capability and can lessen your ability to show initiative. If you are fearful, you will not be able to produce the work you are capable of doing.

Employees fear being

- Foolish before their colleagues or supervisor
- Rejected
- Dominated by another employee
- Overlooked by management
- Surpassed by a younger employee
- Fired
- Criticized

Do not allow fear to control your life and become a barrier to your success. A successful employee realizes that people have fears but learns to control them. Remember, you were hired because you have the necessary skills to do the job.

Importance of Self-Esteem

Good self-esteem is extremely valuable. If you believe in yourself,

- You will be self-confident.
- You will have a greater opportunity to achieve success.
- You will be more enthusiastic about your career.
- Your colleagues will believe in you, too.
- You will have insights that will stimulate you into becoming a leader.
- You will be able to cope with the difficult situations you may find in the workplace.

Human Relations Skills

An essential skill for all employees, regardless of the level or type of position, is the ability to get along with others. Handling difficult human relations problems is an everyday occurrence in an office. As an office employee, you must learn to handle these problems

HINT

Good human relations skills are crucial in the workplace.

diplomatically. This does not mean agreeing with everything that others say to you and doing everything that others want you to do. Everyone should be treated with courtesy, respect, and dignity. Treat others as you want them to treat you. Listen to their views, express your views, and then, if necessary, work out a compromise. Mastery of human relations skills, which are often called people skills, soft skills, or interpersonal relations skills, is important to the success of any employee, but it is especially important for the office employee who interacts with management, colleagues, and clients. More employees are fired from their jobs because they cannot get along with members of the staff than because of lack of job skills. Employers say they can train employees to do the job, but the technical skills are not the only skills employers demand. A workplace where employees do not get along destroys productivity and office cohesiveness. In many cases, mastery of human relations skills is the key to being a success in the work environment. Since human relations skills are essential to a successful career, you will find two human relations exercises at the end of each chapter in this book.

Characteristics of a Successful Employee

All employees, regardless of the type of job they have, should possess basic analytical and communication skills. Although these skills may not be included in a job description, they are essential for a successful career.

Successful office employees must be able to

- Think
- Listen to and understand directions
- Handle office situations efficiently
- Handle a crisis in a logical manner
- Express themselves in a clear and concise manner

FIGURE 1-2 A professional employee at work.

Think before you speak. To communicate so others understand you, organize and plan what you are going to say. Obviously, you cannot plan every comment, but learn not to blurt out irrelevant remarks.

Throughout this book, you will be presented with suggestions and practices which will prepare you to handle the daily challenges you will encounter in the office. Mastering these skills will help you succeed in both business and personal situations.

The following list includes some of the essential characteristics of a successful office employee. Some of these skills can easily be learned in a classroom, while other traits are related to your attitude and personality. If you do not possess the characteristics of a successful office employee, you should work to improve your skills, attitude, or personality. Ask yourself if you currently meet all of these qualifications. If you do not, decide on a specific plan to develop them.

A good office employee

1. Is knowledgeable of office procedures
2. Projects a pleasing personality
3. Is dependable
4. Projects a positive attitude
5. Displays initiative
6. Demonstrates organizational skills
7. Is neat in appearance
8. Is loyal
9. Is sincere
10. Is courteous
11. Is reliable
12. Is honest
13. Is a team worker
14. Is a decision maker
15. Is committed to work
16. Believes in and has a good work ethic
17. Is flexible
18. Possesses a professional demeanor
19. Is interested in and curious about the office
20. Maintains confidences
21. Is punctual
22. Is responsible enough to notify the office when absent
23. Is tactful
24. Follows instructions
25. Asks for clarification of a project when necessary
26. Is confident about personal abilities
27. Is prepared mentally and physically for the job
28. Is self-reliant
29. Works independently
30. Has the ability to think
31. Has the ability to spell correctly
32. Possesses good computer skills
33. Possesses good keyboarding skills
34. Possesses good language arts skills

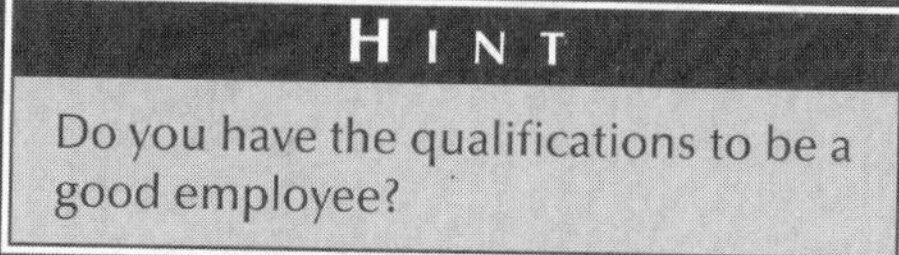

HINT
Do you have the qualifications to be a good employee?

Language arts skills, which include oral and written communications, are essential for all persons who wish to succeed in today's competitive workplace. Knowledge of grammar and punctuation is fundamental for written communications; therefore, a Punctuation Review is included at the end of each chapter. If you are uncertain about punctuation or grammar rules, read the rules found in the Appendix.

Regardless of the economic atmosphere, jobs are available because businesses need workers. The successful employee remembers that, without clients, he or she would not have a job. Therefore, successful employees present an attitude that clients do not interrupt the employee's daily tasks but provide the opportunity for a job.

Personal Traits to Avoid

Some people possess negative personal traits that interfere with job performance. The following list describes some negative behaviors that should be avoided in the office.

A poor employee

- Has a bossy manner
- Is a gossip
- Displays a quick temper
- Chews gum
- Has poor listening habits
- Cracks his or her knuckles
- Brags
- Uses slang
- Is too aggressive
- Is lazy

EFFECTIVE LISTENING

Listening is a skill that most people think they possess, but many people do not listen, comprehend, and remember what they are told. The skill of listening can be strengthened and improved. Listening skills are vital in the office because most office instructions are given orally. Excellent listening skills also help you remember more of what you hear, respond more accurately to what you hear, and understand more of what you hear. When listening, concentrate on what is being said and do not allow your mind to wander. Summarize the important details to yourself, so that you will remember them. You should, of course, feel free to request clarification of instructions if you do not understand them. You should also remember that people can become annoyed if they must continually repeat instructions because you were not paying attention.

Suggestions to help improve listening skills

- Be close enough to the person you are listening to so you can clearly hear what is being said.
- Concentrate on what is being said, and do not daydream. If your mind starts to wander, focus on what is being said.
- If music is played in the office, select relaxing background music. Do not play music that commands your attention.
- Pay attention to what is being said. Also, be aware of gestures, facial expressions, body language, and voice tone—they add to the message.
- Focus your eyes on the person talking to you.
- Do not allow the speaker's personal mannerisms to interfere with your concentration.
- Clarify and verify everything that you do not understand by asking questions.

- Be prepared when someone approaches you with instructions; have paper and pen ready to take notes.
- Do research and obtain background information about office projects, so instructions will be clearer and more meaningful to you.
- Identify the main ideas in the instructions given.
- Repeat the important points to yourself.
- Avoid the pitfalls of biases that cloud the message when listening. Some people have difficulty listening to
  members of the opposite sex
  members of another ethnic group
  persons older or younger than themselves

HINT
Do you have good listening skills?

Duties of an Office Employee

The Job Description

A job description is a list of all of the duties and responsibilities of a particular job. As a new employee, you should be given a copy of your job description. Study your job description carefully, so you will be familiar with your assigned duties and responsibilities. You do not want to be guilty of neglecting a job duty because you are unaware that it is your responsibility.

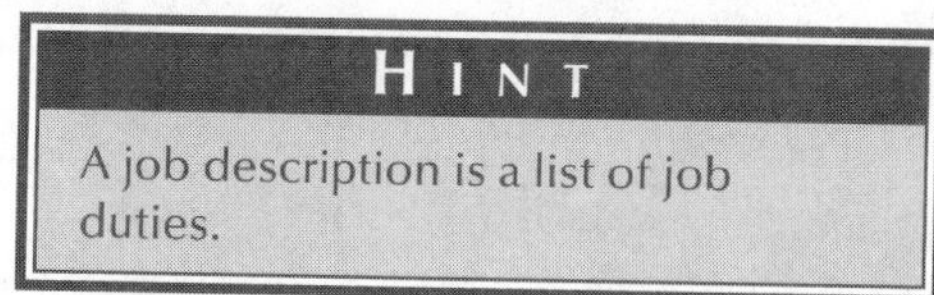

HINT
A job description is a list of job duties.

A typical job description

> The office employee will perform the following duties: greet clients, answer the telephone, prepare expense and travel reports, organize and supervise the daily operations of the office, order and maintain supplies, keyboard documents, write reports, research projects, serve as a member of a team, use the Internet as a resource, and perform additional duties as deemed appropriate by the supervisor.

Most job descriptions end with a phrase such as "additional duties as deemed appropriate by the supervisor." These additional duties can be new and exciting projects, but they may also include making coffee or running personal errands for your supervisor. As the duties of an office employee have changed in the last several years, some office employees have become uncomfortable completing jobs that they feel are personal rather than professional. The decision to complete tasks of a personal nature will be your own. You should base that decision on your work environment. For example, in some offices, coffee making is shared by all employees. If your supervisor is flexible about how you perform your job duties, you should be flexible about taking on additional tasks that you consider a personal chore rather than a professional duty.

The following are typical administrative assistant duties often found in job descriptions. The type of job and company will determine your exact responsibilities.

Typical administrative duties

- Keyboarding reports, letters, and memos
- Writing reports, letters, and memos
- Answering the telephone
- Screening telephone calls and visitors
- Greeting visitors
- Sorting and routing the mail
- Sending and receiving email
- Sending and receiving fax messages
- Maintaining time logs for completion of jobs

- Maintaining employee attendance records
- Preparing expense reports
- Maintaining and scheduling appointments
- Guiding co-workers
- Ordering supplies and equipment
- Calling vendors for equipment repairs
- Making travel arrangements
- Arranging meetings
- Photocopying
- Filing records manually and/or electronically
- Working as a team player with other members of the staff
- Prioritizing work assignments
- Solving office problems
- Using online computer services
- Researching on the Internet
- Using computer application packages to create and revise word processing, spreadsheet, desktop publishing, and database management documents
- Completing other jobs that are necessary for the efficient running of the office

Appointments

As an office employee, one of your responsibilities may be to schedule appointments for your supervisor. Know your manager's preferences concerning days and times for appointments, because certain days or times may not be convenient. For example, the office may have a staff meeting every Monday morning and a top management meeting on Friday afternoon. Frequently compare your appointment calendar with your supervisor's calendar and add appointments that the supervisor may have scheduled without your knowledge. (Even if it is not your fault, it is embarrassing for you to schedule an appointment at a time when the supervisor already has an appointment scheduled.)

Consider the following when making appointments:

1. The name of the visitor (always verify the spelling and pronunciation of the visitor's name; if the pronunciation is difficult or unusual, write a note to yourself with the phonetic spelling of the name)
2. The name of the company where the visitor is employed
3. The reason for the appointment
4. When the visitor wants the appointment and the amount of time that will be needed
5. The visitor's office and cell phone numbers in case the appointment must be canceled
6. The visitor's email address
7. Specific meeting location information when the meeting is not held in the employer's office

Know in advance your employer's policy about scheduling appointments. Know who will be seen and who will not be seen. Diplomacy will be required if you are not allowed to schedule an appointment. For example, your supervisor may not be interested in seeing a particular sales representative who is very persistent about making an appointment.

Computerized Calendars

A calendar is an item that all office workers should use to schedule appointments, organize work, and remember meetings. Prior to the introduction of computers, the traditional office desk calendar was the size of a book and usually was kept open on the top of a desk for quick

Monday, September 1		
	Name	Telephone No.
9:00		
9:30		
10:00		
10:30		
11:00		
11:30		
12:00		
12:30		
1:00		
1:30		
2:00		
2:30		
3:00		
3:30		
4:00		
4:30		

FIGURE 1-3 An appointment calendar.

access. Numerous styles of desk calendars are still available, many of which are designed also to aid in organizing work through the use of to-do lists and sections for notes. Today's technology-driven workers use computerized calendars to organize their personal and professional lives. In many offices, computer calendars have replaced desk calendars.

One advantage of using a computer calendar is its ability to track the schedules of many people. Staff in an office sharing a computer network can share a calendar, thereby making meeting planning simpler. The assistant may have access to the supervisor's calendar to make appointments. Scheduling software can display the calendars of several employees, so time conflicts and open times can easily be identified. Using a shared calendar can eliminate the need to call and recheck the time availability of each person, thus simplifying the process of scheduling a meeting. In addition, computer calendars can easily be revised, printed, and set to give an audio reminder of an appointment. Some computer calendar programs can be stored on the Internet for use by workers in different cities who must have access to the same calendar or by employees who frequently travel. With an Internet-based calendar, they can schedule meetings or check their calendar from any location with access to the Internet.

Computer calendars may be located on the desktop computer or in handheld computers referred to as Personal Information Managers (PIMs) or Personal Digital Assistants (PDAs). Handhelds are very small and can be carried in a pocket or purse, so appointments and notes can be entered at any time. The handheld devices and desktop computer can share the same calendar file, which promotes efficiency. It is important to synchronize the schedule in the handheld with the desktop computer calendar. Some handhelds can be linked with the office computer for synchronizing a schedule by using wireless technology or via a telephone connection. It is often the administrative assistant's responsibility to verify that the supervisor's schedule is kept up-to-date and to coordinate appointments made by phone, computer, and handheld devices. Additional information on handheld calendars is in Chapter 5, Computers in the Office, in the section Handheld Computers, Electronic Organizers, Personal Digital Assistants (PDAs), and Personal Information Managers (PIMs).

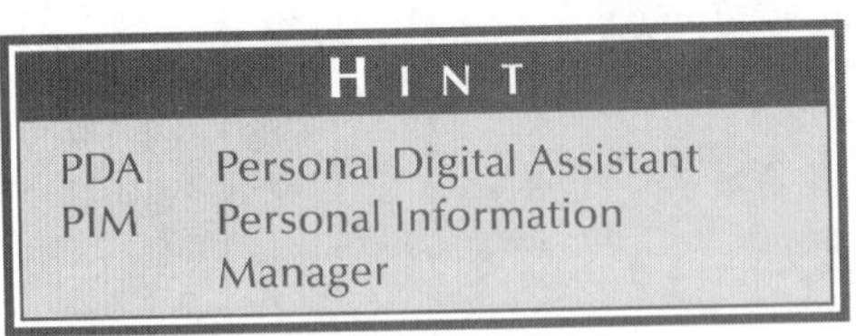

Regardless of the type of calendar system, use your calendar as an organizational and planning device to manage your day. Enter information on the calendar regarding office meetings, vacations for yourself and other employees, deadlines for projects, and where a traveling employee is going to be on a specific date.

Tickler System

A tickler system is a reminder system for due dates and can be set up on a daily desk calendar, computer calendar, handheld computer, large wall planning calendar, or 3" × 5" cards indicating due dates of items. Software tickler systems bring up reminders automatically at the beginning of the day and can easily be modified as dates and events change. If you are using a computer calendar, a tickler system can be included in your calendar, or a separate calendar can be created for the tickler system. If a card box system is used, the card box contains a separate guide for each day of the month. A 3" × 5" card with a description of the project and the due date is placed behind the appropriate guide. For example, a payroll reminder card is placed each month behind the date the payroll is prepared, not the date the payroll is due. A card may be used once or many times.

Visitors

Remembering names and faces is an important skill for office employees. Some people have the gift of being able to easily remember faces and names. If you do not possess this skill, make notes to help yourself remember. Think of ways to associate a person's name and face with something you will remember. It may be helpful to set up a 3" × 5" card file or a computer notepad system with information about your clients. Clients like to feel they are important to the company, so it is good business policy to address them by name.

All visitors should be greeted in a pleasant and professional manner. Invite the visitor to be seated. If a visitor must wait for your employer, offer a soft drink or coffee if your company has these items available for guests. Be pleasant but continue with your work.

Learn your supervisor's preferences concerning visitors who arrive without an appointment. Will your employer see clients, co-workers, friends, or family members if they stop by the office?

Before a visitor is ushered into your employer's office, notify the employer that the visitor has arrived. This can be done by calling on the telephone, taking a note to the employer, or walking into the employer's office and announcing the visitor. Always close the employer's door when you go into the office to deliver your message, so your conversation will be private.

Interrupting your supervisor during an appointment requires diplomacy. Sometimes you may be required to remind a supervisor that there is another appointment waiting or that the supervisor must leave for a meeting. You should be aware of your supervisor's policy regarding interruptions. The manager's personal preference will determine how you handle each situation. Interruptions can be handled by calling the employer on the telephone, delivering a note to the supervisor during the meeting, or walking in and speaking with the employer. Sometimes your employer will ask that you interrupt an appointment at a set time as a way of ending an appointment.

Offices often maintain a visitors log for security purposes or to confirm that a client visited on a specific date and time.

Date	Visitor	Company	Reason for Visit
4/5/XX	Joe Silver	Cakes, Inc.	Discuss June picnic
4/7/XX	Bill O'Dell	S & R Limited	Review project
4/8/XX	Penelope Patterson	Gallery Print Shop	Discuss brochure

FIGURE 1-4 A visitors log.

Chronological File

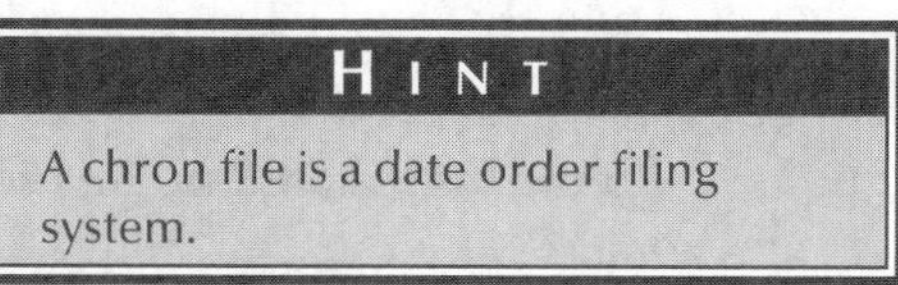

Some offices maintain a chronological file, often called a chron file, which is a date order filing system that contains a copy of everything that has been mailed. This document file is kept in date order, with the most recent date on top. The chronological file is used as a quick reference or review of a project and can be helpful if you do not remember how something was filed but know the approximate creation date.

Charts and Manuals

Organization Chart

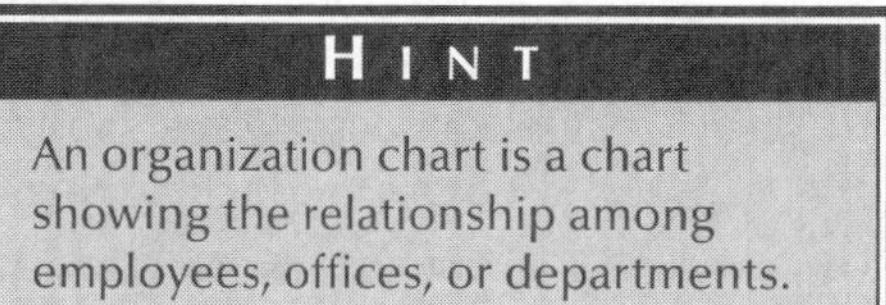

An office organization chart is a chart which shows the relationship among employees, offices, or departments. On your first day on a new job, you should request a copy of the company organization chart and study it carefully. It is important for you to be aware of the structure of the company, so you can understand the chain of command and the relationship among departments. The organization chart will allow you to learn important names and titles quickly and help you avoid mistakes and embarrassment.

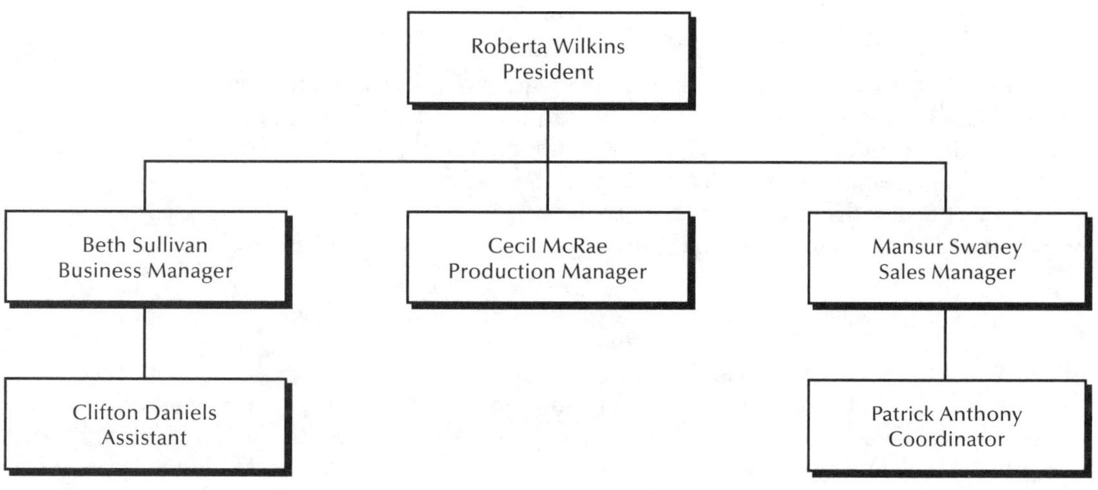

FIGURE 1-5 An organization chart.

Policy and Procedures Manuals and Desk Manuals

When you begin your new job, you may be presented with a company policy and procedures manual or with a desk manual. The policy and procedures manual should inform new employees of company policies, goals, leave policies, health benefits, and grievance procedures. It may also contain company rules and standard company procedures. The examples and explanations found in a policy and procedures manual will help you understand your job and make your work much easier.

A desk manual usually contains information specific to your job or department. It may include examples of forms regularly used in your office, with an explanation of how to complete them; an organization chart of the company; information about the work of your office; phone numbers often used by your office; and information regarding your business. You should frequently consult the desk manual, so you will become familiar with the operation of the office. If you are not presented with a desk manual, immediately begin to compile your own.

Items that should be included in a desk manual

1. Location of company facilities
2. Organization chart
3. Procedures for operating the company telephone system
4. Email and voice mail instructions
5. Letter and memorandum styles
6. Samples of form letters
7. Daily routines
8. Due dates of routine matters
9. Payroll procedures
10. Vendor Web site addresses
11. Important email addresses, such as those of clients, business associates, and relevant government agencies
12. Procedures for handling the mail
13. Additional information to run the office efficiently

Organization and Time Management

Peak Time

Do you have a particular time of day when you are more alert and able to solve difficult problems? Some people have more energy and do their best work early in the morning, while other people are most productive in the afternoon. Your peak time is when you are most productive; therefore, use your peak time to your best advantage. Whenever possible, plan your work so you do the difficult jobs which require problem-solving skills during your peak time and the routine jobs, such as filing, during your nonpeak, or low, times.

Time Management

In an office, work never ends and employees are time-starved. Most office jobs have a continuous flow of work—there will always be another project once the current activity is complete. For that reason, it is important to manage your time carefully, so you can work with maximum efficiency and productivity. Learn to juggle your regular job responsibilities while completing major projects. Set realistic time lines and build in additional time, so you can respond to unexpected delays.

Do not think that your office life is going to be calm—everything will happen at once. It is important to remain flexible to meet the unexpected tasks and crises that interrupt your daily routine.

Managing your time

1. The first step is to plan. Organize what needs to be done and estimate the time it will take to do those tasks. You should do your planning at least once or twice each day. Although last-minute changes may alter your plans, you should prepare daily and weekly work schedules. You should also prepare a master one-month schedule, even if you do not always know in advance what all of the jobs will be.
2. Organize your desk. Place the most frequently used items in easily accessible locations.
3. Do not allow others to control your time with interruptions or unnecessary talk.
4. Establish priorities for completing the most important work first. If you do not set priorities, you will have difficulty completing assignments and may disappoint your supervisor because important tasks are not completed on time.

Priorities

- Know your priorities.
- Your priority projects should be the same as your supervisor's priority projects.
- Create a to-do list based on priorities and follow it.
- Each day review your priorities and reassign a job to other staff, if necessary.
- Focus on each priority.

Avoid Wasting Valuable Office Time

It is very easy to waste time in an office. Your time is valuable to you and the company, so you must not allow others to squander your time. Ten minutes wasted three times a day becomes half an hour of misused time each day. By the end of a week, you have wasted two and a half hours. Think of what you could have accomplished in those two and a half hours.

To avoid wasting time in the office,

- Organize your desk and supplies.
- Delegate work to others.
- Keep telephone conversations to a minimum. Do not let yourself get stuck on a long, nonproductive telephone call.
- Process the daily mail efficiently and rapidly.
- Have the back of your chair face the door. This will discourage people from stopping by to chat.
- Have only one or two chairs in your office. This will discourage people from gathering in your office and wasting your time.
- Stand when people are in your office. (That might discourage them from staying too long!)
- Be concise and to the point when answering questions.
- Make appointments for people to meet with you and stick to your time schedule.
- Be friendly with co-workers but socialize with them in places other than at your desk. Then you have the option of walking away when you want to get back to work.
- If a colleague wants to chat too long, say, "I would love to continue our conversation, but I have to finish this project today."
- Socialize with your co-workers before or after your workday instead of during office hours.
- If you must attend meetings, diplomatically encourage leaders to adhere to the agenda.
- Use email, which is discussed in Chapter 2, to avoid playing telephone tag and to avoid lengthy telephone calls.
- Keep a clock in your office to remind yourself of the current time and the length of time you spend on a project.

FIGURE 1-6 An organized office.

- Accept the fact that it is impossible to read every email, newspaper, magazine, advertisement, memo, letter, and so on that comes across your desk. Prioritize. Decide what you should read, skim, or throw away.

Organize Your Desk

An organized desk is essential to avoid paper clutter and lost materials. Design your desk so you have an in-basket, an out-basket, a pending file, a bring-up file, and a signature file. An in-basket is for incoming materials. Your manager and other employees can leave work for you in the in-basket. Depending on the workload, it may be helpful to have one in-basket for yourself, one in-basket for your supervisor's work, and a separate basket for other staff members' materials. The out-basket is for documents that you have completed and may contain materials to be delivered to other staff members. A pending file is for items that you are processing and for which you need additional information. It may be helpful to have several pending files in a horizontal file holder on your desk. The bring-up file is used for items that you need to discuss with your manager. A signature file is where documents are placed until the supervisor has time to sign them. The use of a signature file eliminates interrupting the supervisor to sign a single document.

At the end of the day, clear your desk and place all working papers in a locked drawer designated for that purpose.

GROUP DYNAMICS

Team Players

Many projects are structured as group tasks in which team members share ideas and work together to achieve a common goal. Teams are formed to complete projects, create new ideas, reengineer company policies, and perform many other functions. Teams often have leaders or facilitators who provide information to help achieve the objectives, solve team problems, and keep the team members focused on the goals. Accordingly, an effective team understands

FIGURE 1-7 Team members working together on a project.

the importance of collaboration. Do you have a team player mentality? Your career and job opportunities may depend on your ability to work as a member of a team.

Team members may come from separate departments, with members at many levels of job responsibility. Therefore, an assistant in purchasing, a coordinator in benefits, and a director in finance may all work together as a team to complete a project.

Expect team members to disagree. Disagreement, when handled properly, can be a productive force, because disagreements provide an opportunity for team members to examine contrasting ideas and thoughts. Disagreement, however, should not develop into hostility, which divides team members. A divided team will not be successful, and the failure of a team often reflects on each of the team members.

The physical environment where a team works can contribute to the success of the project. Sunny and airy conference rooms with computer access, email, flipcharts, white boards, and snack areas with coffee, tea, fruit, sweet rolls, and so on all encourage employees to mingle and share ideas.

When teams are working on a project, they often share files. These files may be kept on a central computer server, which allows access for all team members. In addition, individual members may keep a copy on their personal computer. It is always important to verify dates when saving the shared files, thereby avoiding replacing the newer files with older versions. To avoid problems when using shared files, it is best if the team can use computer software designed for use by several people. This software, referred to as *teamware* or *collaborative software*, permits team interaction by allowing several members of the team to write alternative versions of paragraphs, with each shown in a different font, color, or style.

Suggestions for team members

- Keep project team members focused.
- If possible, select your own team members. Select persons whose ideas are compatible with yours and who will work well with you.
- The team should secure top management's agreement before beginning a project.
- One advantage of working in a team is to showcase your talents to upper management and members of other departments.
- By contributing your ideas at team meetings, you increase your visibility, which can have positive or negative results. You could risk alienating a high-level executive who does not agree with you.

- Before you join a team, research the project and the team's members. Is one colleague the dominant member of the team? Prior to the first meeting, become an expert on the project's background and focus.
- Be diplomatic when you express your opinions.
- When representing your team to other employees, always use the term *we,* not *I.*
- It is important for team members to have an understanding of the diversity of cultures among the teammates and the company's clients.

Brainstorming

Brainstorming is a technique used to develop ideas to help solve a problem. In brainstorming, people try to think of any possible solution to a specific problem. All ideas are recorded and no idea is dismissed or belittled, no matter how silly or outlandish it seems. Since one person's idea will stimulate ideas in others, brainstorming is frequently used by a project team. As one idea prompts another idea, several possible solutions usually develop. Those ideas are then explored and additional information may be gathered before a solution is reached.

Leadership Skills

Employees at all levels need to develop leadership skills, so they will be able to accept the responsibilities of influential roles throughout their career. Depending on the circumstances, an employee may function as a leader or as a team member. The leader is the person who guides organizations or projects through new and innovative enterprises. Also, the leader must motivate the other team members. An effective leader looks to the future and analyzes the current and long-term aspects of the project. In addition, it is important that a leader communicate effectively, because poor communications can doom any project. Since the leader cannot and should not complete the project alone, the leader must be able to delegate responsibilities to others. A leader must have organizational skills, because time is a precious quantity. In addition, the leader must accept the responsibility for the project while meeting the goals of the project. Leadership opportunities abound, so be prepared to accept the challenges.

Work Schedules and Locations

Today's office employee is no longer restricted to a work schedule with a fixed number of hours each day during a five-day week. Work schedules and places of employment have become flexible in response to the demands of modern businesses, employees, and society at large. Many employees have the opportunity to schedule their hours according to alternative work schedules, flextime, or job sharing. Some workers have the opportunity to change their workplace and work from home or alternative work sites via telecommuting.

Alternative Work Schedules

Alternative work schedules permit the employee to work other than the traditional five days a week. With an alternative work schedule, an employee may work four ten-hour days a week to satisfy a job requirement. Another example of an alternative work schedule is a two-week schedule of longer days with alternate Fridays or Mondays off. For example, if an employee works eighty hours over a two-week period, an alternate work schedule may require an employee to work nine-hour days for eight days and one day of eight hours. The employee would then have the tenth day off. In some businesses, all the employees work the same alternative work schedule; in others, the schedules are staggered, for example, so only half the employees are off on any Friday. Alternative work schedules allow flexibility for the employee, save commuting costs, and reduce traffic and air pollution, but the alternative work schedule may cause scheduling problems for the employer.

Flextime

Flextime allows the employees to decide on their own starting and ending times. Usually the company establishes a two- or three-hour time frame within which employees may select the start or end of their workday. With flextime, there are usually core hours when all employees must be present in the office, and all employees must work every day during the standard workweek. When flextime is an option, absenteeism and tardiness are usually reduced, production is increased, employee satisfaction is higher, and employee morale is improved. Flextime allows the employee greater flexibility in scheduling personal appointments and meeting personal needs, such as medical appointments, childcare, and elder care.

Job Sharing

As business has become more amenable to the needs of the employee, job sharing, which is one job shared by two persons, has become more popular. A shared job often has one employee working in the morning and the other in the afternoon. Some companies require overlap time, in which both employees are at work at the same time to discuss shared projects. In job sharing, both workers may receive full or partial benefits. The major advantage to the employee is having time to pursue personal interests and fulfill personal responsibilities, such as childcare or elder care. Companies benefit from job sharing by hiring qualified employees who might not otherwise be available. A downside of job sharing for employers is the increase in record keeping and related costs.

Telecommuting

Telecommuting, or teleworking, allows the employee to work from outside the office with the assistance of communications equipment. Some companies allow employees to work from home a few days a week, a few days a month, or while working on a special project. Another telecommuting option is the use of a satellite office, which is an office where employees can work several days a week in their own region rather than commuting across large metropolitan areas.

Working from a home or satellite office has become easier with the widespread availability of fax machines, computers, and access to the Internet. Telephone services using paging, voice mail, and conference calling allow more people to work from home. Computer groupware software allows employees at home to share email, calendars, and assignments. Also, companies now have computer systems that allow home workers to access company computer files in the same way they access information from the Internet. Voice communication is managed over the telephone, with a telephone at the employee's home office operating as an extension of the office telephone system.

Not all workers are productive while working from home. There may be too many distractions for some employees, while others are unhappy without the social contact an office environment brings to the workday. Employees who work off site may miss being able to bounce ideas off of colleagues and may feel out of the loop on ideas and discussions. In many organizations, telecommuting employees occasionally commute to the office for meetings and to maintain continuity on projects. In addition, it is important for telecommuters to establish frequent contact with the supervisor and co-workers to avoid the misconception that the telecommuter is relaxing at home. The nontelecommuter may be jealous of the telecommuter's apparent freedom.

In some companies, an employee's usual work location may be off site and the employee may not have a full-time company-provided office. To provide office support for these employees, some businesses provide temporary or flexible office space for a few hours or a full day on a call ahead and reserve basis. Another option is "teaming space," in which employees share an office on a scheduled or nonscheduled basis.

A telecommuting employee who works at home should create a work environment with a closed door to secure privacy and quiet. If you are visited by business associates while at home, dress in a professional manner and design an office that looks professional.

It is very easy to waste your business time while at home by allowing your personal life to interfere with your business life. If you work out of your home, establish regular office hours and adhere to them. Inform business associates and friends of your work hours. Since the telecommuting worker is close to the home refrigerator and television, snacking and watching TV may become a problem. To remain focused on your business, you should designate a specific area of your home as your office, and do not allow your family life to interfere with your work activities.

Telecommuting parents have many child-related issues to consider. One of the most important issues is for the at-home child to understand that the parent is working and is unavailable during working hours. To ease the transition from home to work, it may help to say good-bye to the child and close the office door. If possible, establish specific lunch and break times, so the child can look forward to seeing the parent. The parent and child will both benefit from a designated work environment.

To establish an at-home office, you will usually need office equipment, which can include a fax machine, a telephone answering machine, a CD burner, virus protection software, additional telephone lines (one for personal and one for the office telephone), and Internet access. If large files are downloaded, a high-speed computer modem line is very helpful. It is an advantage to configure the office email system to forward email automatically to your home computer. To maintain communications, it may help to have an instant messaging system which allows you, your supervisor, and colleagues to chat via computer in real time.

Employees who telecommute often sign an agreement with their company that describes the conditions under which the employee telecommutes and the responsibilities of the employer as well as the employee. The agreement may include information about the type of work to be done at home by the employee, the hours the employee must keep at the home office, whether the employer will provide a computer and other equipment, the extent of the employee's responsibility for maintaining the home office and equipment, whether the employee may care for children during work hours, and other conditions of the telecommuting arrangement. If you are considering a telecommuting arrangement, carefully review the telecommuting agreement with your employer, so you can fulfill your obligations.

Suggestions for telecommuting workers

- Set a daily work schedule and follow it.
- Designate a workspace.
- Communicate regularly with your supervisor.
- Communicate regularly with your colleagues.
- Organize yourself and decide in advance what materials you need to bring home.
- Make two copies of all computer files being transported.
- Email copies of all files to be used at home or to be returned to work.
- Do not allow personal activities to interfere with work time.

Many employers and employees feel that the advantages of telecommuting surpass the disadvantages. Benefits of telecommuting for the employee include less commuting time and lower commuting costs, more flexible job hours, lower expenses for an office wardrobe, and at-home time with young children or elderly parents. Telecommuting advantages for the employer include hiring of staff who may be unable to work in a traditional office setting and a reduction in expenses because company provided office space may not be required. Telecommuting also provides environmental and quality-of-life benefits to the entire community. Telecommuting decreases the number of automobile trips in a community, which results in improved air quality and reduced traffic congestion.

CONCLUSION

An office employee is a well-rounded individual who possesses the skills and personal traits to succeed in today's turbulent office environment. As you progress through this book, you will develop and expand the skills and traits required for you to reach your goal of being the best office employee you can possibly be.

CHAPTER REVIEW

1. List ten characteristics of a good office employee.
2. List five negative personal traits.
3. Why is listening important?
4. List four suggestions to improve your listening skills.
5. What is a job description?
6. What is a desk manual, and what should be included in it?
7. What is the purpose of an organization chart?
8. List three suggestions for team members as discussed in this chapter.
9. Describe brainstorming.
10. What are the employee advantages of telecommuting?

ACTIVITIES

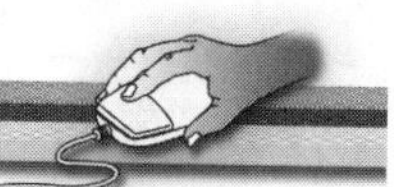

1. Contact five businesses and ask what job titles are used for support staff in each company.
2. Ask three assistants
   a. to name the three most important things they have learned since they have been employed.
   b. to describe three positive aspects and three negative aspects of their job.
   c. how often they have changed jobs.
   d. how they handle difficult situations on the job.

   (Ask any additional questions you feel important.)
3. Write a one-page paper explaining why you want to become an office employee. You may use the Internet for research for this activity.
4. Write a one-page paper explaining the duties of the job you expect to hold five years from now. You may use the Internet for research for this activity.
5. Introduce yourself to two new people this week. Think of a way to remember their names and how to recognize them.
6. Keep detailed records for one week showing how you spend your college-related time. Indicate assignments and deadlines for college projects. Did you meet the deadlines? How much time was spent on each project? Do you feel you used your time efficiently? Did someone interfere with your ability to use your time efficiently? How should you have handled that situation? What changes would you make in your time management techniques?

7. For three days, keep a list of the times when you are full of energy and the times when you are tired. Discover your peak time and learn how to plan important activities around that time.
8. Invite an office employee to speak with your class.
9. Write a two-paragraph report with many important facts. Read the report to the class, and ask questions about the report to determine the listening skill level of the class. You may use the Internet for research for this activity.
10. Read a detailed article to a partner. The listening partner should write a summary of the article. Compare the details in the article with those in the summary. (For additional listening practice, the partners can swap roles.)
11. Request copies of policy and procedures manuals or desk manuals from three companies and review them. Make lists of the contents of each manual and compare them. When contacting a company for information, identify yourself as a student in an office procedures course. Of course, confidential information may be blocked out by the employer.
12. Ask three companies for a job description for an entry-level support staff job. Review the job descriptions and determine whether you would qualify for the positions.
13. Write a job description for the position you hope to obtain when you leave school. You may use the Internet for research for this activity.

PROJECTS

Project 1

Key in the following document.

POLICY AND PROCEDURES MANUAL

L. Levy and Company

Revised June 1, XXXX
By Zev F. Carlton

Topics

- Company Locations
- Organization Chart
- Voice and Email Procedures
- Letter Styles
- Memorandum Styles
- Fax Cover Letter Styles
- Payroll Procedures
- Project Due Dates
- Purchasing Procedures

Project 2

Create the following notice. If possible, include an appropriate graphic.

Time Management Seminar

Monday

December 9

Administration Center, Room 247

9–4

Learn Time Management Techniques

Prepare for a New Job

To register, call Katie at 2477

HUMAN RELATIONS SKILL DEVELOPMENT

HR 1-1 Functioning as a Member of a Team

Working as a member of a team requires that all members be able to work together even though they have different viewpoints. Learning to respect the thoughts of others and to listen to the views of others encourages a good working relationship. Completing your part of a project by the due date is a team requirement. One member of the team who does not complete an assignment on time may hamper the progress of other members of the team.

- What would you do if a member of your team did not complete an assigned project on time?
- What would you do if a member of your team took credit for an idea that you developed?
- What would you do if two members of your team had an argument and refused to work on a project?
- What would you do if a member of your team always needed extra help to complete projects?

HR 1-2 Complaints

When employees gather at lunch, during breaks, or at staff meetings, the conversation can quickly turn into a "complaint session" about the job. While complaint sessions may allow the airing of personal feelings, they are rarely productive in solving job-related problems. Sometimes people try to outdo each other with complaints, which results in increasing employee aggravation and lowering morale. If lunch or office breaks have routinely become gripe sessions, find another way to spend your time. If staff meetings frequently become gripe sessions, try to focus the group on the objective of the meeting.

- You are a member of the support staff and a question and answer session at the end of a staff meeting turns into a gripe session. What would you do?
- You are a supervisor and a question and answer session at the end of a staff meeting turns into a gripe session. What would you do?
- What would you do if your supervisor heard you make negative comments about him or her?
- What would you do if you were the supervisor and you heard negative comments about yourself?

SITUATIONS

How would you handle each of the following situations?

- **S 1-1** You are a receptionist in an office where Phil and Bill both work. When you transfer a telephone call to either one of them, you always seem to transfer the call to the wrong person.
- **S 1-2** Last night your supervisor took a file home and forgot to return it today. You need the file today so that you can complete a report.
- **S 1-3** Jennie is frequently late when returning from lunch. She tells you that she must run errands at lunch and asks you to cover for her.

ROLE PLAYING

Act out the following situations to demonstrate how you would handle each.

1. Assume the role of a receptionist. Greet the person sitting next to you and ask if the person has an appointment.
2. Give a firm, businesslike handshake to the person sitting across from you.
3. Ms. Yee has just arrived for her 10:30 A.M. appointment. Your supervisor has been called out of the office on a personal emergency. You do not know when the supervisor will be back. Explain the situation to Ms. Yee.
4. Your supervisor told you that she does not want to talk to Mr. Bern, an important client. Mr. Bern called to talk to your supervisor at 10 A.M. At 1 P.M. he called again, and at 3 P.M. he called back a third time. What would you tell Mr. Bern each time?
5. Your manager had intended to return a telephone call from Mr. Morales, an important client, but neglected to do so and has left for a business trip. What do you say to Mr. Morales when he calls? Mr. Morales says it is urgent.
6. An irate person arrives at your office and insists upon seeing your employer, who is in a conference with an important client. What would you do?
7. You neglected to tell your supervisor that Mr. Colony called, and now he has called again and is upset.
8. Your supervisor has forgotten his lunch meeting with Ms. Stevens. Ms. Stevens has been waiting at the restaurant for an hour and now she is on the phone. Your supervisor has gone to lunch with someone else. What would you tell Ms. Stevens?

PUNCTUATION REVIEW

Punctuate each of the following sentences.

1. Jerry who was hired last year has received a promotion
2. Because the machine was broken the report was late
3. Our stockholders have earned large dividends and our brokers have been helpful
4. Therefore a conscious decision was made to build up the reserves in the bond fund mutual fund and trust fund so future generations of the family would be financially secure

5. I cannot work late tonight however I can work late tomorrow
6. Zero-coupon bonds pay interest upon maturity but stocks pay dividends quarterly
7. On Friday July 12 the commission intended to vote on the budget for the year but the attorney received a telephone call that called a halt to the vote
8. George Williams Jr an accountant teaches part time at the college
9. Industrial companies on the other hand benefit in the longer term from a dollar that has been stabilized
10. The mortgage rate has risen 1 percent a year but the selling price of most homes has risen 10 percent a year
11. The Dow Jones Industrial Average lost 25 points on Friday but gained 35 points today
12. DuPont General Motors and IBM are blue chip stocks but Florida Power and Lights price earning ratio was better
13. Paul said Bertha wrote the last report
14. Anna said the process of changing the passwords is very complicated
15. Employees from the center met August 23 September 28 and October 15

CD ASSIGNMENTS

CD Assignment 1-1

Open the file CD1-1_Appt on your Student CD and follow the instructions to complete the job. You will also need the file CD1-1_Cal, which is on your Student CD.

CD Assignment 1-2

Open the file CD1-2_Pri on your Student CD and follow the instructions to complete the job.

CD Assignment 1-3

Open the file CD1-3_PA on your Student CD and follow the instructions to complete the job.

The Written Word 2

Objectives

After studying this chapter, you should be able to

1. Compose email messages.
2. Prepare business letters.
3. Prepare reports.
4. Prepare memos.
5. Explain the purpose of a news release.
6. Explain the purpose of a newsletter.
7. Save email.
8. Save documents for placement on the Internet.
9. Save Web page information.

Basics

All businesses, nonprofit organizations, and government agencies rely on letters, reports, email, and other written communications. A written communication may be the only contact an individual or a company has with your office, and it will shape in a positive or negative way the reader's opinion of you and your company.

Depending on the situation, an office employee may be asked to keyboard, rewrite, or compose a variety of written communications, such as a letter, memorandum (memo), report, or news release. The assistant may also write or design a weekly, monthly, or quarterly newsletter describing the events, news, or announcements of the company. All written communications use the same writing techniques. The success of your writing will depend on your ability to make the reader understand your message. Face-to-face conversation allows you to use hand gestures and facial expressions to help convey your thoughts. In addition, your vocal inflections and tone of voice can change the meaning of a sentence and can help the listener understand what you are saying. When you create a document, however, you must use effective writing techniques, because you do not have the benefits of verbal and visual cues to help express your message.

Your writing should be

- Clear
- Concise
- Correct
- Complete
- Courteous
- Concrete
- Conversational

Writing suggestions

- Express thoughts clearly and concisely, so they will not be misinterpreted.
- Come to the point quickly.
- Use easy-to-understand language and verify your facts.
- A completed document should contain all of the information necessary for the reader to respond to it. However, the document should not contain unnecessary information which would overwhelm, confuse, or mislead the reader.
- If you are asking the reader to take some specific action, clearly state the action you are requesting.
- Write in a courteous, friendly, and conversational tone as though you were talking to the reader.
- If you are angry, do not allow your anger to influence your writing style. Since angry people often write in a sarcastic manner, avoid writing when you are upset. If you feel compelled to write while in an angry mood, write the letter, but do not mail it. After you have calmed down, reevaluate the letter and decide if it should be mailed.
- Since important business transactions are at stake, answer letters and memos within two days. Answer emails on the day of receipt or the next day.
- Ending a document with a "thank you" is determined by personal taste. Some people feel it is in bad taste to end a letter with a "thank you" for a future action, while others feel it is a positive reinforcement and encourages the requested action.

HINT
Is your writing clear and concise?

Correcting Common Writing Problems

Clarity

The primary goal of all writing is to clearly convey a message to the reader. Incorrectly placed words and phrases are a common cause of misunderstandings. How would you rewrite these sentences to make them clear?

> Driving a car, the office only was five minutes from the house.
> Office desks are on sale in every store with printer stands.
> Barry ate an ice cream cone walking down the street.

Misused pronouns are another source of misunderstandings. When using pronouns, make sure that the pronoun refers to the noun it is replacing—not another noun in the letter. A reference may have been obvious to the writer but confusing to the reader. The following are examples of confusing sentences:

> June told Kathy that she was late. (Who was late?)
> Linda and Peggy went shopping. She bought a computer. (Who bought the computer?)

Friendliness

In oral communication, the voice indicates the tone of the sentence. In written communication, the words alone must convey a friendly and helpful tone. Here are some examples of a friendly tone:

> We are very happy to be of service to you.
> We greatly appreciate the time you have devoted to our civic project.
> We are truly sorry that we will not be able to be with you to share your joy on the occasion of your daughter's wedding.

Interesting Language

Outdated Words or Phrases with Their Current Equivalents

The English language has changed over the years, and expressions that were correct many years ago are now considered stiff and formal. The following are outdated words or phrases with their current equivalents:

Words to Avoid	*Words to Use*
acknowledge receipt of	received
ascertain	find out
attached please find	enclosed is
enclosed herewith	enclosed is
enclosed please find	enclosed is
endeavor	try
investigate	check
obligation	responsibility
permit	let
peruse	review
terminate	end

Inappropriate or Redundant Words

Many phrases which are commonly used in oral communications are inappropriate in letters. The following is a list of phrases that are inappropriate or redundant and should be avoided in written business communications:

awfully good	close up
each and every	good as gold
seldom ever	upon receipt of
very complete	terribly good

Transitional Words

Transitional words carry the reader from one thought to the next. If transitional words are not used, the sentences do not flow and the letter sounds choppy. Varying the length of the sentences helps a letter read smoothly. The following is a list of transitional words that will help you improve your writing style:

accordingly	also	and
as	as a result	because
besides	briefly	consequently
finally	for example	furthermore
however	if	instead
in addition	in essence	meanwhile
moreover	next	obviously
on the contrary	since	so
therefore	thus	yet

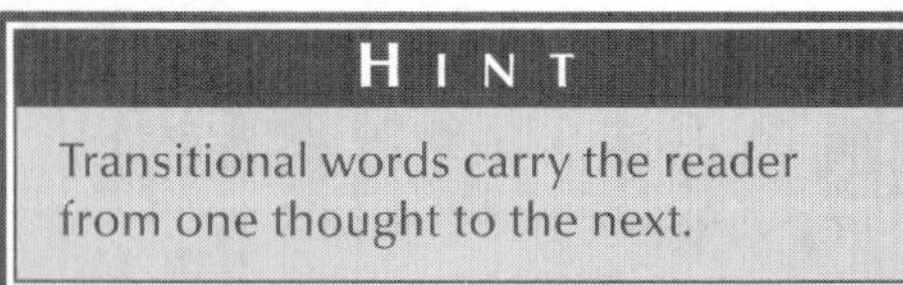
HINT
Transitional words carry the reader from one thought to the next.

Rewrite and improve the following paragraph by using transitional words:

We would like you to speak at the meeting. It will be January 17 at 8:00. The topic is "Foods in the Office." We hope you will come. Write me soon.

Vary Your Language

Repeating the same phrases or beginning every sentence with the same word is boring. People writing about themselves frequently begin sentences with the word *I*. However, constantly using *I* shows insensitivity to the reader, so avoid the *I* syndrome.

Use a variety of descriptive words to add interest to a letter, a memo, or an email. Every sentence should not contain the same adjectives and adverbs. Computer word processing software packages contain a thesaurus to help you select synonyms, which are words with similar meanings.

Gender Bias

HINT
Do not be guilty of gender bias.

Correspondence should be free of gender bias. If the gender of a person is not known, use nongender words instead of *her* or *him* to express general concepts.

If the gender of a person is unknown,

Do not say:	Send the material to him.
Say:	Send the material to the manager. (*Manager* does not imply a gender.)
Do not use the salutation:	Gentlemen
Use the salutation:	Ladies and Gentlemen or Dear Sir or Madam

Moving the Reader to Action

Moving the reader to action requires tact, so the reader is not alienated or offended. When people are told to do something, they often react in a negative way. Accordingly, people are more receptive to suggestions than to demands.

- Always write with the reader's point of view in mind, addressing the reader's concerns. A letter should be reader-oriented—emphasizing what is important to the reader.
- If a negative message must be delivered, accent the positive aspects of the situation. If you must deny a request, place the denial after an encouraging comment, and always end the letter on a positive note.
- Never write "you are wrong" or "you made a mistake." This may anger the reader. Instead, write that there is a problem or a mistake. If this approach is used, you are not placing blame for the error. Never imply that the reader is stupid.

Plain English

In the last several years, companies have adopted the policy of creating documents written in Plain English, which is a writing style that is direct and informative with tight sentence construction. Plain English creates a document that is easy to read and understand. In addition, it uses short sentences containing common, everyday words. Plain English uses the active voice, in which the subject of the sentence does the action, instead of the passive voice, in which the subject receives the action. Readers understand the active voice more quickly

Patrick Brothers Office Supplies
109 Spring Lane
Ft. Lauderdale, FL

June 30, XXXX

Dear Ms. Mendez:

We are very happy that you have enjoyed the service which we have provided you. As you know, our customers are very important to us.

We received your letter of June 12 and have carefully considered your request. Unfortunately, we cannot extend the payment date on your account. Our credit policy is that a minimum payment of only $10 must be made within thirty days of the statement closing date. The remaining balance may then be carried over until the next month. Once the outstanding balance is below your credit limit, you will be able to make additional charges.

We hope that you will resume your visits to our store so we can continue to serve you as we have for the last twenty years.

Sincerely,

L. P. Lewis

skc

FIGURE 2-1 A letter with a negative response placed between two positive remarks.

than the passive voice. Personal pronouns are used to address and inform the reader and create a bond between the writer and the reader.

Example of a sentence in active voice: The employee used the computer.
Example of a sentence in passive voice: The computer was used by the employee.

There are several Internet sites that describe how to write documents in Plain English. For more information on writing in Plain English, view the Internet site *www.plainlanguage.gov*.

Email

Electronic mail (email) is an electronic system for sending and receiving messages. Email is quick and easy to use and is essential in today's business environment. Using email, a business can send an electronic message and attach a report, graphic, picture, spreadsheet, and so on. Delivery is practically instantaneous and the cost does not depend on either the size of the document or the distance traveled. Some computer systems include an email video capability. With video messaging, audio and video files are sent with an email. Picture and sound quality depend on the equipment used.

Email will work between computers in the same office or between computers connected to the Internet located anywhere in the world. With an electronic mail system, the receiving computer will receive and automatically store a message. To send an email, the sender directs a message to the email address of the recipient. Each employee or computer has an assigned email address. (A typical email address is in the form *yourname@businessname.com*.) The message is sent over the Internet and stored in the receiving computer. When the recipient returns to the office, the computer's email software must be checked for messages. Typical email software packages used by many businesses include Outlook and Groupwise. The messages can be read on the computer screen, printed, saved, or forwarded to another mailbox. A major advantage of electronic mail is that recipients can quickly respond to a message and return an answer to the sender. The use of email can speed up business decisions, as the turnaround time for electronic mail messages can be a matter of minutes, while the same message sent by traditional mail could take days.

Because it is an easy and efficient method of communication, email is often used in offices to send short, informal messages. Email allows you to send a message to a person you do not know well and would be uncomfortable approaching as easily as sending a message to someone you know well. Furthermore, email provides a comfort level that may not be felt in a person-to-person telephone call.

To ensure that the email message remains confidential, each user can be assigned an individual password, which must be entered before the user can open his or her mailbox. When you use email, it is wise to change your password periodically to maintain security. Select a password that you can remember, but not a password that is easy for someone to guess. You should avoid using your name, birthday, address, and so on as passwords because they are easy to guess.

Email programs show a list of incoming messages. To read a message, select it. After reading the message, there are usually several options for further action—Reply, Forward, Save, Print, or Delete. The recipient may select one or more of the options. Email programs have a Reply command, which automatically addresses a return email to the person who sent it. Replies can be sent to one person or to an entire distribution list of all recipients of the email, by using the Reply All option. By using the Forward feature, you can send the email to additional persons who would be interested in the message.

Although there are Web sites that provide email addresses, there are few printed email directories. Consequently, you should make your email address readily available. Email addresses can be included on letterheads, placed on business cards, included in the body of a letter, and given verbally. You should create your own directory of business associates' email addresses, which can be kept in database software, organization software, calendar software contact lists, a 3″ × 5″ card file, and so on.

Using notebook computers, wireless handheld computers, or cell phones, employees often retrieve email messages while out of the office. Some computer software programs can convert email into spoken words, so users can dial in to their office computers and listen to audio versions of their email by telephone. When sending emails that will be received by wireless handheld computers, cell phones, or voice systems, the messages must be kept short, since these technologies are not designed to handle long documents.

The advent of email has promoted the electronic sharing of jokes, which can become overwhelming and time devouring. Save time by deleting jokes without reading them, but verify that you are actually deleting jokes, not important office communications.

Although employees think their email is private, it may not be. Companies have a legal right to monitor employee email to ensure that employees are using their time and company equipment appropriately. Learn your company's policy regarding use of company email and its policy on monitoring email. A supervisor who is reading the employee's email should be looking for violations of company policy, but some supervisors may be eager to satisfy their curiosity about the employee's personal business.

Email messages may contain links to Web pages where additional information on a subject is available. Links are created in an email message by keying in an Internet address. The recipient is able to click on the Internet address and immediately view the Web page.

Email Guidelines

- Always verify that you have correctly keyed an email address—even one incorrect letter could send the message to another person. If the message is received by the wrong person, it could be very embarrassing. Some companies use the first letter of a first name with the last name as the individual's email address; therefore, J. Rosen and L. Rosen could easily receive the other person's email if the address is incorrectly keyed.

- Use an appropriate subject line, because the decision to read or delete email is often based on the subject line.
- Do not use all capital letters when composing a message. The message reads as though you were shouting.
- Begin your email with a friendly comment. This sets a courteous tone for the email.
- To save time with email, create a template with frequently used responses that can be quickly pasted into the email.
- Although email may take less time to create than a mailed letter or memo because email does not contain all of the parts of a letter or memo, basic writing skills still apply.
- Compose complex email messages using your word processing software to take advantage of the Save, Edit, and other features. After the message is written, it can be copied into the email message or can be included as an attachment to the email.
- Never send a nasty email, because it may come back to haunt you. Remember that emails can be saved, printed, and forwarded to other people. Decide if your message should actually be sent.
- Respond quickly to email, generally within twenty-four hours.
- Some people spend a lot of time replying to emails to confirm their receipt of the original email. In order to save other people's time, some people end the original email with "no reply needed."
- Do not use the Reply All or Copy features unless the recipients actually benefit from the email. Workers frequently complain about the amount of unnecessary and redundant email received.
- Email can be sent to one person or to a distribution list, which is an efficient method of sending the same email message to several persons simultaneously.
- To avoid missing an important email message, check your email often.
- Use automatic replies when you are out of town. Most email software has an Automatic Reply feature, which you can use to notify the sender that you will be away for a period of time.
- Email can be sent at all hours. It does not interrupt as a telephone does. Therefore, sending communications to a person in a foreign country or to another time zone is not restricted by your local time.
- When sending email internationally or to individuals from other nations who live in this country, be aware of cultural differences. Do not use slang, because it may be misunderstood or may be considered a breach of etiquette. Do not send emails that may be misunderstood or offend persons of other cultures.
- Instead of sending a printed memo, it is now common to send an email message with a memo attachment.
- Email allows the sender to attach a file containing a letter, memo, report, graphic, or picture.
- If the computer is on, most email systems can be set to display a message or sound a beep, so the user will know that a message has been received. The user can be working with any software package, not only email, when the flash or beep is received.
- Do not open questionable emails. If you do not know the sender or if the subject line is strange, it could contain a virus.
- Software developers have created email tools that automatically respond to customer questions by selecting an appropriate response and then sending a return email. If desired, the response can automatically be routed to an employee for verification prior to sending the email.

- Software is available that will generate email based on Web transaction information. Companies use this type of email to market products and services to current or prospective clients. By personalizing email to target audiences, the customer response rate is increased.
- Under United States law (the Controlling the Assault of Non-Solicited Pornography and Marketing Act of 2003, also known as the CAN-SPAM Act of 2003), it is illegal to send commercial email (1) that uses a false address, header, or subject line to mislead the recipient regarding the subject of the email, (2) that does not provide the recipient with the opportunity to request not to receive future emails from the sender, or (3) that the recipient has indicated an objection to receiving.
- For security purposes, some offices use encryption software to protect its email. If your office computer offers encrypted email, use it when appropriate.
- Since words cannot convey hand gestures or facial expressions, symbols called emoticons are used to convey emotions. Emoticons are cute but should be used only sparingly in business communications.

Examples of emoticons

:)	smile
;)	wink
:-o	surprise
:-(	frown
<Grin>	grin
:-\	thinking

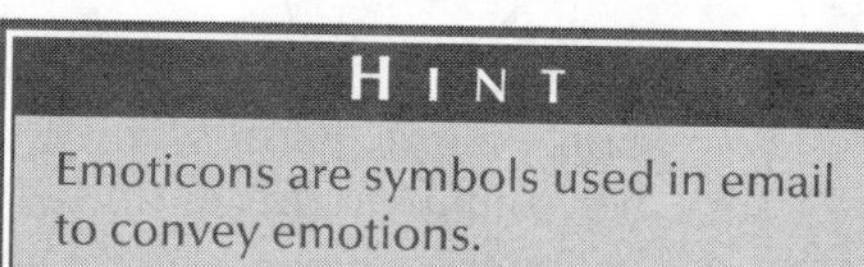

HINT
Emoticons are symbols used in email to convey emotions.

Situations That Should Not Be Communicated by Email

There are many times when it is better to talk with a person rather than send an email, because some messages are too personal or sensitive for email. There are often situations, such as during negotiations of contracts and discussions of personal issues, when the direct give-and-take of a voice conversation is vital. A conversation will also permit your listening to the other person's tone of voice, which can express his or her feelings. If it would be better not to have a written record of a communication, place a telephone call instead of sending an email.

LETTERS

Before you start writing a letter, define the letter's objective and prepare an informal outline. This outline will help to organize your thoughts, so the letter meets your objectives. An outline of the letter should consist of the following three main sections.

1. *Introduction:* This is a short paragraph explaining the purpose of the letter.
2. *Body:* The body includes all of the details necessary for the reader to understand the situation.
3. *Conclusion:* The conclusion is the closing paragraph of the letter. It should end the letter on a cordial note and may remind the reader to perform an action or contact the business for further information.

A letter should

- Be clear and easily understood
- Have an attractive visual appearance
- Contain no errors
- Be pleasant in tone

- Be truthful
- Be sincere
- Be concise but include sufficient information
- Contain no outdated or overused expressions
- Be well organized

All mailed letters require a correctly addressed envelope using the two-letter state abbreviations and ZIP Code, and they must be properly folded. Addressing envelopes and folding letters are discussed in Chapter 4, Processing the Mail.

Format

Today, many new office employees are knowledgeable of their business but are unaware of techniques and formats used in creating written business communications. Employees may prepare letters, memoranda, and reports in their own personal styles because they are unfamiliar with standard document formatting. As an office employee, it may be your responsibility to correct the formatting of documents so they follow accepted business practices.

Letterhead

Business letters are usually printed on letterhead stationery, which includes the organization's name, address, city, state, ZIP Code, telephone number, facsimile (fax) machine number, email address, and Web address. If plain paper is used, a return address must be keyboarded about 1.5 inches from the top of the letter. The return address includes the organization's name, address, city, state, and ZIP Code. Since your name is in the complimentary close at the bottom of the letter, the return address does not include your name.

Letter Margins

Standard paper is 8.5 inches wide by 11 inches long. Paper used for some legal documents is 8.5 inches wide by 14 inches long. Some firms have converted to paper sized in metric measurements, which is slightly smaller than the sizes mentioned.

A letter with equal margins on each side of the text creates an attractive presentation to a reader. The size of the margins you use in a letter will depend on the number of words in the letter. A person usually composes a letter starting with standard margins (1 or 1.25 inches on each side) and then adjusts the margins, depending on the number of words in the letter. If the number of words does not fill the page, you can easily use the word processing software to change the margins. Most word processing packages have a fit-to-page feature, which adjusts the text to the page. This feature is helpful if a document has only one line carried to another page. Another word processing software feature that is helpful in preparing a letter is the ability to count the number of words in the letter. By knowing the number of words in the letter, you can adjust the side margins to create an attractive letter.

The following scale shows appropriate margins based on words in the document:

Number of words	***Left and right margins***
0–100	2 inches
101–200	1 1/2 inches
201 and up	1 inch

Microsoft Word defaults margins to the following settings:

Left	1.25 inches
Right	1.25 inches
Top	1 inch
Bottom	1 inch

Templates

Word processing packages have made document creation easier by offering a letter template feature. The letter template feature guides the writer through the creation of the letter and automatically formats the letter to a specific style. Several templates may be available, providing styles intended to present a casual, formal, or professional appearance. After selecting a template, the user selects a letter part and keys in the letter-specific text. Word processing packages also include templates to assist the employee in preparing reports, memos, faxes, agendas, and other documents. Chapter 4, Processing the Mail, contains a discussion of faxes. While some offices use the word processing templates that are standard in the software, other offices use templates specifically created for their company.

Letter and Punctuation Styles

If the writer does not use a computer template, a letter style must be selected. The letter style defines the letter placement on the page. There are two common letter styles, block style and

THE MARKETPLACE INC.
467 Meritor Drive
Cleveland, OH 45678-0923

May 19, XXXX

Ms. Valerie Jefferson
Linder & Peterson Limited
8009 Union Road
Suite 200
Joplin, MO 64801-1265

Dear Ms. Jefferson

Subject: Software Demonstration

Our sales representative, Joe Goldstein, will be in Joplin in the middle of June to demonstrate to you our new computer software. As we discussed at the Computer Expo in Kansas City, we have several new software application packages that will simplify your office management problems. The packages range from $1,250 to $5,000 and the updated versions will be available by the end of the summer. As part of each package, we provide two days of training for your employees and reference materials. In addition, our company is committed to working with each client to fulfill his or her individual needs, and our staff is available 24/7 to serve you. Mr. Goldstein will call you next week and arrange a convenient time to meet with you. We would like the opportunity to show you how our products can alleviate your office management concerns.

It was a pleasure meeting you and your staff in Kansas City, and I hope to see you at the Dallas Computer Expo in September.

Very truly yours

Ted J. Nicholas
Marketing Manager

skr

FIGURE 2-2 A block letter with open punctuation.

THE MARKETPLACE INC.
467 Meritor Drive
Cleveland, OH 45678-0923

May 19, XXXX

Ms. Valerie Jefferson
Linder & Peterson Limited
8009 Union Road
Suite 200
Joplin, MO 64801-1265

Dear Ms. Jefferson:

Subject: Software Demonstration

Our sales representative, Joe Goldstein, will be in Joplin in the middle of June to demonstrate to you our new computer software. As we discussed at the Computer Expo in Kansas City, we have several new software application packages that will simplify your office management problems. The packages range from $1,250 to $5,000 and the updated versions will be available by the end of the summer. As part of each package, we provide two days of training for your employees and reference materials. In addition, our company is committed to working with each client to fulfill his or her individual needs, and our staff is available 24/7 to serve you. Mr. Goldstein will call you next week and arrange a convenient time to meet with you. We would like the opportunity to show you how our products can alleviate your office management concerns.

It was a pleasure meeting you and your staff in Kansas City, and I hope to see you at the Dallas Computer Expo in September.

Very truly yours,

Ted J. Nicholas
Marketing Manager

skr

c Desi Perez

P.S. I know our software package can solve your application problem.

FIGURE 2-3 A modified block letter with mixed punctuation

modified block style. In the block style letter, all parts of a letter begin at the left margin. In the modified block style, you can place paragraphs at the left margin or indent the paragraph 1/2 inch. In the modified block style letter, the date and closing begin at the center of the paper. Since most stationery is 8.5 inches wide, the center is at 4.25 inches. It may be necessary to reset a tab to center the date and closing.

> **HINT**
>
> In a block style letter, all parts of the letter begin at the left margin.
>
> In a modified block style letter, the date and closing begin at the center of the paper.

Letters written in either block style or modified block style may use open or mixed punctuation. The open punctuation style omits punctuation after the salutation and closing, while the mixed punctuation style includes a colon after the salutation and a comma after the closing. The use of open or mixed punctuation does not change the standard use of sentence punctuation.

Punctuation and language styles evolve in response to current usage. In written communications today, some writers use one space following a period at the end of a sentence, while other writers continue the traditional style of using two spaces following a period at the end of the sentence. People who use two spaces feel that two spaces separate the sentences visually and make the document easier to read.

HINT

Open punctuation omits punctuation after the salutation and closing.

Mixed punctuation places a colon after the salutation and a comma after the closing.

Parts of a Letter

Most of the work in writing a letter concentrates on the text of the introduction, body, and conclusion. The entire letter, however, actually includes several additional parts. Some of these parts are required in all letters, while others are used only when there is a special need for them. An office employee must be familiar with the proper placement of each of these parts.

The chart below indicates the required and optional parts of a letter. An explanation of each part follows the chart. Review the sample letter styles later in the chapter to see the placement of each part of the letter.

Parts of the Letter	Required	Optional
Return address		X
Date	X	
Special notation		X
Inside address	X	
Attention line		X
Salutation	X	
Subject line		X
Body	X	
Complimentary close	X	
Company name in closing		X
Writer's name	X	
Title of writer		X
Initials		X
Enclosure		X
Copy notation		X
Postscript		X

Return Address

If plain paper is used for the letter, a return address should be keyboarded as the first item on the page, approximately 1.5 inches from the top of the paper. For a short letter, the return address can be placed lower on the page to make the page appear almost centered from top to bottom. The return address includes the organization's name, street address, city, state, and ZIP Code.

Date

If plain paper is used for the letter, the date is placed on the line after the city, state, and ZIP Code of the return address. When using company preprinted letterhead stationery, place the date a couple of lines below the letterhead. Depending on the length of the letter, the date may be moved down a couple of lines on the paper to make the letter appear more attractive.

Special Notations

Special notations regarding the mailing—such as CERTIFIED MAIL, REGISTERED MAIL, or special requests for the recipient, such as HOLD FOR ARRIVAL—are placed a double space below the date, at the left margin, and in all capital letters.

Inside Address

The inside address includes the name and full address of the person receiving the letter and is placed on the fourth line below the date. Further information about the two-letter state abbreviation and ZIP Code included in the full address is found in Chapter 4, Processing the Mail.

Attention Line

An attention line is used when a letter is directed to a particular person at an organization. Keyboard the attention line as the first line of the inside address, and keyboard the envelope in the same format.

Attention Ms. Valerie Biltmore
Professional Computer Services
7800 West Fall Lane
Rochester, NY 46219

Ladies and Gentlemen:

Salutation

The salutation is the letter's greeting. It usually includes the person's title and last name. It does not include the person's first name.

Sample salutations

Dear Ms. Silver
Dear Dr. Patterson
Dear Rev. Harrison

If the letter recipient's name is unknown

Ladies and Gentlemen (Note that *Dear* is not included.)
Dear Sir or Madam

Subject Line

The subject line, which quickly explains the purpose of the letter, is keyboarded a double space below the salutation. In a block style letter, it is keyboarded at the left margin. In a modified block style letter, the subject line may be placed at the left margin, indented, or centered. The subject line has increased in importance, because people are busy and quickly glance at mail to determine whether they should read the entire document.

Body

The body of the letter is the main part of the letter. It includes an introduction and a conclusion, and the lines of the body are single-spaced, with a double space between the paragraphs.

Complimentary Close, Company Name, Writer's Name, and Title

The complimentary close includes a closing and the writer's name. It may also include the company name and writer's title. After keyboarding the complimentary close, press the Enter key four times (three blank lines) before keyboarding the writer's name. If the company name is used in the complimentary close, press the Enter key twice after the complimentary close, key in the company name in all capital letters, press the Enter key four times, and key in the writer's name.

Sincerely,

Charles F. Wood

or

Very truly yours,

HARRIS & RUSSEL CORPORATION

Martha Wilson
Assistant Director

An office employee may have the authority to sign a letter in the supervisor's absence. The two most frequently used methods of signing the supervisor's name are as follows.

Very truly yours,

Theodore L. Joseph/RS

Theodore L. Joseph
Assistant Director

The office employee would sign the supervisor's name, Theodore L. Joseph, and then write the employee's initials.

Very truly yours,

Rhonda B. Silver

Rhonda B. Silver
Assistant to Theodore L. Joseph

Initials

The initials of the person who keyed the document are placed at the left margin a double space below the keyboarded writer's name or title. If the writer's initials are used, they are keyboarded in all capital letters before the initials of the person who keyed the document. The initials are important, because they identify who keyboarded the letter.

shc

LLR:shc or LLR/shc

Enclosure Notation

An enclosure notation is used if items are sent with a letter, and the enclosure notation is keyboarded at the left margin a double space below the initials. Several styles may be used.

Enclosure	
Enclosures (3)	(In this style, the number of items enclosed is shown.)
Enclosures Report Check #3456	(In this style, the specific items are listed.)

Copy Notation

A copy notation is used when a copy of the letter is sent to another person, and the notation is keyboarded at the left margin a double space below the initials. If an enclosure is used, the copy notation is keyboarded a double space below the enclosure.

The following copy notations are used:

cc	Was originally used to mean *carbon copy*. Carbon paper is no longer used, but cc is still used by some people.
pc	Is used for *photocopy*
c	Is used for *copy*
bcc or bpc	Is used for *a blind carbon copy* or *photocopy*; this notation is used when a copy of a letter is sent to someone without the knowledge of the addressee. To create a blind copy, print a separate version of the letter for the person receiving the blind copy and keyboard bcc at the bottom of the new letter.

Examples of copy notations

- Copy sent to one person:

  c Tillie K. McNeal

  or

  cc: Tillie K. McNeal

- Photocopy sent to several persons:

  pc Mary D. Johnson
  Rodney H. Gibson
  Rhonda L. Hunter

  If there are several copies, a check mark may be placed beside the copy notation indicating to whom the copy is being sent.

  c Kirk Kong ✓
  c Deanna D. Liggett
  c Jill R. Wood

Postscript

A postscript is used to emphasize an idea. It is the last item keyboarded on the letter and is a double space below the previous section. The postscript may be keyboarded at the left margin or indented to align with the paragraphs. Postscripts are normally only used in sales letters.

Postscript We hope to see you soon.

or

P.S. We hope to see you soon.

Two-Page Letter

The first page of a business letter is usually printed on letterhead stationery. Subsequent pages are printed on plain paper and use the same margins as are used on the first page. There are two styles that may be used for the heading, and they are created by using the header feature in a word processing package. The heading feature does not appear on the first page. All pages of a letter except the first page should have 1-inch top margins.

The following heading is keyboarded at the left margin.

Ms. Janie B. Gomez	(person receiving the letter)
2	(page number)
September 1, XXXX	(date)

The second heading style begins at the left margin, the page number is centered, and the date is right justified.

Ms. Janie B. Gomez 2 September 1, XXXX

INTEROFFICE MEMORANDA

> **HINT**
>
> A memo (memorandum) is correspondence delivered within a company, not mailed to a client. The plural of memorandum is memoranda.

An interoffice memorandum (memo) is correspondence to be delivered within a company or an organization, not mailed to a client or member of the public. An interoffice memorandum may be less formal than a letter, but the same writing rules of clarity, tone, and organization are applicable.

The tone of interoffice memos can vary from casual to very formal. Memos to your co-workers can be written in an informal manner, while memos intended to be sent outside your immediate office or to company executives should use the same tone as a letter. When writing the memo, consider the recipient's personality, interests, likes, dislikes, and needs.

If bad news must be given, deliver it in person rather than in a memo. In addition, consider the implications of any memo that you write. A verbal comment may be forgotten, but the written word lasts forever.

Since memos are internal communications circulated within the office, they are often printed on nonletterhead stationery. In today's technology-driven office, an email with a memo attached is a quick and cost-effective method of distributing information. Memos generally have 1-inch side margins and may have a 1-inch or 2-inch top margin, depending on company preferences.

While the specific format for a memo varies from office to office, the headings of interoffice memos include four basic items:

To:
From:
Date:
Subject:

TO: Sid Bartow

FROM: Rose Henderson
Director of Employee Relations

DATE: September 30, XXXX

SUBJECT: Physical Fitness Center Opening

Mr. Charlton will be out of town on October 15, and he has requested that we postpone the grand opening of our Employee Physical Fitness Center from October 15 to October 17. He has also suggested that we include a demonstration of physical fitness techniques by the Senior Fitness group, which meets at the Grace Community Center. Information about this group is enclosed.

I indicated to Mr. Charlton that we would review the plans for the grand opening by the close of business tomorrow and get back to him with our recommendation.

Please prepare a status report on the plans for the grand opening. We will meet in the conference room tomorrow at 2 P.M. to review what adjustments must be made to reschedule the grand opening to October 17.

jpg

Enclosure

c Arnold Hardy
Sally Moore

FIGURE 2-4 An interoffice memorandum.

When writing a memorandum, do not repeat the subject line in the first line of the memo, since this information is already in the document. A memorandum should be concise, and many offices try to limit memos to one page, if possible. After the body of the memo, the memo concludes with the same sections as letters regarding initials, enclosures, and copy notation. An alternative to keying in the memo format is to use a memorandum template from the word processing software or a memo template created and customized by the business.

Reports

Writing a Report

Report writing is a common office activity. Reports may be directed to potential customers, stockholders, the general public, or senior management. Some reports are based on information internal to the business, such as describing a company project, presenting findings of a research study, or reviewing the progress the business has made in meeting targeted goals. Information for internal reports is usually found in the company's files. Other reports may be based on information from outside the company, such as the preparation of background papers on an industry or information requested by a client. The process of researching and writing reports may be long and complex, and an office employee may be involved in this process at several stages. Today's office employee is often asked to write informal reports, briefing papers, which provide background information in a short summary format, and memo reports.

These papers require the same clarity, conciseness, and completeness as the writing techniques previously discussed.

Whatever your duties are in the preparation of reports, whether you are doing research or are keyboarding the report, you should be familiar with the process of writing a report. The process is the same if the information is gathered from within the company or from outside sources.

The first step in writing any report, after the subject is chosen, is to prepare an informal outline that helps organize your thoughts by listing the points you want to discuss. In the beginning of the project, you may not know what you want to discuss because you are not familiar enough with the topic. The outline should help identify those areas where additional information is required. Also, try to identify sources of information for the report. You should list people in your office whom you would contact in the search for information. If the report relates to company business activities, your supervisor should be able to help you identify the best sources for the information required.

The source of information for internal reports may be other employees or departments directly involved in the specific projects covered by the report. The larger the organization, the more difficult it may be to gather the relevant information required for a report. An office telephone directory and organization chart are useful when trying to locate the people who have the information required for a report. A good assistant is persistent in following leads from one office to another until the proper person is located. Do not be surprised if people are not eager to provide the information you require. Gathering information for your report may be seen as an interruption to another person's busy schedule. A polite but persistent approach may be needed—stressing how important the information requested will be to the report and to the ongoing business of the company.

Gathering information for internal reports based on the company's files can be easy if the files are available and other staff is helpful. Researching information for reports from outside your company's files, however, may be a major task. If you are unfamiliar with the subject, research the topic with the use of books, magazines, newspapers, periodicals, pamphlets, statistical reports, research dictionaries, and other research materials. Information for these reports may be available from references located in your company's research library, or information may have to be sought from outside sources, including public libraries, the Internet, government agencies, or other businesses.

The Web allows businesses to search for information without leaving the office. Since Web sites are frequently updated, it may be easier to obtain current information from them than from printed sources. It is very important to use only information from reputable sources. Anyone can create a Web site and present inaccurate data. Always evaluate the credibility of the Web site you are using. Is the Web site sponsored by a reputable organization, or is it the work of a single individual? Is the Web site endorsed by credible rating organizations, or does it have links from other reputable Web sites? If you find a Web site that is helpful, mark it for future reference by using a bookmark, which is a Web browser feature.

After you have developed the outline, you are ready to begin researching the topic. As you do the research, you should review your outline and revise it to reflect the new information you have found. You should develop your own method of organizing your research. Keep good records, including the name of the book or magazine, date of publication, author, publishing company, and pages used. (Some researchers like to use index cards with notes on one side of the card and reference information on the other.)

To save time, instead of handwriting research information while away from the office, a notebook computer can be used. Then the data can be transferred from the notebook to the office computer system.

If you are using information you found on the Internet, print out a copy of the Web page and keep it in your files for reference. It may be difficult to return to the same Web page if you need to verify the information. Also, information on Web pages is often updated frequently and, if you return to the Web site the next week, the information may have changed. By printing out the Web page, you document the source and accuracy of your research.

Write the report from your notes using your outline as the guide. Where appropriate, use footnotes, which are references printed on the bottom of same page as the quoted material.

Footnotes cite sources of information or give credit for quotations or ideas gathered from documents researched. Word processing packages have removed the drudgery of keyboarding footnotes because software packages automatically place the footnote at the correct location on the page. Another way to simplify the keyboarding of footnotes is to place the references on a separate page at the end of the report and call them endnotes. When footnotes or endnotes are added or deleted, they are automatically renumbered by the word processing package. The completed report may be edited and revised several times to refine the copy and delete errors before it is finalized. As a precaution, create several backup diskettes and store them at several locations. When the report is completed, it should be printed and distributed.

Research Materials

The following are examples of research books and periodicals that are available in a library:

- *ABA Journal*
- Almanacs
- Atlases
- *Best's Insurance Reports*
- *Books in Print*
- *Business History Review*
- *Columbia Journal of World Business*
- *Commerce Clearing House Publications*
- *Consumer Guide*
- *Dow Jones News Retrieval Database*
- Encyclopedias
- *Facts on File Yearbook*
- *Guide to Venture Capital Sources*
- *Harvard Law Review*
- *Industrial and Labor Relations Review*
- *Journal of Research*
- *Journal of Advertising*
- *Justice Quarterly*
- *Moody's Bank and Financial Manual*
- *Moody's OTC Industrial Manual*
- *Moody's Public Utility News Report*
- *Moody's Transportation Report*
- *Nation's Business*
- *New York Times Index*
- *Organizations Master Index*
- *Polk's Work Bank Directory*
- *Reader's Guide to Periodical Literature*
- *Sales and Marketing Management*
- *Standard and Poor's Register of Corporations*
- *The International Who's Who*
- *The Monthly Catalog of U.S. Government Publications*
- *Toll-Free Telephone Number Directory*
- *Who's Who in America*

There are many Internet sites which will help you find information on a specific topic. These Internet sites are called search engines. Search engines change rapidly, so try several search engines when you are looking for information on the Internet and bookmark those you find most useful. The following Internet search engines can be helpful.

www.Askjeeves.com
www.AltaVista.com
www.Google.com
www.HotBot.com
www.Infoseek.com
www.Northernlight.com
www.WebCrawler.com
www.Yahoo.com

The following are sample Internet research sites:

American Stock Exchange	*www.amex.com*
American Institute of Certified Public Accountants	*www.aicpa.org/index.htm*
Barron's Online	*www.barrons.com*
CNN Interactive World News	*www.cnn.com/world*
Congressional Record	*www.gpoaccess.gov*
Consumer Law Page	*www.consumerlawpage.com*
Consumer Product Safety Commission	*www.cpsc.gov*
Federal Communications Commission	*www.fcc.com*
Federal Reserve	*www.federalreserve.gov*
The Gallup Organizations	*www.gallup.com*
Internal Revenue Service	*www.irs.ustreas.gov*
Library of Congress	*lcweb.loc.gov/homepaga/lchp.html*
NASDAQ	*www.nasdaq.com*
Quotations	*www.quotationspage.com*
Quotations	*www.bartleby.com/100*
U.S. Census Bureau	*www.census.gov*
U.S. Department of Commerce	*www.commerce.gov*
U.S. Department of Education	*www.ed.gov*
U.S. Department of Justice	*www.usdoj.gov*
U.S. Department of Labor	*www.dol.gov*
U.S. Department of Transportation	*www.dot.gov*
U.S. Department of the Treasury	*www.ustreas.gov*
U.S. Government's Official Web Portal	*www.firstgov.gov*
U.S. Trade Representative	*www.ustr.gov/index.html*
U.S. Social Security Administration	*www.ssa.gov*

The following are some investment- and business-related sites:

Barron's	*www.barrons.com*
Bloomberg Business News	*www.bloomberg.com*
Business Week	*www.businessweek.com*
Fortune Magazine	*www.fortune.com/fortune*
The Wall Street Journal	*online.wsj.com/public/us*

Reference Materials

In your office, you should have books and/or Web site bookmarks for the following types of reference materials:

- Almanac
- Atlas
- Book of quotations (this is helpful when writing speeches)
- Computer reference books for the software packages you use
- Computer software packages for ZIP Codes, addresses, telephone numbers, encyclopedias, and maps
- Dictionary
- Dictionary of misspelled words (this book lists words the way you think they should be spelled, not how they are spelled)
- *National Five-Digit ZIP Code and Post Office Directory* (USPS Publication 65)
- Office reference manual with letter and memo formatting styles, grammar rules, and punctuation rules
- Specific references for your industry
- Telephone directories of frequently called cities
- Thesaurus

Report Organization

The following format is often used in reports:

Summary:	Most reports begin with a summary. The summary includes the recommendations or conclusions of the report and is helpful to a busy person who does not have the time to read the entire report.
Table of contents:	The table of contents indicates where particular information is found in the report.
Introduction:	The introduction explains what the report is about.
Body:	The body develops the important topics in the report.
Conclusion:	The conclusion reviews the important points and the recommendations of the report.
Bibliography:	The bibliography lists references used in preparing the report.
Endnotes:	The endnotes are references for direct quotes or the ideas of others which are placed at the back of the report. If these references are placed at the bottom of each page, they are referred to as footnotes.

Keyboarding Reports

The format of the report will depend on whether the pages are to be loose (unbound), left-bound (as in a book), or topbound with a single staple.

Guidelines for Keyboarding Reports

Margins

Unbound Manuscript Margins

Top margin

Page 1	2 inches
Subsequent pages	1 inch

Side margins	1 inch
Bottom margins	1 inch

Leftbound Manuscript Margins

Top margin	
Page 1	2 inches
Subsequent pages	1 inch
Side margins	1.5 inches left and 1 inch right
Bottom margins	1 inch

If the pages are to be printed on both sides in a book, the side margins should alternate, so that a 1 1/2-inch margin is on the left side for odd-numbered pages and on the right side for even-numbered pages.

Topbound Manuscript Margins

Top margin	
Page 1	2.5 inches
Subsequent pages	1.5 inches
Side margins	1 inch
Bottom margins	1 inch

Page Numbering. Begin all page numbering on page 2.

News Releases

A news release is publicity or news that is given to the news media. News releases are often used to announce the promotion of an employee, election of officers, introduction of a new product, or hiring of a new employee.

> **HINT**
> A news release is information given to the news media.

Requirements of a news release

1. Double space the text.
2. Use 2-inch side margins.
3. Include a suggested headline.
4. At the top of the page, indicate the date of the press release.
5. Place a notation at the top regarding whether the information is for immediate release or whether it must be held until a specific date and time for release. (A press release may be distributed before the date the information is to be made public.)
6. Include the name and telephone number of a person to contact for further information.
7. Keyboard the word *More* at the bottom of the page to indicate that the news release is continued on another page.
8. Keyboard "###" at the end of the news release.

Newsletters

Many organizations prepare newsletters to distribute information to their employees, their clients, or members of the public. There is no standard format for a newsletter and they vary widely in their size, content, and frequency. Newsletters are intended to be a part of a series of publications which are presented in a similar format and which are distributed on a periodic basis, such as a weekly, monthly, or quarterly. A simple newsletter can be printed on one sheet of 8.5" × 11" paper and include information regarding a single topic. More complex newsletters may be printed on 11" × 17" paper, which is folded in half to result in four pages 8.5" × 11". These newsletters usually contain several articles and may include photos, artwork, and other graphic material. Simple newsletters may be prepared using word

Serobus Incorporated
3500 Executive Drive
Kingsland, GA 31548
Telephone 912-670-8900
FAX 912-670-8901
Email *Sergo@cgo.com*

May 16, XXXX

Hold for Release: 10 A.M. May 21

Director of Marketing for Serobus Incorporated

Patricia Sanez has accepted the position of Director of Marketing for Serobus Incorporated. Her duties begin on June 1. Prior to her move, Ms. Sanez was Assistant Director of Marketing for Taylor Markets in Tacoma, Washington. Serobus Incorporated, which is located in suburban Mayfield, manufacturers door locks and hardware. Serobus Incorporated projects sales of $10 million for next year.

###

For Further Information Contact: Greg H. Castleman
Public Affairs Office
617-555-6666

FIGURE 2-5 A news release.

processing software and consist primarily of text with perhaps the insertion of computer files of clipart or pictures. In addition, newsletters can be prepared using specialized publication software, such as Microsoft Publisher, Adobe InDesign, or QuarkXPress, where the emphasis is on graphic layout and formatting as well as text. Word processing and publication software contain many templates, which can be modified by an office so the newsletter reflects the style and specific interests of the organization.

SAVING FILES FOR AND FROM THE INTERNET

The widespread use of the Internet means that you may be asked to place documents on the Internet or retrieve documents from the Internet.

Posting Files on the Internet

While Web pages are created specifically for posting on the Internet, you can place almost any document, report, brochure, or form on the Internet. Many software application packages can automatically save files in HTML format, the language used to create Internet Web pages. Following are the steps to save a Word file for the Internet.

To save a Microsoft Word file for the Internet

1. Click File.
2. Click Save As Web Page.
3. Key in the file name.
4. Click Save.

Saving and Mailing Files from the Internet

As you use the Internet, you will find specific information and even full documents, reports, or pictures that you will want to save. For example, it is often important to save an email response to maintain a complete history of a project. In addition, you might want to save a photo from a Web page to insert into a written report or spreadsheet. Of course, it is essential to verify that you have permission to use the photo. Also, after completing research on a specific topic, you might want to the save the information to assist you in writing a report. Following are several ways you can save information from the Internet so it can be stored on your computer and used in other documents.

To save an email file

1. Click File and click Save As.
2. At Save in, key in the directory and folder in your computer.
3. At File Name, key in name.
4. At Save as type, choose Text File (*.txt).
5. Click OK.

To save a Web page

1. Click File and click Save As.
2. At Save in, key in the directory and folder in your computer.
3. At File Name, key in name.
4. At Save as type, choose Text File (*.txt) or HTML files.
5. Click OK.

To save an Internet image

1. Place the mouse over the image.
2. Click the right mouse button.
3. Click Save Picture As or Save Image As.
4. At File Name, key in name.
5. At Save in, key in the directory and folder in your computer.
6. At Save as Type, choose either JPEG File (*.jpg), Bitmap (.bmp), or All Files (*.*).
7. Click Save.

To save an Internet link

1. Place the mouse over the image.
2. Click the right mouse button.
3. Click Save Link As.
4. At File Name, key in name.
5. At Save in, key in the directory and folder in your computer.
6. At Save as type, choose either HTML Files or Plain Text (*.txt).
7. Click Save.
8. Click OK.

To Email a Web Page

1. Click File.
2. Click Send.
3. Click Page or Send Frame.
4. Key in the email address to whom it is being sent.
5. Click Send.
6. Web page is automatically sent as an attachment.

CHAPTER REVIEW

1. What is a conversational tone?
2. List six transitional words.
3. Explain how sexual bias is avoided in writing.
4. When is an office memorandum used?
5. What are the requirements of a news release?
6. List six examples of research books and periodicals.
7. Show one example of how an assistant would sign a letter for an executive.
8. List two Internet search engines.
9. Explain why information obtained from a Web site should be carefully evaluated.

ACTIVITIES

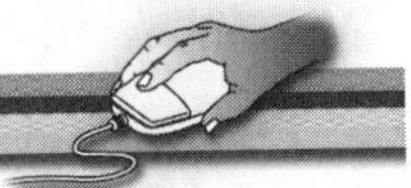

1. Save twenty business letters. Analyze each letter and, on a separate sheet of paper, indicate the good points and the bad points of each letter. Select the five worst letters and prepare a revision to correct or improve them. To maintain confidentiality, block out all names, addresses, and personal information.
2. Consult four of the reference books listed in the chapter. Write a paper describing the items found in each reference book. Indicate under what circumstances a researcher would use those reference books.
3. Visit a library and consult four reference books not listed in the chapter. Write a paper describing the items found in each reference book. Indicate under what circumstances a researcher would use those reference books.
4. Research two topics on the Internet. List the Web addresses used and write a summary of each topic.
5. Use a word processing template to create a letter. Supply the specific letter information.
6. Use a word processing template to create a memorandum. Supply the specific memorandum information.
7. Surf the Web for information about computer calendar software and save a graphic from the Web site. Write a half-page summary of your findings and place the graphic in your summary.
8. Surf the Web for information about your local government and save the Web page.

WRITING ASSIGNMENTS

Supply any information needed to complete the assignments and write your response to the following situations.

1. Write an email congratulating a colleague on receiving a promotion.
2. Write a letter explaining that there is an incorrect charge of $50 on your account.
3. Write a letter to a well-known member of your community inviting the person to speak at a luncheon. Include all necessary information about the event.
4. Assume that you are the invited speaker in assignment 3. Write a letter and accept the invitation.

5. Assume that you are the invited speaker in assignment 3. Write an email and graciously decline the invitation.
6. You received a book order for *Working Keeps Me Happy.* The letter indicates that the check was enclosed, but it was not enclosed. Write a courteous letter stating that company policy will not permit shipping a book without receiving payment in advance.
7. Write a memorandum to your supervisor requesting permission to attend a computer conference in Los Angeles or Phoenix. Explain why the conference would be beneficial to you. Attach the memorandum to an email addressed to your supervisor.
8. Write a letter requesting the completion of the attached survey. Your company is sending a survey to 300 businesses in your area to obtain information about the training opportunities offered to the employees.
9. Order a subscription to *Working in the Modern Office* for yourself and three of your friends. Enclose a check for each subscription. (Include each person's name and address in your letter.)
10. Your employer stayed at the Miami Hotel the nights of December 6, 7, and 8. While reviewing the travel records, you noticed the following: Your employer checked out on December 9 at 9 A.M.; the bill showed a room charge for December 9. Write a letter requesting a credit to the American Express card for the room charge for December 9.
11. Write a news release for your local newspaper announcing that you and two other students have won the local Business Association Scholarship. Include names, information about each person, and the criteria for winning the scholarship.
12. Write a memorandum inviting everyone in your office to the annual company picnic. Everyone should bring a covered dish. The company will provide sandwiches and drinks. Include all details.
13. Write an email notifying all employees that your office will close at 3 P.M. on Friday due to the installation of a new heating system.
14. Write an email notifying your staff that, effective immediately, all visitors will be required to provide photo IDs when entering the building.
15. Write a memorandum to your staff announcing the purchase of a new wireless communication system, which will be installed next month. Training will be available to all staff and registration forms will be distributed shortly. Add information to complete the memo. Attach the memo to an email.
16. You presented a talk at a meeting, and one of the participants requested a copy of your presentation. Write an email attaching a presentation.
17. Answer the following letters after reading the comments in the margins.

Dear Peter,

Write a letter indicating that I will attend

Our annual stockholders' meeting is scheduled for January 15 at 9 A.M. in the Mirror Room of the Charleston Hotel. The hotel is located at 8900 Cosmo Drive, so take the Cosmo Drive exit from Interstate 170.

I will need a reservation for Jan. 14 & 15

After the meeting, the officers of the company will get together for lunch and a discussion of our next project.

We hope you can attend. Let me know what time you expect to arrive and if you plan to stay overnight. I will be glad to make a hotel reservation for you.

Dear Ms. Lighter:

Write a letter

I plan to be in Washington November 7, 8, 9, and 10 for the annual Broadcasters Convention. I will be staying a few additional days to meet with some colleagues. While I am in Washington, I would like to talk with you about the agenda for the next association meeting.

OK, meet in my office

Will you be available to meet with me on November 11 at 9 A.M.? We could meet either at your office or at the Association Building on 7th Street. Either location is fine with me.

Please let me know soon if this date and time are convenient for you.

PROJECTS

Project 3

Send the following letter to Ms. Mary Carmel, Star Real Estate Services, 2207 Lee Lane, Roanoke, VA 22804. Use a block letter style. Make a file copy. Use an appropriate closing and sign the letter from yourself as Associate Director.

I have accepted a new and exciting position with Colony Industries, which has several branch offices in your area. By accepting the position, I have made the commitment to move to your region. Penny Carlton in the human resources department at Colony Industries suggested I contact you to begin the process of finding a new home in the Falls Heights area. She indicated that you have a terrific relocation service.

My wife and I have two children, ages nine and twelve, who will be attending schools in the area, so a home in a good school district is important to us.

We are interested in a house with at least four bedrooms, three baths, and a first-floor family room. We have a deck on our current home and would enjoy having either a screened porch or a deck on our new home.

Since I have already accepted my new position and am extremely busy, my wife, Patricia, will be managing the move. Please contact her at 415-888-1266 to arrange a time when we can view homes in the area.

We look forward to working with you.

Project 4

Send the following memo to the staff and supply all necessary information. The memo is from Alice Garrison, Public Relations Director.

We need your help on a project to honor the 100th birthday of our company. Your help, creativity, and ideas are needed to make our birthday a wonderful celebration.

Put on your thinking caps and decide on a plan for our celebration. Send your suggestions to Walter Mason. Four checks of $25 each will be given to the employees with the best suggestions.

The deadline for suggestions is February 14, so start thinking.

HUMAN RELATIONS SKILL DEVELOPMENT

HR 2-1 Working with People of All Ages

While you may be most comfortable working with people your own age, in the typical office your co-workers will probably range in age from those who have just graduated to those reaching retirement. Your supervisor may be older or younger than you. If the supervisor is older than you, you may be reminded of your parents, or if the supervisor is younger than you, you may be reminded of your children. Some people have difficulty following the directives of a younger person. When you are in the office, disregard the age factor, and remind yourself that the company is paying for the supervisor's expertise in the field, not for the supervisor's age. Above all, you must remember that as an employee you must adhere to the guidelines established by your supervisor.

- How are you going to handle the situation if your supervisor reminds you of your father or mother, and you do not get along with your parents?
- How are you going to create a good working relationship with a supervisor who is fifteen years younger than you are?
- How would you develop a good working relationship if you and your supervisor were the same age?
- How would you develop a good working relationship if your supervisor reminded you of your younger sister, and your sister is a brat?

HR 2-2 Money in the Office

Plan your budget so you always have money with you at the office. You may be asked to attend a last-minute luncheon with a client or another employee. Also, you may be asked to contribute to a retirement gift, birthday gift, wedding gift, or condolence gift. The more employees in an office, the more frequently you may be asked to contribute to an office collection. You should control decisions about how you spend your money but be aware that office collections are a common occurrence. It is not prudent to have a reputation as a person who never gives to anything, but you may have to learn the knack of saying no without offending others in your office.

- How are you going to handle the situation if you are approached to contribute to the going-away gift for a member of another department?
- How are you going to handle the situation if you are approached to contribute to the baby gift for your supervisor's daughter?
- Recently you have encountered many business expenses for lunches, dinners, and gifts. You are now invited to another luncheon. What are your options and how are you going to handle the situation?

SITUATIONS

How would you handle each of the following situations?

- **S 2-1** You sent an envelope to Mrs. Rose and just discovered that your assistant did not include the letter. What action would you take?
- **S 2-2** A sales representative, who will be working with your office for a few weeks, annoys you by making snide remarks.
- **S 2-3** Your supervisor has asked you to talk to Joyce about her clothing. The supervisor feels that Joyce's skirts are too short and tight for an office. Plan your conversation with Joyce. Also, indicate the tone you would use in the conversation.

PUNCTUATION REVIEW

Punctuate each of the following sentences.

1. Ellen was the elevator working when you arrived today
2. After a closed door meeting the company announced that Ms Sheldon the president had resigned
3. The attorney entered a guilty plea and everyone went home to celebrate
4. The trade deficit fuel economy and bank failures were all discussed at the convention
5. The Dow Jones Average rose 5.8 percent therefore the stockholders were pleased
6. The Daniels Center which has its international headquarters in Denver was established on February 20 1974 to promote better public relations among worldwide companies understanding among cultures and cooperation among workers
7. Yes the report was hand delivered
8. The dues which all members pay allow us to fund our scholarship programs
9. As you mentioned the report was late
10. Our manager Mr Lander was sick yesterday
11. Is the photocopier broken again Ted asked
12. Julie said I always attend the department meetings
13. Under a Chapter 13 filing International Footwear will reorganize and reschedule debt payments to its creditors
14. The #5345 womens dress will be available in the following colors peach avocado mauve and lemon
15. Yes the meeting was held at the Coral Marina Resort on 9th Street

CD ASSIGNMENTS

CD Assignment 2-1

Open the file CD2-1_NR on your Student CD and follow the instructions to complete the job.

CD Assignment 2-2

Open the file CD2-2_NRJ on your Student CD and follow the instructions to complete the job.

CD Assignment 2-3

Open the file CD2-3_MG on your Student CD and follow the instructions to complete the job.

CD Assignment 2-4

Open the file CD2-4_EM on your Student CD and follow the instructions to complete the job.

CD Assignment 2-5

Open the file CD2-5_SH on your Student CD and follow the instructions to complete the job.

CD Assignment 2-6

Open the file CD2-6_PR1 on your Student CD and follow the instructions to complete the job.

CD Assignment 2-7

Open the file CD2-7_PR2 on your Student CD and follow the instructions to complete the job.

Workplace Telecommunications 3

Objectives

After studying this chapter, you should be able to

1. Use voice mail.
2. Speak on the telephone in a professional manner.
3. Make long-distance domestic and foreign telephone calls.
4. Understand the use of specialized telephone services.
5. Understand audio and video teleconferencing.
6. Understand techniques for delivering speeches.

Oral Communications

All employees, regardless of the type or level of their position, need excellent oral communication skills. Each day you will speak with people whose knowledge of your company and projects varies greatly. Therefore, it is a mistake to assume that each listener always understands everything you say about your company and its projects. To improve communications, plan what you are going to say and speak distinctly. Good oral communications demand exactness and clarity. If the spoken word is not understood, there is no written reference to consult.

You may need to practice expressing yourself, so others understand what you are saying. Before you speak, organize your thoughts, so they flow in a logical sequence. When speaking, pronounce each word correctly, talk loudly enough to be heard, and pause to indicate the ends of sentences or transitions to new thoughts. While speaking, you must look for feedback from the listener in the form of facial expressions and body gestures. By observing the listener, you will learn how well your message is being received. You can then rephrase thoughts that were not clearly expressed or cite examples to clarify your ideas.

Semantics and perception are barriers to effective communications. Misunderstandings often occur because two people hear the same words but interpret them differently. For example, a supervisor may ask you if you are going to return a telephone call soon. If you answer yes, the supervisor may interpret your statement to mean that the phone call will be returned within a few minutes, whereas you may have meant the next day.

> **HINT**
>
> Barriers to communications: semantics, perception, and withheld communications

Another barrier to effective communications is the withholding of communications. One staff member may not tell other employees important information, thereby causing problems in the office. Information may not be communicated because of busy schedules, forgetfulness, or even a desire to withhold the information from others. Learn to recognize a breakdown in communications before it causes misunderstandings that will be difficult to resolve.

During the past decade, there have been major innovations in communications technology, and the future will bring additional communications changes to the office. This chapter will explain many communications technologies which are present in the workplace.

RECEIVING AND MAKING TELEPHONE CALLS

Answering the Telephone

When you answer the telephone in your office, you are giving the caller an image of yourself and your company. If you speak with a pleasant voice, you create a courteous image of yourself and create goodwill for the company. However, if you are abrupt or rude, you present a poor impression of yourself and your company. We have all experienced rude people, and often rude people make us angry. Most people are reluctant to patronize a company if the employees are discourteous.

To portray the image of a helpful person,

- Speak clearly.
- Vary the tone of your voice.
- Speak directly into the telephone.
- Use a friendly and helpful voice.
- Use professional words, not slang.
- Speak slowly.
- Project a pleasant manner.
- Be courteous.
- Use the caller's name.
- Be alert; give the caller your full attention.
- Talk naturally; use your own words.
- Speak in a pleasant voice.
- Project an enthusiastic personality.

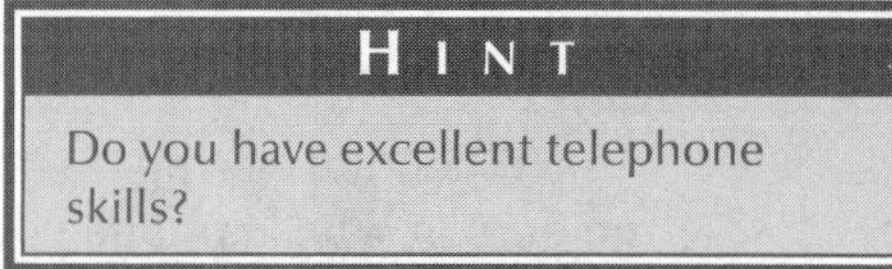
HINT
Do you have excellent telephone skills?

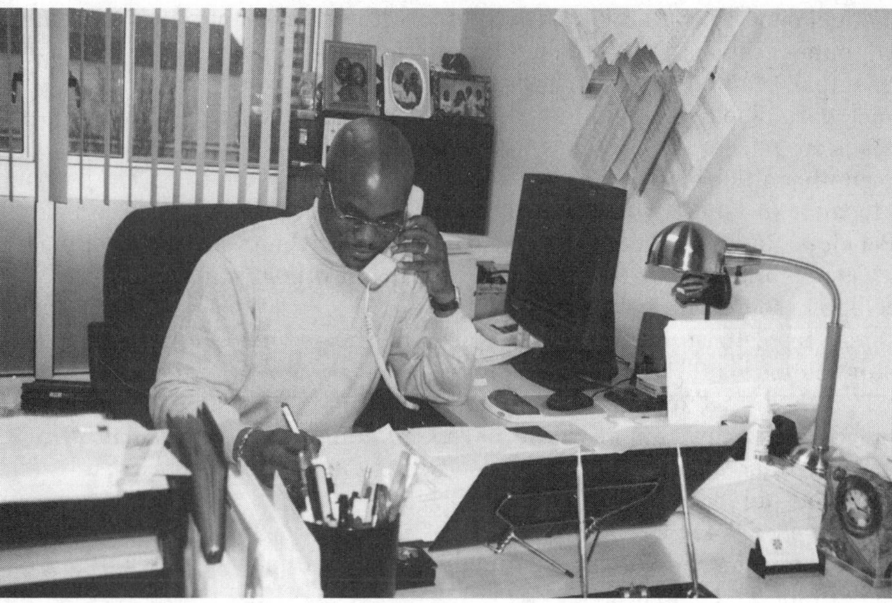

FIGURE 3-1 An employee consulting with a client on the telephone.

FIGURE 3-2 An employee using a telephone headset to talk to a client while using the computer.

When you talk on the telephone, speak loudly enough so you can be heard, particularly if you normally speak softly. It is difficult to talk into the telephone mouthpiece and be heard if you have the telephone receiver wedged between your shoulder and your chin. People who frequently speak on the telephone use headsets, which free their hands for keyboarding or writing the information they are hearing. Never talk on the phone if you have food or gum in your mouth.

When answering the telephone, pronounce the name of the company and the name of the person whose phone you are answering so they can be understood. The way you answer the phone depends on whether your office usually receives calls directly from the public or whether the calls are transferred from a central company operator. In order to provide better service to customers and avoid transferring calls, many organizations distribute the phone numbers of individual departments and even individual offices. An example of one common way to answer a phone received from the outside is to say the company name and individual office—for example, "Clifton and Lewis, Ms. Wood's office."

Many phones have displays which indicate whether a call is coming from an outside phone line or has been transferred from within the company. If you know that the call was transferred from another office in your company, you may say, "Ms. Wood's office" or "Libby Wood's office." In some instances, you may wish to include your name—for example, "Ms. Wood's office, Penelope Rosen speaking." However, do not overwhelm the caller with a long speech, such as "Good morning. This is the Clifton and Lewis Corporation, Ms. Libby Wood's office. I am Penelope Rosen. May I help you?"

If you must ask the caller to wait, speak so the caller hears you. Often people answer the phone and slur "please wait." If additional information is necessary or another telephone rings, say, "May I place this call on hold for a moment?" or "Please hold." As soon as possible, return to the caller and say, "I am sorry to have kept you waiting." Then talk with the caller. Do not keep the caller on hold for a long time. If you cannot quickly get back to a caller, ask for his or her phone number so you may return the call.

If you do not have voice mail and you must leave your desk (even for only a couple of minutes), you should ask someone to answer your telephone. An unanswered telephone does not promote goodwill for the company.

Messages

To ______________________
Date ______________________
Time ______________________
Caller ______________________
Company ______________________
Telephone No. ______________________
Return the Call ______________________
Will Call Again ______________________
Message Taken By ______________________

Message

____
____
____

FIGURE 3-3 A telephone message form.

You may screen telephone calls for your employer because the employer may be too busy to talk or may not wish to speak with a specific person. You must be very clever and skillful when screening calls. Some callers are offended when they know that their call is being screened. When screening a call, do not say, "Who is this?" Instead, say, "May I ask who is calling?" or "May I tell Ms. Wood who is calling?"

Taking Messages

Taking messages is a very important aspect of office work. If the person being called is not available, ask if you can take a message or if the caller would like to have the person's voice mail. Unfortunately, many people do not know how to take messages. First, always have a pencil and paper available when the telephone rings. Do not say, "Wait—I have to get pencil and paper." Taking a message is a standard task when answering the phone, so be prepared. Begin writing notes as the caller speaks. It is easier to write information as it is given, rather than trying to remember a comment a few minutes later.

Immediately write the required information on a message pad. Some companies use a message pad that automatically prepares a copy of the message. If your handwriting is difficult to read, write your notes on scrap paper and immediately rewrite the message on the message pad. As soon as the call is completed, deliver the message or place the message where the recipient will pick it up.

Today, messages may be recorded and distributed via computer systems, and many office email systems have templates designed to record telephone messages. These templates are electronic message forms and will help you record information regarding an incoming phone call. If you have primary responsibility for answering the phone and taking phone messages, you should have a phone messages form always open on your computer, so you can enter the information directly into the computer. Distributing phone messages by email is quick and easy and provides a computerized record of the call.

Telephone messages should include

- Caller's name (verify the spelling of the caller's name with the caller)
- Telephone number, including an area code and extension if applicable
- Reason for the call
- Notation indicating if the call should be returned
- Message, if any

- Date of the call
- Time of the call; the exact date and time can be very important
- Name or initials of the person who took the call (this is needed if a question arises concerning the call)

Before ending the conversation, verify the telephone number and caller's name. For example, you might say, "Thank you, Mr. Bouquet, for calling. I would like to verify that your telephone number is 202-555-5555. I will ask Ms. Paddington to return your call as soon as possible." It is impossible to return a telephone call if the telephone number on the message form is incorrect. Not returning a telephone call creates a bad image of your office.

Each person who answers the telephone should have a copy of the corporate directory with employee names and telephone numbers. This eliminates the need to ask important officials of the company to spell their names and give you their telephone numbers.

Internal Telephone Calls

In some businesses, calls can be placed to company offices in the same building, to an on-site building complex, or to an across-town company facility by dialing only the last four or five digits of the telephone number. Often a company needs quick communications between offices in distant cities. The company may use a dedicated private line service that links the offices. The employee accesses the private line by dialing a simple code, perhaps the number "8," and then dials the office in another city. Large companies with many offices can install their own internal phone system that connects with their local phone company. Some companies have established their own private telephone systems to connect offices in different cities by using satellite communications or leasing long-distance phone lines from commercial providers. In these situations, the company can call offices in different cities without using the regular public telephone system.

Placing Telephone Calls

When you place a telephone call, first identify yourself by saying, "I am Ms. Scott from American Systems" or "I am Katie Scott from American Systems." Then state with whom you would like to speak.

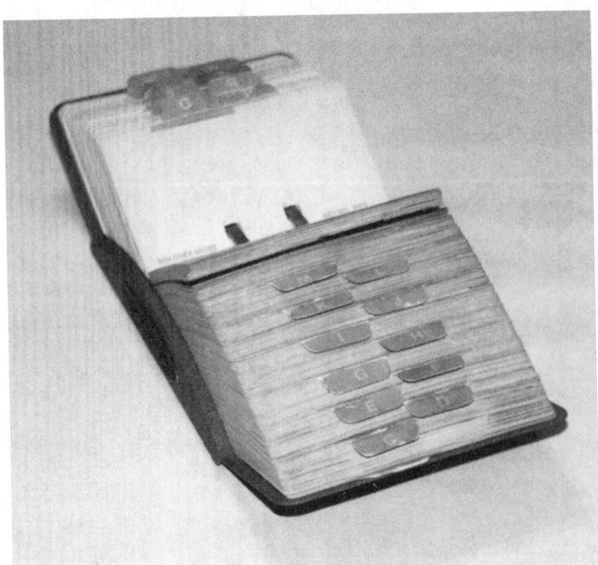

FIGURE 3-4 A card file holder.

Before making a telephone call,

- Verify the telephone number you are going to call.
- Plan what you are going to say. If necessary, prepare a short outline of the points to cover.
- Have reports and letters available for quick reference.
- If the call is long-distance, determine the time at the location you are calling and decide if it is a reasonable time to place the call.
- Plan what action you would suggest if the caller is not available. Do you want to leave a message with an assistant, leave a voice mail message, have the call returned, or speak with someone else?

Personal Telephone Directory

Maintaining a personal telephone directory of your supervisor's and your frequently called numbers increases your efficiency and reduces the number of searches for unknown telephone numbers. There are several personal telephone directory options. Many office employees record phone numbers on a small card kept in a loose card file holder, often called a rotary card file holder. Business cards that you receive can be kept in a similar type of holder. In addition, there are computer calendar and organization software programs that create address books or contact lists, and some software automatically dials the number after clicking the name. If you do not have the telephone number, there are many Internet sites that may be helpful. To find a telephone, address, or fax number, try any of the following Web sites:

> **HINT**
>
> Create a personal telephone directory system.

www.anywho.com
www.infobel.com/teldir
www.smartpages.com

FIGURE 3-5 An employee talking on the phone after using a card file holder to locate a phone number.

Long-Distance Services

Long-distance telephone charges can be a major expense for a business. Businesses can select from several alternate long-distance phone companies and calling plans to reduce their long-distance phone charges.

After a business selects a long-distance provider, the local telephone company automatically sends long-distance calls to the appropriate long-distance company. Many local phone companies now also provide long-distance service. All companies that provide long-distance service use the same phone numbers and area codes and people commonly make long-distance calls without ever thinking of the particular long-distance company being used.

Most of the major long-distance companies provide the same basic services, including long-distance telephone calls to foreign nations. However, if you use a long-distance company that is not your regular long-distance provider, it is important to know the special prefix code required to access the long-distance carrier.

Businesses which are heavy users of long-distance telephone service can seek specialized services tailored to their needs. WATS (Wide Area Telephone Service) provides a business with dedicated lines for outgoing long-distance service at a flat hourly rate. Also, many businesses provide their customers with a toll-free telephone service using an "800" area code. As the 800 area code has filled with more users, the phone system has added 888 and 877 as other toll-free area codes. As the 888 and 877 area codes fill, the phone system will add additional area codes, such as 866 and 855, for toll-free calling.

Some businesses have phone numbers that start with the "900" area code. Phone calls to the 900 area code are not free. Businesses with a 900 area code are selling information or providing a service. The caller usually must pay a charge, which can range from a dollar to several dollars per minute. The per-minute charge is supposed to be disclosed at the beginning of the phone call, and typical charges for a call are sometimes disclosed in written material about the phone service. Use of "900" phone services should be done with care, since the per-minute cost is charged even if the caller is on hold; therefore, the calls can quickly become expensive.

Calling Long-Distance

Most long-distance calls are made by dialing the phone number directly. To make a long-distance call within the United States and Canada, a caller simply dials "1," the area code, and the telephone number. This is a total of eleven digits (e.g., 1-605-555-1212). In the United States, if you do not know the number, you can obtain phone numbers by dialing "1," the area code, and 555-1212. You will be asked for the city and name of the party you are calling. Many telephone companies now charge a fee for locating a telephone number for you. As mentioned earlier, telephone numbers may be found at no charge by searching the Web.

If you would like the party you are calling to pay for your long-distance call, you will place a collect call. This type of call can be made by dialing "0," the area code, and the telephone number. After dialing the phone number, a telephone company operator will ask for your name. Then the operator will ask the party called if he or she will accept the charges from the caller.

Another type of call made through the operator is a person-to-person call. This type of call allows you to speak only with the specific person requested. If that person is not available, there will be no charge for the call. This type of call is very expensive, so many offices do not use it.

Changes in Area Codes

While most local telephone directories contain a list of selected cities and their area codes, they often are not complete and can quickly become out of date. As more people and offices add phone lines for computers, fax machines, and cell phones, area codes are running out of available phone numbers. As a result, many new area codes are being added each year. Sometimes a city will get a new area code or be split between two area codes. Occasionally, there will be two area codes serving the same city or region. New numbers for telephones, faxes, and cell phones in a region may be assigned to the new area code, which means that two people on the same street could have phone numbers with different area codes.

You should be aware that the phone number of an organization can have a new area code, even if the organization has not moved and still has the same street address. Sometimes, the first information you receive about an area code change is when you try to complete a phone call and receive a message that the area code has changed or the phone is not in service. If this happens, call telephone information at the old area code by dialing the old area code plus 555-1212 and verify the area code and phone number. If you find that an area code has changed, change all phone lists as well as any programmed fax machines, computer dialers, or phone dialers. Area codes can be found on the Internet at *www.555-1212.com/aclookup.html*, *www.allareacodes.com*, or *www.nanpa.com/number_resource_info/area_code_maps.html.*

Time Zones

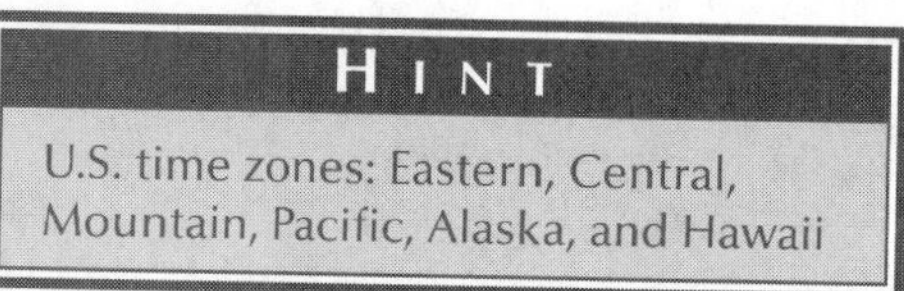

Before making any long-distance calls, determine the time of the place you are calling. The mainland United States is divided into four time zones (Eastern, Central, Mountain, and Pacific). Alaska is one hour earlier than the Pacific time zone and Hawaii is two hours earlier than the Pacific time zone. Canada includes the same four time zones as the mainland United States, plus the Atlantic time zone for the Maritime Provinces, which is an hour later than the Eastern time zone. The time of the Canadian island of Nova Scotia is a half-hour later than the Atlantic time zone. The United States territories in the Caribbean, Puerto Rico, and the Virgin Islands also are in the Atlantic time zone. Many telephone books include a map of the time zones in the United States and Canada. Most of Mexico is in the Central time zone with several western Mexican states in the Mountain or Pacific time zones.

The section of your local telephone book dealing with foreign telephone calls often includes information about the time difference between a foreign country and standard time. Standard time is usually the time zone for the area represented by the telephone book. In a New York City telephone book, for example, France is indicated as "+6 hours" from Eastern Standard Time (9 A.M. in New York City is 3 P.M. in Paris). Japan is "+14 hours," so, when it is 9 A.M. in New York City, it is 11 P.M. in Tokyo. Many countries move their clocks an hour forward in the summer for "Daylight Savings Time." Most of the United States observes Daylight Savings time from the first Sunday in April to the last Sunday in October. In Europe, summer time changes are from the last Sunday in March to the last Sunday in October. If an hour or two time difference is critical for reaching your party and you are unsure of the time in a foreign country, dial the telephone operator and ask for the time in the city you are calling. You also can check the current time in over 500 cities on the Internet. Following are helpful Web sites.

Time and date information

www.timeanddate.com/worldclock
www.worldtimeserver.com
www.worldtimezone.com

Calling Foreign Long-Distance

Making a call to some foreign countries can be as easy as making a domestic long-distance call. Long-distance calls among the United States (including Hawaii and Alaska), Canada,

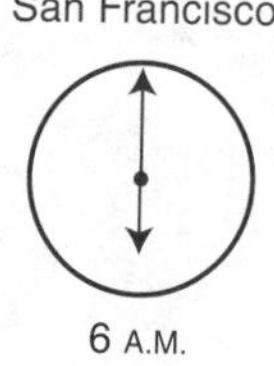

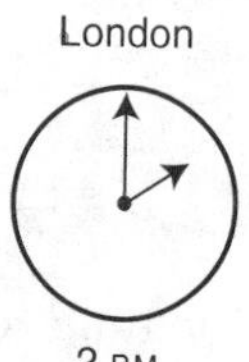

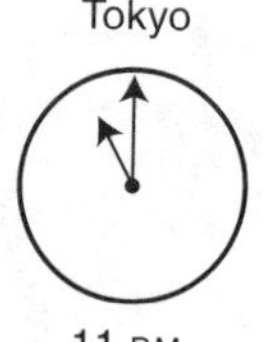

FIGURE 3-6 If it is 9 A.M. in New York, what time is it in Chicago, San Francisco, London, and Tokyo?

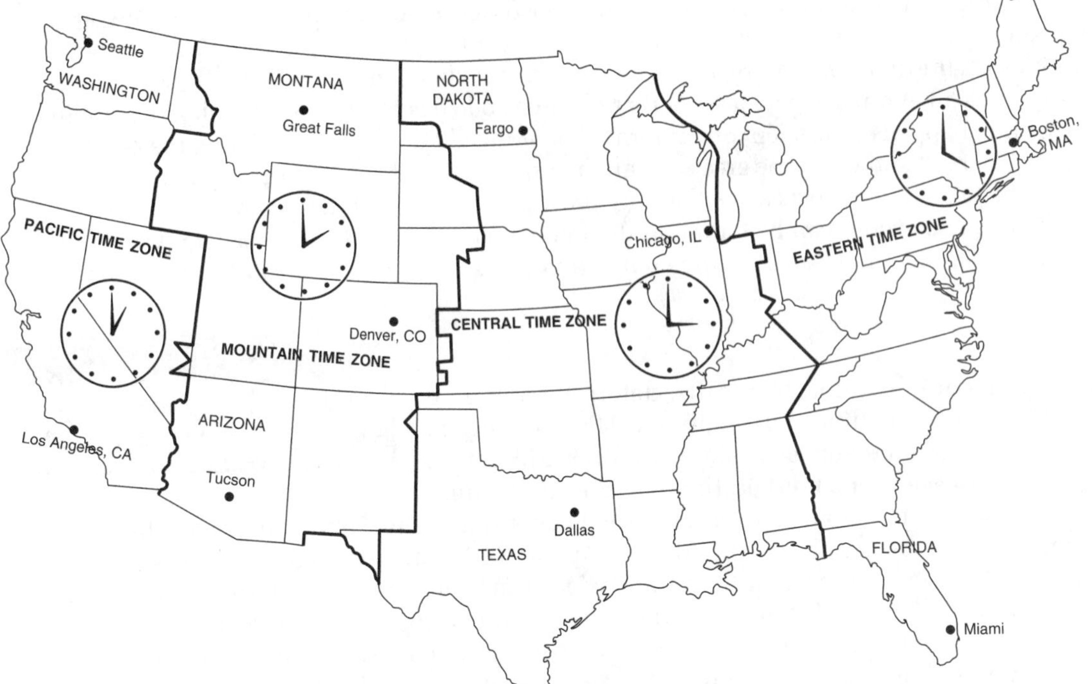

FIGURE 3-7 United States time zone map.

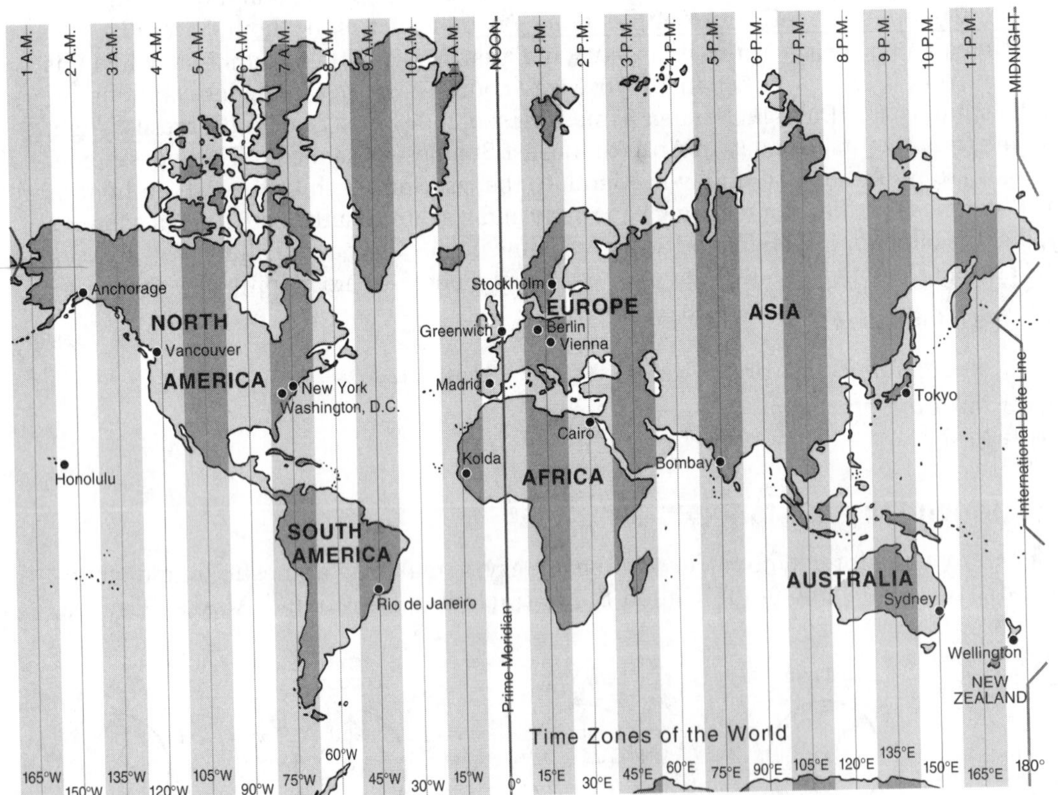

FIGURE 3-8 Worldwide time zone map.

and many islands of the Caribbean are dialed the same as domestic long-distance calls, "1" + area code + phone number.

Many foreign countries can be dialed directly. Foreign long-distance is usually accessed by first dialing "011" (instead of "1" for domestic long-distance). Then a two- or three-digit International Access Code, called a "country code," must be dialed. Some countries then use a "city code" (one, two, or three digits) before the local phone number. For example, calls to Mexico City must use a country code of "52" and a city code of "5" before the local telephone number is dialed. Local phone numbers vary in different countries. In the United States and Canada, all phone numbers are in the format 555-1212.

Lists of country and city codes of foreign nations that can be directly dialed are often included in the front sections of telephone books. Most frequently called foreign countries can be dialed directly. If an International Access Code for a country is not listed in the front of your city's telephone directory, contact the telephone operator and ask if the nation can be dialed directly. If the country cannot be dialed directly, then the operator must place the call. A long-distance operator-assisted foreign call may involve your local operator contacting several international operators to establish a circuit to the country you are calling. Completing an operator-assisted foreign call to a country without direct dialing access can be time-consuming, so you should plan extra time to complete a telephone call of this type.

Long-distance calls to each foreign country are a little different, since the local phone systems are so different. It will be helpful for you to keep a file of foreign long-distance calls made, which includes the local telephone number, a complete set of the access codes required, the time difference from your city, and any special problems encountered in making the call. Because of the time zone differences or the amount of time required to make some international calls, fax and email are often used to send international messages.

Some offices request that a record be made of all long-distance calls. This record is used to verify phone charges that appear on the company phone bill.

Date of Call ________________________________
Telephone Number Called ________________________________
Person Called ________________________________
Name of Company ________________________________
Reason for Call ________________________________
Name of Caller ________________________________
Telephone Number of Caller ________________________________

FIGURE 3-9 A long-distance record.

The following Web sites contain international area codes

www.1discountlongdistance.com/areacodescountry.html

www.countrycallingcodes.com

www.business.att.com/bt/access.jsp?c=a

Credit Card and Phone Card Calls

When you are out of the office, you can make long-distance telephone calls using either a calling card or a pre-paid phone card. A calling card works like a credit card for telephone calls. If your office has established a credit plan with its long-distance company, you will receive a calling card and a Personal Identification Number (PIN). You can then make a long-distance call from any telephone by calling the long-distance company on a toll-free number, entering the PIN, and then dialing the number you want to call. The phone charge will be included on the office's regular monthly phone bill. Calling card plans can also be established with your home long-distance provider so you can easily make personal long-distance calls while traveling.

Many companies sell prepaid phone cards which allow a person to purchase a fixed number of long-distance minutes. With a prepaid phone card, you purchase a card for a fixed cost, such as $5, $10, or $20. Each phone card has a unique authorization number. Using a phone card, you make a long-distance call the same way that you do with a calling card. You can make a long-distance call from any telephone by calling a toll-free number, entering the authorization number, and then dialing the number you want to call. The cost of the call is then subtracted from your account balance. Phone cards can be purchased at many grocery stores, gas stations, and other convenience stores, as well as through the Internet.

Using Voice Mail

Voice mail is a sophisticated telephone answering system that records a caller's voice for later playback. Most offices have a central voice mail answering system which serves an entire office instead of having an answering machine for each telephone. A voice mail system does not require the caller to use any special equipment, since the caller is simply dialing a phone extension. If the person being called does not answer, the caller is asked to leave a message, which is recorded on the voice mail system. The receiving party uses a regular touch-tone telephone to open a private mailbox assigned to that person. The mailbox is opened by keying in an individual access code to ensure privacy and then the recorded message is played. After the person listens to a voice mail message, the message can be deleted, forwarded to another office extension, stored in an archive for future replay, or replied to by dialing an office extension if the message was sent from within the office phone system. Voice mail messages can also be retrieved from a home or cell phone. To check messages while outside the office, the employee calls the office's central voice mail phone number and enters the individual's access code. The user then has the ability to use the features of the voice mail system.

Leaving voice mail messages

- Never chew food or gum when leaving a voice message.
- Speak slowly and distinctly.
- Organize your thoughts before you leave the message.
- Leave your name and telephone number. Your voice may not be recognizable to the recipient, and your call cannot be returned if your telephone number is unclear.
- Leave a short, concise message; do not ramble.
- Indicate why you are calling.
- Indicate when you will be in the office to receive the return telephone call.
- If you leave a long message, repeat your telephone number at the end of the message.

Setting up your voice mail

- Your office will instruct you how to set up your voice mailbox and record your greeting, which is the message a caller will hear if you are out of the office or on another line. Some voice mail systems identify the mailbox for the caller by using a standard greeting and insert the name and voice of the person being called.
- When recording your voice mail greeting, sound professional and enthusiastic. Do not make a cute or humorous voice mail greeting.
- Keep your voice mail greeting brief. People do not want to listen to a long message before leaving their message.
- If you are going to be out of the office for more than a day, change your voice mail greeting so the caller will be able to contact another employee for assistance in your absence.
- Select a personal access code that is easy to remember and easy to enter on a telephone keypad. Do not use an access code that is easy for others to guess, such as your birthday.

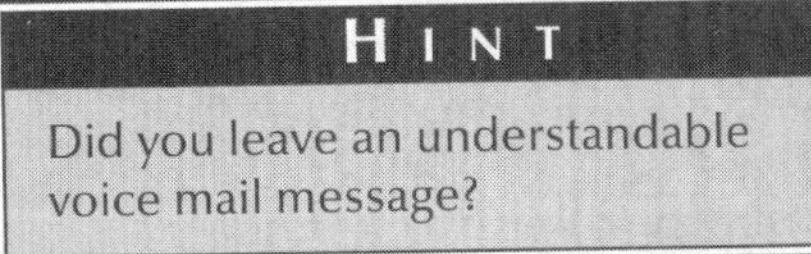

HINT
Did you leave an understandable voice mail message?

Date	Time	Caller	Company	Telephone No.	Message	Returned Call

FIGURE 3-10 A voice mail record.

Listening to Your Voice Mail

Most voice mail systems will alert you that a message is waiting, either by displaying a lighted button or by generating a distinctive sound when you pick up the telephone rather than the usual steady dial-tone. You should check your voice mail early each morning, in case you received messages after you left the office the previous evening, and check your voice mail throughout the day. It is possible to receive a voice mail message while you are talking on the phone with another caller. When you return to your office after a short absence, check your voice mail for messages and frequently check for messages left while you were on the telephone.

Since most offices have voice mail systems, listening to your voice mail messages will be a habitual task. It is common to receive fifteen or more voice mail messages each day, so you should develop a form to record your voice mail messages. The form should include the name and phone number of the caller, the date and time of the message, and information about the call or expected action. At a later date, your records will be available to document that the call was received, to record that you have taken the requested action, or to retrieve a telephone number.

Specialized Telephone Services and Equipment

Specialized Telephone Services

In addition to the standard telephone service, many specialized services have been developed to provide efficient voice communications for the office. This list is not exhaustive and phone companies continually design new services, which they offer to their customers. Be sure you understand your company's policy regarding any phone services that are offered, since these services can be costly to the business.

- *Automatic Callback* is a feature which can be used when a call is made to a phone that is in use. When the phone is free, the system automatically redials the number and notifies the caller.
- *Call Block* sends incoming telephone calls to a recorded message indicating that the call will not be accepted.
- *Call Forwarding* allows calls to be forwarded from one telephone to another. All calls from an unattended telephone can be forwarded to a telephone that is attended.
- *Call Return* automatically dials the number of the last incoming call.
- *Call Waiting* allows a single-line telephone to handle two telephone calls when the phone is in use. A beep signals that an incoming call is waiting. This feature allows the first call to be interrupted while the second call is answered. It is then possible to return to the first caller.
- *Caller ID* displays the caller's telephone number.
- *Different Rings* are available to distinguish internal calls (calls from within the same company) and external calls (calls from outside of the company).

- *Holding* is a feature where a call may be placed on hold while another call is being answered or while information is being found. To place a call on hold, depress the hold button. Telephone receivers should not simply be left open and placed on the desk because the caller can hear office background noises and conversations.
- *Multiline Telephones* permit a telephone to receive calls on more than one phone line. If a line is being used, the telephone displays a steady light. A flashing light indicates that a line is ringing.
- *Preferred Call Forwarding* permits calls from specific telephone numbers to be forwarded.
- *Repeat Number* is a feature where the last number dialed can be dialed again by depressing one key on the telephone.
- *Speed Dialing* of numbers that are frequently called can be coded so that they can be dialed quickly using one or two digits.
- *Transferring* of a call from one phone extension to another extension in the same company is often possible by dialing the last four digits of the number.

Most large offices have established internal telephone systems which provide direct telephone numbers for each extension and include many of these specialized services.

VoIP (Voice over IP—Internet Protocol) Telephones

HINT

In VoIP, the voice message is converted into a computerized sound file and processed using Internet Protocol procedures.

The integration of digital technology and the Internet to voice communications has expanded the services available on the office telephone. Phone service using VoIP technology is available for the modern office. VoIP phones operate very much like standard telephones, but the voice message is converted into a computerized sound file and processed using Internet Protocol procedures.

Because VoIP telephones are digital, they can store and display information about a phone call. VoIP phones usually have a display screen, which can display the length of time of a phone call, as well as lists of calls sent and received. The phone can store a personal telephone directory and selecting an entry can automatically dial the phone call. The VoIP phone makes and receives calls the same way a standard phone operates and can include such features as voice mail and Call Forwarding. An office can have VoIP telephones which use the digital features internally but are still connected to the usual public switched telephone system to complete the calls. The use of VoIP technology is transparent to both the caller and the person called.

If a business implements a full VoIP system, it is able to make long-distance calls using the Internet at almost no charge, since the Internet does not charge for the amount of voice or data sent or the distance between sender and receiver.

Cell Phones

Cell phones are small, wireless phones that permit a person to call and receive telephone calls while away from the office. For the busy office worker, cell phones have become a standard means of communication. People commonly use cell phones while in the car, on the street, in homes, and in offices. Cell phones weigh less than a pound and can fit into a pocket or purse. Most metropolitan areas and many rural areas of North America are served by cell phone services. Cell phone service is also available in many areas of Europe, Asia, and South America. A cell phone operates like a traditional telephone, with its own telephone number, and can receive calls like any other telephone.

Modern cell phones use digital technologies, which permit the storing of personal phone directories in the cell phone, as well as lists of calls sent and received. Cell phones come with many features, including Caller ID and voice mail. Cell phone technology has rapidly changed and many cell phones can receive emails and send and receive text. In

FIGURE 3-11 Using a cell phone.

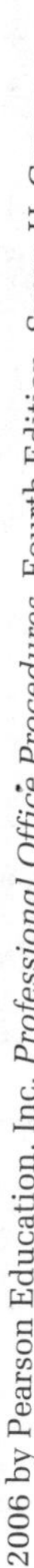

addition, cell phones can be used to connect to the Internet and read Web pages or connect to a fax machine to send written messages. Cell phones can also be used to send or receive music, pictures, and even short video clips. Cell phones are being built into many small PDAs.

One of the reasons that cell phone service has expanded so widely is the lowering of prices through the use of flat-rate pricing. For a single monthly fee, the cell phone user receives a set amount of cell phone minutes, with an extra charge for additional minutes.

Many cell phone plans include free night and weekend service or a family service plan which offers several phones for a specific price. Most cell phone services provide long-distance calling at no extra charge, if the phone number called is within the service area of the cell phone company.

The cell phones that are used in the United States usually do not work overseas, which can be a problem for international business travelers who are accustomed to using cell phone technology. There are literally dozens of different cellular telephone standards used around the world, and a cell phone that works in one country may not work in another. Companies now sell and rent cell phone systems that allow the international business traveler to communicate overseas. Travelers to foreign countries can rent cell phones from stores in the United States, from airport shops in the United States prior to traveling, from airport shops upon arrival in the foreign country, by mail, and online.

As the technology has advanced, cell phones and even PDAs now come with built-in cameras. These small cameras have become a security concern and businesses, manufacturing facilities, and government offices may prohibit taking cell phones and PDAs with cameras into restricted areas. Many people are also concerned about the presence of cell phones and PDAs with cameras in areas of personal privacy, such as bathrooms and health club showers.

Satellite Phones

There are several limitations to traditional cell phones. While cell phone service is very convenient and is available is most areas of the United States, there are still regions of the country where cell phone service is not available. There are vast areas of the world, such as the oceans, that have no cell phone service at all. Persons traveling outside North America, or even within the United States and Canada, may find that the local cell phone service, when available, does not work with their cell phone because of incompatible technology. In the event of natural disaster, cell phones may not work because the electricity which powers cell phone switching equipment may be disrupted. During times or in places where people have the greatest need for telephone communications, such as in remote areas or during emergency situations, cell phone service may not be available.

Satellite telephones have been developed to provide a single, reliable telephone service from anywhere in the world to anywhere else in the world. A satellite telephone is very similar to a cell phone, except that it uses communications satellites orbiting hundreds of miles above the earth as a relay in the phone system. A satellite phone is portable and can be placed in a briefcase or carried in a pocket. Placing or receiving a call on a satellite phone is the same as using a cell phone. Some satellite phones also work as cell phones and will try to use the local cell phone service before accessing the satellite service. Satellite phone service is more expensive than cell phone service but is a way for a busy executive to stay in touch when regular phone or cell phone service does not exist or is unreliable. Satellite phones can be purchased or rented.

Paging Equipment

A beeper, a paging device, is a small receiver that can be carried on the person and which "beeps" to alert the individual that a message has been received. Beepers, or pagers, can also notify the recipient of a message by lighting up or by vibrating. A telephone number or short message is displayed and then the person paged makes contact with the caller by using a regular telephone. Some paging equipment can record a voice message. Paging services cost much less than cell phone services and are usually used where people have relatively easy access to a telephone to contact the person placing the page. Some pagers have the ability to provide two-way communications. These pagers have small keyboards and allow users to send and receive text messages and faxes as well as access email and the Internet. While the use of paging equipment has decreased as the use of cell phones has grown, paging equipment can often be received inside buildings which block cell phone calls. Paging equipment remains an important communications device for many people.

Airline Telephones

Airline telephone service is available while flying in commercial airplanes over the continental United States, Canada, U.S. Virgin Islands, Alaska, Hawaii, and Puerto Rico. Many airlines offer this customer service on U.S. domestic flights and a few airlines are providing such service on flights to Europe and Asia. In some airplanes, the telephones are located at each seat, while other airlines have several phones located in the passenger cabins. The service is operated by the use of a major credit card. To operate the phone, insert the credit card, remove the handset, and place a call. When the handset is returned, the call is charged to the credit card and the credit card is then released. Use of airline telephones is expensive and should only be used when the cost is justified.

Telephone Ethics

Personal telephone calls should not be made from an office telephone. However, it is difficult to avoid all personal telephone calls during office hours. Personal calls should be kept short and limited to those that are essential. Some offices have stated policies regarding making and receiving personal telephone calls on business phones. Ask what the company policy is and adhere to it without exception.

Office telephones should not be used for personal long-distance calls. Occasionally companies will make their long-distance service available to employees for personal use. Be sure of company policy before using the company's long-distance service. Do not simply assume that the company allows employees to use the long-distance service because other coworkers make personal long-distance calls from the office.

TELECONFERENCING

A teleconference is a meeting in which one or more of the participants attend through the use of audio or video equipment, rather than physically being in the same room with the other participants. A teleconference can be conducted quickly and inexpensively using a speakerphone or can be a complex multisite video teleconference. A participant who teleconferences to a meeting saves the time and money of travel to the meeting site. Teleconferences can be successful or can fail, depending on premeeting planning and the willingness of the participants to include the distant attendees in the group.

> **HINT**
>
> A teleconference is a meeting in which the participants are not in the same room but use audio or video equipment to communicate.

Speakerphones

A speakerphone is a telephone with an audio speaker and a microphone so several people can participate in a phone conversation. Many desktop phones have speakerphones built in, and separate speakerphone attachments can also be used so a microphone can be placed in the middle of a table during a group meeting. A speakerphone can also be used without the speakerphone feature activated for regular private telephone conversations. A call from a speakerphone is placed in the usual manner, and then the speakerphone feature is turned on. Using a speakerphone is a simple method of bringing two groups of people together for a meeting.

In addition, speakerphones can be used by one person during a call when holding a telephone handset may be inconvenient or tiring. Speakerphones are often used during audio conference calls, which may last an hour or more. In addition, speakerphones are also useful if you need to get out of your chair or use both hands for other activities during the call.

If you do not have a private office, your end of the speakerphone conversation can be overheard by another person in the room; therefore, you should be considerate of other people in your office when using a speakerphone. You should not interfere with the privacy of others in your office by using a speakerphone and you should recognize that your phone conversation will not be private. It is, therefore, common courtesy to ask your caller if you may put him or her on a speakerphone so the person is aware that the call is not private.

> **HINT**
>
> A speakerphone is a telephone with an audio speaker.

Conference Calls: Audio Conferencing

Travel is expensive in both time and money, so executives frequently use conference calls to allow people at several locations to consult with each other. A conference call is sometimes set up with a telephone company operator in advance of making the call. At the time the arrangements are made, the employee notifies the operator of the time of the call, as well as the names, locations, and telephone numbers of people participating in the call. The meeting participants are provided a telephone number with an access code. Internal telephone systems in many businesses are equipped with conference call capabilities that allow employees to place their own conference calls. Directions for using these systems are usually found in an office telephone manual.

Tips for conference calls

- Prior to the conference call, distribute a list of participants and an agenda.
- Identify yourself the first few times you speak so other participants know who is talking.
- When you speak, face the microphone.
- Remember that the people listening cannot see you. Your words should convey your message, as you cannot use verbal cues or gestures to support your statements.
- Do not interrupt another speaker.
- Do not make a private comment to another person in your room; it could be overheard.
- Use your telephone mute button when you are not talking to reduce background noise during the conference call.
- Do not use your telephone hold button during the conference call if your phone system plays music for calls on hold.
- When the telephone conference is over, thank the person who arranged the call.

HINT

A conference call allows people at various locations to talk with each other.

Video Teleconferencing

Video teleconferencing is usually more expensive than audio teleconferencing but allows the participants to see and speak with each other. Often one-way video teleconferencing is used, so the main speaker is seen by the participants, and the participants can respond to the speaker via voice-only telephone. Video teleconferencing frequently is used for staff training. High-quality video conferencing requires video cameras, camera operators, and costly video channels or satellite communications. It is usually expensive to set up a video teleconference and arrangements must be made for both sending and receiving the video signal. Some companies have established their own full-time video teleconferencing facilities, while, in many large cities, businesses which provide video conferencing services have been established for the occasional user of this service.

Special equipment is used to send video signals over fiber optic lines or telephone lines. This equipment is referred to as codec (code/decode) equipment and compresses the video signal at the sender's end for transmission. Some video conferencing equipment has cameras with remote control built into an integrated unit with a television receiver. The recipient must have compatible decoding equipment to expand the video signal. Using this equipment, video conferencing can be used by businesses on a routine basis. In addition to business meetings, video conferencing is now being used to answer customer questions and solve technical problems.

With advances in computer technology and the increasing availability of broadband, video conferencing is also available on a desktop computer connected to the Internet. Using a small camera clipped to a computer monitor and inexpensive software, the costs of establishing a video conference between several sites is now within reach of many offices. The quality of the video picture, however, will vary with the sophistication of equipment/software used and the speed of the Internet access. The quality of computer-based video conferencing can range from a series of still pictures (called *freeze frame*) occupying a part of the computer screen, to slow scan video (a *slow-motion picture*), to a *full motion video* picture which fills the computer monitor screen. If several sites are involved in the video conference, they may each be seen in a box occupying a portion of the screen. By using video conferencing over the Internet, small businesses can conduct meetings across the country while saving the time and cost of staff travel.

How you dress for a video conference is very important. Avoid wearing bold patterns—they look "busy" on the screen. Also, a solid white or black dress or jacket is not a good choice. Blue and gray are good color choices because they do not blend into the background but do not stand out and attract too much attention.

HINT

A video conference allows participants in various locations to see and speak with each other.

Speaking Before a Group

As you advance up the career ladder, you may be asked to speak in front of a group. At the conclusion of a project, oral presentations are often given to members of the department, supervisors, or members of the board of directors. In addition, community groups may request that you address their organizations. Being comfortable speaking in front of a group is an asset to your career advancement. Each speech should be designed to meet the specific needs of the listeners. The research techniques used when collecting data for a written report are also used when writing an oral report or a speech. When developing the speech, think about the goals and interests of the audience. Then prepare your thoughts to meet the needs of the audience. Never allow personal biases or prejudices to be expressed, and do not use ethnic jokes that may offend someone.

Hints for giving a successful speech

1. Determine your objectives and know your topic well.
2. Organize your thoughts with an outline.
3. Remember that members of the audience have their own interests. Explain how your ideas will benefit them.
4. Include the fundamental points in your speech, but do not overwhelm the audience with too many facts. If you desire, you can distribute a handout sheet with additional information.
5. Do not memorize your speech. Prepare notes on index cards or prepare a sheet of keyboarded notes. List specific words or phrases you want to use. If you know your topic well, your notes should be a guide to keep your thoughts organized.
6. Under some circumstances, the complete speech may be written. It is easier to read a keyboarded double- or triple-spaced speech printed in larger than normal type than reading a handwritten speech.
7. Practice delivering the speech to your family or in front of a mirror.
8. Since you do not want people to look at your clothing instead of listening to you, wear conservative clothing.
9. When the occasion requires your thanking the organization for inviting you, begin your speech by expressing your pleasure at receiving the invitation.
10. Begin each speech with an attention-getter, which can be a joke, an anecdote, a question, or a quotation.
11. Do not talk to your audience in a condescending manner. The audience may tune you out if they feel you are patronizing them.
12. During the speech,
    - Stand so you can be seen and heard.
    - Be enthusiastic.
    - Smile.
    - Appear interested in your audience and in the topic of your speech.
    - Pause between major divisions of the speech. This will allow the audience to better understand your topic.
    - Speak clearly and distinctly.
    - Move your head so that you view the entire audience.
    - Appear to look people in the eye. If gazing directly at people disturbs you, appear to look at them but look slightly over their heads.
    - Do not turn off all the lights in the room. People need some light to take notes. A dark room encourages people to daydream or doze—especially after eating.
13. If you will distribute a handout, decide whether you will distribute the handouts before or after the speech. If the handouts are distributed prior to the speech, the audience will be able to write notes on them. However, if they are distributed before the speech, people may read them during your speech and not listen to you, or they may leave before the speech is completed.

FIGURE 3-12 Making a presentation may require the use of a flipchart, a podium, or projection equipment and a screen.

14. Always ask for questions at the end of the speech. If no one has questions and you still have time, you should have a list of additional thoughts to discuss or questions you can ask the audience.
15. Use charts, large transparencies, flipcharts, white boards, or computer presentation software to illustrate the speech.
16. If you are using computer or projection equipment that is provided by the organization, arrive early and verify that it works. If you are taking your own computer equipment, confirm that you know how to hook it up so it works. Speakers often become nervous and forget how to plug everything into the correct outlets. Also have available an extra electrical strip plug.

Visual Aids for a Presentation

Visual aids enhance a presentation in several ways. People remember more from a picture than they do when they listen to a speech. Visual aids reinforce the oral message, create a mental image which is easy to remember, and create additional interest in the oral presentation. Pictures, displays, and charts add variety and, therefore, simulate the listener's involvement in the presentation. To enhance the effectiveness of your speech, use some of the following visual aids.

Boards

A board may be white or colored, and is used with a specifically designed marker and eraser.

Easels and Flipcharts

Easels and flipcharts hold pads of large sheets of paper. Visuals on the pages can be prepared before the meeting or can be written on during the presentation.

Transparencies

Transparencies are sheets of clear plastic that can be prepared prior to a presentation or written on during it. Transparencies must be used with an overhead projector. A speaker can use colored transparency sheets to add visual variety to the presentation. Transparencies can be mounted in hinged Vugraph frames to permit the overlay of several transparencies in a sequence to create a complex visual. Transparency markers are available in a range of colors and allow the speaker to write directly on the transparency plastic. It is difficult for the audience to read transparencies that are exact copies of keyboarded pages because the print is too small, but many photocopiers have the ability to enlarge text. In addition, word processing software packages easily enlarge the font size of keyboarded text to improve legibility when used to print text on a plastic transparency.

Slides

Slides include photographs or other graphic material and must be prepared well before the meeting. Slides must be shown in a predetermined sequence using a slide projector, and the slides cannot be altered during the presentation.

Computer Presentations

To enhance presentations, many speakers use computer software packages. Computer software packages permit the creation of a presentation which includes graphics, charts, sound, clipart, and animation to capture the attention of the audience and retain their interest. Presentation software must be used with a computer and video projector to project visual material onto a screen for audience viewing. While the audience views the presentation, the speaker explains and reinforces the important discussion points. Computer software presentation packages have become an indispensable business tool used by many speakers. One of the most popular computer presentation software packages is Microsoft PowerPoint.

OTHER OFFICE TELECOMMUNICATIONS

Digital Voice Recorders

A digital voice recorder is another telecommunications tool to assist the busy employee both in the office and out of the office. Most digital voice recorders are small, light-weight, easy to use; have reasonable sound quality; and include software for transfer from the recorder to the computer. Messages are dictated into the digital voice recorder and are stored digitally. The message can be later transcribed or transferred to a computer file. Messages can be saved, edited, or emailed, thus increasing office productivity.

Internet and Intranet

The Internet is a collection of computer networks that communicate together using telecommunication protocols and has become a very important part of most offices. Most people today are familiar with the Internet because they have surfed the Web or received email. The World Wide Web, which is often identified as WWW and called the Web, is a collection of information available from the Internet using a graphical interface. An intranet is for internal communications allowing employees to use hyperlinks to connect to documents, information, and so on. Many companies also provide chat room space on their intranet to encourage sharing of ideas and concerns. Information about the Internet is found in Chapter 5, Computers in the Office.

Wireless Access

In today's high-tech world, immediate information is desired and often critical. Business has moved outside the traditional office to the car, golf course, kitchen table, vacation home, client's office, coffee bar, and other nontraditional locations. On-the-go employees require access to voice mail, email, news, and the Internet. There are several wireless communications technologies that are widely used by businesses. These include cell phones, pagers, airline telephones, and Personal Digital Assistants (PDAs), sometimes referred to as handheld computers. Advances in technology encourage the concept of the virtual office, where the employee is available 24/7. More Information about wireless access will be found in Chapter 5, Computers in the Office.

CHAPTER REVIEW

1. Explain voice mail.
2. Explain how internal telephone systems operate.
3. Explain VoIP.
4. Describe the appropriate voice techniques to be used when answering the telephone.
5. What information should be included in telephone messages?
6. Explain how a speakerphone is used.
7. List two hints for a teleconference.
8. List three hints for a successful speech.
9. Describe visual aids that can be used when speaking to a group.

ACTIVITIES

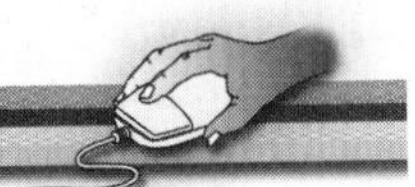

1. Find a telephone partner for role playing. One person will be the caller and the other will be the administrative assistant answering the telephone. In the first role-playing activity, the administrative assistant will be pleasant when the caller requests an appointment. In the second role-playing activity, the administrative assistant will be rude and bored. Notice how the rude administrative assistant causes the caller to become angry and upset. After the two role-playing activities, reverse the caller and administrative assistant roles and role play the calls again.
2. Prepare a personal telephone directory listing all friends and businesses that you call frequently.
3. Visit an office supply store and write a description of three types of telephone directories. Directories may also be called telephone/address books.
4. Visit an office supply store and look at the types of message pads available. Write a paragraph describing each pad and noting the differences. Be sure to note the prices of pads available. You may use the Internet for research for this activity.
5. Keep a record for two days of all of the telephone calls that are received in your home. Indicate which calls are personal and which are business.
6. Create a message form for home telephone calls. Record all telephone calls received during a twenty-four hour period.
7. Ask an administrative assistant to describe three difficult types of telephone calls that are often received. Explain how the calls are handled.
8. Using a tape recorder, prepare a recording of your voice. Speak in a conversational tone. Listen to the tape and analyze your voice. Is it too high-pitched? Does it sound whiny? Is it difficult to understand? Do you speak in an enthusiastic and friendly manner? What changes should you make in your voice?
9. Using the Internet, find two business telephone numbers.
10. Using the Internet, find telephone numbers of two relatives or friends who live in other states.

PROJECTS

Project 5

Key in the following letter to Ms. Mollie C. Hayes, 818 Oakmont Drive, Seattle, WA 98028. Use a modified block letter style and provide any additional information needed to complete the letter. The letter is from J. C. Murray.

Dear Mollie:

I do not know if you have heard the news. At last month's Board of Directors meeting, I announced my intention to retire in about a year. The Board appeared surprised about my announcement, but I have been thinking of retiring for a long time. As you know, I would like to spend more time with my family.

You have several potential candidates for my position in your department, and I hope that you will encourage them to apply for the job. When we met at the Houston convention, we discussed possible employment opportunities with my company. As you know, the company is on the high-tech track and is in a good position to develop and launch a new program. The Director of Personnel is anxious to receive your applications.

I hope you and your family are well. Please give them my regards.

Project 6

Send this memo to the staff. It is from Nicole J. Nelson.

Please join me in welcoming Ms. Laura Berkeley as our new Communications Director. Ms. Berkeley will be arriving next week, and she is very excited about the opportunities and challenges facing her at our company.

Ms. Berkeley, who received both her undergraduate and graduate degrees in communications from Michigan State University, comes to us from Northeast Communications, Inc. Ms. Berkeley is highly respected in the communications field and will be a fine addition to our company.

A reception will be held in her honor on Friday from 2 to 4 P.M. in the Board of Directors Conference Room.

I look forward to seeing you at the reception. Ms. Berkeley is anxious to begin her work here, so take this opportunity to welcome her and offer her your support.

HUMAN RELATIONS SKILL DEVELOPMENT

HR 3-1 Praise

Most people enjoy receiving praise for a job completed satisfactorily. Unfortunately, some managers do not give praise often enough, and some do not give praise at all. Praise increases job satisfaction and demonstrates that the company knows how valuable the employee is.

- What do you say to an employer who praises you for a job well done?
- How can you encourage your employer to reward the staff with positive comments when a job has been completed?
- In your role as supervisor, what would you say to an employee who stayed late to complete an important last-minute report?
- What would you say to praise your employer?

HR 3-2 Prejudice

Do not allow your personal prejudice to influence your work in the office. Here are some examples of unfounded prejudices: Have you always thought that people with certain color hair are rude? Do you think that people who wear unusual or flashy clothing are not professional? Do you think that people who are heavy (or slender) are not as smart as others? Do you have a dislike for people who have unusual accents? Do you dislike persons who have a particular personality trait? Everyone with whom you work should receive your respect and courtesy. Treat every colleague as a professional, and expect to receive the same treatment in return.

- What are your personal biases?
- How are you going to control or overcome your biases?
- Have you demonstrated a negative reaction to a person because of a personality trait? What was the trait?

SITUATIONS

How would you handle the following situations?

- **S 3-1** Your supervisor asked you to arrange a conference call for tomorrow morning, so you set the call for 8 A.M. because your supervisor, who works in Washington, DC, always arrives at work at 7:30. The participants are in New York, Chicago, Dallas, and San Diego. What did you do wrong?
- **S 3-2** This is the third time that you have not received a telephone message. What are you going to say to your assistant?
- **S 3-3** You have difficulty obtaining your supervisor's attention. The last time you approached your supervisor with a question, she continued to work and told you to make your comments quickly.

PUNCTUATION REVIEW

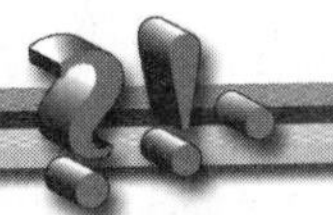

Punctuate each of the following sentences.

1. Due to a recent increase in the cost of materials we must adjust our prices by 3 percent for each unit
2. Mollie who is the manager frequently took the train because it was more convenient
3. Katie also registered for the lecture
4. I need the following items audio tapes video tapes and transparency markers
5. Through a new computerized reservation system that was shown yesterday by Travelers Incorporated business travelers will be able to get information from their travel agents about hotel chains such as Hyatt Marriott and Sheraton
6. For office managers this certificate can serve as a valuable tool for performance evaluations which are the keys to advancement
7. Janie the computer was moved to the new building
8. However Nelson Wagner Jr noted that the action signaled new confidence in the industry
9. Jack asked did interest rates rise

10. Under the new legislation a tax credit was given to students under the age of twenty-five and those earning less than the minimum poverty level wage
11. The stock market had a net gain of 29.34 points but my stock price declined
12. The planned merger of ATEX and METRA which should occur in January is the brainstorm of three individuals Janice Helfstein Olga Rocher and Phillip Francis
13. Since office rents are high in the East they moved the company headquarters to the Midwest
14. Most people prefer to be close to their offices but housing downtown is very expensive
15. Alicia changed the filing system therefore the efficiency of the office was increased

CD ASSIGNMENTS

CD Assignment 3-1

Open the file CD3-1_ISP on your student CD and follow the instructions to complete the job.

CD Assignment 3-2

Open the file CD3-2_IDV on your student CD and follow the instructions to complete the job.

Processing the Mail 4

Objectives

After studying this chapter, you should be able to

1. Process and sort incoming mail.
2. Prepare a mail register of incoming mail.
3. Prepare a chronological register of incoming mail for a traveling executive.
4. List the services offered by the United States Postal Service (USPS).
5. Explain the classes of mail offered by the United States Postal Service.
6. Explain franked and penalty mail.
7. Evaluate express mail services.
8. Recognize the two-letter abbreviations for United States and Canadian provinces.
9. Explain the use of ZIP Codes.
10. Explain the use of postage machines.

Processing Incoming Mail

Mail Delivery

While the use of email and facsimiles (faxes) has increased dramatically in recent years, one of the most important responsibilities of an administrative assistant continues to be the processing of incoming mail. In a small company, the mail is delivered to the office once a day by a United States Postal Service carrier. In a large business, the mail may be delivered first to a company's central mail room, where it is sorted by building, department, or floor before it is distributed to individual offices. Depending on the volume of mail and the size of the company, deliveries may be made more than once a day. While the central mail room relieves the administrative assistant of some of the routine duties of processing the mail, the presence of a central mail room also means that an additional step has been added to the mail-sorting process. This extra step may mean delays of half a day or more in both sending and receiving the mail.

When the mail is received, it should be opened and stamped with the date of receipt. The stamping, which may indicate the time and date of receipt, can be done by hand with a rubber stamp or by a machine. Documenting the date of receipt is critical for many businesses. While most mail is opened by the administrative assistant, company policy may permit mail addressed to specific individuals or mail designated "personal" to be distributed unopened.

Since traditional mail delivered is slower than mail transmitted electronically, traditional mail is sometimes referred to by its slang term, *snail mail.*

Sorting and Distributing the Mail

Depending on the size and layout of the office, the mail should first be sorted according to department, floor, section, office, or similar division. The mail should then be sorted for each

FIGURE 4-1 Putting mail in employee mailboxes.

person within an office. It is usually the administrative assistant's responsibility to sort general mail addressed to the office so that it is forwarded to the proper employees. In many offices, mail is often addressed to the office head, while actually intended for other office staff. The administrative assistant must know how to efficiently distribute the mail so that the proper person quickly receives it. For example, all payments may be forwarded to one person and all invoices to another, and correspondence regarding a specific project may be directed to the person responsible for that project. You should keep a list at your desk of how office projects are assigned to aid in the sorting of mail.

Often, action is taken on the mail by the administrative assistant before the mail is distributed to other employees. Receipt of the item might be entered into a computer log, a tracking number may be assigned, or data entry may be made of the action requested or to whom the mail is directed.

Regular mail and interoffice mail are usually placed in individual mailboxes, often stacked trays, which are in a central location. Express mail and mail for top executives may be taken directly to their offices. Depending on the volume of mail and the procedures of the office, individual mail may also be sorted according to urgency of the item.

Individual mail may be sorted in the following categories

- Express mail, certified, and registered mail
- First-class and personal mail
- Newspapers, magazines, advertising materials, and catalogs
- Packages

In some offices, if the supervisor is out of town, a chronological list of all mail received may be prepared. This list enables the returning executive to quickly review all mail received.

Mail Roster
Clifton Lamb
April 3-7, XXXX

Date	Item	What Was Done With Item	By Whom
4/3/XXXX	Letter P & M Company	Sent to Valerie	Julie
4/4/XXXX	Letter B. G. Corporation	Waiting	Maria
4/5/XXXX	Report Zev Co.	Sent to Ted	Maria
4/7/XXXX	Insurance policy	Sent to Jenny	Julie

FIGURE 4-2 A Mail Roster for a traveling executive.

Coding the Mail

After receiving the mail, some executives code or write notes in the margins indicating what is to be done with the letter. Examples of these notes are "file," "find file folder," "answer this letter," "talk with [another person] about the letter," and "what do you think of this suggestion?"

May 17, XXXX

Ms. Susan Churchill
8934 Jefferson Blvd.
Indianapolis, IN 46260

Dear Ms. Churchill:

I have carefully read the report of your last trip to the South Pacific, and I am impressed with your findings.

I do need clarification of a few points.

1. What is the projected cost to refurbish the lobby of the Island Hotel?
2. How long do you anticipate the renovation will take? *3 months*
3. Would you recommend Polynesian Construction, Inc., or R. N. Woo Construction Company? *Check the file*
4. Do you recommend refurbishing the entire hotel at one time or refurbishing over a period of years?

As we discussed at our last teleconference, I am eager to begin this project. I would appreciate receiving your responses as soon as possible.

Sincerely,

B. W. Biltman

B. W. Biltman

Write a response for my signature

rty

FIGURE 4-3 A coded letter.

Color coding can be used to indicate the processing procedure. For example, a blue check mark may mean "file," a red check mark may mean "hold for response," and a yellow check mark may mean "handle for me."

Rubber stamps can also be used to speed the coding process. A small form containing the most often used codes could be stamped on the mail, permitting an executive to check the code appropriate for the item. To speed the processing of the mail even more, a single stamp with the date of receipt and coding may be used. Today many people code mail by writing on sticky notes and attaching the notes to the letters.

After a manager codes the mail, an administrative assistant completes the action required. In some offices, an administrative assistant opens the letter, reads it, and completes the necessary action. The letter is then filed in the appropriate file. A copy of the letter with a note indicating the action taken is given to the manager so the manager can monitor the action or make revisions before the letter is mailed.

FAXES

A facsimile machine (usually called a fax machine) is a standard piece of equipment in most offices, and it is used to send exact copies of reports, letters, graphics, and so on over a telephone line. A photocell or laser scans a page and converts images text, or graphics into an electronic signal. Information is not rekeyed, so time is saved and the accuracy of the transmission is assured. Graphic and hand-signed materials can be transmitted as easily as typed or printed material. A document, converted into electronic signals, is sent to a receiving facsimile machine. When the document is received, a copy is printed. Some machines send the signals to a computer instead of a fax machine, and the document is stored on a disk. Unless the receiving machine has a computer attached, only the hard copy is available when received—nothing is saved on tape or disk.

Most fax machines conform to international standards and can send a document to a foreign country at the cost of a telephone call. Fax machines which are connected to their own telephone line can answer the telephone automatically and receive the information transmitted. Using fax machines can, therefore, be very useful in sending information during normal business hours in North America to a foreign country where the local time could be the middle of the night.

The advantages of using fax machines, therefore, are similar to those of email. Fax machines are especially useful when you need to send an exact copy of a document, including showing signatures, handwritten notes, letterheads, and date stamps. Faxes are also used when you do not have an electronic version of the document. If you have a document in hand, it is often easier to fax the document than to search for the electronic file and email it. You may also want to fax documents with many graphics, which may be slow to send via email.

When sending a fax, carefully key in the fax number. If the fax is sent to an incorrect number, it will probably be thrown in the trash, and the sender will be unaware that it was not received. Many fax machines will print a transmission log which contains the phone number to which the fax was sent. Check the number on the transmission log to be sure that the fax was sent to the right number. It is also a good idea to keep a copy of the transmission log to document that the fax was sent and that the transmission was completed. Some fax machines will even print the first page of the fax on the transmission log as additional documentation that the correct fax was sent, along with the date, time, and receiving phone number. In addition, various fax machines automatically print monthly reports of faxes sent and received, and companies keep these fax records as part of their office documents.

HINT
A fax sends exact copies of reports, letters, graphics, and so on over a telephone line.

When using a fax machine, remember that anyone at the receiving end can read the document. Obviously, confidential material should only be faxed with care. Some fax machines have mailboxes that store documents until a personal

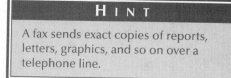

L & J Corporation
14 Lee Street
Washington, DC 20023
Fax 202-488-9000
Phone 202-488-9001

FAX

To: ________________
Company: ________________
Fax No.: ________________
Telephone No.: ________________
Date: ________________
Pages: ________________
Subject: ________________
From: ________________

FIGURE 4-4 A fax cover sheet.

access code is entered. If the document you are faxing is urgent or contains sensitive information, it is wise to notify the receiver that a fax is coming.

Frequently a cover sheet is used when a document is faxed. Companies often create their own cover sheet or use the cover sheet templates which are included with word processing software packages.

To obtain a fax number use a fax directory, which is similar to a telephone directory and lists the company name and fax number. Fax directories are also available as part of online Internet services.

You can fax a document directly from many word processing programs without having to first print the document on paper. If your computer or network is connected to a fax modem and has the proper software, it is easy to fax a message to one person or to a hundred people. You can set up a series of address lists and then fax a document to all people attending an upcoming meeting or to all salespersons in a particular region. This method of faxing is referred to as *broadcast fax* or *blast fax* and is a time-saving way of sending faxes to many people. A broadcast fax is an efficient method of distribution, and it can be scheduled to send faxes overnight or during weekends when the fax machine is not otherwise in use.

If you have a large list of clients to contact, there are companies that offer broadcast (blast) fax and broadcast (blast) email or combined fax and email services. If you provide the company with a computer file or paper document, the service will send mass faxes or emails to many recipients. This relatively low-cost medium is a powerful method of reaching many clients efficiently and quickly. The fax and emails can even be personalized for each recipient. These techniques, however, should be used with care and should only be used to send information to people who request it. Under Federal law, it is illegal to send unsolicited faxes (*spam faxes*), a crime punishable by a $500 fine for every fax sent.

Fax back capability permits a person calling an organization to automatically receive a fax without human intervention. A phone call is answered by a computer, which responds with recorded messages. The caller may have a prepared list of publications available or the computer may use a synthesized voice to recite a listing of information available through the service. Using the telephone keypad, the caller enters the number of the item requested as well as the phone number of the fax machine that will receive the document. The computer then automatically faxes the information to the caller's fax machine or computer. Fax back capability is a service for the distribution of information on demand and is available any hour of the day without the need for live staffing.

FIGURE 4-5 A medical assistant sending a fax.

Sorting Incoming Faxes

In some offices, the administrative assistant is responsible for sorting and delivering faxed material. Many offices place their fax machine near the administrative assistant's desk, so incoming faxes can be quickly processed. Check the fax machine after each incoming fax is received to determine if it is urgent. If the material is routine, the document can be processed as part of the incoming mail.

Often, incoming faxes are sent in response to a telephone call from a staff member who needs the material immediately. You may get a call from a staff member asking that you look for an expected incoming fax. If the incoming fax is not routine, contact the appropriate staff member and ask if he or she needs the fax delivered immediately. Do not be surprised if staff members sometimes linger around the fax machine waiting for an incoming document.

Internal Distribution of Mail

Mail can be forwarded to individuals within an office through the use of a routing slip. This procedure allows the same mail to be sent to one or more employees and indicates what employees should do after receiving the mail. An administrative assistant should develop and reproduce a routing slip that is appropriate for the office.

Interoffice envelopes, which usually are not sealed, are used to send items within the same company. Interoffice envelopes are about 9.5 × 12.5 inches in size, so they can hold several documents. The envelopes can be used several times. Each user crosses out the name of the previous user and writes the name of the new addressee on the next available line. A supply of interoffice envelopes should be made available to employees who send interoffice mail.

Sent to	__________
Sent by	__________
Date	__________
Procedures	
Read	__________
File	__________
Forward to	__________
Discuss with	__________
Handle	__________
Other	__________

FIGURE 4-6 A routing slip.

For Your Information

Sent by __________

Date __________

	Date	Comments
Woo Chang	____	______
Rhonda Chapel	____	______
Brad Cosmo	____	______
Leroy Silver	____	______
Charlie West	____	______
Rodney Healy	____	______
Connie Johnson	____	______

FIGURE 4-7 A routing slip with staff names.

INTERDEPARTMENTAL MAIL

Name __________	Name __________
Dept. __________	Dept. __________
Name __________	Name __________
Dept. __________	Dept. __________
Name __________	Name __________
Dept. __________	Dept. __________
Name __________	Name __________
Dept. __________	Dept. __________
Name __________	Name __________
Dept. __________	Dept. __________
Name __________	Name __________
Dept. __________	Dept. __________

FIGURE 4-8 An interoffice envelope.

PREPARING FIRST-CLASS MAIL TO LEAVE THE OFFICE

For an administrative assistant, processing outgoing mail is a much more complex task than processing incoming mail. You will have to prepare the mail for delivery across your city or across the world. Mail must comply with regulations or standards established by the United States Postal Service (USPS) or other private carriers.

The standard way to send letters, business correspondence, checks, personal letters, and cards is to use USPS First-Class Mail. First-Class Mail is used to send standard-size letters and you should expect delivery within one to three days, depending on the distance the mail has to travel.

Mail that is sent First-Class Mail must meet the following size requirements:

• Shape:	Rectangular			
• Height	Minimum:	3 1/2 inches	Maximum:	6 1/8 inches
• Length	Minimum:	5 inches	Maximum:	11 1/2 inches
• Thickness	Minimum:	.007 inches	Maximum:	1/4 inches
• Weight	Less than 13 oz.			

However, there are many circumstances when you cannot use First-Class Mail. If the mail does not meet the sizing requirements of First-Class Mail, or if delivery must be quicker than the standard delivery time for First-Class Mail, you will need to consider other ways to send mail. The USPS provides several other classes of mail service which can deliver mail or packages larger than the sizes permitted for First Class, faster than First Class, or less expensive than First-Class Mail. There are also private companies that provide next-day mail delivery or that transport packages. The use of next-day delivery or package delivery services is very important to many businesses. Information about these services is contained later in this chapter in the section Next-Day Mail and Package Delivery Services.

The section Using Other USPS Mail Classes and Services also contains information about additional services that can be added to First-Class Mail. For an additional charge, First-Class Mail can be enhanced with the following services: Certified Mail, Certificate of Mailing, Insured Mail, Registered Mail, Delivery Confirmation, Signature Confirmation, and Collect on Delivery.

Whether you use USPS First-Class Mail, use another service from the USPS, or use a private delivery company, you must follow the same basic requirements in preparing the outgoing mail.

Folding the Letter

Most letters are prepared on regular-size stationery, which is sized 8.5 by 11 inches. A letter on paper this size can be folded in thirds and mailed in a standard business-size No. 10 envelope. To fold a letter so it is placed in the envelope properly, start with the letter facing you as you would read it. Pick up the bottom of the letter and fold it about one-third of the way up. Then fold the top of the letter down so that it is about 1/4 inch short of the first fold. This 1/4-inch gap will assist the reader in unfolding the letter. Place the letter in the envelope with the 1/4-inch gap facing you and toward the top of the envelope. Documents of more than about five pages are usually too thick to place in a No. 10 envelope. These thicker documents should be mailed in large manila envelopes.

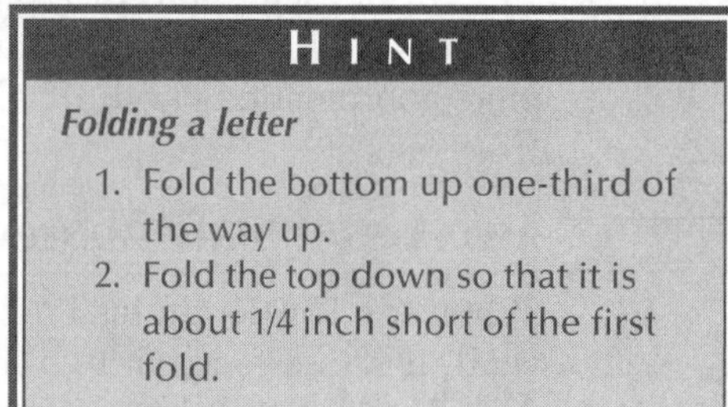
HINT

Folding a letter

1. Fold the bottom up one-third of the way up.
2. Fold the top down so that it is about 1/4 inch short of the first fold.

Addressing Envelopes

The USPS uses computer scanners called Optical Character Readers (OCRs) to read the addresses on envelopes so the mail can be efficiently processed. To enable the computer to read the envelope, follow the USPS suggestions:

- Use a block style for the address.
- Capitalize every letter and do not use commas, periods, or other punctuation.
- Use at least 10-point type with a simple font.
- Use left justification.
- Use black ink on white or light paper.
- A mailing notation—"REGISTERED MAIL" or "CERTIFIED MAIL"—is keyboarded to the left of the stamp or postage meter imprint.
- Use approved abbreviations for street suffixes. The approved abbreviations consist of two, three, or four letters, such as *ST* (street), *ALY* (alley), and *BLVD* (boulevard).
- Approved USPS abbreviations can be found on the Internet at *www.usps.com/ncsc/lookups/usps_abbreviations.html.*
- Place the city, state, and ZIP Code in the last line of the address.
- Use the two-letter state abbreviation. (If the state name is spelled in full, it is too long for the computer to read.) A list of the two-letter abbreviations for states, the U.S. Territories and Affiliated Areas and Canadian provinces appears later in this section.
- Leave two spaces between the two-letter state abbreviation and the ZIP Code.
- Do not use commas or periods in the address. (For example, the last line of the address would be WASHINGTON DC 20001)
- A notation—"PERSONAL," "CONFIDENTIAL," or "HOLD FOR ARRIVAL,"—is keyboarded in all-capital letters two lines below the return address and 1/4 inch from the left edge of the envelope.

The following is an example of an address prepared according to the United States Postal Service guidelines.

ATTENTION MR THEODORE COOPER
COOPER AND SONS
1902 BRANCH DRIVE
DAVENPORT IA 67992

The United States Postal Service suggests that addresses placed on letter-size mail be located within an imaginary rectangle (the OCR read area) on the front of the letter formed by the boundaries as shown in Figure 4-9.

If you send mail by a private mail carrier or use USPS Express Mail, you must prepare special mailing labels that are provided for that service. All companies use the two-letter state abbreviations and ZIP Code developed by the USPS.

Two-Letter State Abbreviations

When the United States Postal Service (USPS) began using scanning equipment to sort the mail, it requested that two-letter state abbreviations be used to expedite the mail. The following two-letter abbreviations for the United States and for Canadian provinces are always capitalized.

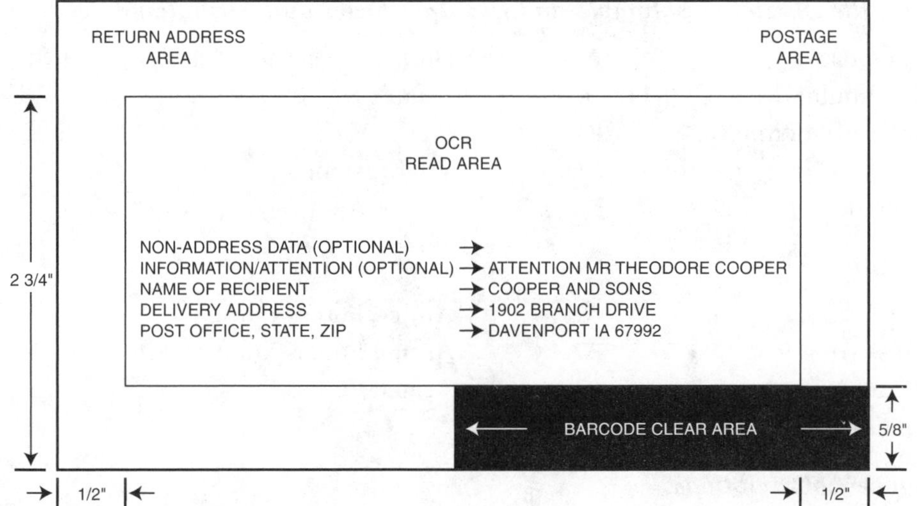

FIGURE 4-9 How to address envelopes.
Courtesy of United States Postal Service.

State Abbreviations

Alabama	AL	Montana	MT
Alaska	AK	Nebraska	NE
Arizona	AZ	Nevada	NV
Arkansas	AR	New Hampshire	NH
California	CA	New Jersey	NJ
Colorado	CO	New Mexico	NM
Connecticut	CT	New York	NY
Delaware	DE	North Carolina	NC
Florida	FL	North Dakota	ND
Georgia	GA	Ohio	OH
Hawaii	HI	Oklahoma	OK
Idaho	ID	Oregon	OR
Illinois	IL	Pennsylvania	PA
Indiana	IN	Rhode Island	RI
Iowa	IA	South Carolina	SC
Kansas	KS	South Dakota	SD
Kentucky	KY	Tennessee	TN
Louisiana	LA	Texas	TX
Maine	ME	Utah	UT
Maryland	MD	Vermont	VT
Massachusetts	MA	Virginia	VA
Michigan	MI	Washington	WA
Minnesota	MN	West Virginia	WV
Mississippi	MS	Wisconsin	WI
Missouri	MO	Wyoming	WY

Abbreviations for the District of Columbia and U.S. Territories and Affiliated Areas

American Samoa	AS	Northern Marianas Islands	MP
District of Columbia	DC	Palau	PW
Federal States of Micronesia	FM	Puerto Rico	PR
Guam	GU	Virgin Islands	VI
Marshall Islands	MH		

Military Abbreviations

Armed Forces Africa	AE	Armed Forces Europe	AE
Armed Forces America (except Canada)	AA	Armed Forces Middle East	AE
		Armed Forces Pacific	AP
Armed Forces Canada	AE		

Canadian Province Abbreviations

Alberta	AB	Nunavut	NT*
British Columbia	BC	Ontario	ON
Manitoba	MB	Prince Edward Island	PE
New Brunswick	NB	Quebec	QC
Newfoundland	NF	Saskatchewan	SK
Northwest Territories	NT*	Yukon Territory	YT
Nova Scotia	NS		

*Both Northwest Territories and Nunavut are abbreviated as NT.

ZIP Code, ZIP+4, and Bar Codes

The ZIP Code is used to expedite mail delivery by assigning a number to each post office and mail carrier route in the country. You must use at least the five-digit ZIP Code; using the nine-digit ZIP+4 Code will result in faster delivery because it can identify specific floors in a building or departments in a large firm. The nine-digit ZIP+4 includes five digits plus a hyphen and four additional digits (for example, 28050-4327). To find the ZIP Code of a United States address, visit *www.usps.com* or call 1-800-275-8777.

Envelope bar codes are also used to assist in the sorting of mail because they can be quickly read by scanning computers. Mailers may use a ZIP Code plus a bar code. The information content of the bar code is indicated by the height of the bars. The bars represent the nine digits of the ZIP+4 Code and an extra digit for error correction. Word processing software can be used to print bar codes on envelopes.

Canadian and Foreign Postal Codes

The Canadian government and other governments have their own postal codes used to speed mail delivery. The forms of these codes differ from those used in the United States and may combine letters and numbers in varying combinations. For example, the postal code for a location in Canada is in the following form: letter, number, letter, space, number, letter, number—for example, L8E 4Y2.

Using Other USPS Mail Classes and Services

In preparing outgoing mail, you should select the most economical service that safely delivers the mail within the time span required by the document contained in the envelope or package.

In order to make this selection, you should understand the services provided both by the United States Postal Service, which handles most of the mail delivered in the United States, and by other carriers that provide specialized services which supplement the services of the USPS.

USPS Special Services

The USPS provides several additional services which can be added to First-Class Mail for an extra fee. These additional services can provide proof of mailing, protection during transit, and confirmation of delivery. These additional services can also be added to other classes of USPS mail, which are discussed later in this section.

The following is a summary of some of the extra services provided by USPS. Many of these services are available for mail classes other than First Class. For current information about the requirements and fees for these services, visit the USPS Internet site: *www.usps.com/send/waystosendmail/extraservices/optionalserviceandfeaturefees.htm#top*.

Certificate of Mailing

A Certificate of Mailing indicates that the mail was received at the post office. It can only be purchased at the time of mailing. It is an inexpensive method of obtaining proof that the mail was received by a USPS employee. The certificate of mailing does not provide proof that the mail was delivered to the addressee nor does it provide insurance coverage for loss or damage to the item.

Certified Mail

Certified Mail provides a receipt stamped with the date of mailing, as well as a tracking number that allows you to go online and verify delivery. For an additional fee, you can order a return receipt, which will be signed by the addressee and returned to the sender. Certified Mail does not provide additional security, and it does not travel faster than First-Class Mail.

COD

COD means "collect on delivery." This service is used to deliver merchandise ordered by the addressee. When the item is delivered, the addressee pays the cost of the item plus postage and a COD fee. This service is not available for international mail or for mail addressed to APO and FPO addresses.

Delivery Confirmation and Signature Confirmation

These two services provide information about the delivery of your mail. Delivery Confirmation will provide you with the date, the ZIP Code, and the time the letter was delivered. This information can be viewed over the Internet or received through the toll-free telephone number 1-800-822-1811. Signature Confirmation adds the name of the person who accepted the mail. If you wish, you can receive a copy of the confirmation from the USPS by fax or mail.

Insured Mail

Mail sent by First-Class Mail, Express Mail, and Parcel Post can be insured for the actual value of the contents, up to $5,000. For items valued over $5,000, you should use Registered Mail. Insured mail must be taken to a clerk at a post office for mailing and cannot be placed in a mailbox or a slot at the post office.

Registered Mail

This is the safest way to send valuables through the mail. Movement of the mail is recorded by a series of signed receipts at each stage of delivery from the sender to the addressee. When the item is mailed, its full value must be declared. Insurance protection for the item up to a total value of $25,000 can be purchased for domestic delivery. Registered mail to Canada is subject to a $1,000 indemnity limit. For all other foreign countries, the indemnity limit is currently $40.45. A receipt of delivery is available at an additional cost. The return receipt will show to whom, when, and where the item was delivered. Registered Mail must be taken to a clerk at a post office for mailing and cannot be placed in a mailbox or a slot at the post office. The delivery date, time of delivery, and number of delivery attempts may be viewed online.

Restricted Delivery

By using a restricted delivery, the sender specifies that the mail can only be delivered to a specific addressee or to someone authorized in writing to receive mail for the addressee.

Return Receipt

A return receipt documents proof of delivery and can be purchased for mail sent COD, Express Mail, mail insured for more than $50, Registered Mail, or Certified Mail. A return receipt provides a postcard with the signature of the person who signed for the item and the date it was delivered.

Return Receipt for Merchandise

By using the Return Receipt for Merchandise, you receive both a mailing receipt and a Return Receipt postcard. It is used when sending merchandise to customers.

Special Handling

Special handling service is required for parcels whose unusual contents, such as live poultry or bees, require special care from postal employees. Special handling service is not necessary for sending ordinary parcels that contain fragile items when the items are packed with cushioning and the package is clearly marked "FRAGILE." The table on page 91 summarizes the extra services available with each postal class.

Other USPS Services and Postal Classes

In addition to First-Class Mail, the USPS provides a wide variety of services to deliver mail anywhere in the world. Fees are charged depending on the class of mail and any special mailing services added to the letter or package. Current information about USPS requirements and fees for any of the following services can be viewed at site: *www.usps.com/consumers/domestic.htm#first.*

Priority Mail

Priority Mail consists of packages up to 70 pounds with a maximum size of 108 inches—which is the combined distance around the largest part of the package and its length. Letters over 13 ounces can also be sent via Priority Mail for preferential treatment at a lower cost than Express Mail. You can obtain free Priority Mail envelopes, tubes, and boxes from the post office. You can send any amount of material that will fit into a Priority Mail envelope for a flat rate. Delivery Confirmation is a feature of Priority Mail at no additional cost.

Periodicals

The USPS has a special postage rate for publishers and registered news agents to mail periodicals, such as magazines.

Service	Can Be Combined with the Following Services	Service Is Available When Using Postal Class			
		First Class	Express	Priority	Parcel Post
Certified Mail	Restricted Delivery Return Receipt	Yes		Yes	
Certificate of Mailing	Special Handling	Yes			Yes
Collect on Delivery	Registered Mail Delivery Confirmation Signature Confirmation Special Handling Return Receipt Restricted Delivery	Yes	Yes	Yes	Yes
Delivery Confirmation	Registered Mail Insured Mail Collect on Delivery Special Handling Return Receipt Restricted Delivery	Yes		Yes	Yes
Insured Mail	Delivery Confirmation Signature Confirmation Special Handling Return Receipt Restricted Delivery	Yes	Yes	Yes	Yes
Registered Mail	Delivery Confirmation Signature Confirmation Collect on Delivery Return Receipt Restricted Delivery	Yes		Yes	
Restricted Delivery	Delivery Confirmation Signature Confirmation Special Handling Return Receipt	Yes		Yes	Yes
Return Receipt	Delivery Confirmation Signature Confirmation Special Handling Restricted Delivery	Yes	Yes	Yes	Yes
Return Receipt for Merchandise	Insured Mail Delivery Confirmation Special Handling			Yes	Yes
Signature Confirmation	Registered Mail Insured Mail Collect on Delivery Special Handling Restricted Delivery	Yes		Yes	Yes
Special Handling	Delivery Confirmation Signature Confirmation Insured Delivery Collect on Delivery Return Receipt	Yes		Yes	Yes

Standard Mail

Standard Mail is used to send printed matter, flyers, circulars, advertising, newsletters, bulletins, catalogs, and small parcels. Standard Mail is used only for bulk mail with a minimum of

200 pieces or weighing 50 pounds. The USPS has several other specialized classes of mail for printed material, including Bound Printed Matter, Media Mail, Library Mail, and Periodical Mail. You can find out more about these special classes of mail at the USPS Internet site: *www.usps.com/send/waystosendmail/senditwithintheus/domesticdeliveryoptions.htm.*

Government Mail (Penalty Mail/Franked Mail)

The federal government sends business letters and checks by penalty mail. Special envelopes for penalty mail sent by the federal government are usually imprinted "Official Business, Penalty for Private Use" and the name of the federal agency. Members of Congress and other government officials are permitted to send mail by franked mail. Franked mail uses the original signature or a facsimile signature of the sender instead of a stamp. Envelopes using penalty or franked mail are only available in offices authorized to use that type of mail.

International Mail

The postal rates for international mail vary with the weight of the envelope and the specific destination. Most international mail is now sent using air mail service. However, packages may be sent by surface mail, which may take several weeks or even months to arrive at its destination. Information about international mail rates is included in a postage chart available from the U.S. Postal Service and is available on the USPS Web site at *ircalc.usps.gov.*

Calculating Postage and Fees from the USPS Internet Site

The USPS provides many different classes of service, many of which can be used at the same time. Estimating the final postage can be a complex matter. The USPS Internet site will help you calculate postage and fees for sending either domestic or international mail. The Web site asks for information about your office ZIP Code, the destination to which the letter or package is to be sent, the weight and size of the package, and any services that you would like to add. Using the calculator, you can change the class of service and can compare postage rates. You may find that it is cheaper to send a package by Express Mail rather than by Priority Mail. Other aids in calculating postage are postal charts and scales, which are discussed later in this chapter. The USPS calculator can be found on the Internet at *www.usps.com/tools/calculatepostage/welcome.htm.*

Post Office Boxes and Drawers

Post office boxes and drawers may be rented from many post offices. Boxes and drawers are located in the post office lobby and mail is placed directly in them after it is sorted by postal clerks. The box holder has a key and can retrieve mail whenever the lobby of the post office is open. A business may use a post office box to receive mail for a specific project or for privacy reasons.

Next-Day Mail and Package Delivery Services

The United States and Canada, like most countries of the world, give government agencies, such as the USPS and Canadian Post, the exclusive right to deliver First-Class Mail. Delivery of other mail or packages, however, may be left open to competition from private companies. Both the USPS and private companies deliver next-day mail and packages.

Next-day mail is a specialized service which provides quick delivery of packages and documents and is used when time-sensitive materials must be sent to another party. The United States Postal Service (USPS) and several private companies, such as DHL, FedEx (Federal Express), and UPS (United Parcel Service), provide next-day mail and package delivery services. The services offered are all very similar but one company may meet your rush or critical delivery needs better than others. Price, convenience of drop-off location, and delivery time may help you make a decision about which company to use. If the delivery time is not critical, some carriers offer reduced rates for an afternoon delivery instead of a morning delivery, or for second-day delivery rather than next-day delivery.

These companies offer a wide variety of both domestic and international delivery services. The Internet sites of these companies include information on drop-off locations, assistance in calculating rates, the ability to track shipments, and the ability to order the company's special envelopes, boxes, and waybills. Since the services each company offers are often updated in response to customers' needs and competitors' offerings, only a few of the services of each company are listed here as examples of the range of services available. For current information, you should check with each company's Web site, which is listed at the end of each paragraph.

USPS Express Mail

The USPS offers Express Mail delivery service 365 days a year, with no extra charge for Sunday or holiday delivery. This is a guaranteed delivery service, which includes tracking information, signature of delivery upon request, and automatic insurance of up to $100 with the option of purchasing additional insurance up to $5,000. You can track the progress of the Express Mail and view confirmation of its delivery on the Internet at the USPS Web site. Mail and packages sent using Express Mail Next-Day Service can be taken to any of over 40,000 designated Express Mail post offices, deposited in one of 26,000 Express Mail collection boxes across the country, or given to a postal carrier. In addition, Express Mail offers a flat rate per stop pickup service by calling 1-800-222-1811. USPS Express Mail International Service is also available to 200 countries around the world, and Express Mail Military Service is available to select U.S. military addresses (APO and FPO addresses) in Europe, Asia, and Panama with two- to three-day delivery. To quickly identify Express Mail, specifically designed envelopes and boxes are available from local post offices with no charge for the envelope or box. In addition, Express Mail labels can be printed from the USPS Internet site, and business customized preprinted labels are available by contacting the local post office. The fees for Express Mail are based on weight (with a maximum weight of 70 pounds) and type of service. However, a 1/2-pound flat rate option is available regardless of weight for mail that will fit into the Express Mail flat rate envelope. More information about Express Mail can be found on the USPS Internet site at *www.usps.com/shipping/expressmail.htm*.

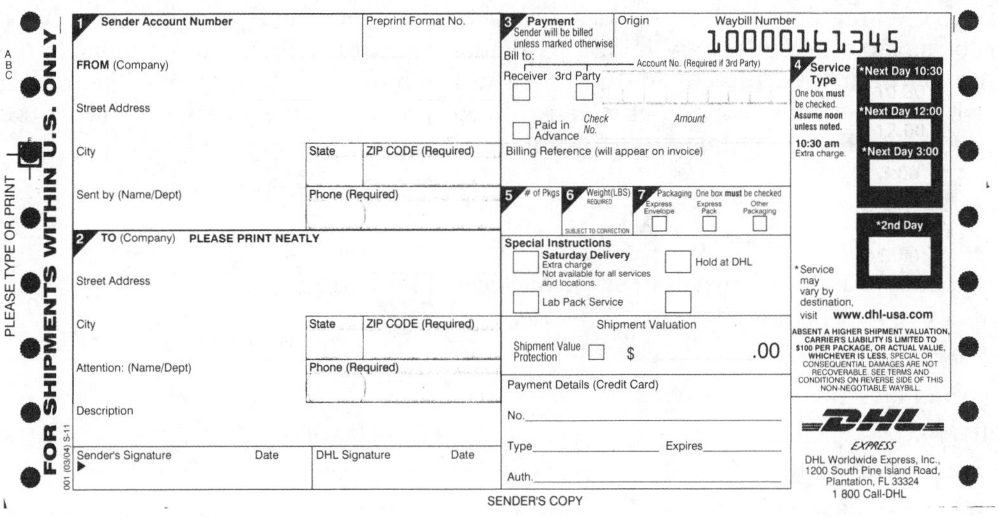
PLEASE TYPE OR PRINT
FOR SHIPMENTS WITHIN U.S. ONLY
1 Sender Account Number
Preprint Format No.
FROM (Company)
Street Address
City
State
ZIP CODE (Required)
Sent by (Name/Dept)
Phone (Required)
2 TO (Company) PLEASE PRINT NEATLY
Street Address
City
State
ZIP CODE (Required)
Attention: (Name/Dept)
Phone (Required)
Description
Sender's Signature ▶ Date
DHL Signature Date
001 (03/04) S-11
3 Payment Sender will be billed unless marked otherwise
Origin
Waybill Number
10000161345
Bill to: Account No. (Required if 3rd Party)
Receiver 3rd Party
Paid in Advance Check No. Amount
Billing Reference (will appear on invoice)
4 Service Type One box **must** be checked. **Assume noon unless noted.** **10:30 am** Extra charge.
*Next Day 10:30
*Next Day 12:00
*Next Day 3:00
*2nd Day
*Service may vary by destination, visit **www.dhl-usa.com**
5 # of Pkgs
6 Weight(LBS) REQUIRED SUBJECT TO CORRECTION
7 Packaging One box **must** be checked Express Envelope Express Pack Other Packaging
Special Instructions
Saturday Delivery Extra charge Not available for all services and locations.
Hold at DHL
Lab Pack Service
Shipment Valuation
Shipment Value Protection $ .00
ABSENT A HIGHER SHIPMENT VALUATION, CARRIER'S LIABILITY IS LIMITED TO $100 PER PACKAGE, OR ACTUAL VALUE, WHICHEVER IS LESS. SPECIAL OR CONSEQUENTIAL DAMAGES ARE NOT RECOVERABLE. SEE TERMS AND CONDITIONS ON REVERSE SIDE OF THIS NON-NEGOTIABLE WAYBILL.
Payment Details (Credit Card)
No.
Type Expires
Auth.
DHL EXPRESS
DHL Worldwide Express, Inc., 1200 South Pine Island Road, Plantation, FL 33324 1 800 Call-DHL
SENDER'S COPY

FIGURE 4-10 A sample next-day delivery form.
Courtesy of DHL.

DHL

DHL provides same-day service for all types of packages. Next-day delivery is guaranteed by noon, with most deliveries made by 10:30 A.M. DHL's USA 2nd Day service provides delivery by 3 P.M. the second business day. Pickup service can be arranged via the Web. DHL also provides ground delivery of package within one to five business days for items up to 150 pounds and 108 inches in length. DHL provides a variety of services for international package delivery to 228 countries. These include Worldwide Priority Express, which ships packages subject to duty worldwide, and International Document Service, which provides for international door-to-door delivery of nondutiable items, such as reports and letters. Through its partner, Deutsche Post Global Mail, DHL can provide mail delivery anywhere in the world. For additional information about DHL, visit *www.DHL.com*.

FedEx

FedEx's quickest service provides for same-day delivery within the United States for packages not exceeding 70 pounds and not larger than 48 inches. Next-day delivery is available, with early morning, mid-morning or mid-afternoon delivery options at additional costs. Also, FedEx offers second-day and third-day deliveries. International delivery service is available to more than 200 countries for packages up to 150 pounds, with delivery choices from one to five days. In addition, FedEx provides a ground delivery service and delivers packages to the home. FedEx offers a large variety of freight shipping options, including same-day service and even truckload shipments. For additional information about FedEx services, visit *www.FedEx.com*.

UPS (United Parcel Service)

UPS's same-day service is called SonicAir and provides pick-up at the customer's location. UPS provides three levels of next-day service, delivery by 8 A.M., by 10:30 A.M., or by 3:00 P.M. Second-day air is available, with a choice of noon delivery or afternoon delivery, and a third-day delivery is available. UPS provides worldwide express delivery service with next-day delivery guaranteed to many cities in Europe and Canada. For many years, UPS has delivered packages throughout the United States through its network of brown vans. Additional information about UPS is available at *www.ups.com*.

Using Next-Day Mail Delivery Services

If you need to send a document or package quickly, first determine if your company has a contract for next-day mail delivery with a particular company. A contract will enable the company to bill your office directly for the delivery. If your office does not have a contract or if you wish to evaluate the cost and efficiency of your present delivery service, you should obtain information from their Internet sites and consider the following:

- Pick-up charges
- Location of mail drop-off boxes
- Whether the customer must deliver the package to the carrier
- Delivery to the community of the addressee
- Delivery by a specific time
- Weekend pick-up and delivery
- Delivery cost
- Insurance availability and cost
- Availability of extra services

Courier and Air Courier Services

HINT

Courier Services deliver within a few hours.

Many large metropolitan areas are served by courier services that will pick up and deliver a package or document within the area in a matter of hours. A phone call is placed to a courier service, and a messenger picks up the package for immediate delivery. In downtown areas, couriers often use bicycles to speed documents through congested city streets.

There are sometimes circumstances when documents or packages must be sent to another city and even a next-day delivery would miss the deadline. As you saw in the previous section, several of the package delivery services offer same-day delivery service. Same-day service is also available from several airlines and specialized delivery services, which can place a letter or small package on the next flight to the destination city. Airline services may only deliver the item to the airport and require pickup of the item at the airport by the receiving party. Specialized delivery services may complete the delivery to the recipient's address. An example of a same-day service provided by an airline can be found on the Internet site of Delta Airlines, at *www.delta.com/prog_serv/cargo/dash/index.jsp.*

Postal Scale and Information Chart

A business sending mail by USPS has responsibility for calculating the correct postage required on each piece of mail. Most businesses use a postal scale, which can accurately weigh envelopes to the half ounce. Use of a postal scale can save up to 20 percent of postage costs, since the correct postal charge can easily be determined, rather than simply placing an extra stamp on an envelope "just in case" the envelope is too heavy. A scale is especially useful for businesses that mail large envelopes (reports, catalogs, and so on) which vary in weight. Many postal scales automatically display the postage required for an item, while older scales may have built-in charts, which must be consulted to determine the amount of postage required for each class and weight of mail. In addition to calculating the item for USPS rates, many digital scales will also determine charges for FedEx or UPS. Postage charts which list the postage required for all USPS classes and services of

FIGURE 4-11 A medical office employee using a compact postage machine.

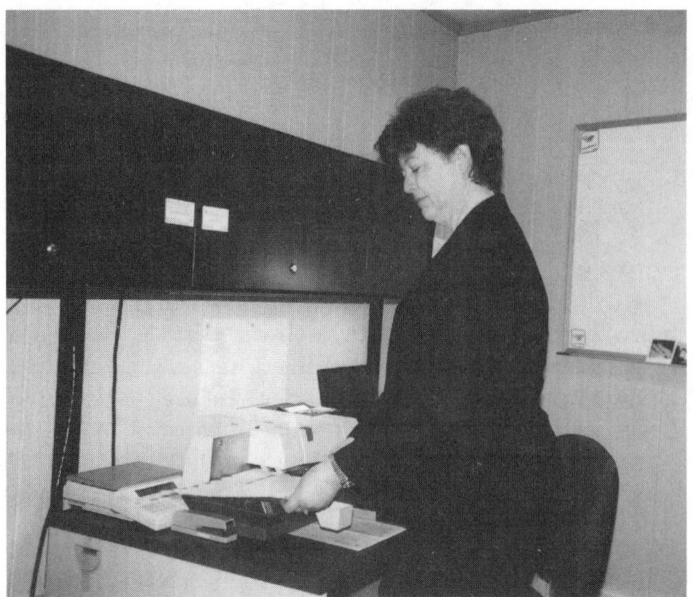

FIGURE 4-12 Using a typical postage machine and scale.

mail are available from the U.S. Postal Service. These charts also list the postage required for foreign countries. The information on the postal charts is revised when postage rates change.

Many post offices have self-service postal scales connected to computers, which you can use to calculate the rate for an envelope. Using a touch screen, you can enter the class of service and ZIP Code. The system calculates the postage and even prints the postage on an adhesive label, which you can place on the package or envelope. Payment can be made using a credit card or cash.

Postage Machines

Instead of placing individual stamps on letters, most businesses use a postage meter to print the postage on an envelope. The postage machine operator can set the proper amount of postage to be printed for each letter or package for different weights and classes of mail. A postage meter prints directly onto the letter or onto a tape that is placed on the letter or parcel. A postage machine contains a base (the envelope handler) used to transport the envelope; a feeder, which guides the envelope through the meter; a meter, which prints the postage; a sealer, which moistens and seals the envelope; and a stacker, which holds the metered mail. Since postage is based on weight, many meters automatically weigh the item. Under federal regulations, meters cannot be purchased but must be rented from a USPS-approved vendor. As postage is used, additional funds can be transferred to the postage meter electronically over the telephone or over the Internet at *postagebyphone.com*. Postage meter vendors charge extra for last-minute and emergency refills, so plan your postage needs in advance.

Collecting Outgoing Mail

Office buildings often have mail-drop boxes or mail slots on each floor, in the lobby of the building, or in close proximity to the building. If this is not the case, outgoing mail will have to be deposited in a blue USPS collection box for pick-up. It is often the administrative assistant's responsibility to deposit the outgoing mail in the collection box. If you are depositing mail, check the collection time posted on the box to determine if the mail will be picked up later that day. Collection times vary from box to box. Locate a box where the pickup is after 5:30 P.M. so last-minute mail can be deposited for pick-up the same day.

In a large office, outgoing mail may be collected for processing by mail room employees before the mail is sent to the post office. Outgoing mail is often collected by the mail room staff when incoming mail is being delivered. Outgoing mail also can be taken directly to the mail room for processing. The office may require that outgoing mail be sorted by the first three ZIP Code digits in order to qualify for discounts on postage. Some offices require that each piece of mail be coded with an office number so postage can be charged to the department originating the mail. It is important to learn the requirements for sending outgoing mail so the mail can be quickly processed and postal costs charged to the correct office.

CHAPTER REVIEW

1. Explain how an incoming letter is coded.
2. Explain the use of a routing slip.
3. What is the purpose of a mail register?
4. Explain the purposes of Registered Mail and Certified Mail.
5. Explain Priority Mail.
6. Define franked and penalty mail.
7. What criteria should be considered when using Express Mail?
8. Explain how postage meters are used.

ACTIVITIES

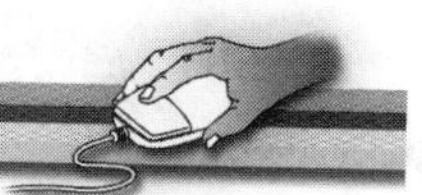

1. How would you send each of the following?
    a. A letter to Paris, France
    b. A gift package to a client in Albany, New York
    c. A letter that must be received by tomorrow
    d. A package that must be received by tomorrow
    e. A stock certificate
    f. A letter to someone in Guam
    g. A package from Boston to Seattle that must be received tomorrow
2. Go to the post office and locate the private boxes available for rent. Check the lobby hours, and ask the price to rent a box.
3. Verify the current rates for First-Class letters and postcards. You may use the Internet for research for this activity.
4. Contact three express mail carriers and compare their rates for mailing a five-page letter. Is the location for mail drop-off convenient for you? Do they have an office pick-up service? By what time do they guarantee delivery? What is the cost for the service? You may use the Internet for research for this activity.
5. What is the cost to mail letters to Mexico, Italy, and England? You may use the Internet for research for this activity.
6. Describe the proper materials used when mailing a package. Where in your area would you purchase the materials and which company would you use to send the package?
7. Ask an assistant how much time is devoted daily to sorting and processing mail.

8. For one week, keep a mail register of all of the mail received in your home.
9. Prepare a routing slip to send a newspaper or magazine article to four members of your class. Attach the article to the routing slip and send.
10. What is the closest post office to your school? What is the last time mail is picked up there? If you miss the last pick-up there, what is the next closest location, and what is the time of the last pick-up there?
11. Where is the main post office in your area? During what hours are the lobby windows open?
12. Address an envelope to each of the following people.
    - Marilyn Horan, Acting Director, Watkins Industries, 3409 Research Lane, Detroit, Michigan 48875
    - Shu Tau, Administrative Assistant, Brandywine Inc., 4877 Garden Avenue, Chicago, Illinois 60067
    - Reynolds Manufacturing, 19 Wood Drive, Columbus, Ohio 43227, Attention of Lucy Wagner
    - Personal letter to Stanley R. Wells, Boyer and Sons, 404 Vine Street, Columbia, Maryland 21045
    - Certified letter to Paula T. Huffman, Managing Director, Birch Systems, Ft. Wayne, Indiana 46815

PROJECTS

Project 7

Create the following form, and write a memo to Peter Bahrami, Ralph Harris, Sarah Rothman, and Pepe Gomez, asking them to complete this form ASAP. The memo is from you and your title is Director.

Activity	*Percentage of Daily Time Spent*
Using email	
Faxing	
Sorting mail	
Filing	
Answering the telephone	
Writing reports	
Writing letters	
Making travel arrangements	

Project 8

Create the following table and calculate mailing costs for each month.

Mailing Costs in Dollars

DEPT	JAN	FEB	MARCH	APRIL	MAY	JUNE
101	2,500	1,875	900	800	2,500	2,500
102	1,600	2,200	800	900	2,300	1,500
103	1,800	2,500	750	700	2,600	2,200
104	2,250	1,300	500	600	1,800	2,700
105	3,600	1,500	900	750	1,700	2,000
106	1,500	2,400	500	900	2,000	2,500

HUMAN RELATIONS SKILL DEVELOPMENT

HR 4-1 Office Friendships

Remember that the office is the place where you work, not the place where you play. Do not tell office friends all the details of your personal life. These individuals may later supervise you, and the details of your personal life may have a negative impact on their evaluation of your work. It is also possible that an office friend, with whom you later have a disagreement, will tell others the details of your personal problems. Be friendly with everyone in your office, but do not divulge all the secrets of your life.

- Have you told someone about an event in your life and later wished you had never mentioned it?
- What would you do if your supervisor began telling you personal information you did not want to know?
- Describe the types of information about yourself that you would like to share with your co-workers.

HR 4-2 Working with Disorganized People

It can be discouraging to work with disorganized people, particularly when their behavior affects you. Postponing the beginning of meetings because a person is always late, waiting for materials to be found, and delaying projects because a person has not completed a portion of the project can be very frustrating. Depending on the individual, there may be little you can do to remedy the situation. You can diplomatically encourage the person to become organized, discuss the importance of being prompt, and tactfully express your frustration about the situation.

- Are you a disorganized person?
- What can you do to become more organized?
- What can you do if your supervisor is disorganized?
- How would you encourage a co-worker who is disorganized to become more organized?
- Do you arrive on time for events?
- Do you have friends who are habitually late for events?
- How can you encourage a person to be prompt?

SITUATIONS

How would you handle the following situations?

- **S 4-1** You arrive on time at your office, but you cannot find your office keys.
- **S 4-2** Your supervisor would like you to do personal errands when the supervisor is too busy to do them. You are told that the errands can been done on company time.
- **S 4-3** Your co-worker loudly chews gum and pops it frequently, which annoys you.

PUNCTUATION REVIEW

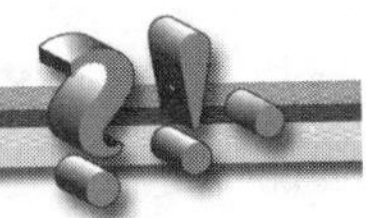

Punctuate each of the following sentences.

1. Edward K Bowman our president has meetings in Virginia Pennsylvania and New Jersey
2. Bill the executive director joined the company in June of this year
3. The most effective manager Ms Engle is well organized
4. Yesterdays price report while representing only a single month gave no indication that inflation is a growing concern to the economic future of the nation
5. Of course we missed the train and were late for the meeting
6. Since fall is here we must reevaluate the project
7. Food prices after increasing 3.6 percent in January declined 2.4 percent last month which is further evidence that the effects of the drought may be less than originally feared by economists
8. The west coast office assistant I understand is the employee of the month
9. No the salary was not the issue
10. Her next interview is in Chicago Illinois on Friday April 17 at 10 am
11. The presentation was a success and we received the contract
12. You will I think benefit from the Friday seminar
13. Several economists cautioned against expecting such price increases to continue Ms Woo for example said that the high costs of raw materials are expected to decline shortly
14. Wendy who will be on a business trip the month of October is the new director
15. The bank was closed yesterday and I wanted to cash a check so I would have sufficient cash for my next business trip

CD ASSIGNMENTS

CD Assignment 4-1

Open the file CD4-1_IPM on your Student CD and follow the instructions to complete the job.

CD Assignment 4-2

Open the file CD4-2_IPS on your Student CD and follow the instructions to complete the job.

CD Assignment 4-3

Open the file CD4-3_Hunt on your Student CD and follow the instructions to complete the job.

CD Assignment 4-4

Open the file CD4-4_FCP on your Student CD and follow the instructions to complete the job.

CD Assignment 4-5

Open the file CD4-5_FML on your Student CD and follow the instructions to complete the job.

Computers in the Office

5

Objectives

After studying this chapter, you should be able to

1. Understand the terms associated with computers.
2. Understand the use of a variety of computer software programs for the office—including word processing, databases, and spreadsheets.

Introduction to Computers

Computers have become an integral part of the everyday life of the office employee. In addition to word processing, computers are used in the office for record keeping, budgeting, retrieval and analysis of data, daily calendars, messages, and many other tasks.

It is almost impossible to function in today's modern offices without the ability to operate computer equipment. Proficiency in computers requires hands-on experience with specific equipment. This chapter presents general computer terminology and concepts and introduces some computer programs commonly used in the office. Many schools offer courses in specific computer programs, in which students gain skills in these and other programs.

Hardware

The terms *hardware* and *software* are often used when discussing computers. Hardware is the physical part of a computer system and consists of several parts. The computer hardware, however, will not operate unless the equipment is used with software. The software consists of various programs (the instructions) that tell the computer equipment what to do. Different software programs permit the same hardware to perform numerous functions, such as word processing, database management, and accounting.

While each computer system is different, a typical computer system may include a central processing unit (CPU), a keyboard, a monitor, disk drives, a CD or DVD drive, a modem, and a printer. The CPU, disk drives, CD, and DVD are usually contained within a single computer case. The monitor, keyboard, and printer are separate items, which are connected to the computer by cables. Many computers are also connected to peripheral devices, such as scanners and audio speakers.

CPU

The central processing unit (CPU) is the part of the computer that interprets the software, performs calculations, and sends instructions to the other hardware in the system. The CPU is actually a small silicon computer chip. This type of computer chip is called a microprocessor and determines the capabilities and speed of the computer. The speed of a computer is based on the number of calculations the microprocessor can do each second. A computer rated at 2.4 GHz will operate faster than one rated at 1.2 GHz. (GHz stands for gigahertz and reflects the speed of the computer microprocessor.) Next to the CPU in the computer case are other computer chips, which serve as the computer's memory. These memory chips are called RAM, for Random Access Memory. (There are several types of RAM chips, and you will sometimes find references to DRAM, SRAM, or SDRAM. The differences are highly technical and do not affect your use of the computer.) The microprocessor only works with information available on the computer's RAM chips. The microprocessor first transfers information to the RAM chips from a computer's mass storage devices, such as a hard drive or disk drive, which are discussed in the Mass Storage Devices section later in this chapter. Once the information is in the RAM chips, it is used by the microprocessor to complete a word processing, spreadsheet, graphic, or other task.

The larger the amount of RAM, the quicker the computer can process information. A typical computer has 126 MB, 256 MB, or 512 MB of memory. MB refers to *megabyte*, which is the unit of measure for computer memory. The computer can store 1 million characters, such as letters or digits, in each MB of memory. Some computers now have even larger memories, which are shown as GB, which stands for gigabyte. A *gigabyte* can store approximately 1 billion characters and is equal to 1,024 megabytes.

Keyboard

A keyboard is the primary input device of the computer system and is used to enter, or keyboard, information into the computer. Most computer keyboards have a number key pad to the right of the alphabetic keys. This key pad is similar to the key pad on a calculator and speeds the entry of numbers. Special function keys are placed above the alphabetic keys. These function keys, usually consisting of ten or twelve keys, are often simply labeled F1, F2, and so on and can execute an instruction automatically with a single keystroke. Computer keyboards also have special keys labeled Alt and Ctrl. The use of the Function, Alt, and Ctrl keys changes with each software program. These keys are used in combination with other keys, such as simultaneously pressing Alt and the letter *P.* Keyboards may also have special arrow keys and Page Up, Page Down keys to help the user move through a document.

Keyboards in desktop computers are usually not built into the computer case but are connected to it by a long cable. The keyboard can then be placed where it is most comfortable for the operator. Some keyboards use wireless technology and are not connected to the computer with a cable. Unfortunately, computer keyboards are not fully standardized and contain from 84 to 103 keys. Check the placement of all the keys before using a new computer keyboard, since manufacturers vary the placement of the specialized keys.

People who use computers for long periods each day sometimes complain of pain in their arms or wrists. A new style of keyboard, called an ergonomic keyboard, has been designed to reduce the stress caused by long-term computer use. An ergonomic keyboard divides the standard keyboard into several parts and angles some of the keys to reduce arm motion and stretching. There are many designs of ergonomic keyboards. While an ergonomic keyboard may look strange and have a different feel than a standard keyboard, many people find these keyboards very useful in reducing computer stress.

Monitors and Displays

The video screen on the computer is called a monitor or display. A monitor is similar to a television set and uses a cathode ray tube (CRT) to bring text and graphic images to the screen. Most monitors can generate from 254 to over a million colors. The minimum useful size for a monitor is about 12 inches, though most people now use monitors of 15 inches, 17 inches, or 19 inches in size. (All screen sizes are measured diagonally.) The larger monitors are useful when viewing detailed graphics.

Many organizations now purchase flat panel displays as part of their computer systems instead of CRT monitors. Flat panel displays use LCD (*liquid crystal display*) technology. These displays were first used in smaller computers, such as notebooks or handheld computers, but now are affordable in larger sizes for use with regular office or home computers. Flat panel displays take up less desk space and are lighter than CRT monitors. LCDs can generate 16 million colors and use only a third of the electricity of a comparable CRT. As the price for flat panel displays decrease, they will be more widely used in offices.

Mass Storage Devices

In order to run the many computer programs used in the office, computers need more information than can be stored on RAM chips. Computer programs and information are saved on mass storage devices, usually using either magnetic or optical technologies. The most common way to store computer programs or information is on magnetic disks, either using diskettes, which are often called disks, or hard disk drives. Other technologies used for mass storage include optical mass storage devices, such as CDs and DVDs, and flash memory computer chips.

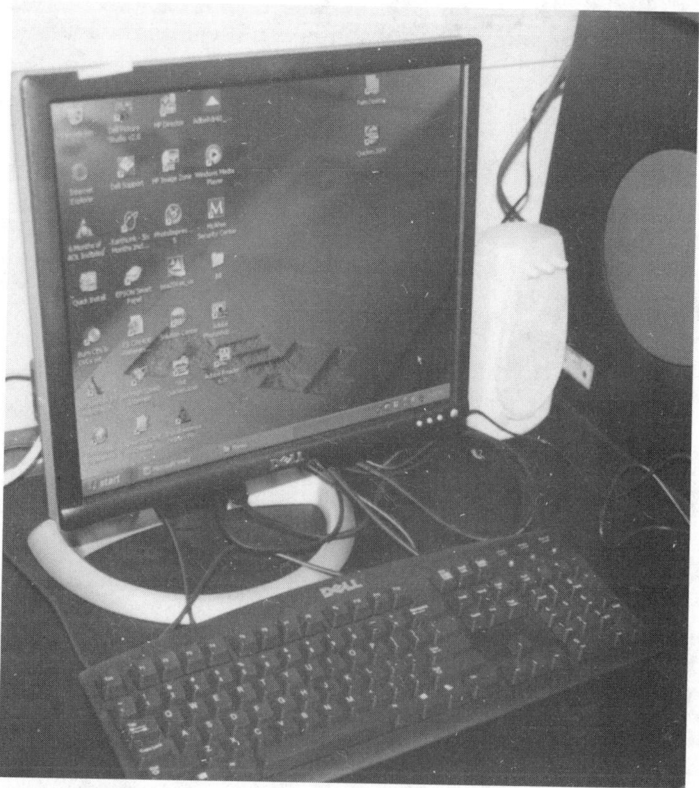

FIGURE 5-1 A flat panel display.

Hard Disk Drives

The main memory storage device on a computer is the hard disk drive, also referred to as a hard drive. A hard disk drive is a magnetic storage device made up of many circular metal disks. Because the information on a disk is read by tiny heads in the disk drive, the computer can quickly retrieve information from any part of the hard disk. Hard drives are usually built into the computer, though portable hard drives are also available. A hard disk can store many programs and thousands of pages of text and other information, including graphics, pictures, and video. As the size of computer programs have expanded, the amount of hard disk storage found on computers has also greatly increased. A typical modern hard drive may have a storage capacity of 40 GB, 80 GB, or 160 GB.

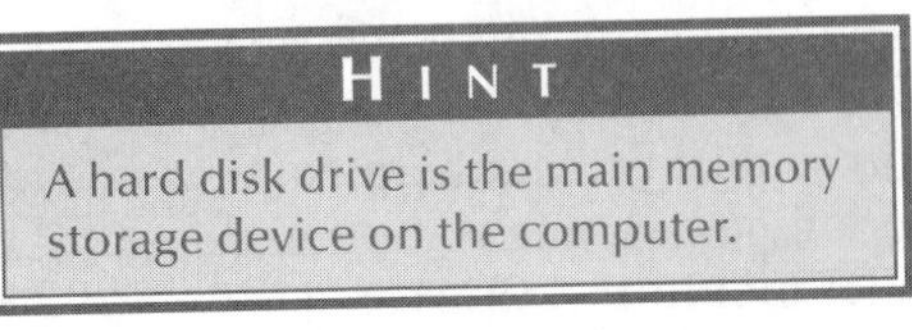

HINT
A hard disk drive is the main memory storage device on the computer.

Disks and Disk Drives

Diskettes are thin, portable disks manufactured in several sizes. Disks are inserted into a disk drive, which is usually built into the computer case, and the information on the disk is "read" by the computer. The original disks were 8 inches or 5.5 inches and were easily bent; therefore, they were called floppy disks. Today offices use a 1.44-MB 3.5-inch diskette (Apple diskettes hold 1.2 MB) or Zip disks with 100-MB or 250-MB capacity. The Zip disks are slightly larger than the 3.5 inch diskette.

All diskettes are very fragile, even the 3.5-inch disks and Zip disks, which are encased in plastic. They can easily be damaged and the information stored on them will be destroyed. It is much easier to take care of a diskette than to try to recreate all the information it contains! If a diskette is partially damaged, it may be possible to retrieve some lost information using special programs. However, retrieving "lost" information is always difficult and often impossible.

Proper care of diskettes

1. Keep dirt, dust, and oil away from the diskette.
2. Coffee or soft drinks spilled on a diskette may damage the disk so it cannot be read by the disk drive.
3. Keep the diskette away from magnets, which can destroy the information recorded on the disk.

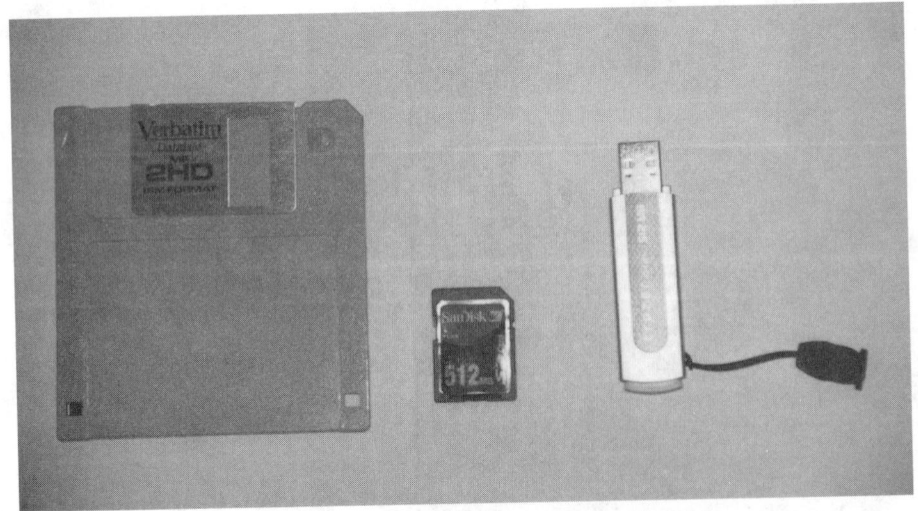

FIGURE 5-2 A 3.5 inch disk, a 512 SD flash memory, and a portable mini-drive.

4. Disk drives have a small light to indicate when the drive is in use. Do not remove a diskette from the disk drive when the light is on.
5. Make backup copies of all material stored on diskettes.
6. Store diskettes at room temperature, keeping them away from extremes of hot and cold.
7. When mailing computer diskettes, place them in specially designed disk mailers.

The storage capacity of any diskette is limited and modern computer programs are too large to fit on a single diskette. Diskettes are, therefore, now used for transporting small files, for transferring small files from one computer to another, or for storing backup copies of data for safekeeping. Many notebook and desktop computers now do not even come with a disk drive.

Tapes and cartridges are also used to store data. Accessing information on a tape or cartridge drive is slow when compared with hard disk drives. Tapes and cartridges are used to store data from a hard disk as a backup in case the hard disk is damaged. Offices may also use a tape to back up all the data on a computer network. These tape backups take several hours and are often completed overnight when the office staff is not using the computer.

CD-ROM Drives

Diskettes and hard disks are magnetic disks that can easily record information from a keyboard or another input device. A *CD* (compact disc) is a storage system that saves information optically. A CD which contains programs or large reference databases and is meant only to be read is called a *CD-ROM* (compact disc—read only memory). CD-ROM computer discs are often referred to as CDs, and it is possible to play a standard audio CD on a computer CD drive. The benefit of a CD-ROM is that it can store sound, video, and thousands of pieces of computer information. A CD-ROM disk can store 640 MB of information, an encyclopedia's worth of information on a single disk. Most software programs are distributed on CD-ROM and many computers come with CD drives as standard equipment.

It is also possible to record a large amount of information on an optical CD by using a rewritable CD drive (*CDRW*). A rewritable CD drive can record as much as 450 diskettes on a single CD. Another type of CD is a *WORM* (write once, ready many). A WORM CD is designed to be written once by an organization, and then the information is protected from changes as it is read many times by multiple employees. A CD is a useful way of storing large amounts of information in relatively little physical space.

DVD

HINT

DVDs are designed to store large amounts of data or video information.

DVD (digital versatile disc or digital video disk) disks and disk drives are another type of optical storage that can be used by computers. DVDs are designed to store large amounts of data or video information and were originally designed to store movies for home entertainment. The most common DVD holds 4.7 GB, which is the equivalent of seven CDs. Because of their vast storage capacity, the DVD provides the immense storage space necessary for picture, audio, and video files which may be used for creating computer presentations or other uses. Most DVD drives also read standard CD-ROM and audio CD disks. It is also possible to create your own DVD disks using the proper DVD-writable drive. As with CDs, some DVD disks can be written on only once; others can be written upon many times. Unfortunately, there are several DVD writable formats available in the marketplace. One format is known as *DVD+R* and *DVD+RW*. The DVD+R disk can be written on only once, while the DVD+RW disk can be written on many times. The other format is shown as *DVD-R* and *DVD-RW*. Again, a DVD disk ending in *R* (DVD-R) can be written on only once, while the other disk (DVD-RW) can be written on many times. Each DVD format (+R and −R) is supported by a group of DVD manufacturers. DVDs prepared in both formats can usually be read by older read-only DVD drives.

> **HINT**
>
> Flash memory consists of a recordable computer chip which can store information in a very small physical space.

Flash Memory Storage

Flash memory consists of a recordable computer chip which can store from 8 MB to over 2 GB of information in a very small physical space. There are several formats of flash memory, including Compact Flash, Memory Stick, MultiMediaCard, SD Card, and SmartMedia. Flash memory units are available on cards smaller than a matchbox; some the size of a postage stamp. The unit can be inserted into an appropriate slot in a desk or notebook computer, a digital camera, a printer, a handheld computer, or another digital device. Adaptors are available so you can use several types of flash memory with your computer. Flash memory cards are reusable; therefore, they can be used for permanent or temporary storage.

Another flash memory format is a unit about the size of a pen or a person's thumb. These units are often called portable mini-drives, thumb drives, pen drives, or keychain drives because they can be attached to a keychain. These drives fit into USB ports which are available on most computers. These drives are useful to quickly store and transfer large amounts of information from one computer to another.

Modems and Other Connections

An office can use several technologies to connect computers to the Internet. Regardless of the method used in your office, technology has developed so your connection to the Internet will probably be done automatically with a few mouse clicks. Many computers connect to the Internet through the use of a modem, a small device which allows one computer to talk to other computer. It is usually inside the computer console (internal modem), though it can be a separate box (external modem) connected to the computer by a special wire.

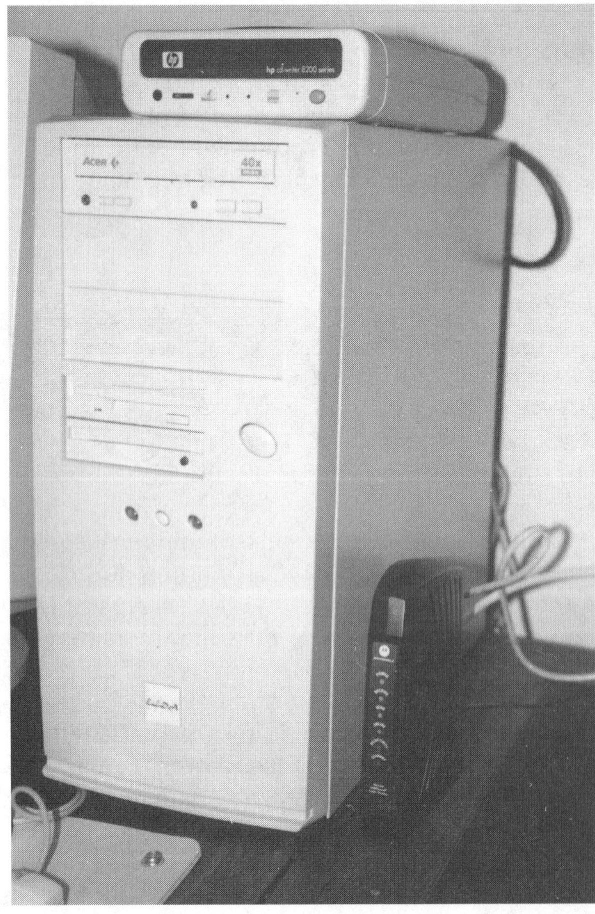

FIGURE 5-3 An external cable modem (lower right corner of photo) and an external CD drive on top of a CPU.

Dial-Up Telephone Modems

A dial-up modem permits a computer to interconnect to other computers or to the Internet over regular phone lines. With a dial-up modem, the computer dials a telephone number each time it wants to connect to another computer or the Internet. Most dial-up modems purchased today follow the V.90 standard, which permits transfer of data over phone lines at 56 kbps. Kbps stands for kilobits per second (where one kilobit is 1,000 bits of information). Using a dial-up modem is the least expensive way of connecting to the Internet, though the data speed is slower than other methods. Dial-up modems are usually too slow to be efficiently used in the modern office.

Broadband Connections

The term broadband refers to high-speed connections that are possible using technologies, such as cable modems, ISDN or DSL telephone lines, and optical fiber communications. A cable modem connects computers to the Internet using special channels on a cable television system. ISDN and DSL are two types of services offered by telephone companies and other providers. Using optical fiber provides the fastest connection with the Internet. Cable, ISDN, DSL, and fiber-optic technologies permit a full-time connection so the Internet is always available. The cost of service usually increases as the data speed increases. Companies with many employees using the Internet often have an optical fiber connection because it can serve many users at the same time.

Wireless Technology

> **HINT**
>
> To use wireless technology, the computer must have a special wireless communication card and must be within the range of a compatible wireless transmitter.

Another way to connect to a local area network or to the Internet is by using wireless technology. Many portable computers, which are discussed in the next section of this chapter, have wireless cards so a person can access the Internet or receive email when the computer is out of the office. Wireless technology can also be used within an office or a home to connect a portable computer to a network or to the Internet. To use wireless technology, the computer must have a special card which supports wireless communications and it must be within the range of a compatible wireless transmitter. (In a portable computer, the wireless card can often be inserted into a slot in the side of the computer.) Different wireless cards are available for use with different wireless technologies. Some computers have cell phone cards and act as cell phones to provide voice connections and to connect to the Internet. Another wireless technology used in computers is called Bluetooth. Bluetooth technology is used in computers, printers, cameras, cell phones, and other devices. Bluetooth technology is best used for connecting devices within 30 feet of each other, although sometimes it can be used for longer-distance interconnections. Perhaps the most popular wireless technology is called Wi-Fi (short for Wireless Fidelity). This technology is sometimes referred to as 802.11b or 802.11g, which refers to the international standard on which it is based. Wi-Fi cards are available for a wide variety of computer, cell phone, and other electronic equipment. Many airports, hotels, coffee shops, bookstores and other businesses and public places have established Wi-Fi connections where people with portable computers can connect to the Internet for free or for a modest fee. These locations are often referred to as Wi-Fi "hot spots." Wi-Fi equipment can be purchased for homes and businesses so portable computing equipment can connect to the Internet and to local area networks. More information about Bluetooth technology can be found on the Internet at *www.bluetooth.org* and *www.bluetooth.com*. Information about Wi-Fi technology can be found at *www.weca.net/OpenSection/index.asp*. For information about Wi-Fi locations, check *www.wi-fizone.org/zoneFinder.asp* or *www.wififreespot.com*.

Even faster wireless connections to the Internet will be possible through the use of WiMAX technology. WiMAX is the next generation of wireless technology and will implement the international 802.16 standard. WiMAX technology will cover larger areas than WiFi hot spots and will be available for use in portable computers for direct access to the Internet beginning in the near future.

Network Card

If your computer is connected to a computer network within your office, your computer has a network card inside the computer case. This card contains several computer chips so your computer can exchange information with the computer that controls the network.

Audio Speakers

Computers which are used for multimedia are often connected to external audio speakers. While full-size computers may have small built-in speakers, external audio systems are often used to provide the volume and sound quality required in systems where audio and video is an important part of the computer experience. External speakers can range from small, inexpensive speaker boxes to full stereo systems.

Scanners

A scanner is an input device that reads printed or graphic material, including photographs, prepared art, and business logos; it converts the scanned material into a computer file. The file then can be stored and processed. With a scanner, a photograph can be scanned into a computer and then inserted into a document or report. A page of text can be scanned into a computer, rather than having to be entered by the keyboard. If the computer has Optical Character Recognition (OCR) software, the text can then be inserted into a word processing package for editing. Scanners can be separate units or can be built into photocopy machines or printers. Some electronic scanners are so small that they can be held in one hand.

> **HINT**
>
> A scanner is an input device that converts printed material or art into a computer file.

FIGURE 5-4 A scanner.

Printers

A printer is a primary output device of the computer and provides the hard copy—a single-page letter or a multipage report—that can be distributed throughout an office or around the world. Printers can also create transparencies for overhead projectors or print detailed graphs and complex engineering drawings. Printers with various capabilities are available in many price ranges to serve a variety of needs. Printers can use different widths and types of paper. Printers that use single-sheet feed paper can use special paper, such as letterhead, and can quickly select from a variety of paper sizes or colors.

Two types of printers are commonly used in offices:

- A laser printer is a printer that uses a beam of light to form images on paper. Laser printers are high-quality printers, but they are expensive. Laser printers can reproduce high-quality graphics and letter-quality documents and can easily print a variety of fonts and font sizes. Furthermore, a laser printer can print letters sideways on paper, called landscape printing, in addition to regular printing, which is called portrait printing. Laser printers can print detailed graphics and are, therefore, used to print documents created with desktop publishing programs. Some laser printers can print in color as well as black and white.
- An ink-jet printer is a printer that sprays the ink onto paper to form letters and characters. Ink-jet printers have many of the same capabilities as laser printers but are lower in cost, though the quality of the printing is not as exact as that of laser printers. Ink-jet printers are often used for color printing, since the cost per page is less than using laser color printers.

FIGURE 5-5 A printer.

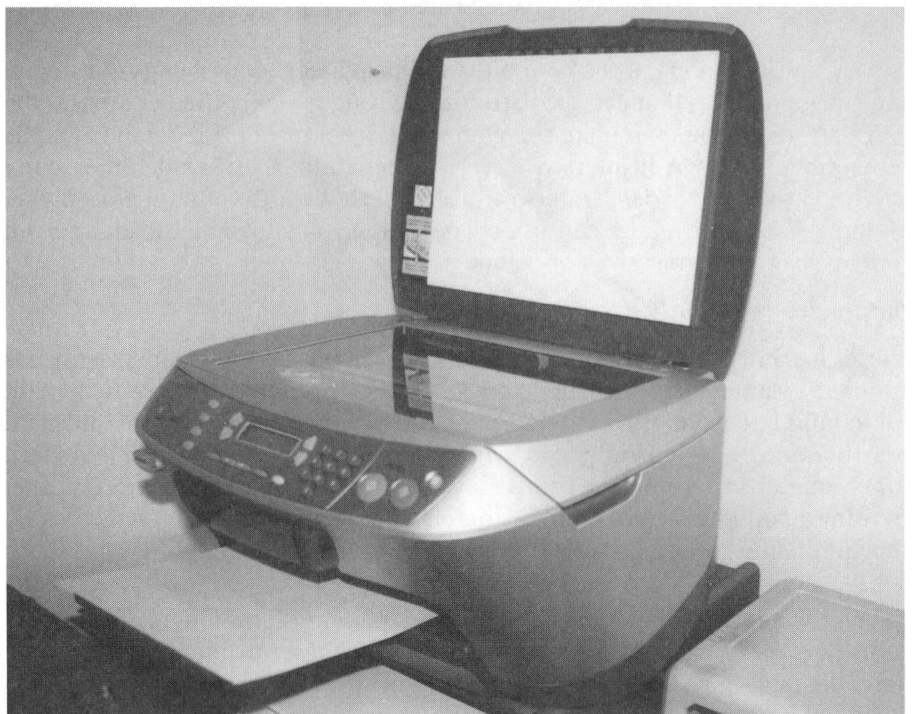

FIGURE 5-6 A combination scanner, printer, and copier.

Printers do not need to be directly connected to a computer but can be connected to an office network or the Internet. In this way, several employees or offices may share the use of an expensive printer. Many office printers have internal memory to store many pages of text or graphics until the printer is ready to print. Printers can also have adaptor slots where flash memory cards or digital cameras can be connected to print without the printer being connected to a computer or computer network. Some printers can also be used as a photocopier or scanner.

Digital Cameras

Digital cameras have become popular because they can quickly save a picture in digital format. Digital cameras do not use film but replace the traditional roll of film with a reusable

FIGURE 5-7 A video screen on back of digital camera.

memory card, which is used to store pictures. Digital cameras have a small video screen on the back where the user can immediately view pictures that were taken. While older digital cameras store the picture on 3.5-inch diskettes, most modern digital cameras store pictures using flash memory cards, such as CompactFlash, SmartMedia, MMC, SD, xD, or a Memory Stick. Digital cameras may have an optical or a digital zoom and a movie mode, which allows a person to record a short video. After the pictures are taken they may be stored or printed. If you use an expensive digital camera to obtain quality photos, but print the photos on a low-quality printer, you may not produce high quality prints. Purchasing an expensive, high-quality printer is one option, but another option is to send the digital photos to a photo-finishing site, which will print the photo. Photos can be uploaded to a photo-finishing Web site or sent by email. Photos taken with a digital camera can easily be inserted into email; word processing, spreadsheet, desktop publishing, and presentation software packages. The following are sample Web photo finisher sites: *www.printmypicture.com*, *www.printroom.com*, *www.activeshare.com*, and *www.ofoto.com*.

Hardware Operating Systems

The parts of the computer, the monitor, CPU, and disk drives, require an operating system which connects them together and allows them to work. The operating system is a specialized type of software which directs information between each of the pieces of hardware and the CPU. When the computer is turned on, the operating system on a hard disk drive is usually automatically run (booted). The most commonly used operating system is the Windows family of software, from Microsoft Corporation. This software (Windows 98, Windows 2000, Windows ME, Windows XP, Windows NT, and so on) is used in computers using microprocessor chips compatible with those developed by Intel Corporation. Computers built by Apple Corporation use the PowerPC chip built by Motorola and uses the MAC OS X or next generation operating software. Linux is another operating system and is an open operating system that is available free or at little cost. Linux can operate computers using either Intel-compatible microprocessors or Motorola microprocessors.

Types of Computers

As electronics become smaller and less expensive, a wide variety of specialized computer and computer-like devices have been developed to serve the needs and wants of businesses and the public. A computer no longer needs to sit on a desktop with a monitor, CPU, and hard and/or disk drives. There are now a whole range of computers, many designed to perform a specific function or to attract the user by being smaller than comparable units.

In addition to the "standard" desktop computer, there are several categories that are commonly used to distinguish the varieties of computers available. The terminology used to categorize computers is often confusing, as different manufacturers may refer to the same type of computer with different terms, in part to try to distinguish their product from their competitors'. For example, the terms *handheld computer, PDA (Personal Digital Assistant),* and *PIM (Personal Information Manager)* all refer to the same type of product. What many people call a laptop computer is now usually referred to as a notebook computer.

Network PCs

Network PCs are computers that are designed to work on a local area network (LAN) that links computers within an office. Network computers may appear to be standard desktop computers but are designed to be operated in a network. The software used by each computer may reside on a central network computer, and the network will manage, limit, or monitor the performance of each computer. The hardware configuration of each network computer will be the same, reducing the maintenance costs of the system. The network provides access to mass storage, email, and the Internet. Information on the hard drives of individual networked computers can be backed-up from the central network computer. Use of network computers reduces the cost and increases the reliability of the computer system.

Notebook Computers

Notebook computers combine the CPU, a flat panel display, and a hard drive into a single, small, portable unit. The miniaturization made possible by modern electronics provides a full computer system in a single package the size of a briefcase. Notebook computers usually weigh less than 10 pounds and include a battery so the computer can be operated anywhere. While notebook computers may cost more than a comparable full-size computer and may not be as powerful as the latest office computer, their portability has made notebook computers very popular. Notebook computers can operate the same software as full-size desktop computers. The configuration of notebook computers can vary widely. Some manufacturers do not include a disk drive built into the computer in order to save weight and conserve power. In these cases, the disk drive may be a peripheral (add-on device) that can be connected to the computer when needed. Many notebook computers include a writable CD or DVD drive. Another peripheral which is common in notebook computers is a wireless card to connect to the Internet.

Today many businesspersons carry a notebook computer when they travel, and offices may have a supply of notebook computers that are available for use by the traveler. Prior to the trip, always check the configuration of the notebook computer to verify that the computer can handle the software needed. You should always charge the computer's battery before a trip. It is wise to take the following extras when traveling: extra battery and battery charger, electrical extension cord, electrical adapter to convert a three-hole to a two-hole plug, diskettes, and emergency startup disk. To protect the computer, use a good-quality carrying case. Unfortunately, these extra items add considerable weight, which can become a problem to the traveler.

Many hotels frequented by business travelers have updated their wiring systems by adding additional electrical, phone, and broadband outlets to accommodate computers and to provide high-speed connections to the Internet. These modifications allow travelers to check email and complete projects. Many business hotels also provide access for their guests to send and receive faxes.

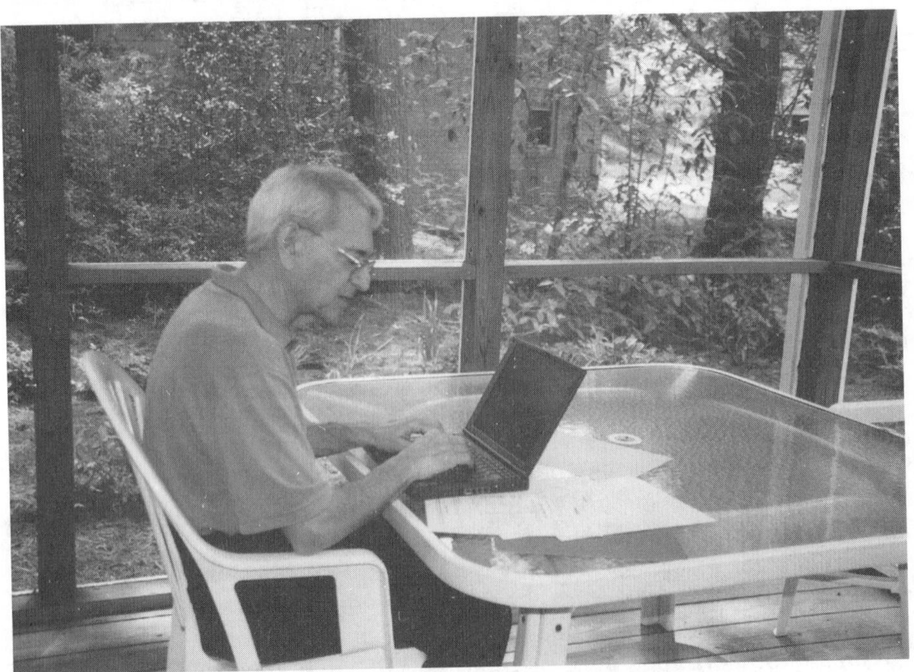

FIGURE 5-8 Working at home using a notebook computer.

Handheld Computers, Electronic Organizers, Personal Digital Assistants (PDAs), and Personal Information Managers (PIMs)

As electronics have become smaller each year, computers have shrunk and are now small enough to fit into one hand. These computers may be referred to as handheld computers, Personal Information Managers (PIMs), electronic organizers, or Personal Digital Assistants (PDAs). Sometimes they are called Palm computers, after the name of one of the most successful brands of this type of computer. All of these handheld computers are so small and light they often fit into a coat pocket or purse and can be carried throughout the day. These computers can be as small as 6 by 4 1/4 inches. Handheld computers have no floppy drives or hard disk but store their information in built-in memory. Flash memory cards can be inserted into some handheld computers to increase the memory or load additional programs.

Handheld computers were originally designed to keep information previously stored in a pocket calendar, address book, memo pad, or scheduler. While the screens on these handheld computers display only a few lines of text, the information can be organized, searched alphabetically, searched by date, and so on because the information is kept in digital format. Handheld computers have become very popular, and there are now thousands of computer programs that can be used on handheld computers. Many of these programs allow a user to download information from a regular computer. You may be asked to keep your executive's schedule on a desktop computer, which can be transferred to the handheld computer so the executive can have an updated schedule when going to a meeting or on a trip. Word processing documents, spreadsheets, presentation software, and other programs can also be downloaded from a desktop computer and used on handheld computers.

There are several types of handheld computers. One type includes a small keyboard to input data. The keyboards on these computers are so small it is difficult to touch type, as one does on a regular computer keyboard. The keyboards of some handheld computers are actually designed so a person can type using his or her thumbs. The second type of handheld computer does not include a keyboard but, instead, uses software that understands letters which are handwritten on a touch-sensitive screen.

As technology has developed, the capability of handheld computers has dramatically increased. Some handheld computers have wireless capability and can access the Internet. Various handhelds have telephone capability and can

HINT

Personal Digital Assistants (PDAs) are carried in pockets or purses and are often used for calendars and contact lists, which contain names and telephone numbers.

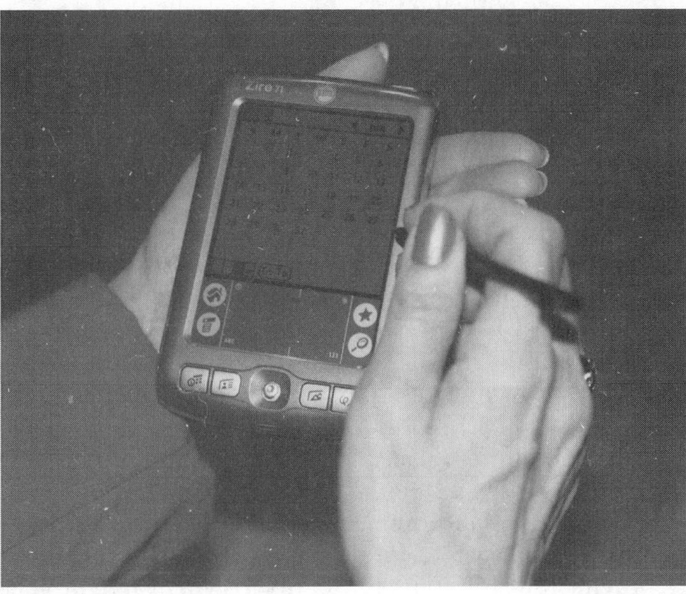

FIGURE 5-9 A handheld computer.

send and receive phone calls like a cell phone. (In competition, the cell phone community is adding calendar, scheduling, address, and memo programs into many cell phones; cell phones and wireless handhelds may merge into a single product.) Several handhelds take pictures with built-in small cameras. These pictures can be saved on flash memory cards or, if the handheld is wireless, can be immediately sent over a phone call or over the Internet. Some handheld computers have GPS (Global Positioning System), which can locate and display exactly (to within 20 yards) the user's location. A handheld with a GPS and a mapping program can be very useful for a traveler. In addition to the telephone or Internet capabilities, some handheld computers are designed to perform specific functions, such as taking orders.

SOFTWARE

Computer Programs for the Office

A large variety of programs are available to efficiently organize and run an office. Commercial programs can be purchased from a computer store and programs can be written by a computer programmer to meet the unique needs of a particular office. The needs of an office will determine the computer programs used. For example, a travel office will use a reservation program to book airline flights, an auto parts store will use an inventory program to aid in the reorder of sold parts, and a doctor's office will use a scheduling program to schedule patient appointments.

There are several types of computer programs commonly used to support the basic functions of the office: word processing, desktop publishing, database management, spreadsheets, presentation, graphics, scanning, project management, and electronic calendar software. Office efficiency can be improved by transferring information created in one program into another program. Often this can be done by using the Copy-Paste feature. In addition, some software permits files created in one program to be inserted into another. For example, an employee can create a budget in a spreadsheet and then copy it into a word processing document which contains a three-page explanation of the budget. The word processing document can be edited, saved, and printed. Furthermore, text created in a word processing document can be copied into a desktop publishing or presentation document. Likewise, graphics created in a desktop publishing or presentation document can be copied into a word processing or spreadsheet file. The integration of various software packages increases productivity and saves time for employees. As you learn to use computer software, be alert for the ability to exchange information from one computer package with another.

Word Processing

The major activity of most offices is the processing of information: ideas, data, and policies expressed in words or numbers. Modern offices have invested in a wide variety of electronic technology designed to speed the processing of words so information can be prepared, analyzed, distributed, and stored efficiently.

Word processing software is the most common computer program used in offices. Today's word processing software does more than just assist the office worker in preparing reports and letters. Word processing includes many features which increase the productiveness of the office worker and enhance the quality of the finished product. These features include spell checks, thesauruses, and clipart. Many word processing packages also create Internet Web pages.

Word processing software packages contain templates, which are a set of predefined styles for word processing projects. Most packages have templates for letters, reports, memos, newsletters, calendars, faxes, envelopes, and many additional documents. Microsoft Word is a commonly used word processing software package.

Word processing programs also provide the office with the ability to design and produce its own newsletters, brochures, forms, and manuals. Word processing software usually can be used by people, who possess little artistic ability or design background, to produce a professional-quality product. Many word processing software programs permit the operator to perform basic desktop publishing without the need for specialized software. Word processing programs provide numerous font styles and sizes and include draw features and pictures used to enhance the document. In addition, text can be printed in columns or around illustrations for a professional appearance.

Desktop Publishing

Desktop publishing programs are available with advanced or specialized features that provide capabilities beyond those found in standard word processing packages. Programs are available for designing office forms, banners, and cards. More complex software programs are used for designing newsletters and brochures. The printing of brochures, forms, or other material developed with desktop publishing programs usually requires the use of laser printers which can reproduce the full graphics capability of the program. Microsoft Publisher, a desktop publishing package, is part of the Microsoft Suite. Adobe InDesign and QuarkXPress are sophisticated publishing packages.

Database Management

Before computers arrived in the office, offices manually kept records for each customer, employee, project, or item inventoried. In today's office, a computerized file using a database management program would be used instead of manually maintaining records. Databases are commonly used where consistent information is required for a large number of items, such as personnel records, inventory records, and sales records.

The value of a database management program is its ability to store and organize large amounts of data. A handwritten file folder can be organized in only one way. The data in a database management system, however, can be organized, sorted, and reported in many ways.

The data in a database program are organized into *fields*, with each field containing one piece of information. For example, a college student database could contain information such as the student's last name, first name, college identification number, number of credit hours earned, and date of enrollment in the school. The collection of fields (piece of information) for each student would be called a *record* (student record), and all of the student records would be considered a *file*.

Entering information into a file can be done at any time using a data entry screen. Data entry screens are written to ask for the specific information required for the file, and they can be designed to minimize operator errors. For example, the attempted entry of the date of February 20 would not be accepted if the data entry screen were programmed to accept only valid calendar dates in the format 02/20/2006.

After data entry, the information in the file can then be sorted by several fields, selected, analyzed, summarized, and printed into reports. A variety of reports can be programmed in advance and printed whenever required. A college, for example, can use the database to review the progress of all students who entered school in a specific year by retrieving such information as which department students are enrolled in, how many are still enrolled, and how many credit hours they have earned toward graduation. A report of this nature can be prepared in a matter of minutes using a computer, while the same report prepared from handwritten records could take days to prepare.

One of the most powerful aspects of database management systems is the ability to link the data from more than one file. If two database files have a field with identical information, such as a student identification number, they can be linked and new database files can be created. Reports can be created from the new database file without having to reenter information into the computer.

Database programs have the ability to create custom menus, screens, and reports. Many employees who use a company system or an inventory system are actually using a database management system in which the screens have been customized for use by that specific office. Microsoft Access is a commonly used database program.

FIGURE 5-10 A medical employee performing data entry.

Spreadsheets/Worksheets

Computer spreadsheet programs (often called worksheet programs) are useful to persons working with figures or money. Spreadsheets are constructed of grids consisting of horizontal rows and vertical columns. A single spreadsheet can consist of hundreds of rows and columns. Each blank space on the spreadsheet is called a cell and can be identified as the intersection of a row and column. Numbers in any cell can be added, subtracted, multiplied, or divided by any other number, or cell, on the spreadsheet. Each cell can also represent a complex mathematical formula.

Companies use worksheets to analyze financial data. The main advantage of a spreadsheet is the ability to change any number and have that change reflected automatically in all of the other numbers or formulas on the spreadsheet. This spreadsheet feature is used to consider "what if," and it is very useful in making projections. In seconds, an operator can see the effect of changing a single number or of changing a series of numbers. Then a decision can be made to accept the "what if" or not to accept it. Spreadsheets are, therefore, very useful in preparing budgets and sales projections.

Because cells and rows can be easily changed within a spreadsheet, spreadsheets are also often used to create tables just consisting of normal text. The editing features of spreadsheets are usually more powerful and flexible than the table features of word processing software, and the resulting table can be inserted into word processing and other software.

Worksheets are usually printed with columns of text and numbers, but spreadsheets can display the data in the form of graphs as well. Spreadsheets can exchange information with word processing software so the information can be incorporated into the text of another document, such as an annual report or a presentation. Also, spreadsheets can be formatted to accept changes in font, point size, row height, and column width. Clipart may be inserted and borders and shading may be added to enhance the appearance of a presentation. Two commonly used types of spreadsheet software are Microsoft Excel and Quarto Pro.

Presentation Software

Speakers at conferences or meetings often use presentation software to prepare visuals to highlight the main points of their speech. An effective presentation can quickly inform an audience, persuade listeners to accept a new idea, or to purchase a product. With presentation software, graphics, text, and artwork can be combined into a display that is quicker to prepare and more flexible than using slides or overhead transparencies. By linking a desktop or notebook computer to a projection system, a presentation can be displayed to the audience directly from the computer. Sound and moving video can be added to text and graphic material to enhance the presentation. Using computer software, an employee can easily create a powerful presentation that an audience will remember. Microsoft PowerPoint is one of the most commonly used presentation software packages.

Clipart and Drawing Software

The expanding graphics capabilities of computers can be used to create artistically attractive documents. Clipart can be inserted into word processing, desktop publishing, spreadsheet, and other software programs. With the appropriate software, anyone can draw perfect circles, squares, shapes, and straight lines. The imaginative use of graphics can make reports and other printed materials more interesting.

Computer-Aided Design (CAD)

Computer-aided design software uses the computer to assist in the creation of technical drawings. CAD software is often used for the creation of engineering and architectural drawings and can create views showing two dimensions (2D) or three dimensions (3D). The computer can rotate a 3D CAD design so it can be viewed from all perspectives. CAD software is a quick way to fully visualize a design.

Scanning Software

Scanning software allows documents to be scanned using scanning equipment and saved to a computer file. Scanning software permits each scanned image to be given a name so it may be filed and easily retrieved. A page scanned into a computer usually will be stored as a single image. For text, however, it is often more useful if the resulting computer file can be edited. By using Optical Character Recognition (OCR) software, the computer will be able to recognize each letter in a document so it can be edited by word processing software. OCR software is not perfect, however, so the scanned document must be carefully checked against the original document and corrected before it is used in word processing or other software.

Project Management

Project management software is used to develop timetables for completing projects. With project management software, a project is broken down into many steps, and each step is assigned the amount of time needed to complete it. Using project management software, time lines can be created for a project. When project management software is used, it is easy for the user to determine the effect a delay in any step of the project can have on the overall completion of the project. Project management software is often used to plan complex projects that are completed by several team members.

The Internet and Internet Browsers

The Internet is one of the most significant computer developments which links millions of computers around the world to permit easy exchange of information. Most people use a part of the Internet referred to as the World Wide Web (or more simply, the Web). The Web uses a special computer language called HTML (HyperText Markup Language) for display of graphics and text. Internet browser software is used to connect to the Internet, search for information in HTML on the network, and download the results to the individual user's computer. The two commonly used Internet browsers are Microsoft Explorer and Netscape Navigator.

Web Development Software

Web pages can be created using a variety of software and codes. While special development software is available, word processing, spreadsheet, presentation programs, and so on can save a file as an HTML document for posting on the Web. Using this software, literally everyone can become a worldwide publisher by posting his or her own information on the Web.

Anti-Virus Programs

A virus is an extremely dangerous computer program designed to interrupt or damage your computer or files. Viruses can destroy computer data or even erase all data on a hard disk. Viruses can be received from an email message or a shared diskette or can be downloaded from an Internet site. It is important to use an anti-virus program to safeguard your computer. An anti-virus program should be used to check a diskette and hard drive to determine if it contains a virus. Updates to an anti-virus program should be downloaded from the Internet frequently so your computer is protected against new viruses. If a virus is detected, the anti-virus program will remove the virus from the computer before it causes damage.

Firewall

A firewall is a security software program or computer hardware that protects a computer from access by unauthorized users. Firewalls are used to protect the integrity of computers and networks from people who wish to steal information from the computer, change information in the computer system, or harm the computer system.

HINT

Protect your computer with virus protection software.

Email

One of the most common types of software used in business today is a program that exchanges electronic mail (email). Email programs handle the composing, sending, receiving, and storing of email messages and their attachments. Email programs include an address book where you can store the email addresses of people with whom you normally exchange messages. Furthermore, addresses can be organized into group lists so a single email message can be sent to all of the people on the list.

Instant Messaging

Instant messaging, often called IM, is an almost instant text messaging feature which appears via pop-up windows on computers. By using IM software, customers can click on icons on emails or Web pages and immediately connect with a sales representative. The instant chat option increases communication between the customers and the company, provides immediate answers to the customer, and demonstrates that the company cares about its customers.

Additional Computer Terms

It is essential that you understand the following terms if you are going to work with computers.

- *Artificial Intelligence* consists of technologies that try to achieve humanlike attributes of intelligence, such as reasoning.

- A *backup* is a duplicate of information or a program which is saved in case the original is damaged. A backup may be made on a hard disk drive to save the original data before making changes in a document. Backups may also be placed on diskettes, Zip disks, CDs, DVDs, or flash memory for storage away from the computer. Since copying all files for all employees to disks takes time and could become a storage nightmare, companies often use a tape backup system. A tape backup system is an efficient and reasonably priced method to back up files on a large hard drive. There are three types of backups—total, modified files only, and selective files. A *total backup* backs up the entire hard drive to a tape. A *modified-files-only backup* backs up only those files that have been changed since the last backup was done. A *selective backup* backs up only those files that are selected by the user. Some systems make backup copies automatically in the middle of the night, while other systems do the backup at the end of the day.
- A *bar code* is a series of spaces and lines which the computer translates into a number. Bar codes are often used for inventory control. In Chapter 4, you saw that bar codes are also used to address mail.
- A *bit* is a single binary digit. Computers store all information as the binary digits "0" and "1." Eight bits of memory are called a byte.
- To *boot* is to start the computer and load a program. A "cold," or "hard," boot is performed by turning the computer on. A "warm," or "soft," boot, which restarts the operating system after the computer is on, can be done in some operating systems by pressing several keys, such as the Control, Alt, and Delete keys, all at the same time.
- A *byte* is eight bits of memory which are used to represent a single letter, number, or other computer character. Bytes are used as a measurement of memory storage. A kilobyte is 1,024 bytes; a megabyte is 1 million bytes; and gigabyte is 1 billion bytes.
- *Cache memory* consists of high-speed memory chips that hold the most frequently used data and instructions. By having this information on hand, the computer saves the time required to access the data on a hard disk.
- A *chat board* or *chat line* permits a person to use a computer to communicate with another person by keying in text and having the other person respond by keying in text.
- A *communications satellite* is a satellite that acts as a relay station by receiving data from equipment on or near the ground (earth station), amplifying it, and then retransmitting it to another earth station. The earth station can actually be an antenna on the top of a building, a small satellite telephone, or an antenna located in an airplane or on a ship. Using communications satellites, computer networks can reach locations unserved by regular phone lines or cables.
- A *cursor* is a highlighted area on the monitor or flat panel display which marks the place where data entry will begin.
- *Documentation* is an instruction manual explaining how to operate computer hardware or software.
- *Downtime* is time when the computer is not working. It can be scheduled (for example, downtime for maintenance) or unscheduled (when the computer has a problem and is not operating).
- A *fiber-optic cable* is a transmission medium which includes a glass cable that transmits data as pulses of light. A LAN (Local Area Network) or Internet connection using a fiber-optic cable can exchange data much faster than one using phone lines or coaxial cable.
- A *file server* is a computer that has enough memory and speed to store programs for quick access by many computer users.
- A *gateway* is an item of computer hardware that connects a LAN to outside computer systems.
- *Groupware* is software that helps several users to work together on projects and share information.
- A *home page* is the screen that welcomes a user to a Web site and often has text and/or graphics.

- *HTML* (HyperText Markup Language) is a specialized programming language used to create Web pages.
- *Image processing* systems use scanners to capture and electronically file an exact copy of a document. In addition to recording the document, these systems can record pertinent information about the document—for example, the date the file was created or handwritten notations attached to the document.
- The *Internet* is the worldwide group of connected networks that allows the public access to information on thousands of subjects. The user may view, print, or save the information. Business research may be conducted quickly and efficiently without leaving the office.
- An *intranet* is an internal network that uses Internet and Web technologies.
- *Internet relay chat* (IRC) is chatting or holding a live conversation on the Internet by keyboarding messages while reading responses on the screen. This service allows the user to have a real-time written conversation with several people on the Internet. Persons in different locations converse with each other by the use of an Internet Relay Chat program.
- An *ISDN* (Integrated Services Digital Network) is a technology that allows images, voice, and data to be transmitted simultaneously as digital signals over regular telephone lines.
- An *Internet Service Provider* (ISP) is a business that provides people and businesses a connection to the Internet. Some ISPs just provide a connection to the Internet. Other ISPs also provide news, travel information, weather, and information on a multitude of topics in addition to providing a connection to the Internet. America Online (AOL) is an example of a national Internet service provider that provides information services as well as connection to the Internet.
- *Java* is an object-oriented programming language specifically designed for use on the World Wide Web.
- A *license* authorizes the use of computer software. The purchaser is only authorized, or licensed, to use that software; the purchaser cannot change the software or copy the software without permission from the copyright owner. The illegal copying of software, also referred to as software piracy, is a concern in many offices. Most software packages provide a license for use on only one computer. Instead of purchasing an individual software program for each user, offices may purchase a site license, which allows a specified number of computers to use the same software package.
- A *Local Area Network* (LAN) is a communications network that connects two or more computers in a limited geographic area. LANs are usually contained within a single building but can connect computers in different buildings if they are close together. The LAN allows each computer on the network to share hardware, software, and information resources. For example, a client file may be stored on the file server and all computers connected to the LAN may access the file. See also MAN and WAN.
- *Mapping software* consists of computer software that uses graphics, database management, and spreadsheet features to display data geographically. Information can be presented in a map to display differences in income, education, or age level by using mapping software.
- *Metropolitan Area Networks* (MANs) are exchanges that are located in large metropolitan areas that carry Internet communications traffic. A MAN is used to transfer data from one provider to another.
- A *Mouse* is a pointing device that allows the operator to move the cursor and input commands without using the keyboard. A small box about 2 inches by 3 inches is rolled on a tabletop to move the cursor around the computer monitor.
- *Multimedia* refers to the combination of text, graphics, sound, and video in one project.
- A *network* is a group of computers that are electronically connected so they can communicate with each other. Examples of networks include the Internet, as well as LANs, MANs, and WANs.
- A *network printer* is a printer that is connected to a network and has many users printing to it.

- A *network server* is the central computer that manages a local area network or that provides information to the Internet.
- A *PC fax* is a computer that can perform as a fax machine. The computer must be turned on in order to receive a fax.
- *Pop-up ads,* or advertising banners, may appear when surfing the Web or viewing email. These ads promote products or services and are designed to encourage the purchasing, downloading, or installing of software but may also cause the computer to slow down or crash. In addition, the ads may be inappropriate for children or adults. A computer code delivers the pop-up ads or advertising bars so they automatically appear on the computer screen. Proponents of adware feel it helps to recover programming development costs and minimize user costs. Some adware contains codes that track a user's personal information and that share it with others without the user's knowledge or authorization. This software, called *spyware,* may be a violation of personal confidentiality and could also lead to fraud if the spyware obtained a person's or company's financial information. Pop-up blocker software is available to help diminish pop-up advertising.
- A *plotter* is a printing device used to produce graphics using a moving pen.
- A *presentation monitor* is a computer monitor 25 to 36 inches in size that is used when making presentations to midsize groups.
- *Random access memory* (RAM) is the working memory of a computer that is used to store programs temporarily. When the computer is turned off, the information in RAM is lost.
- *Read only memory* (ROM) is internal memory that is built-in to the hardware and cannot be changed by the operator. When the computer is turned off, the information in ROM is not lost. ROM usually contains the program which boots (starts) the computer when it is turned on.
- *Search engines* are computer programs found on the Internet that help users search for information. After the user enters a word or phrase, a search engine will review thousands of computer sites to find sites that may contain the type of information requested. If the user is too general when requesting information from a search engine, the results may be thousands of possible sites which contain the requested information. Two commonly used search engines are *www.google.com* and *www.yahoo.com.*
- *Shareware* consists of software programs that are distributed at little or no charge, often by user groups. The programs can be distributed online, on diskette, or on CD. The user is frequently asked to pay for a shareware program after receiving the program. Shareware programs often mimic features of popular commercial software, but the quality of the program is usually unknown.
- *Touch screen monitors* permit data or requests to be entered into the computer by touching the screen instead of using the keyboard. Touch screens, which are often found in public places such as shopping malls and airports, allow the user to easily obtain information. Some Personal Digital Assistants use touch screens to input data, since they are too small to have keyboards.
- A *trackball* is a pointing device and performs the same function as a computer mouse. Since notebook computers are not used on a desktop, there is often no surface on which to place a mouse to move the cursor. A trackball is like a large marble located near the notebook computer's keyboard. The top of the ball is rotated by a finger, which moves the cursor on the screen. A trackball can also be part of a keyboard for use with a desktop computer.
- *URL* (Uniform Resource Locator) is a special code which gives the address or location of the Web site or page. Many Internet addresses begin with "www" and the parts of the address are separated by periods. Web addresses typically end with designators which indicate the type of organization sponsoring the computer site. Typical designators are .com for commercial organizations, .edu for educational institutions, .org for nonprofit organizations, .gov for government agencies, and .net for networks.
- *Virtual reality* is a computer-created environment which places the user in the middle of a computer-generated image. Virtual reality software creates a three-dimensional

display and is often used for three-dimensional electronic games. In this type of game, the user wears special glasses to see the computer-generated environment. Sensors in the game machine record the user's body gestures and the view of the scene changes as the viewer moves.

- *Voice recognition software* provides a way to enter information into a computer directly from spoken words. Using a small microphone, the computer converts spoken words into digital information that can be entered into a word processing package or other office software.
- A *Wide Area Network* (WAN) is a communications network that covers a large geographical area. These networks use satellites, microwaves, and telephone cables to interconnect computers across the country or around the world.
- The *World Wide Web* (often simply called the Web) is a part of the Internet that uses computers, which are Web servers, to store files called Web pages. A person seeking information locates an appropriate Web page.

The Paperless Office

Imagine an office in which everyone is linked via a computer network. All information is received electronically directly into a computer and work is done on documents in the computer. Computers are used to rearrange information using word processing, spreadsheet, database, presentation, scheduling, graphic design, and a variety of other programs into required reports. These documents are edited on the computer and sent directly to the users over the office Local Area Network. People read documents on their computer screen and respond via email. Documents are stored in computer files. The use of computers, in this vision, results in the "paperless office."

Unfortunately, while computers have become universal in offices, and the power of computer programs has multiplied, the result has not been the paperless office. Indeed, the ability of computers to churn out documents has in some respects resulted in more paper being used, not less. The ability to easily revise documents with word processing software often results in more time and paper spent in editing documents. The usefulness of databases to sort data into a report often results in more requests to sort the data a little differently than before. Printing a report on a computer laser printer is no more difficult for ten copies than for five copies and just takes a few more minutes. While many offices have made great strides in using computers, the paperless office has not arrived.

CHAPTER REVIEW

1. Define hardware and software.
2. Explain flash memory.
3. Describe printers.
4. Explain the advantages of desktop publishing.
5. Explain the "what if" feature of a spreadsheet.
6. List six types of computer software used in an office.
7. What is an anti-virus program?
8. Explain six computer terms listed in the text.

ACTIVITIES

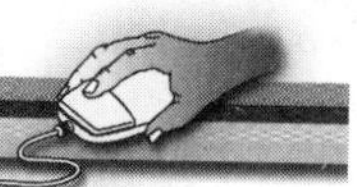

1. Read an article about the features of the newest version of a popular word processing program. Prepare an oral and a written summary of the article. You may use the Internet for research for this activity.
2. Survey several computer magazines and list the names of database management, word processing, and spreadsheet programs which are advertised or discussed.
3. Read the advertisements in computer magazines and compare the price of three computer software packages.
4. Ask an office employee to describe two software application packages. Write a report describing the features they like and the features they dislike.
5. Go to a computer store and see what electronic calendar programs it carries. Write a short report about the features of the different programs. You may use the Internet for research for this activity.

PROJECTS

Project 9

Keyboard the following letter and make all decisions concerning the letter style. Supply any additional information necessary. The letter is from Van Quieret, President of Russell Corporation.

Send this letter to Phyllis Maller with a copy to Daniel Kinsley, Meeting Coordinator. Ms. Maller's address is 324 Dixie Street, Moscow, ID 83843, and Mr. Kinsley's address is 8912 Columbia Blvd., Tucson, AZ 85701.

> There will be a stockholders' meeting on Monday, June 4, in my office, which is in the Dalton Building, 2004 K Street, NW, Washington, DC.
>
> We would like all stockholders to be present, as there will be a discussion of changes in the bylaws. After the discussion, a vote will be taken on the proposed new bylaws. If you cannot be present, please send your proxy to me prior to the meeting.
>
> In addition to the discussion of the bylaws, we will review the Meadman Report and make a final decision on it. I am enclosing a summary of that report.
>
> I hope to see you on June 4.

Project 10

Keyboard the following letter and make all decisions concerning the letter style. Supply any additional information necessary.

Send this letter to the attention of Raymond A. Barron, Truax Corporation, 3859 Plains Drive, Chicago, IL 60627-1057. Include a subject line. The letter is from Denise D. Berlin, Purchasing Manager.

> Thank you for the demonstration of your communications software package. Also, I appreciated the specification sheets and computer documents you left with us. They have been helpful in reviewing your product. The operational procedures and documents have already

been sent to our regional offices for their analysis and input. As you can imagine, we are eager to begin the project.

If you have any additional information to add to your proposal, please fax it to me immediately.

As I mentioned, we are evaluating several packages, and we have a committee already studying the proposals. As soon as a decision is made, I will call you.

HUMAN RELATIONS SKILL DEVELOPMENT

HR 5-1 The Employee in the Middle

It is possible to have two supervisors with conflicting ideas supervising one person. Receiving conflicting directions, projects, and assignments can put you in a difficult situation. If possible, arrange a meeting with both supervisors and yourself to discuss the project. Continue to meet as a group during the project. If you find yourself meeting individually with one supervisor in a decision-making session, write a for-your-information memo for the other supervisor or talk with the other supervisor before proceeding with the project.

- What would you say to two supervisors who continually give you conflicting directions on a project?
- Describe personal reasons that may cause two supervisors to have opposing views on all projects.

HR 5-2 Dealing with an Angry Client

You may need to calm an angry client on the telephone or in person. Identify why the client is angry but do not react to the anger personally. When you become angry, you lose your ability to handle the situation objectively. Once you have determined the reason for the client's anger, encourage the client to discuss the problem even if the client needs to shout to do it. The anger should dissipate as the client discusses the problem. Once the client calms down, a solution to the problem can be discussed.

- Discuss the last instance when you were an irate client or customer.
- What types of business situations make you angry? Why?
- How would you handle an agitated client who had several times spoken to you in an angry voice?
- What tone of voice would you use with an irate client?

SITUATIONS

How would you handle the following situations?

- **S 5-1** You made a mistake and scheduled two appointments at the same time on the same day. Both clients are now waiting to see your supervisor.
- **S 5-2** As a supervisor, you must deal with the problem of personal use of the company copy machine. Company regulations prohibit personal use of the photocopier,

but employees have been using the machine. While walking past the copy room, you notice Jennifer copying a cookbook. What would you do?

- **S 5-3** The refrigerator and coffee pot in the lunch room are dirty, and no one wants to clean them. As a supervisor, what should you do?

PUNCTUATION REVIEW

Punctuate each of the following sentences.

1. Sue asked when is the annual meeting
2. Yes I have an account at that bank
3. Ralph asked if we joined the Wellness Program
4. Marcie Ross who prepared the communications has been with the company since March 17 1996
5. I transcribed the affidavit replied Martin
6. Based on our projections income should rise at least 25 percent each for each of the next three years
7. Whether you are expanding your computer network system creating new databases or developing new application packages you most continually update your skills
8. We service the geographic areas of the U S Virgin Islands Puerto Rico and Hawaii
9. After working in the health services field for over twenty years she was ready for a career change
10. In managing this project Ms Wingate demonstrated considerable skill and professionalism
11. As you mentioned the duties were not explained
12. Our director Mr Wood attended the University of Rochester
13. Max said I cannot locate the executive director
14. Charlton Corporation is located at 289 West Field Drive Sarasota Florida
15. We offer a flexible reporting service which allows the customer many options

CD ASSIGNMENTS

CD Assignment 5-1

Open the file CD5-1_ITM on your Student CD and follow the instructions to complete the job.

CD Assignment 5-2

Open the file CD5-2_IHC on your Student CD and follow the instructions to complete the job.

CD Assignment 5-3

Open the file CD5-3_Scan on your Student CD and follow the instructions to complete the job.

Information and Records Management: Filing

6

Objectives

After studying this chapter, you should be able to

1. Set up a file drawer and prepare file folders.
2. Understand the concepts of subject and geographic filing.
3. Understand the concepts of electronic filing.
4. Apply alphabetic filing rules to a filing system.

Technology in Records Management

One of the ways that the Internet is revolutionizing office procedures is in the receipt of data and processing of records. As you saw in the section on Database Management in Chapter 5, many offices use database management software to maintain information and to organize and retrieve data. In a database system, data can easily be stored, added to, deleted, sorted in many different ways (such as sorted alphabetically, sorted by number, sorted by amount), and reorganized. As use of the Internet continues to grow, people and businesses are completing more transactions electronically. When people use the Internet to purchase items from *Amazon.com*, register a software purchase, view a credit card bill on the Internet, or apply for a government benefit, they are entering information into a computer database. These computer databases handle the filing and retrieval of information quickly and accurately without human intervention. As more transactions are performed over the Internet, records management in the future will increasingly be done using the computer. However, as long as people and businesses continue to use paper documents, there will be a need to record, store, and retrieve documents in the office.

Why File?

Every office receives information, letters, reports, applications, or orders which relate to the business. After these documents are processed, they must be stored in an organized way, so they can be quickly and easily retrieved when they are needed. The ability to locate these documents is vital to the efficiency and success of an office. Documents or files that cannot be found when required cause many problems:

- Valuable office time is wasted looking for lost files.
- It is embarrassing to tell clients that their files cannot be found.
- A file that cannot be located may contain valuable information that will require considerable time and expense to reassemble.

File Cabinets

The most common way to store paper documents in an office is to use either a vertical or lateral file cabinet.

> **Hint**
> Standard file cabinets are vertical or lateral.

- Vertical file cabinets are available in two-, three-, four-, and five-drawer models, with one drawer stacked on top of the other. Each drawer is approximately 28 inches deep and can be pulled forward to its entire length. Vertical

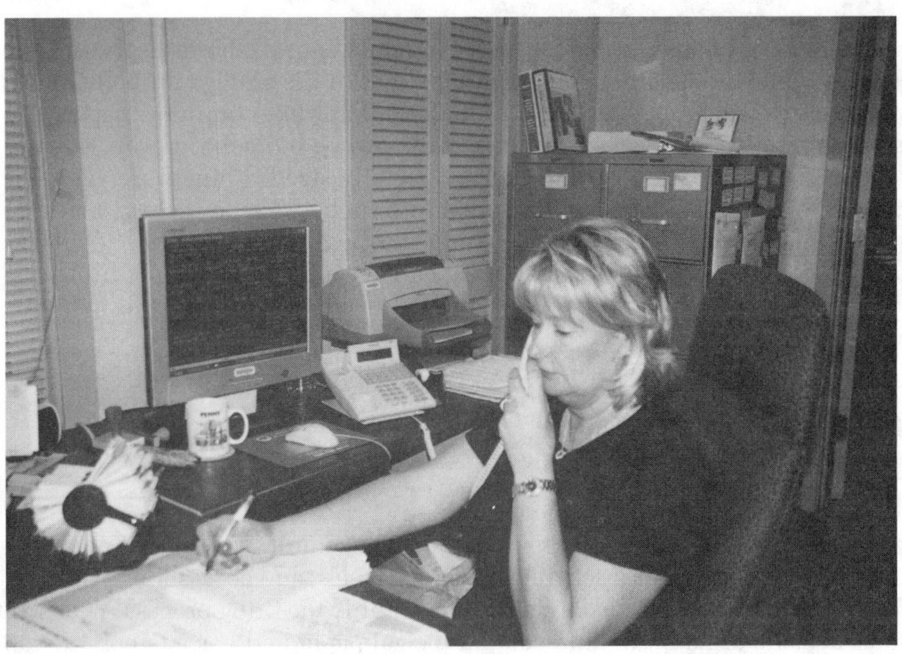

FIGURE 6-1 An office with vertical file cabinets.

FIGURE 6-2 An employee using a lateral file cabinet.

cabinets, therefore, must be placed where room is available for a person to work when a drawer is fully extended. Vertical files may be purchased in legal-size widths, for papers 8.5 inches × 14 inches, or in letter-size widths, for papers 8.5 inches × 11 inches.

- Lateral file cabinets are approximately 15 inches deep and from 36 to 42 inches wide. Opening a drawer exposes all files in the drawer at once. Lateral cabinets take up more wall space than vertical files, but they can be used along walkways because of their design. Lateral files are available in models which contain two, three, four, five, or six drawers and they are available for the storage of legal- or letter-size papers. Lateral file cabinets can contain a shelf located at a comfortable working height, so papers can be processed while standing at the file cabinet.

File storage units have changed to meet the requirements of different users and the need to store new technologies. There are many other styles of file storage units that meet specific needs, such as cabinets for storing microfiche, microfilm, computer paper, and computer disks and tapes. In addition, file storage units can be built into a wall, such as small pigeon-hole units used to store working files. Specially sized cabinets are available to store papers, cards, brochures, and so on that are 3 by 5 inches, 4 by 6 inches, 8.5 by 11 inches, and 11 by 14 inches. Open shelves can be built into a wall to store files, or shelves can be placed on rollers to expose many files at once. Large, wall-size electronic filing systems can utilize all the space from floor to ceiling and electronically retrieve files with the touch of a button.

SETTING UP FILES

File Folders

Before you place a document in a file cabinet or another storage unit, you should prepare a file folder and label. There are a large variety of file folders, labels, and accessories available, each designed for a specific purpose and all intended to simplify the filing process. The most common file folder is made of heavy manila-colored (beige) paper and has a tab on the top

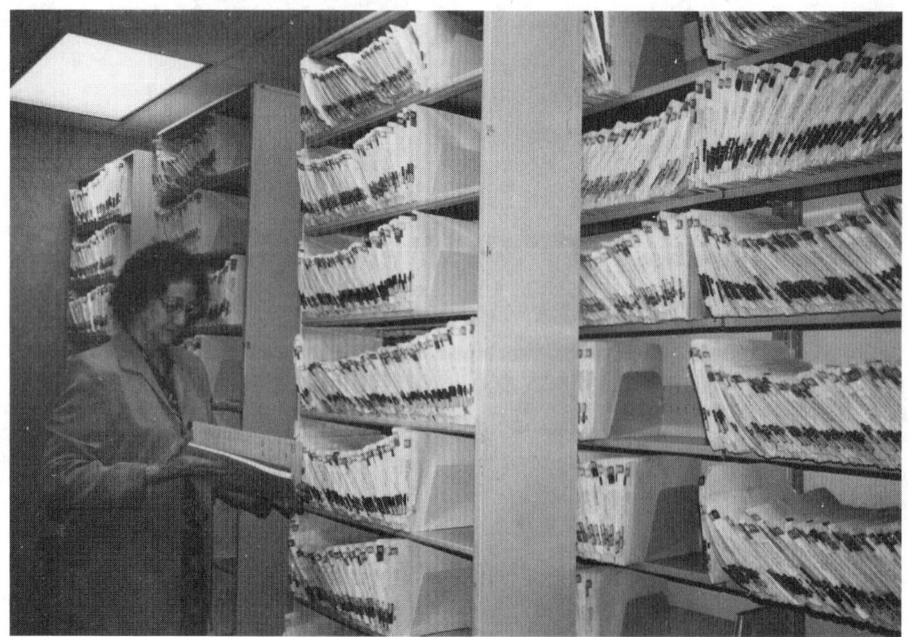

FIGURE 6-3 Electronically moveable file cabinets.

FIGURE 6-4 A pigeon-hole filing cabinet.

on which to place a label. The tab may extend across the entire top of the folder (full-cut), across a third of the folder (third-cut), or across a fifth of the folder (fifth-cut). The use of third-cut or fifth-cut folders enables filing personnel to stagger the labels for easy reading or to designate subdivisions of a project. File folders are creased on the bottom, so the folder can expand to hold more paper without blocking the folder label. Folders are available in a multitude of colors other than the standard manila. The use of colored folders can reduce errors and save time when filing or retrieving documents by using folders of the same color for a particular project, type of activity, or year.

Some offices use hanging folders, which are suspended from tracks along the sides of the file drawer. Documents can be filed directly in a hanging folder, or documents can first be placed in a file folder and then related file folders can be grouped by placing them together in a hanging folder. Color coding of the file folder or hanging folder improves organization and quickly locates a specific file. Other types of folders include plastic file folders which are good for heavy files, and expanding folders which are designed with expansion folds at the bottom to accommodate several inches of documents. Also, file folders may contain fasteners to secure papers. Some folders have a fastener in the front for a limited number of pages, while others fasten all of the papers in the folder. File folders with internal panels are available, so papers can be grouped together for easy reference.

Folder Labels

File folder labels are small slips of paper attached by adhesive to a backing sheet and are available in a variety of colors, sizes, and shapes. While many offices use standard white labels, color-coded labels are often used as a method of organizing a filing system. If a label has a line of color, the label should be prepared so the color is at the top of the label.

Prepare the label by writing or keyboarding the file name while the label is still attached to the backing sheet. Labels can also be generated by computer software packages and printed on file folder label sheets purchased from an office supply store. After the label is prepared, it is removed from the backing sheet and quickly placed on the file folder. Information about the various types of labels available can be obtained on the Internet at such sites as *www.avery.com*.

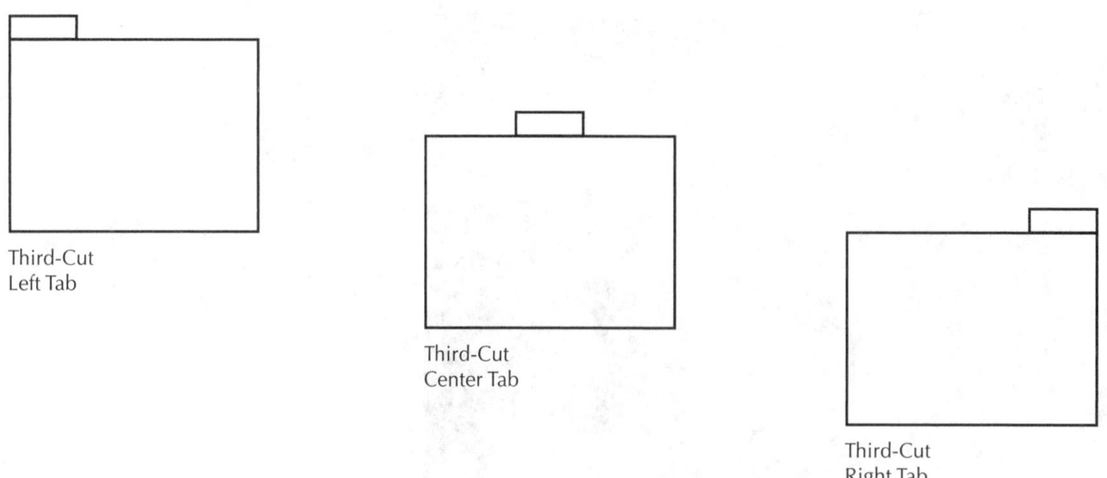

FIGURE 6-5 Third-cut file folders.

When keyboarding a folder label for the name of an individual, key the last name, a comma, a space, the first name, a space, and the middle name or initial. Labels for company names are keyed according to the indexing units discussed later in this chapter.

Organizing the Filing System

An efficient filing system should contain guides which organize and subdivide the contents of the file drawers. The guides are made of heavy cardboard or other substantial material and direct the eye to the desired file. For example, if the business uses a chronological filing system (date order), the guides may divide the files into months. In a geographical filing system, guides may be organized by state with city subguides. The labeled file folders are then placed in the drawer using the guides and divisions.

A well-organized filing system goes beyond the preparation of file folders and takes into account how the files are used in the office. In many offices, employees borrow files from the cabinets. When files are borrowed, there is always the question of when and if the files will be returned. To ensure the return of file folders, a check-out system should be established. When files are borrowed, only complete folders should be taken. Individual items should not be removed from file folders. A designated employee may be in charge of a file check-out system, or each person who borrows a file may be responsible for completing a check-out slip. The check-out slip may be a 3" × 5" card kept in a box or a large cardboard sheet placed in the file where the folder was kept. Regardless of the system used, an established procedure should be followed to encourage the prompt return of file folders.

File Folder Label ____________________
Date Borrowed ____________________
Borrower ____________________
Telephone Ext. ____________________
Department ____________________
Date Returned ____________________

FIGURE 6-6 A file folder check-out slip.

Because filing space is usually limited and expensive, inactive or old files should be moved to an inactive storage area, so active files are easily accessible. Files can be moved at a specific time or whenever the file drawers are full. The beginning of the calendar or fiscal year is a common time when offices move older files created before a specific date to inactive storage, so there is ample room for the new files. Inactive files can be placed in corrugated or plastic storage boxes, which are purchased from office supply stores. These boxes are available in legal and letter size.

Storage of Document Images

While most offices store original paper documents in large filing cabinets, technology can assist in the storing of documents as images in electronic or photographic form. Storing documents electronically or photographically saves significant space, and a copy of a document can be easily printed when a paper copy is required.

Microfilm

Microfilm photographs documents on high-resolution film and stores the information in miniature form. Thousands of pages of documents can easily be photographed and stored on a single piece of microfilm. This process greatly reduces the requirements for storage space, and a room full of paper documents can be contained in a single microfilm drawer.

Microfilm is available in several forms:

- Microfiche is a 4" × 6" sheet of film on which the pages are photographed in columns and rows. Each page can easily be located without having to go through all the previous pages.
- Cassettes, cartridges, or reels of microfilm contain as many as 5,000 pages of copy, which are photographed consecutively. Microfilm comes in two sizes, 16 millimeter and 35 millimeter, and is loaded on long rolls or spools of film.
- Aperture cards are keypunch cards that have an opening in which a frame of microfilm is mounted. Aperture cards are often used for engineering drawings.
- Microfilm jackets contain clear material sealed together on at least two sides. Inside the jacket are channels where the microfilm can be placed. Individual frames can be inserted easily, and updating of files is a simple task.
- Microfilm must be placed in a microfilm reader, which enlarges the image so it can be read. Many microfilm readers can also print a page from the microfilm.

Today existing microfilm, microfiche, and aperture cards are being digitized, so the information can be stored on CD-ROMs, DVDs, or PCs and then filed, faxed, and networked. This digitized information can easily be updated and shared with many users through standard computer technologies. Microfilm is still used because the information can be archived for 500+ years and the life of digitized information is unknown. The Library of Congress and the Smithsonian continue to microfilm data to ensure its long-term retrieval.

Computer Storage

Computers are used to store files electronically. As discussed in Chapter 5, Computers in the Office, documents can be entered into a computer using a scanner, and each page of the document is stored as an image. Computer software treats the documents as though they were stored in a filing cabinet. Documents can be organized in folders, drawers, and cabinets. Electronic notes can be attached to the documents, just as handwritten notes are attached to paper documents.

Electronic storage of document images requires considerable memory and would overwhelm the hard drives of most computers. Copies of documents generated by computers are stored in several ways.

- CD—either a CD-ROM (used only once) or a writeable CDRW (can be rewritten and used again). Documents can be stored on a CD, they can be read on the computer, and a paper copy can be printed.
- A DVD is the same physical size as a CD but holds more information. The storage of document images requires large computer files, and the use of DVDs is now replacing the use of CDs for large storage needs.
- An optical disk stores a large amount of text on a rigid, 12-inch plastic disk. More information can be stored in a smaller area on an optical disk than can be stored on microfilm. Since information stored on an optical disk can be retrieved randomly, it is an efficient method of storage and retrieval.
- Computer Output Microfilm (COM) allows the computer to process data and store it on magnetic tape or on a microfilm recorder. The microfilm recorder converts the data to images and stores it on film. After the film is developed, it is viewed at a microfilm reader.

Photocopier Reduction

Many photocopiers can reduce images. Some digital photocopiers have the ability to automatically reduce and store several pages of original images on a single sheet of paper. The copier then can enlarge the image back to the original size. Some copiers, however, can reduce an image, such as storing twenty images on a single sheet of paper, without the ability to enlarge an individual image so it is legible. If you intend to use a photocopier to reduce images for storage, verify that the copier can enlarge the images so you have a legible copy if needed in the future.

Filing Systems

There are five types of filing systems that are commonly used to organize documents for easy retrieval. They are the chronological, subject, geographic, numeric, and alphabetic filing systems. A chronological filing system maintains a copy of all documents by the date the document was sent. A chronological filing system was discussed in Chapter 1, The Successful Employee.

Rules for consistent filing have been developed by many organizations, but some offices use their own filing procedures instead of following standardized procedures. Therefore, when you are working with a new filing system, review the system carefully before filing or retrieving documents.

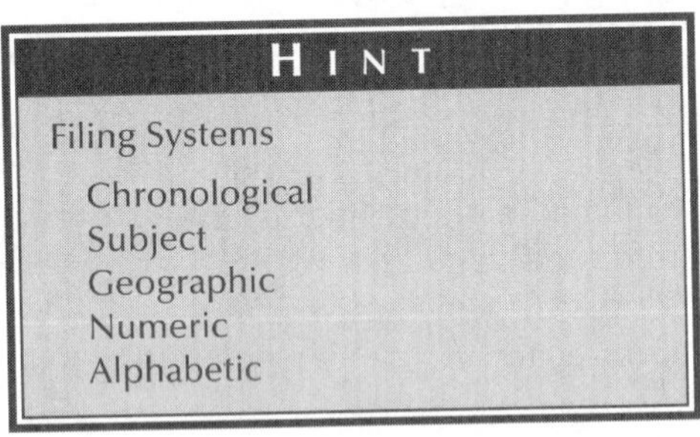

If a file could be placed in several locations or you are uncertain as to how to file it, cross-reference it. A cross reference indicates alternate methods of filing a document. For example, if you are unsure of how to file a document with a company name, you can file the document where you think it should be placed, then place a sheet of paper, the cross reference, at the location of your second filing option which informs the user where the folder is located. A list of all cross references can be kept in the file drawer directing the user to look at alternate filing locations.

Subject Filing

Subject filing is a system in which files are arranged by the topic of the document rather than the name of a person or company. When using a subject filing system, a letter concerning the purchase of the Webster Building would be filed under the topic "Webster Building." Within the topic, the files are arranged alphabetically or chronologically. To facilitate locating files, create a cross-referencing system listing all subjects.

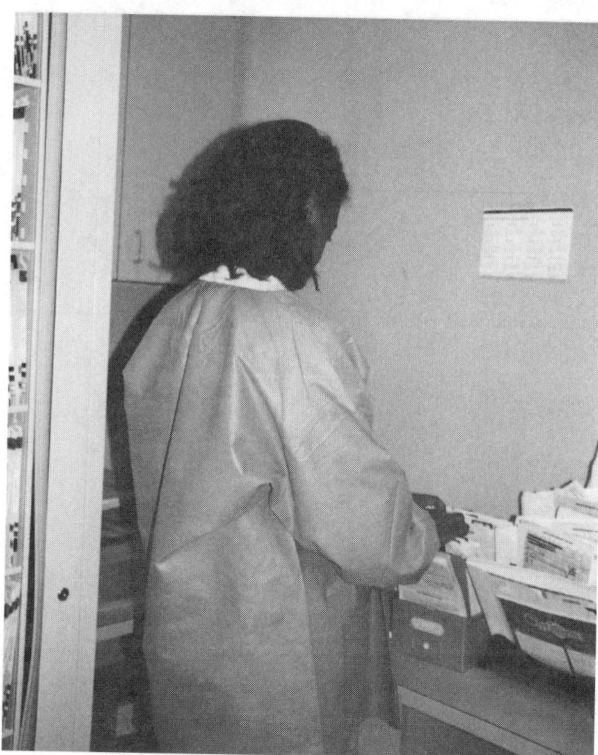

FIGURE 6-7 An employee using a cross-reference filing system.

Geographic Filing

Geographic filing is a system in which files are arranged according to geographic location. Businesses that are organized by geographic locations, such as sales districts, often use geographic filing. Files are arranged alphabetically within the geographic divisions.

File drawers are usually established with the main geographic categories as the primary guides. Secondary guides are used for subdivisions. For example, this system would use the state as the primary guide and the city as the secondary guide. The file folder would first list the state, then the city, and then a specific client in that city.

Numeric Filing

Numeric filing assigns a number to each company, person, or project. The numeric code is placed on each document to be filed. Numeric files are often used in banking, credit card accounts, and accounts receivable in which each client has a separate account number. The account numbers are a quick way to identify persons who have similar names. To assist in locating files, the office must have a cross-referencing system using a card-file index or computer list of clients and their numeric codes.

Alphabetic Filing

Although alphabetic filing is the most commonly used filing system, there is no single set of alphabetic rules used by all offices. While some offices use filing rules developed by the Association of Records Managers and Administrators (ARMA), alphabetic rules vary from office to office. As an employee, you should study the filing system used in your office prior to filing documents.

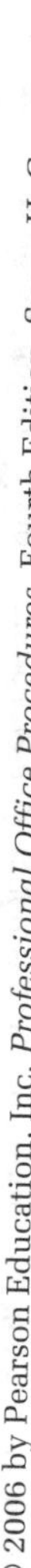

Budgets
- Year 2004
- Year 2003
- Year 2002
- Year 2001
- Year 2000
- Year 1999

Company Forms
- Employee Assistance Programs
- Employment
- Evaluations
- Leave
- Local Travel
- Long-Distance Travel

Personnel Files
- Baldwin, Jenny
- James, Tammy
- Lewis, Sally
- Peterson, Julie
- Potter, Laura
- Tran, An
- Zhou, Dave

Seminars
- Budget Forecasting
- Computer Software
- Environmental Safety
- Human Relations Skills
- Management Techniques

Vendors
- Brooks & Sons
- Lee Industries
- Robertson Supplies

FIGURE 6-8 A subject filing system.

Florida
- Ft. Lauderdale
- Ft. Myers
- Miami
- Sarasota

Maryland
- Baltimore
- Frederick
- Rockville

New York
- Buffalo
- Rochester
- Syracuse

FIGURE 6-9 A geographic filing system.

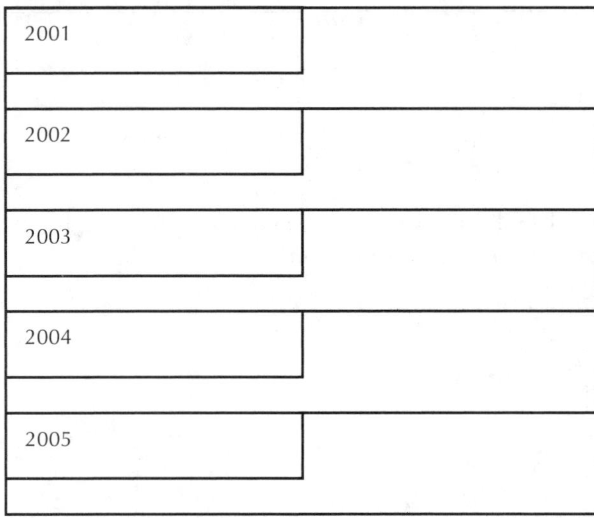

FIGURE 6-10 A numeric filing system.

Cross-Reference List

2001	McHale, Laura
2002	Livingstone, Mary J.
2003	Kanawha Industries
2004	Fernando, Maxwell
2005	Amos Enterprises

FIGURE 6-11 A cross-reference for numeric filing.

An understanding of the alphabetic filing system is also required to establish and use subject and geographic filing systems. This chapter will contain common alphabetic filing rules used in many offices, examples of the filing rules, practice exercises for each rule, and a continuous review of previously learned rules.

The first step when filing is to index the name. Indexing means dividing the name of an individual, company, or a title into separate units.

Filing rules follow alphabetic order. Since *a* comes before *b, apple* is filed before *banana.*

When filing two names, look at the first letter of each name to determine which should be filed first. If the two first letters of each name are the same, look at the second letters and follow the alphabetic order of the second letters. If the second letters are the same, look at the third letters, and so on. This procedure will determine which name should be filed first.

Alphabetic Filing Rules

Rule 1 Simple Personal Names

- When filing personal names, divide the name into the following indexing units.

Unit 1	Last name
Unit 2	First name
Unit 3	Middle name or initial

Names	*Unit 1*	*Unit 2*	*Unit 3*
Lillian Kay Martin	Martin	Lillian	Kay
Edward Fairfax	Fairfax	Edward	
Stacy Ann Moore	Moore	Stacy	Ann
Kenneth Ted Hardy	Hardy	Kenneth	Ted

- After determining the indexing units, alphabetize the names according to unit 1. The previous group of names would be filed in the following order:

Unit 1	*Unit 2*	*Unit 3*
Fairfax	Edward	
Hardy	Kenneth	Ted
Martin	Lillian	Kay
Moore	Stacy	Ann

- If you have two unit 1's that are exactly alike, unit 2 will determine which name will be filed first. If units 1 and 2 are exactly alike, alphabetize according to unit 3.

Names	*Unit 1*	*Unit 2*
Patricia Dunlap	Dunlap	Patricia
Roger Dunlap	Dunlap	Roger

Patricia Dunlap would be filed before Roger Dunlap.

- Individual letters are considered as indexing units. The period following the initial is ignored.

Names	*Unit 1*	*Unit 2*	*Unit 3*
Emma B. Ball	Ball	Emma	B
Doyle R. Beyer	Beyer	Doyle	R

- If a name is abbreviated, index it using the abbreviation.

Names	*Unit 1*	*Unit 2*	*Unit 3*
Bill O. Levy	Levy	Bill	O
Joe C. Rose	Rose	Joe	C

Rule 2 File "Nothing Before Something"

- Consider the following names. Since Orlans is the last name for both persons, look at each person's first name—L. and Libby. The initial L has nothing following it, so L would be filed before Libby.

Names	*Unit 1*	*Unit 2*	*Unit 3*
L. Orlans	Orlans	L	
Libby Orlans	Orlans	Libby	

- Consider the following two similar names.

Names	*Unit 1*	*Unit 2*	*Unit 3*
Robert France	France	Robert	
F. Frances	Frances	F	

France is filed before Frances.

France_	(File the blank space [nothing] before the *s*.)
Frances	

Practice 6-1

Use one 3" × 5" card for each folder to be filed. Divide each name in the following list into its indexing units, and write the names on the 3" × 5" card. Move the cards around, so that the first card in alphabetical order is on top, the second card in alphabetical order is next, and so on. After all of the cards are alphabetized, open the Practice Filing Form, CH6_FF, which is located on your Student CD. On your Filing Form file, key in the information from your 3" × 5" cards. Key the information from the first card in alphabetical order onto line 1, key the second card in alphabetical order onto line 2, key the third card in alphabetical order onto line 3, and so on. Use Save As to save the file with the name Practice 6-1. Print the file.

Folders to be filed

1. Holly Arnold
2. Amos J. Homer
3. Norma Joan Pendell
4. Anne Elizabeth Anderson
5. Donna Emily Parker
6. Louis K. Yeager
7. Donna Emilyann Parker
8. Louis Kenneth Yeager
9. Greg Snyder
10. Randy Ray Tuckwillar
11. Martha R. Norris
12. Norma Jean Pendell
13. Lillian Phyllis Martin
14. Henry R. Feliciano
15. Cyrus Martine
16. Argelio F. Fellows

FIGURE 6-12 A wall-mounted filing system.

Rule 3 Identical Names

- If people have identical last, first, and middle names, the city, then state, then street name, and then street address are used to determine the filing order. Consider the following two similar names.

Suzy Gomez
890 Butler Road
Ft. Wayne, Indiana

Suzy Gomez
712 Grazing Drive
Chicago, Illinois

Ms. Gomez of Chicago would be filed before Ms. Gomez of Ft. Wayne.

Unit 1	*Unit 2*	*City*
Gomez	Suzy	Chicago
Gomez	Suzy	Ft. Wayne

Rule 4 Seniority Titles

- Seniority titles are used as the last indexing unit in a name. Seniority titles include Junior, Senior, Jr., Sr., II, and III. Companies differ on spelling in full or abbreviating Jr. and Sr. Always cross-reference if necessary.

Names	*Unit 1*	*Unit 2*	*Unit 3*	*Unit 4*
Richard B. Davis	Davis	Richard	B	
Richard Davis, Jr.	Davis	Richard	Junior	
Richard Davis, Sr.	Davis	Richard	Senior	
Donald R. Miller, Jr.	Miller	Donald	R	Junior

Rule 5 Organization Names

- Index names of organizations according to how the names are written on the letterhead.
- However, if the company name contains a person's first and last name, some organizations use the person's last name as the first indexing unit and the first name as the second indexing unit.
- If a company name contains single letters, index each letter as a separate indexing unit.
- If a business name contains an acronym (a word formed from the first letters of several words) or an abbreviation which is printed in capital letters on the letterhead, index the unit as one word. For example, in the name MGM Grand Hotel, the first indexing unit is MGM.
- The rules in your office may vary when indexing company names containing a person's first and last names. Review your company's procedures before filing materials.

Names	*Unit 1*	*Unit 2*	*Unit 3*
Broad Equipment	Broad	Equipment	
Shady Road Hospital	Shady	Road	Hospital
Costal Resorts	Costal	Resorts	
Sunny Day Deli	Sunny	Day	Deli
L J Enterprises	L	J	Enterprises
LAJ Enterprises	LAJ	Enterprises	
MGM Grand Hotel	MGM	Grand	Hotel
Ronald Watson Jewelers	Ronald	Watson	Jewelers
(Alternate method)	Watson	Ronald	Jewelers

Rule 6 Abbreviations

- Abbreviations in business names should be spelled in full. Examples of abbreviations in business names include *Incorporated (Inc.), Company (Co.), Limited (Ltd.),* and *Manufacturing (Mfg.).*
- *Mr., Mrs.,* and *Ms.* preceding personal names are not considered abbreviations and are not used as an indexing unit. They may, however, be placed in parentheses at the end if necessary for clarification.

Names	***Unit 1***	***Unit 2***	***Unit 3***
Champagne Interiors Inc.	Champagne	Interiors	Incorporated
Mrs. Sally Rogers	Rogers	Sally (Mrs.)	
Mr. William Rogers	Rogers	William	

Rule 7 Possessives

- If a name is possessive, ignore the apostrophe.

Names	***Unit 1***	***Unit 2***	***Unit 3***
Chuck's Garage	Chucks	Garage	
Frances' Gift Shop	Frances	Gift	Shop
Royce's Fruit Market	Royces	Fruit	Market

Practice 6-2

Use one 3" × 5" card for each folder to be filed. (You may reuse the cards from the previous practice by drawing a line through the names.) Divide each name in the following list into its indexing units, and write the names on the 3" × 5" card. Move the cards around, so that the first card in alphabetical order is on top, the second card is next, and so on. After all of the cards are alphabetized, open the Practice Filing Form, CH6_FF, which is located on your Student CD. On your Filing Form file, key in the information from your 3" × 5" cards. Key the information from the first card in alphabetical order onto line 1, key the second card in alphabetical order onto line 2, key the third card in alphabetical order onto line 3, and so on. Use Save As to save the file with the name Practice 6-2. Print the file.

Folders to be filed

1. Martin J. Davis III
2. Elmer I. Elliott, 900 Pear Drive, Austin, TX
3. Dennis K. Watson, Senior
4. Paul R. Bates, Senior
5. Lottie Russell, 8934 Crown Avenue, Tacoma, WA
6. Phil W. Morgan, 5810 Earlston Drive, Seattle, WA
7. Floyd Haque
8. Phil W. Morgan, 3478 Albia Road, Portland, ME
9. Cecil's Department Store
10. Horn's Antiques, Ltd.
11. C. Jay Istar, Junior
12. Kelly's Leather Shop
13. Jerry's Garage
14. Elmer I. Elliott, 1723 Eagle Court, Atlanta, GA
15. Martin J. Davis II
16. Lottie Russell, 700 Fordham Drive, Salem, OR

17. Paul R. Bates, Junior
18. Ronald Freeman, Jr.
19. Eugene Frederick, Jr.
20. J. Elmer Elliott, 3078 Veirs Road, Bethesda, MD
21. Dennis K. Watson, Jr.
22. S. Hanson
23. Shamsul Hanst
24. Floyd D. Haque
25. Phil S. Morgan, 2309 Diamond Avenue, Portland, OR
26. M. Shamsul Hanst
27. Samuel Hanson
28. C. Jay Istar, Senior
29. Krammar's Grocery
30. Randy's Bakery

Rule 8 Personal Titles

- If a name contains a title, disregard the title if it is used with a complete name. Place the title in parentheses at the end.

Names	*Unit 1*	*Unit 2*	*Unit 3*
Dr. George Quade	Quade	George	(Dr.)
President Harold Roselli	Roselli	Harold	(President)
Sylvia Walters, Ph.D.	Walters	Sylvia	(Ph.D.)

- If a title is used with an incomplete name, the title is the first indexing unit. An incomplete name does not have first and last names.

Names	*Unit 1*	*Unit 2*
Father Malone	Father	Malone
Rabbi Wise	Rabbi	Wise

Rule 9 Married Women's Names

- When indexing a married woman's name, include her first name as an indexing unit, if it is known.

Names	*Unit 1*	*Unit 2*	*Unit 3*
Joyce M. Davis	Davis	Joyce	M
Brenda Sue Morell	Morell	Brenda	Sue
Mrs. Fred Sikes (Linda)	Sikes	Linda	

- Some companies place the husband's name in parentheses.

Names	*Unit 1*	*Unit 2*
Kate Mullens (Mrs. Harry Mullens)	Mullens	Kate (Mrs. Harry)

- *Ms.* or *Mrs.* may be placed in parentheses at the end.

Name	*Unit 1*	*Unit 2*	*Unit 3*
Ms. Helen C. Harvey	Harvey	Helen	C (Ms.)

- If only the husband's name is known, index using the husband's name and place the personal title at the end.

Name	*Unit 1*	*Unit 2*	*Unit 3*
Mrs. Harry Mullens	Mullens	Harry (Mrs.)	

Rule 10 Hyphenated Names

- A hyphenated name is considered as one indexing unit, and the hyphen is ignored.

Names	*Unit 1*	*Unit 2*	*Unit 3*
After-School Plaza	AfterSchool	Plaza	
Jane Bailey-Starr	BaileyStarr	Jane	
Mason-Todd Garage	MasonTodd	Garage	
Peck-Boyd Shop	PeckBoyd	Shop	
Kay Stone-Albert	StoneAlbert	Kay	

Rule 11 Directions

- If a business name contains a directional word, index it as written.

Names	*Unit 1*	*Unit 2*	*Unit 3*
Northwest Business	Northwest	Business	
North West Foods	North	West	Foods
Southwest Service Center	Southwest	Service	Center

Practice 6-3

Use one 3" × 5" card for each folder to be filed. (You may reuse the cards from the previous practice by drawing a line through the names.) Divide each name on the following list into its indexing units, and write the names on the 3" × 5" card. Move the cards around, so that the first card in alphabetical order is on top, the second card in alphabetical order is next, and so on. After all of the cards are alphabetized, open the Practice Filing Form, CH6_FF, which is located on your Student CD. On your Filing Form file, key in the information from your 3" × 5" cards. Key the information from the first card onto line 1, key the second card in alphabetical order onto line 2, key the third card in alphabetical order onto line 3, and so on. Use Save As to save the file with the name Practice 6-3. Print the file.

Folders to be filed

1. Judge Richards
2. Adkins-Anderson Clothiers
3. Leslie Pratt-Wallace
4. Senator Robert C. Byrd
5. Mrs. Sharon Salamon (Mrs. John)
6. Sister Melissa
7. Judge Raymond Rebuck
8. Mini-Mart Stores
9. Louise Abbott-Lawford
10. Mary-Rose Foods
11. Congresswoman Barbara Jordan
12. W. Richard-Hardkins
13. Ms. Hanna Haye
14. South East Movies
15. Dr. Mary Salcetti
16. Reverend Iverson

FIGURE 6-13 A card filing cabinet.

17. Edward Recht, Senior
18. North West Cleaners
19. Judge S. Rebuck
20. Reverend Daniel P. Villegas

Rule 12 Minor Words and Symbols

- Minor words and symbols are indexed as separate units. The following are examples of minor words: *the, and, for.* The following are examples of symbols: &, #, $, *, and @. If *The* is the first word in a name, place it as the last indexing unit.

Names	*Unit 1*	*Unit 2*	*Unit 3*	*Unit 4*
The Clays	Clays	The		
Kids on the Move	Kids	on	the	Move
Young & Bates	Young	&	Bates	

Rule 13 Prefixes

- If a name begins with a prefix, consider the prefix and the word that follows as one unit. Examples of prefixes are *l', el, la, las, mac, mc,* and *o'.*

Names	*Unit 1*	*Unit 2*	*Unit 3*
Jose DeSardo	DeSardo	Jose	
El Grande Hotel	ElGrande	Hotel	
Pierre La Piana	LaPiana	Pierre	
Belle LaPlante	LaPlante	Belle	
Richard N. LeVan	LeVan	Richard	N

Rule 14 Numbers

- Business names with numbers are divided into indexing units as written. If the number is spelled out, index it spelled out in alphabetical order. Numbers in digit form are

considered one unit and written in digit form. Business names in digit form are filed in numerical order before alphabetical names are filed.

Names	*Unit 1*	*Unit 2*	*Unit 3*
24 Hour Shop	24	Hour	Shop
500 Lounge	500	Lounge	
Big Ten Shop	Big	Ten	Shop
Biglerville 2000 Club	Biglerville	2000	Club
One Market Place	One	Market	Place

Practice 6-4

Use one 3" × 5" card for each folder to be filed. (You may reuse the cards from the previous practice by drawing a line through the names.) Divide each name on the following list into its indexing units, and write the names on the 3" × 5" card. Move the cards around, so that the first card in alphabetical order is on top, the second card in alphabetical order is next, and so on. After all of the cards are alphabetized, open the Practice Filing Form, CH6_FF, which is located on your Student CD. On your Filing Form file, key in the information from your 3" × 5" cards. Key the information from the first card onto line 1, key the second card in alphabetical order onto line 2, key the third card in alphabetical order onto line 3, and so on. Use Save As to save the file with the name Practice 6-4. Print the file.

Folders to be filed

1. The Ladder Store
2. Peter W. LeBrun
3. P & R Incorporated
4. 52 Week Travel
5. The Big Men
6. Nancy McDonald
7. Hartz & Porter
8. T. M. LeBlanc
9. Martha Sue O'Connor
10. Luigi Ira LeBow
11. Amy McCabe, D.D.S.
12. U. S. Construction
13. Atkins and Jackson Associates
14. Women for Success Inc.
15. Rollins Shoes
16. Young at Heart Golf
17. Clay's Bed and Bedding
18. 300 Sovern
19. Come and Go Cleaners
20. Jose's Books
21. J. W. Rollins Shoes
22. Romeo Design Interiors
23. Cooking 24 Hours
24. Dr. Amy Sanford
25. Books on Travel

Rule 15 Banks

- Index banks according to the most important word.

Names	*Unit 1*	*Unit 2*	*Unit 3*	*Unit 4*
Maine Federal Bank	Maine	Federal	Bank	
Reid Thrift Bank	Reid	Thrift	Bank	
Saving Bank of Roanoke	Roanoke	Savings	Bank	of

- If the bank names are exactly alike, use the city, state, street, and building number in that order to determine the filing order. Consider the following three branches of the Chain Savings Bank:

Chain Savings Bank
200 Williams Drive
Boston, MA

Chain Savings Bank
500 Colonial Drive
Boston, MA

Chain Savings Bank
3200 Hampton Lane
Braintree, MA

Unit 1	*Unit 2*	*Unit 3*	*Address*
Chain	Savings	Bank	Boston, MA Colonial Drive
Chain	Savings	Bank	Boston, MA Williams Drive
Chain	Savings	Bank	Braintree, MA

Rule 16 Radio and Television Stations

- Radio and television stations are indexed as though the call letters were a word. When *AM, FM,* or *TV* are included with the call letters, they are unit 2.

Names	*Unit 1*	*Unit 2*
KANG	KANG	
KONG-FM	KONG	FM
KONG-TV	KONG	TV
WZTF(FM)	WZTF	FM

- Some companies use the words *Radio Station* or *Television Station* as the first two units.

Name	*Unit 1*	*Unit 2*	*Unit 3*
KANG	Radio	Station	KANG

Rule 17 School Names

- A school name is indexed in the order written unless it contains a person's first name and last name. In that case, the last name is the first indexing unit. Some companies use *University* as the first indexing unit and others place the most important word in the title as the first unit. For example, *University of Washington* may be filed as *University of Washington* or as *Washington University of.* Always cross-reference the file when there is a question about how to file it.

Names	*Unit 1*	*Unit 2*	*Unit 3*	*Unit 4*
Arnold Junior High School	Arnold	Junior	High	School
The John Dewey School	Dewey	John	School	The
Maine Academy	Maine	Academy		
University of Washington	University	of	Washington	
(Alternate)	Washington	University	of	

- Schools with identical names are first indexed by the school name. After the school name, index by city first and then by state if necessary.

  Green Elementary School, Dayton, Ohio
  Green Elementary School, Fairmont, West Virginia

Unit 1	*Unit 2*	*Unit 3*	*City*
Green	Elementary	School	Dayton
Green	Elementary	School	Fairmont

Practice 6-5

Use one 3" × 5" card for each folder to be filed. (You may reuse the cards from the previous practice by drawing a line through the names.) Divide each name on the following list into its indexing units, and write the names on the 3" × 5" card. Move the cards around, so that the first card in alphabetical order is on top, the second card in alphabetical order is next, and so on. After all of the cards are alphabetized, open the Practice Filing Form, CH6_FF, which is located on your Student CD. On your Filing Form file, key in the information from your 3" × 5" cards. Key the information from the first card onto line 1, key the second card in alphabetical order onto line 2, key the third card in alphabetical order onto line 3, and so on. Use Save As to save the file with the name Practice 6-5. Print the file.

Folders to be filed

1. McArthur Federal Savings, 2200 Lake Street, Dayton, OH
2. Berkeley Springs Country Inn
3. Williams Resort and Inn
4. Washington Federal, 702 Russell Avenue, Seattle, WA
5. Valley Bank, 307 Jefferson St., Rockville, MD
6. McArthur Federal Savings, 300 Wilkins Blvd., Cincinnati, OH
7. WETA-FM
8. Oaklands High School, 3789 Spring Drive, Norfolk, VA
9. WKZA-TV
10. Captain Standish Motor Lodge
11. Kensington Elementary School
12. Rochester High School
13. San Diego High School
14. Oaklands High School, 3200 Luck Road, Houston, TX
15. Valley Bank, 3000 River Rd., Bethesda, MD
16. Oahu High School
17. William Howard Taft Elementary
18. WCHS
19. The Bank of Cincinnati, 1775 Hughes Drive, Cincinnati, OH
20. WWVA-TV

FIGURE 6-14 A filing cabinet designed to hold pamphlets.

Rule 18 Churches and Synagogues

- When indexing churches and synagogues, the first unit is the word that identifies the organization. Do not use *church* or *temple* as the first word. When in doubt about how to file a church or synagogue, cross-reference the file.

Names	*Unit 1*	*Unit 2*	*Unit 3*
B'nai Israel Temple	Bnai	Israel	Temple
Church of Hope	Hope	Church	of
St. John's Church	Saint	Johns	Church

- Some companies do not spell out *Saint* and file the name as written.

Rule 19 Organizations

- When indexing organizations, use the most distinctive word as the first unit.

Names	*Unit 1*	*Unit 2*	*Unit 3*	*Unit 4*
United Guild of Barbers	Barbers	United	Guild	of
Networking Associates	Networking	Associates		
Retired Teacher's Club	Teachers	Retired	Club	

- Most telephone directories do not index using this rule. Telephone directories usually list organizations in the order the names are written. For example, *Association of American Planters* would be listed in the telephone directory under *Association*. Also, common abbreviations and acronyms are usually listed in the telephone directory without spelling out the words.

Rule 20 Magazines and Newspapers

- In most instances, magazines are indexed in the order in which the names appear. Newspapers should be filed with the name of the city as first indexing unit. If the name of the newspaper does not begin with the city name, place the city name first, followed by the name of the newspaper.

Names	*Unit 1*	*Unit 2*	*Unit 3*
Journal of Accountancy	Journal	of	Accountancy
Newport City Journal	Newport	City	Journal
Daily News (Tilden, UT)	Tilden	Daily	News
Time Magazine	Time	Magazine	

Rule 21 United States Government Agencies

- United States government agencies are indexed as

Unit 1	United
Unit 2	States
Unit 3	Government
Unit 4	main word in the name of the division

Note: The Cabinet department is not indexed.

United States Government will be units 1, 2, and 3 in all of the following examples.

United States Government Department of Labor, Bureau of Labor Statistics

Unit 4	*Unit 5*	*Unit 6*	*Unit 7*
Labor	Statistics	Bureau	of

Note: Department of Labor is the Cabinet department and is not indexed.

United States Government Department of Commerce, Patent & Trademark Office

Unit 4	*Unit 5*	*Unit 6*	*Unit 7*
Patent	&	Trademark	Office

Note: Department of Commerce is the Cabinet department and is not indexed.

Rule 22 Political Subdivisions

- Index political divisions by the name of the state, county, or city. Then index by the name of the department or division, using the most important word first. Some companies may use *Department of, Bureau of,* and so on only when needed for clarification.

Names	*Unit 1*	*Unit 2*	*Unit 3*	*Unit 4*
Board of Education, Houston	Houston	Education	Board	of
Idaho Department of Parks	Idaho	Parks	Department	of

Practice 6-6

Use one 3" × 5" card for each folder to be filed. (You may reuse the cards from the previous practice by drawing a line through the names.) Divide each name on the following list into its indexing units, and write the names on the 3" × 5" card. Move the cards around, so that the first card in alphabetical order is on top, the second card in alphabetical order is next, and so on. After all of the cards are alphabetized, open the Practice Filing Form, CH6_FF, which is located on your Student CD. On your Filing Form file, key in the information from your 3" × 5" cards. Key the information from the first card onto line 1, key the second card in alphabetical order onto line 2, key the third card in alphabetical order onto line 3, and so on. Use Save As to save the file with the name Practice 6-6. Print the file.

Folders to be filed

1. First Baptist Church
2. Association of Engineers
3. Department of Water and Sewer, Knoxville, TN
4. St. Mark's Church
5. Mapping Agency, U.S. Department of Defense
6. American Association for Counseling
7. U.S. Department of Commerce, Bureau of Economic Analysis
8. Anaheim Examiner
9. First Montrose Church
10. Institute of Cardiology
11. Department of Recreation, Nashville, TN
12. Church of Christ of Danville
13. Dallas Daily Reporter
14. American Psychology Association
15. Department of Travel, Chattanooga, TN
16. Housing and Community Development, KY
17. The New York Times
18. Temple Shalom
19. Maryland Boating Association
20. The Pasta Depot

FILING HINTS

1. Develop a master index of the filing system and make it easily accessible to everyone who uses the files. The master index should include the divisions of the filing system. It is also useful to have a list of all folders in subject and geographic files.
2. Repair torn pages before filing them.
3. Remove all paper clips before filing and staple the pages of multipage documents. (Paper clips can attach pages that should be placed in different files.)
4. To simplify the filing process, code documents before filing. As the code, use the name or number of the folder where the document should be filed. Use the master index to assign the code and write the code in the top right corner of the first page of the document. On an incoming letter, you might simply underline the name of the company in the letterhead with a red pen. On a copy of an outgoing letter, you might underline the name of the company in the inside address.
5. Prior to filing, arrange all papers in the order in which they will be placed in the file cabinet. This prior planning eliminates the constant opening and closing of alternate file drawers.
6. Establish a specific time each day to file, because a large stack of unfiled documents may become so large that it becomes a major project. In addition, a seemingly lost document may actually be in the to-be-filed pile.
7. If a file folder is too full, divide the contents into two folders.
8. Use a miscellaneous folder for each file subdivision until there are sufficient documents to establish a separate folder. The minimum number of documents to start a new folder is usually five.

HINT
Create a master index. Make it accessible to everyone.

Master Index

Burgess	Gerald	S	
Cincinnati	Enquirer		
Cleveland	High	School	
Glassblowers	Guild		
Herandex	Gloria	R	
Heritage	Associates		
Kearney	Donald	M	
Libby's	Restaurant		
Lore	Ronald	Thomas	
Maxwell	Lana	Maria	
Miami	County	Animal	Research
Ottenberg	Rhonda	Connie	
Rose	Accounting	Incorporated	
Saint	Marks	Church	
Schwartz	Jewelers		
Simons	Pharmacy		

FIGURE 6-15 A master index showing all files in the file cabinet.

9. Allow about 4 inches of free space in each file drawer for working room.
10. Stagger the heading tabs on file folders to make it easier to find materials.
11. To locate missing papers,
    - Carefully check the folder where the paper is supposed to be.
    - Check the folders in front of and behind where the lost item should be.
    - Consider alternate ways the item could have been filed and look in those folders. For example, it could have been filed under a person's first name instead of the last name.
    - Ask other employees if they have the folder.
12. Create a color-coded "Important Information Folder" and place copies of documents in this folder. Select a specific color and only use it for this type of folder. This is an easy method of quickly locating important documents.
13. As part of your personal filing system, keep a file of people you meet. Put information about everyone you meet in your file. These contacts can be very helpful if you have a problem, and a last-minute crisis may be solved by a person on your contact list. This file list can be kept in your business card file, 3″ × 5″ card index system, word processing file, computer database file, calendar software file, organizer file, or computer software contact list file.

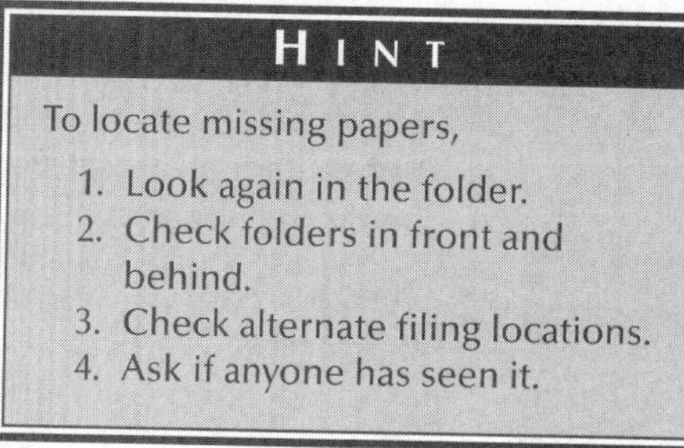

HINT
To locate missing papers,
1. Look again in the folder.
2. Check folders in front and behind.
3. Check alternate filing locations.
4. Ask if anyone has seen it.

CHAPTER REVIEW

1. Explain subject filing.
2. Explain geographic filing.
3. Explain numeric filing.
4. Explain the nothing-before-something rule.
5. Explain the rule for filing a hyphenated name.
6. Explain the rule for filing a United States government agency.

ACTIVITIES

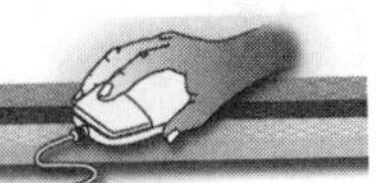

1. Visit an office supply store and look at the variety of file folders, labels, and filing storage units available. Prepare a written report describing your findings. Be prepared to give an oral summary of your report in class.
2. Ask three businesspeople:
   a. What type of filing systems they use
   b. What type of filing storage units they use
   c. If they use a cross-reference system

   Prepare both an oral and a written report describing the comments you receive.

PROJECTS

Project 11

Create the following memo from Michelle Kaplan, Managing Director, to Theodore Nash, Executive Director, concerning file cabinets.

> This memorandum is being prepared in response to your request for reorganization of the filing system.
>
> As we discussed, the reasons to reorganize are
>
> 1. The need to archive files that are crowding the office environment
> 2. The need for additional filing cabinets
>
> The staff appreciates the opportunity to provide input in meeting this challenge. We are well aware of the unsightly conditions which exist in the file cabinet space adjacent to the offices. The current conditions not only are very inefficient in locating files but also reflect poorly on the staff in the eyes of those in industry who visit us. The following recommendations, if adopted, will increase the efficiency of the files, will reflect a proper image of the department, and will provide a more pleasant office environment for the staff.
>
> The current files are retained in the individual offices. All other files are kept in the outer offices entered through the reception area. Currently, this room has 26 file cabinets, varying in type, size, and color. These cabinets are used to store the following:
>
> - Files for approximately 1,000 projects
> - Approximately 300 new proposals
> - Approximately 200 projects which are not reactivated from the previous year
> - Records of the 20 years of the department
> - Stock of forms
> - Stock of miscellaneous publications which are distributed to other departments
>
> There is an increasing need for space to contain the files for these projects.
>
> 1. More projects are entering the department than are leaving.
> 2. The size of the files has increased dramatically from the original projects.

With the increased requirements of recent years, the folder size of current projects is twice the size of those projects processed in the 1990s. Therefore, removing the inactive folders does not provide sufficient file space for all active folders.

As a result of these factors, there is not enough room in the existing 26 file cabinets for files, storage of forms, and historical or processing information on the most recent projects. Files of every nature are placed on the top of cabinets, in boxes, or in stacks on the floor.

Information in these files must be readily accessible to the staff. These files are used to monitor the current projects.

Recommendation for Reception Room

The following recommendation provides for more efficient use of the space in the reception room to ensure that sufficient file space is available for the files, forms, and information.

- Obtain 20 uniform lateral files, 5 drawers high, for placement in the outer offices. To accommodate the available space, 11 of these lateral files should be the 42-inch size, while the 9 others should be the 36-inch size.
- Relocate 3 cabinets which do not have pull-out drawers and are 6 shelves high to Building 800. These cabinets will be used for storage of forms and will not interfere with the use of this area as a miniconference room and office for visiting associates.
- Relocate the 5 lateral files in this room to employee offices to create additional storage in those locations.

The 20 new lateral file cabinets will be a much more efficient use of space and will actually provide 46 percent more shelf space than currently occupied by the 26 file cabinets in this room. Additional storage space will be created in the staff offices and in the reception room.

As a result, file space will be available for both the current folders and those files which are projected to enter the system in the next several years. Also, the appearance of the room would be greatly improved.

Room 1810

Since there are no chairs for visitors, a chair should be provided in the redesign of this area. One file cabinet can be removed and replaced by a small chair for a visitor.

Project 12

Send this memo to the staff. It is from Mary C. Putnam, Director.

We are happy to announce the opening of our employee day-care center.

On January 6, our new $2 million-day care center will open. Children three months and older will be accepted into the all-day program. In addition, there will also be a program to meet the needs of children in school. Bus service from the elementary schools in the community will be provided, thus eliminating a transportation problem for parents.

Registration will begin October 1, and forms may be obtained from the benefits department in Suite 205.

Costs for the program will be shared by each participating employee and our company. Therefore, the employee cost will be very reasonable.

At 9 A.M. on September 1, there will be a meeting in the auditorium to explain the details of this service. We hope all employees who have children will be able to attend this discussion.

HUMAN RELATIONS SKILL DEVELOPMENT

HR 6-1 Standing Up for Your Rights

Being agreeable in the office is important, but being agreeable should not interfere with your principles. You should not allow a colleague to take advantage of you. Assertive behavior (standing up for your rights) is acceptable; aggressive behavior (influencing others by physical or emotional force) is not acceptable.

- When was the last time someone took advantage of you?
- Describe the personality traits of the last person who took advantage of you.
- When was the last time you asserted yourself?
- How did you feel when you asserted yourself?
- Describe the last time you used aggressive behavior.

HR 6-2 Accepting and Rejecting Advice from Co-Workers

During your business career, you may work with someone who freely gives advice about all situations. Unsolicited suggestions can be annoying. Dealing with this advice in a diplomatic manner can be the difference between a comfortable working relationship and an antagonistic one. It is not essential for you to accept the advice, but it may be wise for you to listen to it. First of all, the suggestion may be beneficial to you. If you choose not to follow the recommendation, that is your decision. Consider the reason the counsel is given. Perhaps the giver's objective is to get attention and recognition. If that is the case, just listening should solve the problem.

- Describe the personality traits of the people from whom you accept advice.
- Describe the last time you were wise to accept someone's advice.
- Describe the last time you advised someone. Were your recommendations followed?
- Describe how you would handle an overbearing person who is attempting to counsel you although you did not seek the guidance.

SITUATIONS

How would you handle the following situations?

- **S 6-1** Your boss, Ms. Canton, is with Ms. Taylor and has asked you to bring Ms. Taylor's file to her office. Although you saw the file yesterday, you cannot find the file now.
- **S 6-2** Although you left your office in plenty of time to pick up your supervisor at the airport, there was an accident on the interstate and traffic was delayed. When you finally arrived at the airport, your supervisor was furious at you for being late.
- **S 6-3** You were invited to your supervisor's house for dinner, and you spilled coffee on the new oriental rug in the living room.

PUNCTUATION REVIEW

Punctuate each of the following sentences.

1. Economic expansion is often accompanied by rising costs but the consumer continues to purchase goods and services
2. Jack asked did interest rates rise
3. Have you planned the convention Sara asked
4. My attorney Laura Reston is well known in the community
5. Web City for example is a large retail discount store located near Interstate 15
6. The director Phil Joseph moved from Houston to San Diego
7. The new employee Patricia Wilson was late for work
8. We are sorry that you did not receive your supply order by your due date therefore we will credit your account for $100
9. The office supply store which is on Route 28 is open after work
10. Doug said the computer paper arrived damaged
11. No the package was not delivered
12. The meeting is scheduled for Monday August 6 XXXX
13. Her office was in an old dingy building
14. Jane Kipper Ph D will address the next session at the conference
15. John Tasky II was my roommate in college

CD ASSIGNMENTS

CD Assignment 6-1

Open the file CD6-1_IFS on your Student CD and follow the instructions to complete the job.

CD Assignment 6-2

Open the file CD6-2_ME on your Student CD and follow the instructions to complete the job.

Meetings and Conferences

7

Objectives

After studying this chapter, you should be able to

1. Plan on short notice a meeting that is to be held in the office.
2. Plan a meeting using a conference room.
3. Plan a meeting at a facility outside your office.
4. Plan food for a meeting.
5. Evaluate sites for a meeting.
6. Prepare minutes of the meeting.
7. Understand the use of audio and video conferencing.

INTRODUCTION

When discussing meetings, it is important for you to understand the following meeting terms:

Attendee:	A person who attends the meeting
Organizer:	The person who plans the meeting
Facilitator:	The person who eases the transition from one session or speaker to another
Presider:	The person who speaks or introduces other speakers at the meeting
Participant:	Another term used for a person who attends the meeting

While meetings are a fact of modern business life, many people look upon meetings as a waste of their time. Unfortunately, this is often true. Some meetings are unproductive, or the limited results of the meeting do not justify the time invested by all of the participants.

Meetings are very common in today's workplace, and a suitable facility will enhance the success of the meeting. The number of participants and meeting purpose will determine the meeting room. Most face-to-face business meetings have a small number of participants and usually can be held in a private office. When more than six participants attend a meeting, they are generally more comfortable sitting around a table in a conference room than sitting in a private office. Also, most private offices do not have a sitting area for more than six people. In addition, meeting in a conference room setting with attendees sitting around a table aids note taking and encourages conversation, because all participants can easily see everyone.

A meeting or conference with more than twenty participants may have special requirements in regard to type and number of rooms required for the meeting. Meetings with more than twenty participants are usually held in special meeting rooms, often in a conference center or hotel. Larger meetings with many attendees may require a large meeting room, where all attendees may gather to listen to opening remarks or a keynote speaker, and several

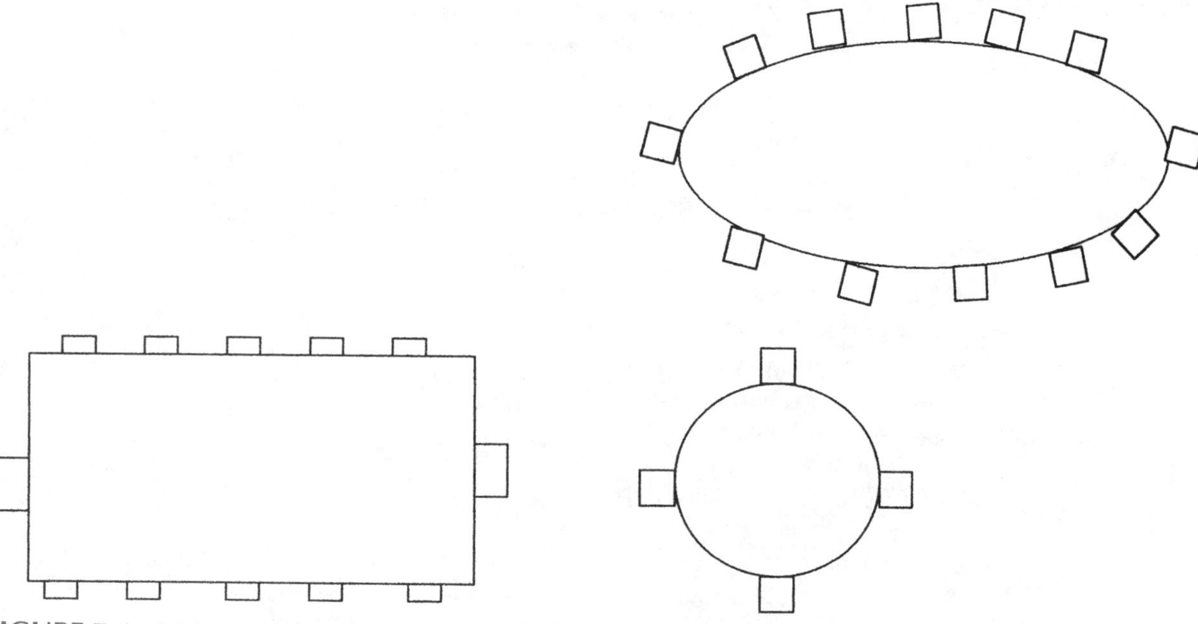

FIGURE 7-1 Meeting room tables.

smaller rooms for breakaway or concurrent sessions, where participants can focus on a specific task or topic.

Many businesses send their employees to meetings and retreats away from the office to strengthen team building while addressing the meeting objectives. Furthermore, businesses often feel that off-site meetings improve communication and camaraderie between the participants. Often there is a greater sense of accomplishment with an off-site meeting than from weekly staff meetings.

Meeting and conventions are big business and most communities have a local Convention and Visitors Bureau, which can provide meeting planning assistance and information about community facilities.

Agenda

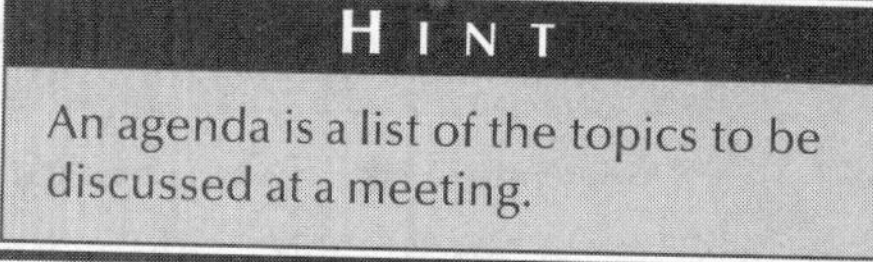

HINT

An agenda is a list of the topics to be discussed at a meeting.

All meetings, whether a small informal gathering in an office or a large, formal, day-long conference, require careful preparation. When planning the meeting, estimate the length of time required to complete the meeting objectives, but keep the meeting as short as possible, because people are busy with their own projects and responsibilities. Most people feel an obligation to attend meetings but would prefer not to attend. If the meeting lasts more than one and a half hours, people become restless and may need a break, so include a break when planning the meeting. Meetings that run an entire morning or afternoon should have a fifteen-minute restroom/coffee break.

Every meeting, regardless of the size, should have a planned agenda, which is a list of items to be discussed at the meeting. The agenda should include start and ending times for the meeting, so participants can plan their schedules. Be realistic when determining how long a discussion will last. It is important to remember that most people like to share their views, so allow a sufficient amount of time for each participant to talk. Prior to the meeting, send a copy of the agenda to all participants, so that they will have an opportunity to prepare for the items to be discussed. If the agenda is not sent in advance, it should be distributed at the beginning of the meeting. Even if it is sent in advance, additional copies of the agenda should be available at the meeting for those who did not bring one. The agenda will be determined by the supervisor, but the administrative assistant will be responsible for the keyboarding, duplication, and distribution of the agenda.

Patrick Research and Management
324 Research Drive
Suite 600
Charleston, WV 25311

2 P.M. on May 19, xxxx
Room 620, Central Building

Agenda

1. Minutes of the last meeting
2. Review of Ms. Harris's proposal
3. Review of computer purchase
4. Review of marketing plan
5. Discussion of annual charity ball
6. Discussion of proposed health benefits package
7. Date of next meeting
8. Adjournment

FIGURE 7-2 An agenda.

The Informal Office Meeting

Informal office meetings are usually scheduled by telephone or email. A supervisor asks you to contact several people and arrange a short meeting for a specific date and time. Prior to contacting other participants, you should review the supervisor's calendar to determine several alternate times when the supervisor is available. You should discuss with the supervisor which of the alternate times would be preferable and which participants are essential to the meeting. Shared calendars can make meeting planning easier. If all the meeting participants are from your office and your office uses calendar computer software, you may be able to schedule the meeting by comparing the calendars of the participants and selecting a time when everyone is available. You should send emails or call the participants and ask that they confirm their availability. It may take several emails or phone calls and rescheduling of the meeting to ensure that your supervisor and the essential participants can attend. You should also consider where to have the meeting. If the number of participants is too large for the supervisor's office, a conference room should be scheduled.

For a successful meeting to occur, it is also important for "key participants" to be in attendance. Therefore, you must know the "key participants" when attempting to schedule the meeting. If a decision maker cannot attend, then the meeting must be rescheduled. A meeting without the key players is wasteful. For the meeting objectives to be successful, it is important to know who must "buy into" the agenda items, so arrange the meeting time to accommodate the schedules of key people.

The time of a meeting can influence the discussion and meeting results, so knowing when to schedule a meeting can impact the outcome. Sometimes meetings drag on and on, so, to keep a meeting short, schedule it before lunch or near the close of the business day. People are usually eager to leave for lunch or to go home.

The day before the meeting, remind your supervisor of the meeting schedule and verify that sufficient copies of meeting materials have been prepared.

Conference and Meeting Rooms

While it may be obvious that the number of attendees determines the size of the meeting room, meeting rooms vary in purpose and design. Rooms can often be rearranged to meet the specific requirements of a particular meeting. A room with a large central table is often called

FIGURE 7-3 A meeting room.

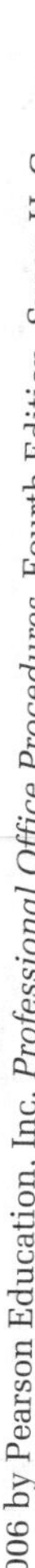

a conference room, and it may have a marker board on a wall and a built-in screen for use with slide, film, and overhead projectors for computer displays or transparencies. Flipcharts can be brought in if they are required. An electronic whiteboard is very similar in concept to the traditional board in classrooms where notes and information are recorded, but an electronic whiteboard also allows the recording and storage of notes written on it during a meeting. In addition, the electronic whiteboard may be attached to a computer and projector, so the notes are projected on a screen for greater viewing by all meeting participants. Notes made on an electronic whiteboard can also be printed out after the meeting.

Conference rooms may have built-in microphones to record a meeting or for audio conferencing. Some conference rooms have television equipment and/or equipment for two-way video conferencing. If a wireless microphone and cordless mouse are available, the speaker will have greater freedom of movement when making computer presentations.

A larger room with chairs set in rows is frequently called a meeting room. Meeting rooms usually are designed for flexibility and may have film and slide equipment located in a small projection booth at the rear of the room. Podiums with microphones are available, so all participants can see and hear the speakers. Additional equipment can be brought in if required.

Some meeting rooms have fixed chairs on a sloping floor, like those in a theater. Other meeting rooms, especially those located in hotels, may have movable walls and portable chairs, which can be rearranged to meet a variety of needs. Meeting rooms in hotels are often arranged in rows of chairs with a long table, which facilitates note taking.

Large conventions may use rooms with an audience response system, which allows participants to use a keyboard to respond to questions by keying a specific number or to signal the chairperson that they wish to speak.

Arranging for Food

Often it is an assistant's responsibility to order or purchase food for an office meeting. If your company has a cafeteria or restaurant, you may make food arrangements with them. For a small, early morning meeting, you may be required to stop on the way to work and pick up donuts, pastries, or bagels.

FIGURE 7-4 A conference room with flip chart and whiteboard.

A meeting that continues longer than anticipated may require a last-minute food arrangement. You may need to call a restaurant close to the office and make a reservation for lunch, or you may go to the cafeteria or local delicatessen (deli) and purchase sandwiches. You should be familiar with your manager's preferences regarding carry-out delicatessens or restaurants, in case last-minute lunch arrangements are required.

In addition, you should be aware of the company's policy regarding food purchases. Procedures for paying for meals should be worked out between you and your supervisor before the meeting to avoid embarrassing discussions while clients are present. Will the company pay the entire bill? Will a company credit card be used to pay the entire bill? Will each participant pay? Will separate checks be provided?

Attending a Meeting

Suggestions for the presider/organizer

- Do not schedule meetings the day before a holiday or Friday afternoons when people are anxious to leave for the weekend.
- Distribute the agenda well in advance, so your associates can read and think about the agenda.
- In advance, decide how long to wait for late participants.
- Begin the meeting by stating the meeting's objective and the desired outcome.
- Be aware of the nonverbal communication from participants.
- Be aware of any tension between participants, and do not allow the tension to alter the meeting's purpose.
- Do not allow verbal attacks on other attendees. Remind attendees that verbal attacks are unprofessional and will not be tolerated.
- Do not allow a discussion to ramble on. Always stay focused.
- Do not allow the meeting to divert from the agenda.
- Use flip charts to organize the discussion, and use one piece of paper for each topic. This procedure also helps keep the group focused on one topic since the topic under discussion can be seen by all participants.

- If one person monopolizes the conversation, encourage others to speak.
- Always summarize each agenda item prior to moving to the next item.
- Avoid belittling an individual's comments.
- If a problem occurs, respond with diplomacy and move on to the next topic.

Suggestions for the attendee

- Prepare for the meeting by reading background material about the agenda items.
- Always arrive on time. Your colleagues may feel that your arriving late is inconsiderate and a waste of their time.
- Bring key documents, such as the agenda and pertinent reports, to the meeting but do not overburden yourself with background material.
- Always be courteous to all attendees.
- Since you will not remember everything, make notes during the meeting.
- Meet new business associates at the meeting. Do not talk only with co-workers you know. This is your opportunity to expand your network of business associates.
- Do not talk privately to the person sitting beside you. Always talk to the group.
- New employees attending meetings should follow a "wait and see attitude." Do not jump into the conversation immediately; you may not know all of the facts or background of the items under discussion. Listen and watch first. Also, observe the meeting tone, gestures, and climate before venturing into the discussion.
- Thank the meeting organizer.

Why meetings are not successful

- The meeting chairperson and the attendees differ on the topics to be discussed.
- The timing of the meeting is poor, because attendees have other projects that must be completed.
- The participants are not interested in the meeting topics.
- The attendees feel that there is no reason to have the meeting other than the custom of having a meeting at that time. Weekly staff meetings often fail because there is no real reason to have a meeting.

PLANNING A LARGE MEETING OR CONFERENCE

Another name for a meeting is a conference. While the term *meeting* may be used for a small or large gathering of participants, the term *conference* often refers to a meeting attended by a large group of people. Conferences may have several hundred participants or more.

Meetings require careful preparation, but having sufficient time to plan a small or large meeting is usually a luxury. Before you make any definite decisions about a meeting, review your company's meeting policy and bring any questions you have to your supervisor's attention.

You should establish a basic plan for meetings and keep it in your computer files. When you are asked to arrange a meeting, your plan will be available. In addition, whenever you visit potential meeting facilities in your area, always request brochures and information about the facility. If you need to plan a meeting at the last minute, that information will be in your files. In addition, keep all of your planning lists and information about completed meetings, because they could be useful in planning the next meeting.

In addition to maintaining your meeting files on your computer system, put a computer diskette which contains all information about the meeting in the meeting file folder, so it will be easily found the next time you plan a meeting. At a future date, your office computer may have been replaced, and your computer meeting file may not have been transferred to the new disk drive.

Your basic meeting plan should include a checklist, so you are sure that every detail is covered. You should not assume any aspect of the meeting will be taken care of by someone else. Do not leave any question unanswered. If you omit important details, any resulting mistakes will reflect upon you and your supervisor.

Anticipate what could go wrong with your meeting arrangements, and then create a plan to solve it. If something does go wrong, keep calm.

Factors to consider when planning a meeting

1. What is the purpose of the meeting? What is the hoped-for outcome of the meeting?
2. When will the meeting be held? Before a final date and time are selected for the meeting, contact important individuals who will attend the meeting to verify that they are available.
3. Where will the meeting be held? The location for the meeting will be determined by the number of participants, the facilities available, the length of the meeting, and your office budget.
4. How many participants will attend and who are they? If a similar meeting has been held in the past, how many people have attended? What does the follow-up report for that meeting indicate?
5. What is the planned length of the meeting? Will the meeting be scheduled for an hour, several hours, one day, or several days?
6. How many meeting sessions will be planned? If this is a large meeting with concurrent sessions, how many meeting rooms will be required?
7. When will the meeting begin and when will it end?
8. Will food be served? If food is served, money must be included in the budget to cover its cost. You will also need to determine whether the food will include a full meal or just a snack. An early morning meeting often begins with coffee, donuts, pastries, bagels, fruit, and so on.
9. Will water pitchers and glasses be provided for the speakers? Will they be provided for the attendees?
10. Is presentation equipment required for the meetings? If so, what equipment is necessary—a computer and projector, an overhead projector, or a slide projector? Are any other items needed? How will the equipment be obtained? Who will operate the equipment? During what sessions will the equipment be needed?
11. Will there be an audio or video recording of the meeting's sessions?
12. What is the budget for the meeting?
13. Will there be exhibits or displays?
14. Will there be out-of-town guests for the meeting? If so, will your office be responsible for making hotel accommodations? Will transportation costs need to be included in the budget?
15. Will RSVP notes be sent out?
16. How will the meeting be evaluated?

After the preceding factors have been considered, you are ready to begin implementing the meeting plan. If the meeting will be held at a location other than your office, arrange to visit the facility. The visit will provide information regarding the site, as well as a sense of the site management's responsiveness to your needs.

Today, the Web sites of many hotels and conference centers provide virtual tours of their facilities. While these online tours may be helpful in eliminating possible sites, the final decision on a site should be based on an in-person tour, not a virtual tour.

Computer software and the Internet have made meeting planning easier by creating Web sites that provide assistance in planning meetings. In addition, software is available to organize and maintain the paperwork of meeting planning. As the number of large meetings has grown, event planning has become a common activity. Many hotels and restaurants have Web sites which include maps, basic information about the facility, specific information about the meeting rooms, sample menus, and other helpful information. View the following Internet sites for more information about planning a meeting.

Meeting-planning Web sites

www.meetinglocators.com
www.event-master.com
www.meetingsource.com
www.mpiweb.org
www.marriott.com/meeting
www.event.com
www.forgent.com
www.iacconline.com
www.resortsonline.com
www.cruisemeetings.com

Where to Have the Meeting

Meetings can be held at hotels, motels, restaurants, private clubs, resorts, state parks, conference or convention centers, and similar locations. Many large companies have their own attractive meeting facilities. Past experience and recommendations from friends and business associates will help you select a good facility for your meeting. If your company has held a similar meeting in the past, pay particular attention to the meeting facility evaluations and feedback from meeting participants.

Factors to be considered when selecting a location for your meeting

1. Is the facility available when you need it?
2. Is the facility in your price range?
3. Is the location convenient for those attending? Is it close to main roads or interstate highways? If attendees are flying in, is the facility conveniently close to an airport?

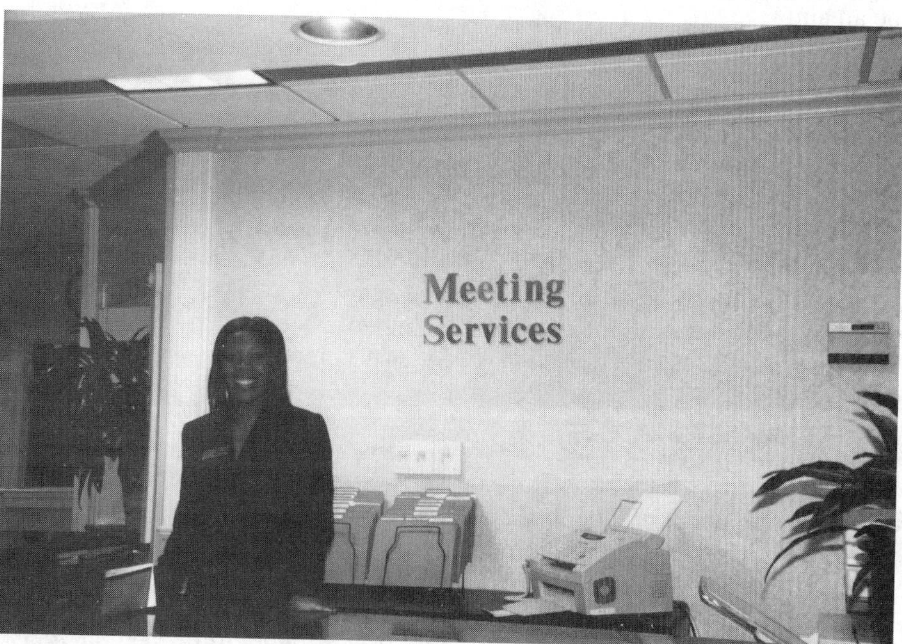

FIGURE 7-5 A meeting services coordinator.

4. Are there a sufficient number of meeting rooms?
5. Are the chairs in the room comfortable? Are tables available if necessary?
6. Will the meeting room accommodate the anticipated number of participants?
7. Are meeting rooms comfortably climate-controlled? Rooms that are too hot or too cold can detract from the success of a meeting.
8. Is there sufficient lighting?
9. Are there shades or drapes to block the sun?
10. If equipment such as computer projection units, overhead projectors, or slide projectors is needed, will the facility supply them? What is the cost of supplying this equipment?
11. If a broadband connection is required to connect to the Internet, is it available?
12. Is a sound system available? Are microphones handheld, lapel style, wireless, or on a podium?
13. Are there sufficient electrical outlets for the equipment?
14. Is there a technician available if there is a problem with the equipment?
15. Are the employees pleasant? Do they seem to be efficient and interested in servicing your meeting?
16. What is the quality of the food? Is the food served quickly? What is the cost for food service?
17. Is the site clean and attractive?
18. Is parking available? Is it adequate for the size of the meeting? Is there a parking fee?
19. If a loading dock is necessary, is it available and convenient?
20. Is there a lobby or registration area available? Is the area large enough, and is it convenient to the meeting rooms?
21. Is there an area for displays or exhibits?
22. For longer meetings, will the meeting room be available for twenty-four hours, or will someone else use it a portion of the day? What security is available to protect equipment and other important items?
23. Are the facilities fully accessible to people with disabilities, as required by Americans with Disabilities Act?
24. Is there a satellite hookup?
25. Is the meeting room near distractions, such as an elevator with a constantly ringing bell?
26. Is the meeting room near the kitchen, so the clatter of dishes is heard?
27. Is the meeting room near a window with street noise and distractions?
28. If the meeting is being held in a hotel, does the hotel have a block of rooms available at a reasonable price for participants staying overnight?

Not all of these questions may be relevant to your meeting, and a negative response on any one item should not necessarily disqualify a facility from consideration. Remember that there is no perfect meeting site; therefore, the meeting organizers will have to determine which of these criteria are most important in selecting a meeting site.

When evaluating potential meeting sites, it is a good idea to complete a site evaluation form.

Food Service

When planning a meeting, decide if food will be served. The time of day and length of the meeting will often determine whether food will be served, and your food budget will impact the choice of menu. In addition to providing food at normal mealtimes (breakfast, lunch, and dinner), food can be served as snacks during meeting breaks or before and after the meetings.

If food is going to be served, the availability and cost of food should be considered before making a decision on the location of the meeting. If a meal is served, the charge for the meeting room may be reduced or even free. A free meeting room usually requires that

SITE EVALUATION FORM

Date of Visit ________________________________

Facility ________________________________

Address ________________________________

City ______________ State __________ Zip __________

Telephone Number ________________________________

Email ________________ Fax ________________

Contact Person ________________ Title ________________

Date(s) Facility Available ________________________________

Overall Appearance of Facility ________________________________

Atmosphere of Facility ________________________________

Desirable Features ________________________________

Description of Meeting Rooms ________________________________

Number of Meeting Rooms __________ Per-Day Cost __________

Number of Sleeping Rooms __________ Per-Night Cost __________

Food Quality ________________ Food Cost __________

Special Equipment/Services/Available (Lectern, Audiovisual, etc.) __

Accessible to Physically-impaired ________________________________

Additional Comments ________________________________

FIGURE 7-6 A site evaluation form.

a specific number of meals be served. Since many convention or meeting facilities will not allow you to bring in any food, confirm their policy regarding outside food if you intend to provide your own. Outside food may include a special cake, candy, nuts, or mints, so it is important to be aware of the facility's policy.

The cost of the food is usually based on a per-person charge. Sometimes, the more meals served, the lower the cost per person. Before you select the food to be served, review with the proposed facility sample menus and the prices for each menu item. When selecting menus do not limit your choices to only your favorite foods; select foods that appeal to everyone. It is important to consider alternative diets when selecting food for a meeting. Today many people are on special diets—for example, low-sodium, low-fat, low-carbohydrate, or vegetarian diets. Be sure to ask if it is possible to prepare a vegetarian meal or if the facility can accommodate people on special diets.

Hotel/Motel Rooms

Meeting participants who plan to stay overnight will require hotel reservations. If only a few participants need hotel reservations, your only role may be to recommend hotels that are convenient to the meeting site. You should, therefore, be familiar with hotels that are convenient, their quality, and the facilities they have available for guests. If the meeting is being held in a hotel, most participants staying overnight will want the convenience of staying in the conference hotel.

If a large number of participants are staying overnight, you may need to reserve a block of rooms at a hotel. One of the advantages of reserving a block of rooms is that hotels usually reduce the price of rooms when they are reserved in quantity.

There are several different arrangements that companies can use regarding the making of hotel reservations and payment of hotel bills. If meeting participants pay for their own hotel rooms, you will need to decide whether the participants or the company will make hotel reservations. Meeting participants usually are encouraged to make their own hotel reservations. If you have reserved a block of rooms, the participants should tell the hotel that they are attending your meeting in order to receive any special room rates you have arranged.

If the company makes the reservations, you may need to get credit card numbers (with expiration dates) from the participants, so you can guarantee the reservations when you make them. The participants pay for the hotel room and may seek reimbursement for the hotel bill using their expense account.

It is also possible for the company to contract with the hotel for rooms and pay the base room rate directly. In such cases, the participant may still be required to pay the hotel for personal expenses, such as room service or phone calls.

More information about hotels and motels is found in Chapter 8, Business Travel.

Contracts for Meeting Rooms

After a meeting location has been chosen, a contract usually is signed with the facility. Although you may not be the person who signs the contract, read it carefully to verify that the contract includes everything you discussed about the meeting's arrangements. Nothing should be omitted. For example, if a reception table is promised, it should be written into the contract. Your contact person at the hotel or restaurant may have changed jobs by the time you have the meeting, and the new employee may be unaware of an oral promise.

HINT

Read the contract before signing. Verify that all details are included in the contract.

Very Important People

If VIPs (very important people) will be attending your meeting, they may be given special treatment. These VIPs may include company officials, honored guests, or invited speakers. Discuss with your supervisor whether any individuals should be given VIP treatment.

Dealing with VIPs

- Who are the VIPs?
- Will the VIPs be met at the airport or train station? Who will meet them?
- Will there be baskets of candy, fruit, nuts, or flowers in their hotel rooms?
- Will you need a car and/or driver for the VIPs?
- Tell the bell captain and meeting services manager who the VIPs are.
- As an extra gesture, you might want to gather information about the likes and dislikes of the VIPs.

Meeting the Needs of All Participants

If your meeting will include participants who are hearing-impaired, wheelchair-bound, or visually-impaired, ask what accommodations you should provide for their assistance. Be sure the meeting facility is fully accessible, as required by the Americans with Disabilities Act. You may need a sign language interpreter, materials translated into Braille, or someone to provide personal assistance to the participants who are wheelchair-bound or visually-impaired. You should be able to locate a sign language interpreter by contacting your local sign language interpreter association, contacting your local convention bureau, or conducting a Web search for local interpreters. The following national Web sites will also be helpful:

Americans with Disabilities Act
www.usdoj.gov/crt/ada/adahom1.htm

Registry of Interpreters for the Deaf
www.rid.org

National Association for the Deaf
www.nad.org

National Association for the Blind
www.nfb.org

HINT
Does your meeting accommodate all participants?

Foreign Visitors

Since most large corporations operate in a global environment, there is a good possibility that foreign visitors will attend meetings. An international population may require interpreters or additional assistance to meet the needs of those not familiar with the area or local customs. When meeting with business associates from foreign countries, gifts are often exchanged. Also, foreign visitors may appreciate receiving a list of embassies with addresses and telephone numbers. Under security procedures implemented after the 9/11 attack on the World Trade Center, there are new procedures regarding the entry of foreign visitors into the United States. You may need to become familiar with visa and entry requirements for foreign visitors to assist them in attending your meeting. Additional information about working with foreign visitors is included in Chapter 13, Tips of the Trade. Working with Foreign Cultures.

For information about visitor visas to enter the United States, go to the Web site: *www.travel.state.gov/visa;visitors.html.*

HINT
Plan for foreign visitors.

Identification Badges (Name Tags, Name Badges)

People attending meetings often wear name or identification badges to help them remember names and meet new business associates. Name tags can be prepared in advance for those participants who are preregistered for the meeting, but pens and extra name tags should be available for persons who register at the meeting. To make it easy to read the name tag, it should be printed in a large font size; often the first name is

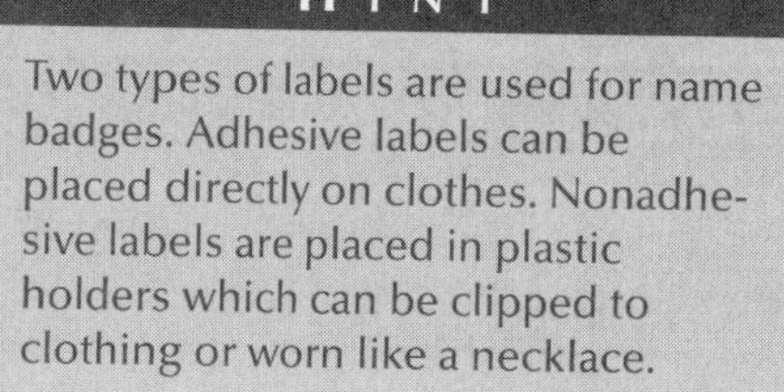
HINT
Two types of labels are used for name badges. Adhesive labels can be placed directly on clothes. Nonadhesive labels are placed in plastic holders which can be clipped to clothing or worn like a necklace.

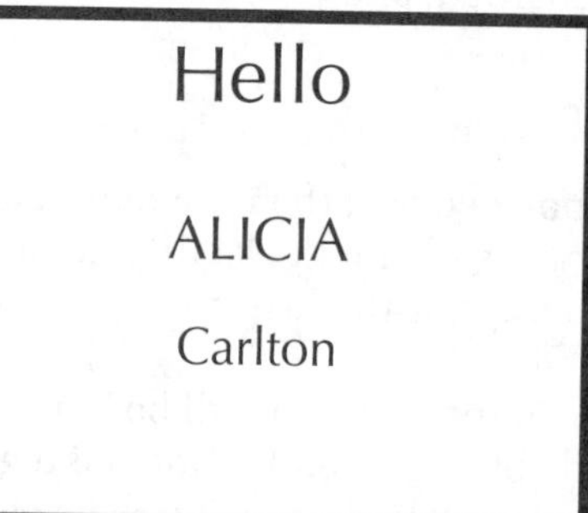

FIGURE 7-7 A name badge.

printed larger than the last name. Some badges include the name of the company where the person is employed in addition to the person's name. Wearing the tag on the right shoulder allows another person to easily see your name while shaking your hand.

The use of a name tag is not limited to a large meeting or conference. Identification badges can be helpful for a small group in which the participants are not acquainted.

Web Site

To assist your meeting attendees, create a Web site or add additional pages to your current Web site with information about the meeting. This will allow attendees to obtain information at their convenience without additional staff time and costs for your organization. The Web site should contain details about the hotel accommodations and location, the meeting agenda, airfare, and auto rental. It should also contain an online meeting registration option. The meeting Web site should also have city and hotel maps and links to Web sites of appropriate organizations.

Cell Phones

Since cell phones have become entrenched in today's business and personal world, cell phone etiquette at a meeting is a significant issue. A ringing cell phone is an interruption to everyone at a meeting. If you anticipate receiving an urgent telephone call while meeting with a few people, inform them that you are expecting an urgent call and will leave the meeting for a moment to receive the call. Do not allow your telephone call to interrupt the meeting, and do not talk on the telephone in the presence of others. Many cell phones have a vibrating signal, which can silently signal a call. Use caller ID and voice mail to reduce the interruptions of cell phones during a meeting. To avoid interruptions, some large meetings require the participants to check their cell phones at the door. Then if the phone rings, an assistant answers the phone and records messages. Also, be aware that, since meeting rooms are often placed in the center of large buildings, cell phone reception may be unreliable.

Adding Special Interest to the Meeting

A large meeting may have a theme or slogan, which can be used on decorations, on printed materials, on the Web site, and at banners at meeting sessions. The theme may also include the company logo or have its own graphic identifier. A theme can focus the meeting atmosphere, thus making the meeting more productive. If a meeting is small or has no theme, you can create a theme for the meeting by using local attractions or a holiday if a meeting occurs near a holiday. A meeting that occurs during fall, on Valentine's Day, or around July 4, for example, would use appropriately colored napkins, plates, and table decorations.

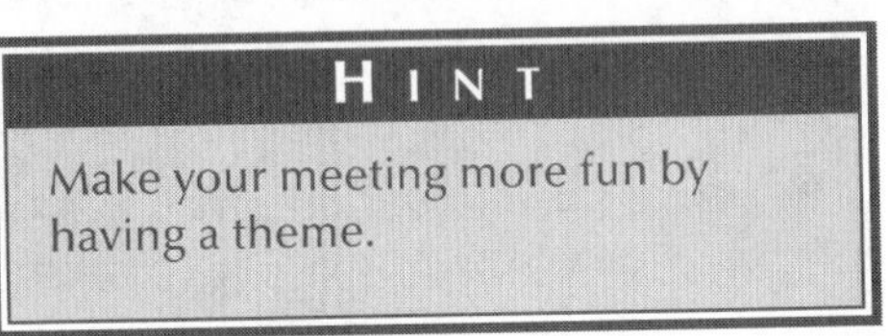
HINT

Make your meeting more fun by having a theme.

Meeting Evaluation

Many large meetings conclude by having the attendees evaluate the meeting. Therefore, prior to the meeting, an evaluation form must be designed, keyboarded, and printed.

Additional Thoughts

Inform the facility of all changes in the meeting plans as they occur. If the number of participants changes, notify the facility immediately. It may be impossible for the facility to include additional attendees or to remove unoccupied luncheon tables at the last minute. A room with many unoccupied tables looks uninviting.

Will a packet of meeting materials be given to each participant? What will be in it? Who will prepare and distribute the packet? Will paper and pens be provided for note taking?

Decide in advance who will pay the bill for the meeting and decide how it will be paid—cash, check, credit card, or direct billing.

Consider transportation needs. Must someone be picked up at the airport? If the guest and the driver do not know each other, identification will be necessary. Prepare a sign for the driver with the name of your organization or a sign with the guest's name.

Send a map and information about ground transportation to out-of-town participants.

Meeting Day and Follow-Up

The Day of the Meeting

Arrive early and verify that everything is completed to your satisfaction. Have available extra copies of the agenda, pens, meeting packets, maps of the area, and anything else that would be helpful to the attendees. If flowers, candy, nuts, or similar items have been ordered, verify that they have been delivered and that they are placed where you want them.

When the meeting begins, try to adhere to the time schedule you have set. Deviating from the schedule could cause problems for the service staff. If lunch is scheduled for 12 noon and the meeting runs late, the food service may have difficulty serving the lunch at 1 P.M. If the meeting runs late, check with the service manager and see what adjustments can be made in the food service. Also, take breaks when they are scheduled, because during breaks the service staff may straighten the meeting room or deliver refreshments.

Meeting Conclusion

At the end of the meeting, summarize the meeting discussion; review findings, conclusions, and recommendations; remind participants of assignments; solicit involvement for other projects; and announce the date of the next meeting, if appropriate.

After the Meeting

After the meeting, write thank-you letters to everyone who helped you. In some instances, a gift or tip should be given to those who assisted you.

Meeting Follow-Up

A working meeting where the participants are asked to complete specific projects or research particular ideas needs a follow-up. If the work assignments or decisions arrived at during the meeting are not implemented, the meeting did not accomplish its objectives. It may be the administrative assistant's responsibility to follow up and contact the participants to determine if they have completed the materials they agreed to prepare, if they have talked with the people they were to communicate with, or if they have reached the goals that were established.

After the meeting, the person who sponsored the meeting should have a summary prepared. Notes may have been taken by the assistant or by one of the meeting's participants. It is often the administrative assistant's duty to prepare the minutes of the meeting, which is a written report of the meeting, and then to send a copy to all of the participants.

In addition, the assistant may be responsible for organizing and reviewing the meeting evaluation forms.

Minutes of Meetings

Each organization uses its own preferred format for minutes of a meeting, so you should review past minutes to determine the standard format used by your organization. Usually the minutes include the date, time, and place of the meeting. The minutes should also include names of those attending, and the names of absent members. The minutes are routinely written in the past tense, and they include a summary of the discussions and actions taken.

MINUTES OF THE ORLANDO BUSINESS ASSOCIATION

March 1, XXXX

The monthly Board of Directors meeting was held at Mike's Seafood House. The Board of Directors meeting was called to order at 7 P.M. by Vice-President Sue Phong.

Present: Stephanie Coffman, Eli Stone, Najar Pooser, Marcia Pearce, Sue Phong, and Earl Button

Absent: Stella Meyer, Anita Bradford, Mike Beller, and Libby Wayne

Minutes of the February meeting were read and approved.

Treasurer's report showed that $1,500 was raised by the calendar sale.

Eli Stone moved, seconded by Marcia Pearce, that an honorarium of $200 be approved for guest speakers. The motion unanimously passed.

Stephanie Coffman moved, seconded by Earl Button, that July 25 be selected as the date of the art auction. The motion passed unanimously.

Stephanie Coffman moved, seconded by Najar Pooser, that the president appoint a committee to plan the fall fundraiser. The motion passed 3 yes, 2 no.

Meeting was adjourned at 9 P.M.

FIGURE 7-8 Meeting minutes.

Minutes may be taken at informal staff meetings and business gatherings or at formal business meetings, such as those held by a board of directors. Minutes are usually prepared immediately after the meeting. Prior to the next formal meeting, each member should receive a review copy of the minutes of the previous meeting. At the next meeting, members vote either to approve the minutes as written or to make corrections. The approved version of the meeting minutes is usually signed by the secretary of the board or the president of the organization.

The preparation of the minutes of a meeting requires the combination of highly developed listening skills, concentration, and note-taking ability. During the meeting, an assistant must be able to listen, take notes, and summarize the points being discussed while the discussion continues.

Since the minutes should be accurate, the person taking the minutes must be alert and must concentrate on the subjects discussed. The note taker should be familiar with the participants, because the minutes of a meeting indicate the names of the individuals who attended the meeting, participated in the discussions, made motions, and seconded motions. If the note taker is unfamiliar with the attendees, name plates may be helpful. You can make a name plate by folding an 8.5″ × 11″ sheet of card stock paper in half and writing or printing a person's name on it. Office supply stores carry name plate paper with a perforated folding line for easy writing and printing. When taking minutes, quickly record all important comments, discussions, motions, and resolutions. To eliminate uncertainty concerning what was said at a meeting, tape recorders are often used to record the entire meeting. When the minutes of the meeting are prepared, information not essential to the minutes can be omitted.

Virtual Meetings

Audio and Video Conferencing

As discussed in Chapter 3, audio and video conferencing are often less expensive alternatives than bringing participants together at a meeting. These technologies are also used within a traditional meeting setting to bring in participants who could otherwise not be present. An expert, a high-level government or a business official may be able to participate in your meeting for an hour via audio or video conferencing when he or she would otherwise be unavailable. Many meetings are held for the purpose of being able to hear from people via audio or video teleconferences when it would be impossible to schedule a personal visit from those individuals. If audio or video teleconferences are on the agenda a major requirement in the selection of a meeting site will be the availability of equipment required to support these teleconferences.

Web Meetings

Another technology-based meeting option is Web conferencing. With Web conferencing, participants are directed to your Web site to view a presentation. The participants can communicate via computer instant messaging or a telephone conference call. As with a traditional meeting, thought should be given to the scheduled length of a Web meeting. Since many participants have short interest spans, they may easily become bored and allow their minds to wander. Therefore, Web meetings should not exceed two hours. Looking at a computer screen can become boring, so keep participants active and focused by initiating questions and actions that require responses.

Although Web conferencing may be slow or stiff, it is often used because it is relatively inexpensive to set up. Be aware of the technology limitations of your system. For example, some systems experience a transmission delay in communications. It is important to stay close to the camera for a full-face camera view instead of a small face against a large background. Instead of being only a "talking head," use the technology to your advantage by displaying photos of other events and include computer-based presentations, other demonstrations, flip charts, equipment, and so on. If participants in a Web conference are connected by an audio conference call, they should use the mute feature on their telephone to avoid noise clutter. Also, never place your phone on hold if your phone system plays music when callers are on hold. To avoid embarrassment, never say anything during a Web conference with audio talk-back that you would not want overheard.

Whiteboards can also be used as part of Web conferences to focus the attendees' attention. There are two types of whiteboards: (1) wall-size whiteboards with an Internet connection where pictures or graphics can be viewed and (2) wall-size or personal drawing tablet size, where presenters can draw or write during the meeting. Virtual whiteboards allow the use of shared files, and attendees can modify the drawing during the actual meeting.

Web Conferencing Sites

www.thinkofit.com/webconf/realtime.htm
www.meetingplace.net
www.thinkofit.com/webconf/wcchoice.htm
www.web-conferencing-central.com
www.main.placeware.com

CHAPTER REVIEW

1. Define the terms *attendee, organizer, facilitator,* and *presider.*
2. Describe the desirable features of a meeting room.
3. Define an agenda.
4. List five suggestions for the presider.
5. List five suggestions for the attendee.
6. List five points that should be considered when planning a meeting.

7. List six points that should be considered when selecting a location for a meeting.
8. List three points that should be considered when planning for VIPs.
9. List two suggestions for accommodating participants who are visually or physically impaired.
10. What information should be included on a name badge?
11. What information should be included in a meeting Web site?
12. Define minutes of the meeting and list what should be included.

ACTIVITIES

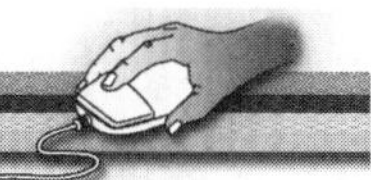

1. Call or visit the Web site of three hotels/motels and investigate charges for
   a. A meeting room
   b. Sleeping accommodations
   c. A lunch meeting for 50 people
   d. A dinner meeting for 100 people
2. Call or visit the Web site of three restaurants and ask about
   a. Lunch costs for 20 people
   b. A sample lunch menu
   c. The charge for a meeting room
3. Call a bakery and request prices for donuts, croissants, and pastries to serve 25 people.
4. List 10 facilities in your area where you could hold a one-day meeting. You may use the Internet for research for this activity.
5. Plan a retreat a couple of hours from your home. Where would you hold the retreat?
6. Ask two administrative assistants how often they plan meetings. Also, ask them to comment about planning large and small meetings. Write a summary of their comments.
7. Make all of the plans for an informal one-day meeting at a facility other than your office. There will be 15 participants but none of them will be from out-of-town. Submit a detailed list of your plans.
8. Make all of the plans for a four-day meeting. There will be 12 out-of-town guests, 1 out-of-town VIP, and 4 in-town participants. Submit a detailed list of your plans.
9. Use the Internet to find information about three restaurants in your city. Write a summary of your findings.
10. Attend a meeting of a local organization (college, social, garden, political, and so on) and take minutes of the meeting. Prepare a copy of the minutes using the correct format.

PROJECTS

Project 13

Create the following table. Add a column for the cost of exhibition space. O'Brien, Community, and Power each will pay $1,200. Blackstone will pay $1,500, Chamber and Fairdale will pay $2,475, American Donations will pay $1,300, and McFarlin will pay $1,250. Prepare a total cost figure.

Convention Exhibitors
Chicago
Spring XXXX

Company	Contact	Phone
American Donations, Inc.	Eugene Hartzell	703-555-8613
O'Brien Engineering	Barbara Wilmore	703-555-8153
Chamber Designs	Treva Semanick	703-555-7765
Power Technology	Jody Peerke	202-555-7514
Blackstone, Inc.	Colleen Storch	202-555-2493
Community Appliances	Andrew Knowles	703-555-4487
Fairdale Atlantic	Saba Tollie	202-555-1014
McFarlin Agency	Victoria Gannon	202-555-2556

Project 14

Send the following memo to the staff. It is from you, and your title is Training Director. Send a copy to Sharon Barber, Marcia Morton, and Sang Seegars.

> Computer training classes will be offered as follows. If you have questions, please call Clifton at extension 6177.
>
> All classes are held from 9 to 4, with a lunch break of one hour. The classes will be held in room 809.
>
> I encourage you to register as soon as possible, as classes fill quickly.

Date	Class	Instructor
January 15	Introduction to Access	Hainer
January 28	Intermediate Access	Hainer
February 10	Intermediate Word	Leroy
February 20	Introduction to PowerPoint	Perez
March 4	Introduction to Excel	Zang
March 8	HTML Fundamentals	Anderson
March 15	Advanced HTML	Anderson
March 22	Introduction to Digital Imaging	Powers

HUMAN RELATIONS SKILL DEVELOPMENT

HR 7-1 Working with Pessimistic People

In your working environment, you may encounter a person who sees the negative side of everything. When dealing with this person, do not permit yourself to become pessimistic also. If possible, keep your contact to a minimum and encourage other workers to be present when the two of you are together. After being with this type of person, make a list of positive thoughts.

- Who among your acquaintances has a pessimistic outlook?
- Describe your feelings when you are around pessimistic people.

HR 7-2 Problems with Your Supervisor

Never take a problem to someone above your supervisor without first discussing the problem with your supervisor. If the situation persists after several unsatisfactory attempts to solve the problem with your supervisor, it can be taken to a higher level. Depending on the circumstances, it may be wise to tell your supervisor that you are seeking a response from another person. Whenever you discuss a problem, respect the other person's opinions and be tactful with your comments.

Before taking your problem to a higher level, decide if the situation is important enough for you to pursue it. Taking a problem to a higher level could alter the relationship between you and your supervisor—no matter how the problem is resolved.

- What tone of voice would you use when discussing a problem with your supervisor?
- Describe your approach when taking a problem to your supervisor's manager.
- Describe three types of problems that are too petty to take to a higher level.
- What are you going to do if the supervisor's manager does not agree with you? What will be your reaction to this situation?
- Describe a problem that your supervisor cannot resolve and explain how you would handle it.

SITUATIONS

How would you handle the following situations?

- **S 7-1** A meeting is continuing longer than you anticipated and everyone is hungry.
- **S 7-2** Your supervisor asked you to attend a meeting on the same day as your sister's college graduation. You had planned to attend the graduation.
- **S 7-3** Last weekend at a party you heard confidential information about a project you are completing.

PUNCTUATION REVIEW

Punctuate each of the following sentences.

1. The community needs affordable housing and a balanced budget
2. Patrick of course understands the importance of completing projects by the due dates
3. I received the Outstanding Employee of the Year award and I was very surprised
4. Cincinnati my hometown is the site of the next annual meeting
5. While Max was in Paris his mail was forwarded to him
6. As you mentioned the minutes of the meeting were incorrect
7. Hedys mother Mrs Hoffman was the director responsible for the revised budget
8. Opal Marshall Executive Manager for Personnel has a large office
9. While the Marketing Department remains on the third floor the Administration Department has been moved from the first floor to the second floor

10. Ed who is active in community affairs is an excellent speaker
11. Rachel who exercises daily has lost 20 pounds as a result of her involvement in the Employee Wellness Program
12. When it comes to management skills demonstration is more important than paperwork
13. As previously noted the statistics are valid
14. This notion of course runs counter to all you have learned in the seminars you have attended
15. Every department has a desk manual and it is your job to locate it and to become familiar with it

CD ASSIGNMENTS

CD Assignment 7-1

Open the file CD7-1_AG on your Student CD and follow the instructions to complete the job.

CD Assignment 7-2

Open the file CD7-2_ICE on your Student CD and follow the instructions to complete the job.

Business Travel 8

Objectives

After studying this chapter, you should be able to

1. Make airline reservations.
2. Make hotel and motel reservations.
3. Use the Internet to plan a business trip.
4. Determine the rental car that best meets your needs.
5. Apply for a passport.
6. Prepare an itinerary.
7. Prepare an expense report.

Fundamentals of Office Travel

Travel is an integral part of today's business world. Business trips planned at the last minute are often the norm, not the exception. If your company has a travel department, your only responsibility may be to notify that department of the impending trip, including location, date, and travel preferences.

However, as an office employee it may be your responsibility to make travel arrangements. The first requirement is to be aware of your company's travel policies. The second requirement is to know the preferences of the traveler. Personal preferences include the method of transportation, particular airline, preferred auto-rental company or chain of hotels or motels, desired room location, time of day of travel, airline food preferences, and so on. If you do not know your supervisor's travel preferences, you should ask. Usually you will be given the information regarding the destination and time for a trip, and you will have to arrange the itinerary yourself.

If it is your responsibility to prepare the travel arrangements, first organize your thoughts. Arrangements can be made through a travel agent; directly with airlines, hotels, and auto-rental agencies; or via the Web. Knowing the specifics of the trip is important before proceeding. For example, will the person be traveling by air, rail, or personal car? In some organizations, the use of a company airplane is also an option.

Your company may have a contract with an airline, an auto-rental company, or a hotel chain which provides discounts from the standard rates. If so, check with the airline, auto-rental company, or hotel chain to see if it serves the city to be visited.

Travel by rail or air will require ground transportation to a hotel or a business meeting location. Most airports are served by a variety of ground transportation services, including taxis, auto rentals, or shuttle vans to and from downtown locations or the suburbs. Hotels near airports often have free shuttle service between the airport and the hotel. Call the hotel or check the hotel Web site to determine if it provides a courtesy van or if an airport shuttle service is available.

Prior to a business trip, check the weather forecast for the area. Daily weather forecasts or average temperatures can be obtained from newspapers, television weather channels, or Internet sites, such as *www.weather.com.*

TRAVEL ASSISTANCE

Travel Agencies

Travel agencies can be very helpful in planning a trip. Instead of your contacting each airline individually, travel agents use their computer systems to review schedules and prices of all the airlines flying to the destination. They will find pricing and alternative routes and will wade through the thicket of restrictions which apply to many airfares. Through their computer reservation systems, travel agents also can give you information about auto rentals, hotels, and other travel costs. You can request that the travel agency make a reservation on a specific flight, at a specific hotel, and with a specific auto-rental agency.

Many companies have contracts with travel agencies to make reservations for all of their traveling personnel. Before using a travel agency which does not have a contract with your company, ask if there is a charge for services. Some travel agents now charge a service fee of $10 and up for each airline ticket they prepare, because they no longer receive a payment from the airline for each ticket they book. If you find a travel agent who provides current information, good service, and reasonable airline prices, the agent's fees will be worthwhile. Many travel agents specialize in travel to particular locations or in specific types of travel. A good travel agent can prevent aggravation and save time for you and your office.

In today's business climate which stresses cost reduction, many businesses allow employees to ignore the traditional corporate travel office in favor of using low-cost online travel sites. Use of these sites is discussed further in the section titled The Internet.

Toll-Free Telephone Numbers

Airlines, railroads, auto-rental agencies, hotels, and motels all have centralized reservations systems with toll-free telephone numbers. Lodging reservations can be made through a hotel

FIGURE 8-1 Travel agents can be very helpful when planning business trips.

chain's toll-free centralized system or directly with the hotel. An efficient office employee should record frequently called numbers in a personal telephone directory or in a computer contact/telephone list software program.

Travel Guides

There are many travel guides that provide information and recommendations for visitors to a city or country. Travel guides recommend hotels, motels, and restaurants. The guides often discuss topics such as airlines serving an area, how to travel from the airport to downtown locations, traffic conditions, parking, and area attractions. There are travel guides available for specific cities, regions, and countries throughout the world.

The following are examples of travel series which publish guides for many areas of the United States or the world.

- *AAA TourBook* (available to members of travel clubs affiliated with the American Automobile Association)
- Frommer's guides
- Fodor's travel guides
- *The Green Guide*
- *Insiders' Guide*
- Michelin travel guides
- Mobil guides
- Stephen Birnbaum guides
- Rick Steves' guides

Since there are many other travel books available, check the travel department of your library or bookstore for additional sources.

The Internet

The Internet can be very helpful for obtaining information on travel and destinations around the world. You can use the Internet to find information and make reservations for airline, auto, and rail travel. Hotel rooms and even dinner reservations can be made directly from your computer.

Finding travel information on the Internet is usually very easy. Many of the common Internet browsers have sections devoted to travel. Selecting a travel link will bring you to a world of travel information. If your Internet browser does not have a travel link, entering the name of a destination in a search engine will usually bring up many relevant Web sites. You will be able to find city maps, lists of hotels, city services, restaurants, and special events in an area. Frequently you will be able to link to Web sites sponsored by hotels or events in the area you are researching.

The Internet gives you access to searches for numerous airline reservations. Airlines have Web sites where you can enter the name of the city you wish to visit and the dates of travel. The program will search and provide a selection of airline schedules and prices. While you can make a plane reservation directly over the Internet, you may want to check several alternatives with your supervisor before actually making a reservation and sending payment via the computer. Often after a reservation is made, either it cannot be canceled or there is a penalty for canceling.

There are several Web sites that will provide information from numerous airlines, auto-rental companies, and hotels, so you do not have to check the Web site of each company individually. Several of these general travel sites are

General Reservations (Flight, Hotel, Car)

www.aol.com
www.expedia.com

www.orbitz.com
www.travelocity.com
www.yahoo.com

These sites can sort the flight schedules of many airlines by time of departure or in order of increasing price. Many of the lowest-cost flights may be available for only a short period of time or have restrictions which limit their use. Be sure to check the restrictions before you book a flight, and be aware that some sites charge a booking fee. Several low-fare airlines are not listed in these Web travel sites, so you may find a lower fare by checking directly with a low-fare airline Web site.

Airline tickets, automobile rentals, hotel reservations, and train tickets all can be reserved on the Internet. For some reservations, you will have to connect directly to a specific company's Web site. When you deal directly with an airline's Internet site and with many of the general reservation sites, you will be able to enter the passenger's frequent flyer membership number, make seat selection, or request a special meal. Making travel arrangements on the Web has proved to be a major use of the Internet. The Web-based services provided by airlines, auto-rental agencies, hotels, and the general travel sites are continually being expanded and upgraded. Each travel site is unique and presents its information in a different manner. You may find some sites easy to use and other sites cumbersome. You may need to use a site several times before it truly becomes useful. If one site does not meet your needs, there are many alternatives on the Internet.

Many Internet travel and airline Web sites send weekly emails to subscribers announcing last-minute bargain opportunities. Since travel can be a costly business expense, receiving these travel announcements may be helpful when planning last-minute trips. However, you should limit the number of travel sites you sign up for, or you will have to deal with many email travel messages.

You should keep a file of useful travel Web sites. These sites can change often, so always be on the lookout for new and interesting Web sites. To get started, ask co-workers or your supervisor for sites they have found useful. New sites are recommended in newspapers and magazines or are listed in a company's advertisements. You will find new useful sites as links from older sites. When you find a useful Internet site, you should bookmark the site on your Internet browser, so it is easily available. You should also write the site's address on a list which is not kept on the computer. You do not want to lose Web addresses to a computer crash or an upgrade of your Internet browser software.

The following Web sites have specialized information that may be helpful for travel planning.

Airport codes	*www.flyaow.com/citycode.htm*
Centers for Disease Control and Prevention	*www.cdc.gov/travel*
Currency conversion chart	*www.oanda.com/converter/travel*
Country-specific health reports	*www.tripprep.com/index.html*
Global airports	*www.quickaid.com*
International security news	*www.airsecurity.com/hotspots.htm*
Occupational Safety and Health Administration health risks	*www.osha.gov/dts/tib*
Passports	*www.travel.state.gov/passport_services.html*
Tipping suggestions	*www.tipping.org/TopPage.shtml*
Travel books	*www.fodors.com*
Travel delays	*www.fly.gov*
Travel health risks	*www.travel.state.gov*
Travel opportunities	*www.bestfares.com*
Travel opportunities	*www.cheaptickets.com*
Travel opportunities	*www.expedia.com*
Travel opportunities	*www.orbitz.com*
Travel opportunities	*www.travelocity.com*

Travel safety	*www.internationalbenefits.com/travel-tips/travel-safety-abroad2.htm*
U.S. Department of Commerce country advisory desks	*www.travel.state.gov/travel/warnings.html/*
U.S. State Department	*www.travel.state.gov/travel*
U.S. State Department travel warnings	*www.travel.state.gov/*
Visas	*www.travel.state.gov/visa/index.html*
Weather	*www.weather.com*
World current time zones	*www.timeanddate.com/worldclock*
World current time zones	*www.worldtimeserver.com*
World current time zones	*www.worldtimezone.com*

Computer Maps

Computerized maps will help orient travelers to new surroundings and are available from many Internet sites or on CD-ROMs and DVDs. When you use a computer-generated map, you can often select the exact area and scale you want to view. A computer-generated map can be customized to include the features most important to the traveler. County designations, roads, terrain profiles, schools, and museums can often be included or excluded from the map, depending on the traveler's need. Because the Internet is continuously updated, a map on a Web site can be more current than a printed map, which may have been created and printed a year ago. However, do not assume that a map or any other information on the Internet is up-to-date; look for information on the Web page which indicates when it was last updated. Maps obtained from the Internet or from CD-ROMs and DVDs can be printed on paper and often can be downloaded to notebook computers and PDAs.

People traveling by auto can use the Internet or CD-ROMs to obtain maps with personalized driving directions to help them reach their destination. The traveler enters the starting location and the desired destination, and a computer program provides both a map and written directions all along the route, including mileage and route numbers. Map programs can also calculate the driving distance and time that should be allotted for the trip. Some computer programs are very detailed in their maps and driving directions and will pinpoint street addresses and provide such detailed instructions as "Turn left at Rt. 5, drive 1.4 miles, right on Rt. 343." These maps can be printed or can be downloaded to a PDA for use during a driving trip. Cell phone users are also able to obtain driving directions on cell phones which have a text display screen. Two widely used Internet mapping sites are *www.mapquest.com* and *www.maps.yahoo.com*.

As computers and satellite technology become more widespread, more automobiles will come equipped with computer navigation systems and built-in display screens which can show a map and highlight the current location of the car. The computer will calculate the route to be followed, and the driver can follow the car's progress made during the journey.

Automobile Clubs

Automobile clubs such as the American Automobile Association (AAA), Exxon Driver Card, Shell Motorist Club, and Allstate Motor Club offer travel information concerning hotels, motels, restaurants, and places of interest. They also offer maps, roadside assistance, and towing services to their members. Membership usually begins at about $50 per year.

Airline Travel

In recent years, air travel has undergone a revolution. In the new world of travel, airlines change fares, schedules, and even cities of service with little advance notice. Some changes are made seasonally in response to travel patterns; other changes are made in response to competing airlines or changing economic conditions.

Making Reservations

If airline reservations are made through a travel agent, the tickets are issued by the agent. Tickets may also be ordered by calling the airline, using the Internet, or purchasing them at an airport ticket counter. Purchasing tickets at an airport ticket counter can require waiting in long lines and should be avoided except for last-minute emergencies.

If a travel agent is not used, either surf the Web for airline schedules and prices or call an airline and ask if it serves the area. After reviewing all possible schedules and prices, discuss the schedules with the traveler and then make a reservation. Always verify all information prior to paying for the tickets. Airline tickets may be paid for with cash, credit card, or check, but since most tickets are ordered over the phone or on the Internet, most airline travel is paid by credit card.

Although airline travel today is often discounted, there are many restrictions on discount fares. Examples of airline restrictions include issuing nonrefundable tickets, requiring the immediate purchase of tickets or within twenty-four hours after the reservation is made, and purchasing tickets seven to thirty days in advance of travel in order to get a special fare. Since business travelers frequently do not have enough advance notice before traveling, they usually are not able to take advantage of the best discounts. A common restriction to secure a discount airfare is the requirement that the traveler stay at the destination city over a Saturday night. Many businesses now require that travelers include a Saturday night stay on their trips in order to obtain a lower airfare. Whether your traveler qualifies for a discount, the important point to remember is always to ask about airline restrictions before making a reservation.

When making reservations, be sure to give the airline the home, office, and cell telephone numbers of the traveler. If there is a schedule change or flight cancellation, the airline may try to contact the traveler. Airline reservations should be reconfirmed a couple of days prior to traveling and again on the morning of departure. Airlines try to notify travelers of schedule changes, but it is best to verify flight times and reservations to avoid last-minute problems.

Frequent-Flyer Programs

Many airlines offer free frequent-flyer bonus programs that encourage a traveler to use one particular airline. If the traveler has a frequent-flyer number, be sure to give it to the airline when making the reservation. By frequently flying on one airline, the traveler accumulates points, which may be used toward free travel, upgraded accommodations, or other gifts. Many airlines have joint programs with hotel and car-rental agencies, where the traveler may earn extra points and obtain discounts for using those hotel or car-rental companies. Also, airlines have partnerships with credit card companies which award the traveler bonus points by using the credit card for restaurant meals, shopping, medical bills, and so on. Business travelers often use a particular airline to increase the number of frequent-flyer miles in their account to generate a free trip or an upgrade to a better seat. Many companies permit the traveler to use the frequent-flyer miles for personal travel, but some companies require that frequent-flyer travel points be used only for business purposes.

In addition to the free frequent-flyer programs, many airlines have membership clubs which provide quiet lounges in many airports. In addition to a quiet place to wait or work between flights, the lounges may provide free coffee and snacks, Internet access, fax machines, and travel assistance. The cost for these clubs may be several hundred dollars, but membership can also be purchased using frequent-flyer miles. If the traveler is a member of an airline club, check the airline's Web site to determine where the club lounges are located.

Electronic Airline Tickets

As mentioned earlier in this chapter, many airline tickets are now purchased using the Internet. Airlines are moving to new technologies beyond just using the Internet to reach the consumer. Some airlines are installing automated kiosks located at grocery stores, shopping malls, and other locations where they may sell tickets. When you purchase a ticket by using the Internet or an automated kiosk, you will receive an electronic ticket. When you purchase a ticket over the phone or through a travel agent, you may have the option of receiving a paper ticket, but most airlines are strongly encouraging the use of electronic tickets. Some airlines are even adding an additional charge for paper tickets or for tickets purchased by telephone.

Electronic tickets are less expensive for the airlines than the standard paper forms. In electronic ticketing, the passenger receives a confirmation number for a flight itinerary and uses that confirmation number to board an airplane. Electronic ticketing is quicker than using paper forms since the entire booking and ticketing transaction can be done via phone or computer. There is no need to go to an airline or a travel agent or to wait for a ticket to arrive through the mail. If a paper ticket is lost, the traveler absorbs the loss. Depending on the airline policy, lost tickets may be refunded, minus a service fee of approximately $70. If electronic tickets are lost, they can easily be reissued without a penalty.

Luggage

Airline travelers on a trip lasting a few days face a choice regarding luggage, whether they should carry their luggage into the airplane cabin or check the luggage with the airline. The two main reasons for carrying luggage on the plane are to save the time spent waiting for luggage to arrive at the end of the trip and to ensure that the luggage does, in fact, arrive. The disadvantage of taking luggage on the plane is carrying heavy luggage, often down endless corridors through airports, through security, and then trying to find a place for the luggage on the plane. Suitcases with built-in wheels and briefcases with wheels are very popular to help people transport luggage through airports.

There is very limited space on aircraft, and airlines are very restrictive on the size and amount of luggage they will permit to be carried aboard the aircraft. Airlines differ on size limitations for carry-on luggage, so it is wise to contact the airline you are using to determine its luggage standards. A typical airline limitation might be one carry-on bag and one personal item. Personal items include coats, purses, handbags, umbrellas, cameras, and laptop computers. The carry-on bag typically is limited to a combined dimension (length + width + height) of 45 inches. Most airlines have sizing boxes at airport counters, which show the dimensions of luggage that is permitted on the plane. If planes are full, travelers may have to place the suitcase underneath the seat in front of them, thereby using most of their leg space. This can result in a very uncomfortable flight.

Airlines also have restrictions on the number and size of checked luggage. The limitations on checked luggage typically include the number of bags (usually two or three per person), the size per bag (such as 62 inches combined dimension), and the weight per bag, such as 50 pounds per item. Airlines may charge travelers a fee from $50 to $100 for each piece of luggage over the airline's luggage limit, size limit, or weight limit. When checking luggage with an airline, always have your personal identification tag on both the inside and outside of the luggage and be sure that the airline has placed a baggage tag with the proper airport code on the suitcase. Each airport in the world has a unique three-letter identifier code. This is done to avoid confusion between airports serving cities with the same names: for example, Charleston, West Virginia (code CRW) and Charleston, South Carolina (code CHS). The code also distinguishes among multiple airports serving the same city. For example, three airports serve the Washington, DC, area: Ronald Reagan Washington National Airport (code DCA), Washington Dulles International Airport (code IAD), and Baltimore-Washington International Airport (code BWI). If a baggage tag with the wrong airport code is placed on your suitcase, it will have a nice trip without you.

Be sure you keep the luggage check receipts that are given to you. If your luggage does not arrive at the end of your trip, immediately go to the airline's baggage office, usually located next to where you pick up the luggage. You will need the check receipts to complete the claim form, which the airline will use to trace your lost luggage. Usually the airline will deliver your luggage to your home or hotel when it is found.

Boarding Passes and Checking In

Boarding passes are issued by the airline to serve as a security measure, to reserve seating, and to ensure that only ticketed passengers enter the plane. You can obtain a boarding pass several ways. You can request a boarding pass at curbside when you check in your baggage or when you check in with the airline reservation agent at the ticket counter. You may also print a boarding pass from home or the office using the Internet. Boarding passes can usually be printed up to twenty-four hours in advance of a flight by entering passenger and flight information at the airline's Web site. Also, you can often print a boarding pass from an automated kiosk near the airline ticket counter. To use a kiosk the traveler may have to enter his or her airline mileage program account number into the keypad or insert a credit card for identification.

At the airport, the traveler must check in with the airline prior to boarding. Check-in procedures vary from airport to airport. Travelers with electronic tickets may complete check in when they obtain their boarding pass at curbside check-in or via the Web. Passengers with paper tickets may have to check in at the departure counter. Even with a boarding pass, travelers who are not at the departure counter well before flight time can lose their seat. The requirement for check-in time varies with the airline, and many airlines suggest that passengers arrive at the airline departure gate an hour before scheduled departure. For security reasons, check in time for international flights can be several hours before the scheduled flight departure time. Always check with the airline regarding how long before the flight you should arrive.

To improve their on-time schedule record, many airlines begin boarding passengers a half an hour before departure time and closing the airplane doors ten minutes prior to departure. Therefore, late-arriving passengers may not be allowed to board the plane. Maintaining airline on-time arrival and departure schedules is important to the airlines and to their passengers. In addition, the United States Bureau of Transportation Statistics publishes airline on-time statistics, which indicate which airlines meet their schedules and which flights are frequently late. For specific data, visit *www.bts.gov/ntda/oai/index.shtml.*

Airport Security

After the terrorist attacks of September 11, 2001, the United States government instituted many changes in airport security, which affects every airline traveler. All persons and items carried on an airplane must pass through a security inspection system operated by a United States government agency, the Transportation Security Administration (TSA). Only ticketed passengers are permitted in airline boarding areas, and, to reach the boarding area, a traveler must pass through a TSA security checkpoint. To enter the airport security area, the traveler will need to display a boarding pass and a government-issued photo ID. After showing the boarding pass and photo ID, the traveler will pass through a metal detector to search for weapons or items that can be used as a weapon. Remember, items that can be used as weapons cannot be carried onboard an airplane. These include guns, knives, box cutters, baseball bats, spear guns, scissors, razor blades, and hockey sticks.

Before passing through the metal detector, you should place metal objects, such as cell phones, PDAs, watches, coins, and keys, in small baskets, usually available in the security area. Metal detectors will also detect metal in clothing, such as metal in some shoes. If some of your clothing has metal, it is better to pack the clothing or take shoes off before going through the metal detector. If you travel with a computer, it will have to be removed from its carrying bag and placed on the scanner conveyer belt. Since notebook computers look alike, always label your computer with your name, company address, and telephone number. TSA will allow passengers with medical needs requiring diabetes-related supplies and equipment to carry the items if they are labeled with the manufacturer's name or pharmaceutical label.

In addition, checked baggage is examined by an electronic screening device and/or screened by TSA employees. The TSA recommends that checked baggage not be locked to avoid breaking the locks for inspection. To secure the luggage, some travelers use small, plastic, cablelike strips which can be easily cut by TSA inspectors. There are now locks available that are TSA-compliant. TSA personnel have the keys or combinations to these locks, so, if they need to open luggage, they can do so without destroying the locks. Packing suggestions for checked baggage include (1) not packing film or food, (2) spreading heavy items so the contents can easily be viewed, (3) putting personal items in plastic bags to reduce touching by TSA inspectors, and (4) not overstuffing the luggage so opened luggage can be closed by TSA inspections. Additional security information can be obtained from the TSA at *www.tsa.gov/public/*.

While airport security measures have increased passenger safety, the screening process has created a haven for thieves. It is important to watch your personal possessions when passing through airport security scanning equipment. If you are not alert, someone could easily grab your personal items. Pay particular attention to your notebook computer as it moves on the conveyer belt, because computers are attractive to thieves.

> **HINT**
>
> Visit *www.tsa.gov/public/* for travel security information.

Travel Safety and Security Precautions

- Do not divulge travel plans unnecessarily. For example, do not tell the grocery clerk, gas station attendant, restaurant personnel, and so on of your travel plans.
- Do not discuss travel plans where you can be overhead.
- Do not discuss travel plans with strangers.
- Be aware of pickpockets. Pickpockets may work in groups of adults or children and create diversions so you become an easy target. Techniques used include asking you for the time, a match, a cigarette, or extra change and spilling food or drink on your clothing.
- Secure money using a hidden money belt worn under your slacks or shirt.
- Carefully watch and secure purses and wallets that are in back pockets.
- Keep your hotel/motel door locked at all times. Only open the door if you are expecting someone, and look through the peephole prior to opening the door.
- Know where the hotel stairways are located. Count the number of doors from your room to the exit. In an emergency, you may not be able to see the exit.
- If you are uncomfortable in an area, do not walk alone.
- If the area is questionable, limit your activities, especially at night.
- If you see a suspicious individual, do not enter an elevator or a subway with that person.
- Be alert for carjackers and thieves.

How to Pack for Your Business Trip

- Take the least amount possible.
- Take neutral-colored clothing that mixes and matches, thus extending your wardrobe.
- Take sample-size cosmetics and put them in plastic zip bags so nothing will spill and soil your clothing.
- Many hotels and motels provide shampoo and hairdryers. If you check with the hotel, you may not need to carry your own.
- Take a small folding suitcase to pack meeting handouts, souvenirs, and so on.
- Since most luggage looks alike, attach a ribbon or another distinguishing item to the outside of your luggage.

Jet Lag

People who travel across time zones often experience jet lag—a change in the body clock. The symptoms include exhaustion, loss of sleep, too much sleep, disorientation, loss of appetite, lack of motivation, and lack of concentration. In some cases, the symptoms last for several days or even weeks. Since jet lag muddles the thought processes, it can be a major problem for business travelers who must make business decisions upon arriving at the destination. Many travelers feel traveling east is worse than traveling west, but either direction can be a challenge. To help combat jet lag, some business travelers arrive the day before an important meeting to give the body time to adjust to the time change. Some experts believe when traveling east it helps to go to sleep an hour earlier each night for several nights prior to the trip. Others recommend eliminating caffeine for several days to help the body adjust. For additional information view the following Web sites: *www.bodyclock.com*, *www.nojetlag.com*, and *www.nlm.nih.gov/medlineplus/ency/article/002110.htm*.

Choices of Airline Services

Types of Service

Most airlines offer at least two types of service. They are usually called first-class and coach, although some airlines call their two services business-class and coach. First-class service (or business-class service) is considerably more expensive than coach, but the seats are wider, and first-class service provides better-quality food, free alcoholic beverages, and more service from flight attendants. First-class passengers sit at the front of the plane and can enter and exit the plane before other passengers. Companies usually purchase first-class seats only for top executives; increasingly, business travelers are not permitted to travel first-class at company expense. Some airlines offer a business-class service, which offers larger seats and more amenities than coach for a price between that of first-class and coach. The discount tickets widely advertised by the airlines are usually for coach seats. Airlines that fly smaller planes, such as commuter airlines, may offer only coach-class service.

Travelers' Personal Preferences

Check with the travelers to determine their personal seating preferences when flying. Some people prefer to sit toward the front of the airplane, others over the wing, and others prefer to sit toward the back. Also determine whether a window or an aisle seat is preferred. An aisle seat provides more leg room, and a window affords the traveler a sky view of the trip. Always avoid seating a business traveler in the middle seat of a three-seat row if at all possible. Smoking sections are no longer an option on flights in the United States and Canada, as U.S. and Canadian airlines have banned smoking on domestic and foreign flights. Many foreign airlines, however, continue to have a smoking section for their travelers.

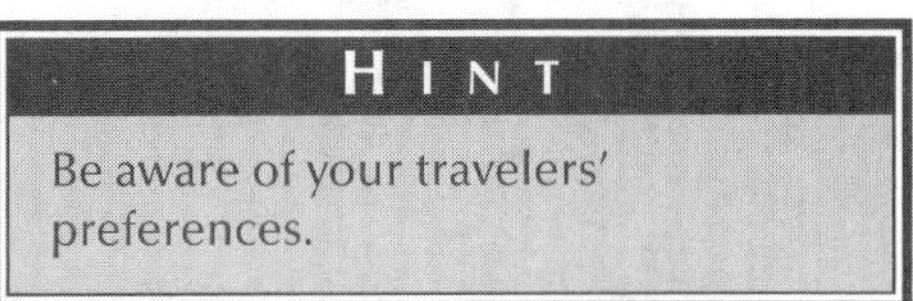

Types of Flights

Airline flights can be classified as nonstop, direct, and connecting. Nonstop service means that the flight flies between two cities with no intermediate stops. A direct flight means that the flight has an intermediate stop, but the passenger remains on the same plane the entire trip. A nonstop flight could, therefore, leave at 8:15 A.M. and arrive before a direct flight that left at 7:30 A.M. and made several stops along the way. The final type of flight is the connecting flight, on which the traveler must change planes at an intermediate city.

Many airlines encourage connecting flights by routing passengers through a hub, where as many as twenty or more airplanes will land and depart within an hour. Each airline has a minimum connecting time that must be available at a particular airport for a passenger to transfer from one flight to another. Airlines will only accept reservations for connecting flights that meet their connecting time requirements. However, even with a flight itinerary meeting the minimum connecting time, there is always the danger that a delay in the first flight may cause a passenger to miss a subsequent flight. If you book a connecting flight, try to book an itinerary for which both flights are on the same airline. If the first flight is late and the traveler misses the connecting flight, the traveler will deal only with a single airline to complete the trip.

Meals

A wise traveler always tries to eat before getting on a flight rather than relying on airlines for food. Most airlines no longer provide a full meal service in coach, except on transcontinental and foreign flights. Even flights during a normal meal time may consist of a sandwich served in a tote bag. Some airlines now have a "Buy on Board" program and charge passengers an additional payment for meals. If you do not wish to purchase the airline meal, you can take your own food. Some low-cost airlines have only a beverage and snack service, the snack being a bag of peanuts or pretzels.

Most airports have an eatery where you can purchase a sandwich or snack food to eat during a flight. Some airports have restaurants which will take reservations and will deliver the order to the airline gate before your flight. Check with the airline to see what food service will be offered during the flight; then check with the airport Web site to see what other food alternatives are available.

When airlines provide a meal service, they usually offer special meals, such as kosher, vegetarian, fruit plate, low-sodium, and low-carb. Since special meals must be ordered at least twenty-four hours prior to the flight, determine in advance if your traveler wants a special meal.

Airline Flight Guides

Airline schedules are available via the Internet, either from an individual airline or from travel reservation sites that list many airlines. Seasoned travelers often carry airline flight information on alternate flights, in case they have a change in plans or flights are delayed. Many airlines provide electronic schedules, which can be downloaded to desktop computers, notebook computers, or handheld computers. Travelers can also check airline schedules using PDA's which have wireless connections or cell phones that can access the Internet. Some airlines provide printed guides of their flights. These guides are usually sized to fit in a traveler's pocket and may be available at airline counters.

LODGING

Selecting a Hotel or Motel

Selecting lodging can be the most difficult part of preparing a travel plan. The choice of hotels and motels is usually greater than the choice of airlines or car-rental agencies. In a large metropolitan area, the choices can be overwhelming.

Very often, however, a traveler who visits a destination frequently has a preference regarding lodging. Travelers attending a convention or large meeting will usually be given information about suggested hotels. If an administrative assistant is not given specific hotel recommendations, the selection of a hotel is usually based on the following criteria: location, price, accessibility to clients or meeting sites, and accommodations desired.

Location and price are the two most important criteria in selecting accommodations. Usually, except in resort areas, the closer a hotel is to the city's central business district, the more expensive the room rate. Hotels that are convenient to an airport, particularly those hotels with courtesy transportation to the airport, can also command a premium room rate. Often the most reasonably priced accommodations are on the fringes of cities and are near major highways. However, a traveler staying in such a hotel or motel may need to rent a car to reach clients and meeting sites. People with meetings in a city center area can use taxis or mass transportation to travel from the hotel to meetings. Ideally, the hotel or motel should be accessible to the business appointments and to transportation. This, however, is not always possible.

Today some hotels and motels offer a free continental breakfast, which is convenient for the traveler and saves time and money. The breakfast usually consists of at least juice, donuts, sweet rolls, and coffee. Some facilities offer more elaborate breakfasts, which also include cereal, toast, bagels, eggs, fruit, yogurt, waffles, and other foods. Generally the free continental breakfast is not available at expensive hotels that cater to the business traveler.

Hotels

Hotels that cater to the business traveler are found in a city center, at resorts, near industrial parks, and near airports. They offer a variety of restaurants, meeting rooms, airport transportation, and additional services that are not found in most motels. Hotels are often used by travelers who do not arrive by car; therefore, they provide a variety of services and entertainment at one location. A hotel may include shops, travel desks, business center services (fax, photocopy, and so on), a swimming pool, or a health club. These services may be very important or have no value to the individual traveler. You should determine which, if any, of these amenities are important to your traveler.

Many hotels have broadband computer access in each room. In some hotels, the cost of broadband is included in the nightly room charge; in other hotels, it is available for an additional charge, either on an hourly or a daily basis.

Motels

Motels are usually smaller than hotels with an informal atmosphere and limited food services or no food services on site. Motels are frequently located near major highways, and they usually offer extensive parking. Travelers planning to do a lot of driving to meeting facilities and appointments may prefer a motel convenient to major highways rather than a hotel in the center of a city.

Other Lodging

The lodging industry is continually developing new variations on the concept of hotels and motels. Some hotels offer two-room suites, which may include a sitting room suite or kitchen facilities in addition to the usual bedroom. Bed and Breakfast (B & B) facilities, which are

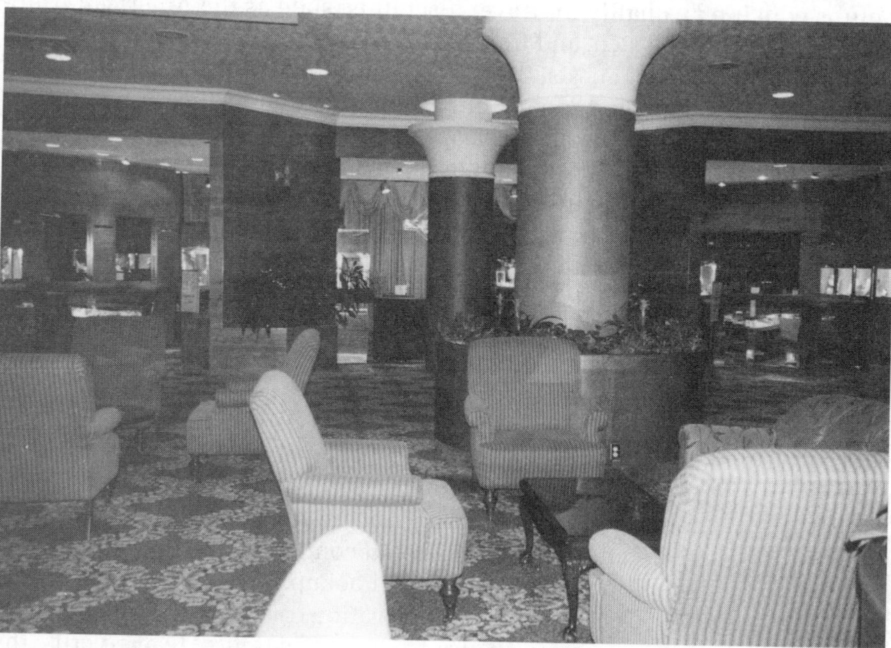

FIGURE 8-2 A hotel lobby.

usually small inns or restored properties, are also available. To meet the needs of the business traveler, extended-stay facilities with kitchens and sitting rooms are being built throughout the country to cater to travelers who may need to stay for extended periods.

Nationwide Lodging Chains

There are many national hotel and motel chains that specialize in a particular type of accommodation. These chains have toll-free central reservation services and most provide free directories with maps indicating their locations and the services offered at each hotel or motel. Many of the national and worldwide lodging chains operate facilities in one or more of the following categories of lodging: luxury, medium-priced, and budget. Examples of national chains are Hyatt, Marriott, Hilton, Holiday Inn, Ramada Inn, Hampton Inn, Quality Inn, and Comfort Inn. Most of the national lodging chains have a frequent-stay program similar to airline frequent-flyer programs. Guests earn points for each night's lodging. The national chains also work with airlines, and guests can receive airline frequent-flyer miles from the hotel's partner airlines. Check with the traveler to determine whether the traveler is a member of any of the frequent-stay programs and if this should be a factor in selecting lodging.

In addition to national chains, accommodations are available through regional chains and local hotels and motels. As an assistant who makes reservations for a supervisor, you should keep records for future trips regarding your supervisor's travel preferences, hotels and motels that were suitable, and car rental agencies that were reasonable. In addition, keep records on problems encountered, so you will know what to avoid.

Reservations

Hotel and motel reservations are usually made by calling the facility's toll-free telephone number. While it may be quicker to use the chain's central reservation number, less expensive rates can often be obtained by making reservations directly with the hotel or motel where the traveler will be staying. Whether you call the central reservation number or the hotel directly, never accept the first rate quoted; always ask if there is a lower rate available. Hotels often list many different prices for the same room. It is helpful to ask if the hotel has any special rates that can be used. Be sure to ask if there is a special convention rate or if the hotel has a corporate rate for your business. Ask if the supervisor belongs to any organizations or clubs which may qualify for travel discounts, such as the American Automobile Association (AAA), AARP, Costco, and travel clubs. If the traveler is a member of the hotel or motel chain's club for frequent guests, the traveler may qualify for special discounts, upgrades, or other amenities. Hotels and motels often participate in airline frequent-flyer programs, and this information should also be checked when making a reservation.

Hotel reservations can also be made over the Internet, and it is wise to check the hotel's Web site for Internet special rates. You can try the hotel's Web site or the travel Web sites mentioned in the section The Internet. Web travel sites have become some of the largest travel agencies in the country and, because of their buying power, can often book hotel rooms cheaper than you can reserve from the hotel itself. Some Web sites will book rooms in general locations and then will tell you which hotel is booked only after receiving payment. Check the Web site before you complete the reservation to be sure you reserve a specific hotel if location or a specific hotel is important.

As an administrative assistant, you should know your supervisor's preferences in lodging accommodations. Nonsmoking rooms are available in most hotels and motels. Some travelers prefer one king-size bed; others prefer a queen-size bed or two double beds. If the traveler intends to work in the room, you should ask the reservation agent if the room contains a desk and if the room has a broadband computer hookup.

When making a reservation, request either a confirmation number or a written confirmation. Always verify the

HINT

When making a reservation, always ask for the best price.

confirmation number by repeating it to the reservation agent. Written confirmations are now often sent by email. The traveler should be given a copy of the written confirmation or confirmation number, and a second copy should be kept in the office file. All confirmation numbers should be included in the itinerary, which is discussed later in this chapter.

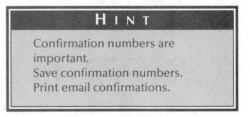

HINT

Confirmation numbers are important.
Save confirmation numbers.
Print email confirmations.

Guaranteed Reservations

Most hotel and motel reservations are held only until 4 P.M. or 6 P.M. on the day of arrival. As a precaution against having a reservation canceled, it is best to guarantee a reservation by using a major credit card. Giving the credit card number to the hotel guarantees that a room will be available, regardless of how late in the evening the traveler arrives. This also means that the room must be paid for if the reservation is not canceled by the hotel's deadline. Always ask the hotel's cancellation policy when making a guaranteed reservation and be sure to get a cancellation number from the hotel or motel if you must cancel a reservation. Also, be aware that some facilities have a policy requiring cancellations two or three days prior to the arrival date and some charge a cancellation penalty.

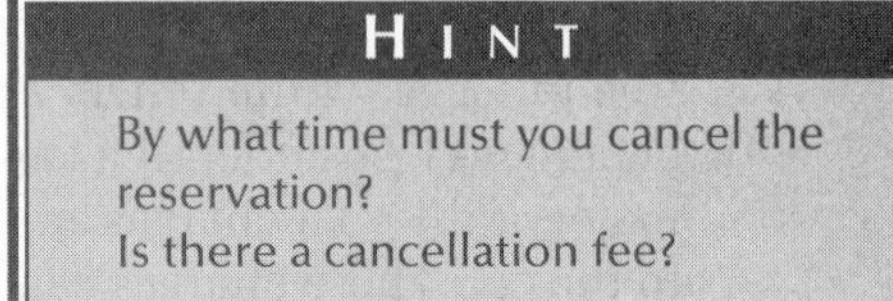

HINT

By what time must you cancel the reservation?
Is there a cancellation fee?

AUTOMOBILE TRAVEL

Personal Car

Many times a personal car will be used for business purposes. In that case, the traveler will complete an expense report form, so the employee will be reimbursed for expenses. Reimbursement is usually based on a per-mile rate—usually not more than the Internal Revenue Service allows per mile traveled for business purposes. The employee should keep accurate records of the dates and purposes of business travel and the number of miles traveled. You will find information regarding expense accounts later in this chapter.

Auto Rental

Organizations frequently have a contract with a specific nationwide rental-car company, and they expect all traveling employees to use that company. In exchange, the company gets a better rate on the auto rental. If your company or the traveler does not prefer a specific auto-rental company, you can call a company's toll-free-telephone number or search for a rate on the Internet. There are many nationwide auto-rental companies, as well as local agencies, and all have toll-free phone numbers and/or Internet sites. Several of the auto-rental Internet sites are listed at the end of this section. In addition, you can also obtain auto rental information from the general travel sites listed. Also, most airlines have partnerships with auto-rental companies and usually have direct links from the airline's Web site. The auto-rental rate quoted through an airline Web site may or may not be less expensive than the rate obtained by making a reservation independently.

Auto-Rental Base Rates

Auto rates are based on the size of the car and the number of days of the rental. The smallest auto available for rental, the economy size, often has a trunk too small for the traveler's luggage or an uncovered trunk, which can be seen from outside the vehicle. Most business travelers prefer to rent a compact or midsize auto. Cars may be rented by the hour and by the day, but the daily charge is usually the same as for a few hours, and the weekly charge is usually equal to the charge for four days. Auto rental agencies will always check a driver's license.

They may check driving records and may charge a higher rate for drivers who have poor driving records or who are under twenty-one or twenty-five years of age.

Auto-rental rates vary widely and often discounts are offered. As when making airline or hotel reservations, never accept the first rate quoted. Ask about corporate rates or discounts for memberships in the company's auto club. Discounts are also available from AAA, AARP, Costco, and so on. Auto-rental companies often have coupons which provide an upgrade to a larger car at the same price as a smaller vehicle. Coupons or other discount offers may be available from the Internet or enclosed with monthly credit card bills.

In addition to the base daily rate, the final auto rental charges will also include additional user taxes imposed by local governments and airport user fees. Make sure you know all the required fees and taxes before you make a reservation.

Additional Charges

Auto-rental companies offer and charge for a variety of other services. Some companies offer free mileage, while others charge for the number of miles traveled. An additional drop-off charge may be added if a car is left in a city other than the one where it was picked up. The major additional charges are for personal liability insurance and insurance to cover damages to the car. These charges can significantly increase the cost of the auto rental. Insurance coverage for rental car damage is often included in services provided by credit cards at the gold or platinum level. In addition, the insurance you have on your own car may cover personal liability on a rental car, but check carefully for an exclusion for cars used for business purposes. The traveler should check with his or her insurance and credit card companies to determine coverage. If coverage is available from either of these sources, it may not be necessary to purchase auto insurance from the rental company. In addition to insurance, gasoline is a standard auto-rental charge. Some companies ask the traveler to return the car empty of gas, while others ask the driver to fill the car before returning it. The traveler should be aware of which gasoline method is used by the rental company. Some companies charge an additional fee for a second driver.

Frequent-Traveler Clubs

The company, or the traveler, may also participate in a program run by auto-rental companies which is similar to an airline frequent-flyer program. Membership in most auto-rental clubs is free and provides several benefits. Reservations can be easily made, since the auto-rental company has information on file about the traveler and his or her auto preferences. Being a member of an auto-rental company's program, the traveler can take advantage of speed check-in and check-out. Often travel club members can bypass the check-in procedure at the auto-rental counter and go directly to their car, which can easily save them a half-hour when picking up a car. In addition, members can quickly return the car by dropping off the keys and indicating the number of miles driven.

Picking Up a Car

The primary location to rent a car is at an airport. In most airports, auto-rental check-in counters are located near luggage pick-up. If a traveler does not have an auto-rental reservation, the traveler can try to locate a car at the airport. However, this will probably require standing in

Date	Beginning Mileage	Ending Mileage	Destination	Parking	Other Expenses
6/1/XXXX	32,457	32,489	Wood, Inc.	2.00	
6/2/XXXX	32,489	32,529	B. K. Supplies	5.00	1.75 toll

FIGURE 8-3 An auto expense report form.

several long lines and, perhaps, not locating a car. While the auto-rental company may have a check-in counter inside airport terminals, in larger airports the cars are often picked up and returned at a location several miles away. The traveler must use a courtesy bus or van from the terminal to the auto-rental agency. Once at the rental location, the traveler will be given directions with maps of the area and directions on how to return the car. In addition to the small area maps available, some auto-rental agencies rent cars with satellite navigation systems, which provide electronic maps and directions, which can be continually revised for the next destination, thus making travel easier for their clients.

When making a reservation, you should confirm the operating hours at the auto pick-up location. This is particularly important if the auto rental is set for very early in the morning or very late in the evening. Most auto-rental agencies request the incoming flight number. If the flight is delayed, the agency will continue to hold the car until the traveler arrives.

While most cars are rented at airports, auto rentals are also available in downtown areas, resorts, and suburban areas. The selection of rental companies in these areas, however, may be limited. If you need to rent a car for pick-up other than at an airport, ask where they have rental sites. An auto-rental company that is within walking distance or a short taxi ride from where the traveler is staying is preferable.

Sample Auto Rental Agencies

Alamo Rent a Car
www.alamo.com/

Avis Rent a Car
www.avis.com

Budget Rent a Car
www.budget.com

Dollar Rent a Car
www.dollar.com

Enterprise Car Rental
www.enterprise.com

Hertz
www.hertz.com

National Car Rental
www.nationalcar.com

Thrifty Car Rental
www.thrifty.com

RESPONDING TO THE TECHNOLOGICAL DEMANDS OF BUSINESS

Business travelers rely on the Internet and cell phones to keep in touch with their offices and clients. Prior to a trip, it is prudent to determine whether the traveler's usual Internet access and cell phone service will be available in the locations to be visited. It may be best to call the traveler's cell phone provider or check the web to determine if the cell phone operates in the city the traveler will be visiting. Many cell phone systems are nationwide; others are regional but have affiliations with carriers in other cities. Also check with the traveler regarding the type of calling plan being used. Some cell phone plans include calls made throughout the country as part of the base plan, while others add a roaming charge if the phone is used out of the usual service area. Roaming charges can be very expensive. In many airports, visitors can rent a cell phone by the day, so they can avoid roaming charges and be in contact with their office. In many cases, the common cell phones people use in this country will not work in Europe, Asia, South America, and elsewhere. Therefore, international travelers often rent a wireless phone in the country they are visiting or rent a phone in the United States specially designed to work in the region visited. In some states and outside of the United States, cell phones cannot be used while driving, and this restriction includes hands-free wireless phones.

It is also important to verify if the traveler's usual Internet provider has an access phone number in the city being visited or if it provides a toll-free telephone number that can be used while on travel. Making a long-distance telephone call to complete an Internet connection can be very expensive. Many large airports have shops where a traveler can connect to the Internet for a per-minute fee. In some cities, travelers can visit an Internet-wired café, where for a fee they can check their email. Many public areas are now being equipped with WiFi wireless technology. Subscribers to WiFi services can access the Internet with portable computers at airports, hotels, coffee shops, restaurants, bookstores, and many other locations. Information about places served by WiFi technology can be found on the Internet through sites such as *intel.jiwire.com/hot-spot-directory-browse-by-state.htm?country_id=1* (note: www is not used at the beginning of the address).

Hotels are meeting the demands of business clients by providing on-site technology in many ways. Since most business travelers want to check their email when they are away from the office, most hotels that cater to businesspeople provide connections in rooms where lodgers can easily connect to the Internet. Some hotels now provide unlimited long distance phone service and high-speed Internet connections for a fixed, daily rate. Some hotels/motels have computers available for rental and have experts on staff who can solve computer problems in a meeting or guest room. Many hotel/motels that cater to business travelers have business centers that provide the following services: complete computer systems on moveable carts; small offices with a computer, fax, telephone, and table; and fast Internet access. If these features are important to your traveler, check with the hotel before making a reservation.

Conventions are a good opportunity to gather information and materials, but the materials must somehow get home. Therefore, convention hotels often provide mailing services, which are important because of weight and luggage restrictions when flying.

TRAVEL FUNDS

Expense Accounts

Travel can be a major cost, so companies limit the travel expenses which they will pay. Usually, companies will pay only for approved travel expenses for such items as transportation (including cabs, parking, or tolls), food, and lodging. At the completion of the trip, the traveler completes an expense account report and is reimbursed by the company for approved expenses. Companies may advance cash or travelers checks to employees, which are used to cover the anticipated costs of a trip. At the end of a trip, the expenses of the trip are compared with the funds given in advance to the traveler. If the approved expenses are more than the travel advance, the traveler will receive additional money from the company. The traveler will refund money to the company when the cost of the trip is less than anticipated.

Some companies allow employees a per diem, which is a fixed amount for travel expenses per day. The per diem amount usually includes meals but may also include lodging expenses. Employees generally do not have to submit receipts to their employers for those items covered by the per diem allowance. Many companies issue corporate credit cards to employees who travel, and these cards simplify employee travel records. Since the card is used solely for company travel and not used for personal expenses, the credit card statement can be submitted with an employee travel reimbursement request. Some companies pay the funds to the employee and then the employee pays the credit card company, while other companies directly pay the credit card invoice.

As mentioned earlier, business travelers often receive corporate rates at hotels, motels, and auto-rental agencies. These are discounted rates offered to frequent users. Often a corporate identification card is all that is necessary to qualify for these discounts. When making a reservation, ask if your company qualifies for a corporate discount.

Expense Reports

One of the duties of an assistant is to help the traveler prepare the expense report at the end of a business trip. A detailed list of expenses must be available to complete the expense report accurately. For that reason, a business traveler should make a daily listing of expenses while traveling.

Have your supervisor use a personal record of travel expense while traveling. Most PDAs contain expense account forms as one of the built-in features. If receipts are required, the traveler should take an envelope, where receipts can be stored, so they are easily available to be attached to the expense record.

HINT

For reimbursement, keep detailed expense records.

PERSONAL RECORD OF TRAVEL EXPENSES

Date ____________________

Hotel/Motel ____________________ Amount ____________________

Mileage Begin ____________________ End ____________________

Breakfast ____________________

Lunch ____________________

Dinner ____________________

Taxi ____________________

Parking ____________________

Tips ____________________

Additional Expenses

____

____

____

____

FIGURE 8-4 A personal daily expense worksheet.

Date	Lodging	Meals	Mileage	Misc.	Daily Total
8/14	$60	$35		$5	$100
8/15	$60	$42		$8	$110
8/16	$60	$33		$9	$102

Method of Transportation airplane
miles @ .25

Airline Ticket **$300**

Trip Total **$612**

Traveler's Signature ____________________ **Date** ____________________
Supervisor's Signature ____________________ **Date** ____________________

FIGURE 8-5 A travel expense record.

After a trip, an administrative assistant would complete the company expense reimbursement form using the information the traveler has provided. Company expense report forms vary, but the information required is essentially the same.

Travelers Checks and Corporate Credit Card Numbers

Travelers checks can be purchased from a bank, a credit union, or an auto club, as well as on the Internet. To ensure the validity of the check, the purchaser signs each travelers check twice—first when purchasing the check and then again when using the check to pay for an item. The merchant can then compare both signatures to determine the validity of the check. Each travelers check has a serial number printed on the front of the check. Prior to each trip, verify that the administrative assistant has a list of the numbers of all travelers checks and corporate credit cards as well as their related toll-free phone numbers. If the travelers checks or corporate credit cards are lost or stolen, the administrative assistant can notify the travelers check or credit card companies and obtain replacements.

ITINERARY

HINT

An itinerary is a day-by-day travel plan.

An itinerary is a day-by-day travel plan. It includes dates, hotels, telephone numbers, times and locations of meetings, methods of transportation, airline schedule and flight numbers, hotel and car-rental agency rates and confirmation numbers, and any other information necessary to help the traveler. If the traveler is flying, transportation to and from the airport must also be considered. If special airport pick-up

Itinerary, Wilma Sugarman
6/1/XXXX to 6/4/XXXX

June 1	Delta Airlines flight 347 Departs Baltimore-Washington International Airport (BWI) at 9:15 A.M. Arrives Los Angeles Airport (LAX) at 12:02 A.M. Hertz car rental, confirmation # 2988345S Meet at 3 P.M. with Max Rodman at his office, 3400 Western Blvd. (map is enclosed) Reservation at California Best Western, 3704 Western Blvd. Confirmation #BW43775, Telephone No. 831-555-6714
June 2	Meet with Bill Snowdon at 9 A.M. Reservation at California Best Western, 3704 Western Blvd.
June 3	Drive to Newport Beach Meet at 11:30 A.M. with Marilyn Rose at 2380 Beach Way Reservation at Newport Beach Villa, 1215 Beach Drive Confirmation #2318LP. Telephone No. 831-555-8977
June 4	Delta Airlines flight 782 Departs Los Angeles (LAX) at 11:30 A.M. Arrives Baltimore-Washington International Airport (BWI) at 8:04 P.M.

FIGURE 8-6 An itinerary.

service is used, it should be noted on the itinerary. Since some cities are served by more than one airport, the itinerary should indicate which airport is being used. The administrative assistant should file a copy of the itinerary. Copies of the itinerary should be given to the traveler and to the administrative assistant. In addition the itinerary should be available to the traveler's family if so desired.

PASSPORTS AND VISAS

Travelers to most locations outside the United States require a passport. A passport is used by a government to grant permission for international travel and is the internationally recognized way to identify the traveler. Citizens of the United States obtain passports from the Department of State. Passport applications are available from passport agencies, major post offices, and some county and municipal offices. The first time an applicant applies for a passport, the applicant must appear in person. Applicants for a passport must furnish proof of citizenship with one of the following documents: certified birth certificate issued by a city, county, or state; consular report of birth abroad or certification of birth; naturalization certificate; or certificate of citizenship. In addition, two 2″ × 2″ photographs taken within the past six months, showing current appearance, must be attached to a passport application. Passports are issued for a ten-year period for persons over eighteen years of age. Depending on the passport application location, the fee may be paid by check, cash, credit card, money order, or bank draft. Passports may be renewed by mail if (1) the passport is not damaged, (2) it was received within the past fifteen years, (3) the applicant was over sixteen when it was issued, (4) you still have the same name as the passport or you can legally document the name change. When renewing a passport, you must provide your old passport along with your application and fee.

Information on obtaining United States passports and current fee information is available via the Internet at *www.travel.state.gov/passport*. Information on obtaining Canadian passports is available from the Canada Passport Office Internet site at *www.dfait-maeci.gc.ca/passport/menu.asp*. Some airlines are now scanning passenger passports and comparing them with immigration and customs databases to identify forgeries and tampering.

A visa is a document permitting a visitor entry into a foreign country. Not all countries require a visa for entry. Information regarding visa requirements can be obtained from travel books, travel agencies, and airlines serving foreign countries. Visas are usually obtained from the embassy of the foreign country a visitor plans to visit. Visa fees and the time required for processing applications vary, so it is best to check on visa requirements as soon as foreign travel is known.

Before traveling to another country, it is prudent to investigate whether any medical precautions are necessary. The U.S. government's Centers for Disease Control and Prevention (CDC) maintains an Internet site (*www.cdc.gov/travel*), which is the standard reference for medical information of interest to travelers. The CDC Internet site includes information on vaccinations required and medications recommended to be taken as a precaution when traveling to specific countries.

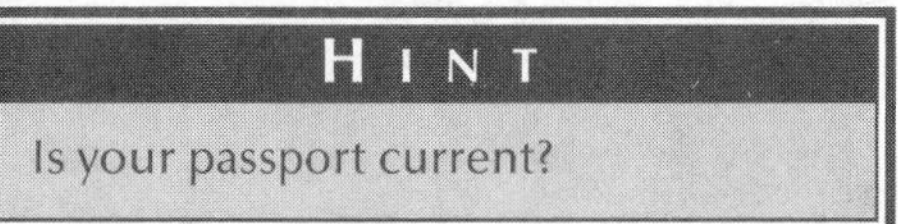
HINT
Is your passport current?

TRAVEL HINTS

When traveling on business, check the weather forecast for your destination using newspapers, television, or the Internet. One source to check is *www.weather.com*. Since the weather may be unpredictable, it is wise to take a folding umbrella when you travel.

Many hotels offer dry-cleaning services or have irons available for last-minute touch-ups. However, you can eliminate the need for ironing by carefully packing clothes. To avoid wrinkling your jacket while traveling, remove it and hang it or carefully fold it.

U.S. Department of State

APPLICATION FOR A ☐ U.S. PASSPORT ☐ REGISTRATION

(Type or print in capital letters using blue or black ink in white areas only.)

1. NAME (First and Middle)

LAST

2. MAIL PASSPORT TO: STREET / RFD # OR P.O. BOX APT. #

CITY STATE

ZIP CODE COUNTRY / IN CARE OF *(if applicable)*

☐ 5 Yr. ☐ 10 Yr. Issue Date ______

☐ R ☐ D ☐ O ☐ DP

End. #______ Exp.______

3. SEX ☐ M ☐ F

4. PLACE OF BIRTH (City & State OR City & Country)

5. DATE OF BIRTH Month Day Year

6. SOCIAL SECURITY NUMBER (SEE FEDERAL TAX LAW NOTICE ON PAGE 4)

7. HEIGHT Feet Inches | 8. HAIR COLOR | 9. EYE COLOR | 10. HOME TELEPHONE | 11. BUSINESS TELEPHONE | 12. OCCUPATION

13. PERMANENT ADDRESS (DO NOT LIST P.O. BOX) STREET/R.F.D.# CITY STATE ZIP CODE

14. FATHER'S FULL NAME Last First | BIRTHPLACE | BIRTHDATE | U.S. CITIZEN ☐ Yes ☐ No | 15. MOTHER'S FULL MAIDEN NAME Last First | BIRTHPLACE | BIRTHDATE | U.S. CITIZEN ☐ Yes ☐ No

16. HAVE YOU EVER BEEN MARRIED? ☐ Yes ☐ No | SPOUSE'S OR FORMER SPOUSE'S FULL NAME AT BIRTH | BIRTHPLACE | BIRTHDATE | U.S. CITIZEN ☐ Yes ☐ No

DATE OF MOST RECENT MARRIAGE Month Day Year | WIDOWED/DIVORCED? ☐ Yes ☐ No Give Date Month Day Year | 17. OTHER NAMES YOU HAVE USED (1) (2)

18. HAVE YOU EVER BEEN ISSUED A U.S. PASSPORT? ☐ Yes ☐ No IF YES, COMPLETE NEXT LINE AND SUBMIT PASSPORT IF AVAILABLE.

NAME IN WHICH ISSUED | MOST RECENT PASSPORT NUMBER | APPROXIMATE ISSUE DATE Month Day Year | DISPOSITION ☐ Submitted ☐ Stolen ☐ Lost ☐ Other

It is necessary to submit a statement with an application for a new passport when a previous valid or potentially valid passport cannot be presented. The statement must set forth in detail why the previous passport cannot be presented. Use Form DS-64.

STAPLE STAPLE 2" x 2" STAPLE STAPLE SUBMIT TWO RECENT, IDENTICAL, COLOR PHOTOGRAPHS

19. EMERGENCY CONTACT. If you wish, you may supply the name, address and telephone number of a person not traveling with you to be contacted in case of emergency.

NAME

STREET

CITY STATE ZIP CODE TELEPHONE

20. TRAVEL PLANS *(not mandatory)* Date of Trip Month Day Year Length of Trip

COUNTRIES TO BE VISITED:

21. **STOP!** DO NOT SIGN APPLICATION UNTIL REQUESTED TO DO SO BY PERSON ADMINISTERING OATH.

I have not, since acquiring United States citizenship, performed any of the acts listed under "Acts or Conditions" on the reverse of this application form (unless explanatory statement is attached). I solemnly swear (or affirm) that the statements made on this application are true and the photograph attached is a true likeness of me.

X ______ Applicant's Signature - age 14 or older

X ______ *Father's/Legal Guardian's Signature (if identifying minor)*

X ______ *Mother's/Legal Guardian's Signature (if identifying minor)*

22. FOR ACCEPTANCE AGENT'S USE

(Signature of person authorized to accept application) Month Day Year (SEAL)

☐ Clerk of Court; Location ______ ☐ PASSPORT Agent ☐ Postal Employee ☐ (Vice) Consul USA

FOLD

23a. Applicant's or Father's Identifying Documents ☐ Driver's License ☐ Passport ☐ Other (Specify) ______ Issue Date: Expiration Date: Place of Issue: Name ______ ID No. ______

23b. Mother's Identifying Documents ☐ Driver's License ☐ Passport ☐ Other (Specify) ______ Issue Date: Expiration Date: Place of Issue: Name ______ ID No. ______

24. FOR ISSUING OFFICE USE ONLY (Applicant's evidence of citizenship)

☐ Birth Certificate ☐ SR ☐ CR ☐ City Filed/Issued:
☐ Passport Bearer's Name:
☐ Report of Birth:
☐ Naturalization/Citizenship Cert. No./Issued:
☐ Other:
☐ Seen & Returned:
☐ Attached:

APPLICATION APPROVAL

25. FEE ______ EXEC. ______ EF ______ OTHER ______

DS-11 OMB No. 1405-0004 Expires: 03/31/2005 Estimated Burden - 20 Minutes Page 3 of 4

FIGURE 8-7 A passport application.

It is wise to carry a small snack with you on a plane. If meals are served on a long flight, they are usually served a couple of hours after the departure time. Therefore if you have a 12 P.M. departure, you may not be served until 2 P.M. It is also a good idea to carry something to read. With the uncertainty of airline travel, your travel time may be several hours longer than you anticipated.

Always take a road map with you even if you are not going to drive. The map will assist you in becoming familiar with the area you are visiting.

In addition, you should carry small bills and change for tips and be aware of your company's policy on telephone calls home. Some companies will reimburse employees, within set limits, for calls made to their families.

CHAPTER REVIEW

1. Name four travel guides that would be helpful when planning trips.
2. What factors should be considered when renting a car?
3. What is meant by the term *corporate travel rates?*
4. Explain the term *guaranteed reservation.*
5. Explain how the Internet is involved in travel reservations.
6. What information should be included in an itinerary?
7. What is the purpose of a passport?
8. What is the purpose of a visa?

ACTIVITIES

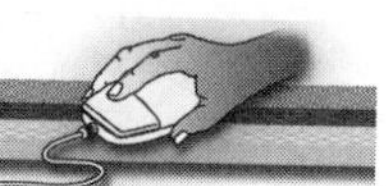

1. Call three airlines and compare the travel times and prices for a trip from your home to a city of your choice. Create a report with this information.
2. Use the Internet to determine the time and cost of a trip from your home to the city of your choice. Include in your report three possible time schedules, airlines used, and a cost comparison for your trip.
3. Call two airlines or visit their Web sites and request that they send you information about their frequent-flyer bonus travel program.
4. Call two airlines and ask what kinds of special meals are available. You may use the Internet for research for this activity.
5. Go to a library and look at the travel book section for books by Birnbaum, Mobil, Frommer, Fodor, Michelin, or others. Select a city you would like to visit. Then select two hotels or motels that appeal to you. Also select three restaurants where you would like to eat. Explain why you made your selections.
6. Select two cities which are in different states about 500 miles apart. Call two auto-rental agencies or visit their Web sites and inquire about renting a car for a trip between the two cities. The trip should take a week. You have not decided if you want an economy car or a midsize car. You are going to leave the car in the second city. What are the charges? Remember, you must be concerned with drop-off charges, mileage charges, gasoline charges, and insurance fees. Explain why you made your final selection.
7. Get a passport application and complete it. If you do not currently have a passport, you might actually apply for one. You may use the Internet for this activity.
8. Prepare a detailed itinerary for a three-day trip to a city of your choice. Contact several airlines to determine the best schedule and fare. Contact several car-rental agencies to compare rental costs. Select a hotel that is a member of a national chain. Determine if there is a limousine service to the hotel from the airport. After deciding on the hotel, inquire about room costs and the reservation cancellation policy. Keyboard

a complete itinerary, including dates, times, locations, hotel and rental-car rates, telephone numbers, and method of transportation. You may use the Internet for research for this activity.

PROJECTS

Project 15

Complete the following travel expense report from the receipts. If needed, add rows to the table.

Travel Expense Report						
Date	City	Lodging	Food	Tips	Taxi	Daily Total
Total Amount to Be Reimbursed						
Date			Traveler's Signature			
Date			Supervisor's Signature			

8230 87235 23789 2076
VISA
Lucy R. Castle
3 Nights
$295
Inns of Tomorrow, Tampa, FL 33606
7/27/XX

8230 87235 23789 2076
VISA
Lucy R. Castle
Food $23.95, Tip $4
The Sea's Delight, Tampa, FL 33607
7/26/XX

8230 87235 23789 2076
VISA
Lucy R. Castle
Food $27, Tip $5.50
Hawaii at Night, Tampa, FL 33607
7/24/XX

8230 87235 23789 2076
VISA
Lucy R. Castle
Food $27, Tip $4
Pedro's Best, Tampa, FL 33607
7/25/XX

Taxi Receipt
$22
7/25/XX

Lunch at a Fast-Food Restaurant $4.25
Tampa
I forgot to get a receipt.
7/25/XX

Project 16

Prepare the following itinerary.

> Mary, I am going to be traveling to Denver on May 1 (United Airlines flight #478), which leaves at 10:01 A.M. It arrives at 12.33 P.M. I will be staying at the Sheraton Convention Center (Confirmation #7182409). I will then fly to San Francisco on American Airlines (flight #326) and will stay three nights at the Mark Hopkins Hotel. The flight leaves Denver at 9:02 A.M. and arrives in San Francisco at 11:17 A.M. The confirmation number at the Mark Hopkins is #221684. After two nights in Denver and three nights in San Francisco, I will be returning on United's 8:07 A.M. flight (#602), arriving at Chicago O'Hare at 3:59 P.M.

HUMAN RELATIONS SKILL DEVELOPMENT

HR 8-1 Scents

Men and women who wear perfume, cologne, aftershave, scented hair care products, or scented cosmetics can offend others without realizing it. Fragrances should be light enough that they do not disturb other workers. Working in close proximity to others and in closed or windowless offices can compound the problem of a heavy fragrance. In addition, people with allergies can become physically ill from breathing strong scents. After using a product for a period of time, the user becomes less sensitive to the smell and may not be aware that the scent is disturbing to others.

- Ask a friend to honestly tell you if your fragrances can be smelled by a person near you. Are your fragrances too heavy or offensive?
- How would you tell a co-worker diplomatically that you find a scent too heavy?

HR 8-2 Restoring an Injured Relationship

Getting along with other workers is important, but a relationship can be damaged by a misunderstanding or insensitivity to a situation. If a friendship existed and then cooled because of a problem, the problem must be solved before the friendship can continue. Unfortunately, one person may not be aware of what caused the problem, and getting the other person to talk about the problem may be difficult. To begin solving the problem, remove yourself from the office environment. Suggest meeting for lunch, going for a walk at lunch, or meeting after work to talk. Start by saying that you would like to continue your friendship and explain that you are not aware of what created the problem. Repairing a damaged relationship can take time, but it can be worth the effort.

- Have you lost a friendship?
- Discuss a friendship that you lost.
- How would you restore a damaged relationship with your supervisor?
- If your co-worker is not interested in remaining friends, how would you handle the day-to-day work situation?

SITUATIONS

How would you handle the following situations?

- **S 8-1** Your employer asks you to go to the airport to pick up Ms. Kahn, whom you have never met.
- **S 8-2** Your supervisor is attending a business meeting in Cheyenne, Wyoming, and immediately needs a folder that she did not take with her on the trip.
- **S 8-3** Your employer is on the third day of a 14-day trip. You have just received a telephone call informing you that the hotel for day 12 has been destroyed by fire.

PUNCTUATION REVIEW

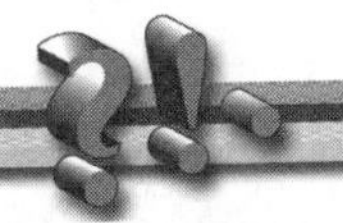

Punctuate each of the following sentences.

1. He wore a dark blue suit and he impressed the manager
2. The budget office estimated that because of the new regulations the cost of maintaining the equipment would be very expensive
3. Rodney who has a pleasing personality worked in a small office on the 10th floor
4. Because most persons who receive outplacement counseling are anxious to continue working they actively search for jobs
5. Penny has a large office with an impressive view of the city and a private elevator
6. At one time my mentor was Ted Lincoln the manager
7. With all of their credentials the applicants also have many shortcomings that must be considered
8. William I believe received the outstanding employee award at last years ceremony

9. Yes I saw the results of the advertising campaign
10. If business takes a hands off attitude the problem will not be solved by next June said the Mayor
11. The reigning theory about career development was discussed at the last board meeting and Samuel said lets stop talking and implement it
12. Such a policy would create what many of our departments drastically need a think tank
13. In our view Thomas Costello took the initiative developed the project and brought it to a successful conclusion
14. The petroleum company which is incorporated in Kentucky transferred the stock to three members of the board of directors
15. Joseph Peerless the witness stated I have never seen a corporation run with such a lack of courtesy

CD ASSIGNMENTS

CD Assignment 8-1

Open the file CD8-1_MG on your Student CD and follow the instructions to complete the job. You will also need the file CD8TF, which is on your Student CD.

CD Assignment 8-2

Open the file CD8-2_LD on your Student CD and follow the instructions to complete the job. You will also need the file CD8TF, which is on your Student CD.

CD Assignment 8-3

Open the file CD8-3_JL on your Student CD and follow the instructions to complete the job. You will also need the file CD8TF, which is on your Student CD.

Terminology of Business and E-Commerce

9

Objectives

After studying this chapter, you should be able to

1. Explain the impact of globalization of business.
2. Explain e-commerce.
3. Explain market systems.
4. Explain the four types of business ownership.
5. Define and use basic business terms.
6. Define and use basic financial terms.
7. Define and use basic legal terms.
8. Define and use basic accounting terms.
9. Define and use basic real estate terms.
10. Read and use a stock listing.

INTRODUCTION

If you hope to advance to a job with greater responsibilities, it is essential that you understand the business and economic terms used to describe the American economic system. Business and economic terms are not only important in the business world but also have become an integral part of modern society. An understanding of these terms, therefore, will help you be successful in your personal life as well as in your professional career. While the professional terms used in a real estate office are quite different from the specialized terms used in a medical office, both offices use the same language for general business activities. In this chapter, you will review standard economic and business terms used by many offices, as well as specialized professional terms used in several types of businesses. Mastering the language of business will improve your ability to work in any office.

The Globalization of Business

The *globalization* of the world economy has created a new business culture and has changed businesses across the country. The rise of a global economy is the result of many political, technological, social, and economic factors. These include the lowering of trade barriers between nations, privatization of many nations' economies through the encouragement of private businesses, and an increase in telecommunications technologies such as the Internet. Business decisions made in Europe or Asia can affect the availability of supplies and raw materials available to your business, can provide competition to your company, or can open new markets for your employer's product. Today, businesses are no longer limited to one locality and often operate in many countries.

HINT

Globalization has changed the business world.

Business globalization requires an interaction of people from numerous cultural backgrounds. Cultural diversity and its implications on business are discussed in Chapter 13, Tips of the Trade.

E-Commerce/E-Business and the Internet

The Internet provides an electronic marketplace where buyers and sellers meet to conduct business. This electronic marketplace has flourished and grown immensely in the last few years and, while it is expected to undergo changes, it will continue to grow in the future. Electronic commerce (*e-commerce*) is the selling and buying of goods and services using the Internet and is changing the way business is conducted in this country and globally. E-commerce has become very successful in the sale of retail goods and services throughout the country. *Amazon.com*, *eBay.com*, and *Travelocity.com* are notable Internet pioneers in electronic commerce.

Although e-commerce is still in its early stages of development, several types of e-commerce have developed.

Business-to-Consumer Transactions

Business-to-consumer (B2C) transactions are the selling of products or services between business and the consumer using the Internet. E-commerce, which is also known as e-business, has advantages for both the buyer and the seller. From the seller's viewpoint, e-commerce is an efficient way to present a business's goods and services to a large group of buyers. The cost to sell an item can be very low. Buyers appreciate the twenty-four-hour-a-day, seven-day-a-week (often called 24/7) easy access to a large selection of items. Purchases can be completed from the comfort of one's home or office and payment can be made using a credit card, taking only a few minutes. B2C Web sites may combine products from many vendors in one location for easy consumer access. Once the consumer has purchased one product, Web links can be established to encourage the consumer to purchase additional products. In addition to offering online buying, many online merchants enhance the Internet experience by supporting chat boards, where customers have electronic real-time conversations to ask questions, discuss issues, or review products. Many Internet business Web sites also provide FAQ (Frequently Asked Questions), Q&A (Questions and Answers), support systems, and email customer support.

E-commerce has empowered the purchaser in ways unthought of several years ago. Buyers use Web sites to obtain a wide array of product and service information. These might include product reviews from other users, information about financing the product, information from manufacturers' Web sites, and government-sponsored sites which contain safety information Purchasers can easily check specifications and prices from competitors to determine the best item and price for their needs. Both purchasers and retailers appreciate the ability to use the Web to obtain answers to questions and other public feedback.

Many traditional businesses are moving to e-commerce, as the Internet has become a growing segment of today's technology-driven society. Traditional companies are rethinking their business practices to compete in a market in which communication and the purchase of products are accomplished over the Internet. There are many opportunities but also pitfalls for companies that enter the e-commerce arena. Companies that are innovative and successful will be the e-commerce leaders of the future. E-commerce requires a redesign of product marketing and distribution. Moreover, e-commerce can alter an enterprise's entire sales approach and can dramatically change its records management process. In addition, business and computer security is very important to the conduct of e-commerce, to protect both a business's information and the consumer's privacy.

Business-to-Business Purchases

Government and private industry are joining the private consumer in purchasing through the Internet. This type of e-commerce has become known as business-to-business, also referred to as Business 2 Business (B2B). B2B is the selling of products or services between businesses using the Internet. Businesses buy products, which they in turn use to build their own products, and then sell the products to another business or to the consumer. E-commerce can help automate the production and distribution system for a company. In addition, B2B has the potential to decrease costs and increase revenue. Furthermore, B2B has created partners who both profit from the partnership and provide additional services to the customer. An example of a B2B partnership is an electronic catalog that sells products from many vendors. With this service, the customer can search the electronic catalog and view products from several vendors according to the item type, cost, and feature.

Internet Auctions

Online auctioning is another sales opportunity for the vendor to provide a product to the purchaser, and many companies, such as eBay, have embraced this opportunity. In an online auction, the highest bidder purchases products or services. The online marketplace auction has been very successful.

Global E-Commerce

E-commerce is a business without the restrictions of a building, a time, or a place. Web sites can be viewed wherever the Internet is available around the world. Use of the Internet has opened new foreign markets to American businesses for the selling and purchasing of products and services. These markets are now available twenty-four hours a day (24/7). Since the Web page presents the company's image to the viewer, many companies design their Web pages to increase sales and promote the company's objectives. Web sites for companies that wish to create an international business should be designed with a global audience perspective, so they can be easily understood and used by people and diverse cultures all over the world. Therefore, slang words, which may not be understood in different parts of the United States or in foreign nations, should not be used.

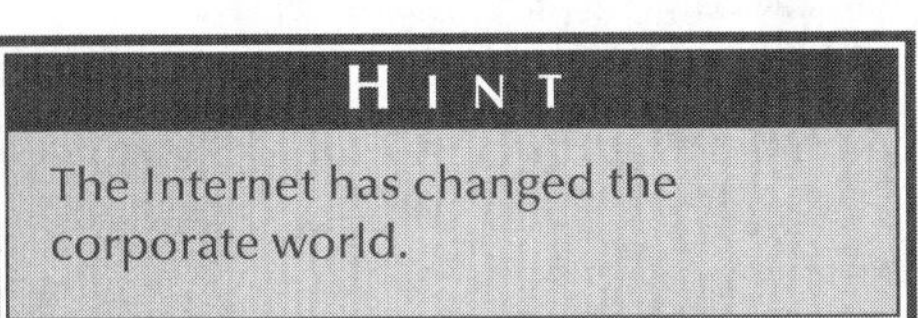

HINT
The Internet has changed the corporate world.

E-Government and the Internet

Governments at all levels have joined business in using the Internet to improve their services and to reach their clients efficiently. Government clients include both business and the general public.

Most businesses in the country interact with the government on several levels. Governments provide information that may be useful to the business, such as employment information, information about trends in the business's industry, and new research in the business's field. Governments now use the Internet for more than distribution of information about their services. However, the range of government services on the Internet can vary widely. Most businesses can now file taxes and reports with the local, state, or federal government using the Internet. The Internet can be a source of new opportunities for business, as many governments list their major purchase procurements on the Internet and invite businesses to submit proposals or bids. Businesses can apply for many government benefits or permits using the Internet. Governments post proposed regulations and legislation on the Internet prior to adoption. A wise business, therefore, regularly checks the Web sites of government agencies to be aware of current policies.

Sources of Business Information

Reading daily newspapers and business publications or their online services will help keep you informed of current events. A political or an economic event in another part of the country or in another part of the world may affect the business where you work. A change in economic conditions or new legislation could alter the business environment in which your employer functions, and could affect your job and the operation of your office.

Many offices subscribe to well-known business publications, such as *The Wall Street Journal,* which contain news about business ventures, stocks, taxes, politics, marketing, and other subjects that affect the business environment. Other important business publications include *Business Week, Fortune, Barron's,* and *Financial World.* In addition, there are many specialized services, such as Standard and Poor's and Moody's, which report on the stock, bond, and municipal markets. You should become familiar with these publications or their online services and skim them for information related to your business. If your office does not subscribe to the business newspapers or magazines that interest you, check the selection available at your library or purchase your own subscription.

Each industry also has specialized publications and newsletters that contain information directly related to that industry. These publications may be monthly, weekly, or daily; some are available over the Internet or can be sent via email. Examples of these specialized publications are *Journal of Accountancy, Journal of Taxation, Accounting Review, Administrative Management, Telecommunications Reports, Communications Daily, Satellite News,* and *Best's Insurance Reports.* These publications are excellent sources of news about the industry specified. By reading specialized publications and newsletters, you will be well informed about events in your field.

Television provides up-to-date business and financial information by broadcasting programs about financial and business issues. There are full-time financial news services, such as CNBC which is distributed by cable and by satellite television, as well as daily business programs, such as *Nightly Business Report,* and weekly financial programs, such as *Wall Street Week.*

Also, the Internet is an up-to-date reference for business information. Many business publications, newspapers, cable television networks, and financial television programs have created their own Web sites to extend their services to their readers and viewers. Additionally, many financial institutions, mutual fund companies, and brokerage firms have established Web sites that contain business information. Data can be obtained from newsletters, newsgroups, and emails, as well as individual company Web sites. Always bookmark interesting Web sites and click on the links from site to site to expand your knowledge of a specific topic.

Sample Web sites for general business information

CNBC	*www.moneycentral.msn.com/investor/home.asp*
Merrill Lynch	*www.ml.com*
SalomonSmithBarney	*www.salomonsmithbarney.com*
Yahoo	*www.yahoo.com*

Sample Web sites for information about a specific company

3M	*www.3M.com*
Citigroup	*www.citigroup.com*
General Motors	*www.gm.com/company/investor_information/*
Kodak	*www.kodak.com*
Palm, Inc.	*www.palm.com*
Unisys	*www.unisys.com*
Zurich Financial Services	*www.zurich.com*

Sample list of business publications

- *Barron's*
- *Business Week*
- *Business Month*
- *Columbia Journal of World Business*
- *Commerce America*
- *Credit and Financial Management*
- Daily business sections of newspapers
- *Forbes*
- *Fortune*
- *Harvard Business Review*

- *High Technology Business*
- *Industrial and Labor Relations Review*
- *Money*
- *Nation's Business*
- *The Wall Street Journal*

Economics

Economics is the study of how a community manages its income, expenditures, labor, and natural resources. The production, distribution, and consumption of goods and services are all included in the study of economics. No person, business, or government can produce or purchase everything it needs or desires. People and organizations continually make choices about how to spend their money. As individuals, we often have to choose whether to spend our money going to a movie, eating in a restaurant, or buying clothes. In the same sense, each business must make a choice concerning allocation of its resources of money, people, and raw materials. For example, to earn a greater profit, should a business continue production of an old item (and risk being overtaken by competitors with new products), or should it invest its money in the production of a new product? As this question implies, economic decisions can be very complex with far-reaching results.

HINT

Economics is the study of how a community manages its income, expenditures, labor, and natural resources.

Market Systems

One aspect of economics is the *market system.* A market occurs when buyers and sellers exchange goods or services for money. In economic terms, a market is not simply one store but includes the entire community.

We live in a *free-market system* where people are free to go into whatever type of business they choose. A business tries to attract consumers to the business's products or services, so the owners of the business will earn a profit. Profit is the difference between the cost to manufacture an item and the price for which it is sold.

In a free-market system, businesses are free to set the price of any product or service they sell. Consumers are free to choose from any product or service available in the market. A sale occurs when a consumer is willing to buy an item at the same price at which the business is willing to sell it.

Consumers have a major role in deciding the type of products manufactured and their selling price. People will not purchase goods or services if they do not need or want them or if the price is higher than they are willing to pay. While a manufacturer chooses to make a product in the hope that it can be sold for a profit, the consumer has the final choice—deciding whether to purchase or not to purchase.

When a new product is developed, consumers have no knowledge of the item. Marketing involves the selling of goods and services and often uses advertising to influence consumers to purchase a product. Advertising the product creates demand. In many cases, consumers do not know that they want a product unless advertising convinces them that the product is desirable.

The price of most new products is very high because of the expense of developing and producing only a limited number of items. As larger numbers are produced through mass production, the price of the products can be reduced. As larger numbers of a product become available, and as more people know about it through marketing, more people will want to purchase it.

Since the business owner, or *entrepreneur,* is in business to make a profit, the owner has an incentive to produce items efficiently in response to consumer demand. The more efficiently the product is produced, the greater the potential profit. *Competition* limits the profit of a company, because it involves rivalry between companies selling the same products or offering similar services. Competition regulates the price that can be charged for a product or service. The producer or retailer can raise the selling price of a product when there is a lack of competition or when the limited quantity of a product is insufficient to meet consumer demand. If a consumer can find the same item at a lower cost, the consumer will purchase it at the lower cost. The entrepreneur who is the most efficient producer or retailer of a product or service can lower the selling price and attract more customers. Selling more of the item can then increase profits.

The free-market system encourages *specialization,* which results in the most efficient use of time and resources. Specialization is producing one particular item or delivering one type of service. Companies specialize in those products that are most profitable for them.

The government does not directly control the economy in a free-market system. A free-market system, however, does not mean a total absence of a government role in the nation's economy. Governments may regulate some industries, such as requiring the treatment of hazardous waste material or prohibiting the sale of dangerous toys to children. The government's ability to tax businesses and the government's own spending have a major effect on the nation's economy. The extent of government regulation, tax policies, and spending levels are major political and economic issues in our society.

Business provides goods and services for the consumer to purchase. The income received from the sale of these goods and services allows a business to pay workers a salary. Workers spend the salaries for food, shelter, clothing, and other products. This spending, in turn, produces other jobs and the money continues to flow through the economic system. This process is called the *circular flow of goods and services.* If jobs are terminated, workers do not receive a salary. Consequently, their ability to purchase goods and services must decrease. This change in spending patterns is felt throughout the business community.

Types of Business Organizations

Several types of business ownership have developed to meet the financial and management requirements of different-size businesses. Business ownership can be divided into four categories: sole proprietorship, partnership, corporation, and cooperative.

> **HINT**
> Types of business organizations include sole proprietorship, partnership, corporation, and cooperative.

Sole Proprietorship

A *sole proprietorship* is a business owned by one individual. The owner provides all of the money for the investment in the business and receives all of the profits. The owner manages the business, makes all of the policy decisions, and is personally responsible for all of the business's debts. If the business has financial difficulties, the owner can be required to sell personal property to pay the debts. An example of a sole proprietorship is a small business such as a photographer's studio, a farm, an accountant's office, or a business operated from a home.

Partnership

A *partnership* is a business owned by at least two people. While the decisions of the business are made by the partners, each partner may have an area of expertise for which that partner is responsible. Ownership in the business may or may not be equally divided. Ownership and profits are divided according to an agreement between the partners. Each partner, however, is legally responsible for the debts of the business and the promises of the other partners. Therefore, one partner may be forced to pay the business debts of other partners. Examples of a partnership include a restaurant, an attorney's office, and a supply store. It may be difficult for a consumer to know whether a business is a sole proprietorship or a partnership.

Corporation

A *corporation* is a business which is created under state law and is a legal entity separate from its owners. Ownership in the corporation is represented by shares of stock. When a person purchases shares of stock, a *stock certificate* is issued. The certificate states how many shares of stock were purchased. The stockholder can sell the stock to another individual at any time without the consent of the corporation. Stocks are often purchased through stock exchanges, such as the New York Stock Exchange or the American Stock Exchange. Stockholders have no personal liability in the business. If a corporation fails, the stockholders lose only their investment. Their personal money is never used to pay the debts of the business.

People usually buy shares of stock in a company because they expect the company to grow and to earn a profit. The profit can be reinvested in the business or it can be returned to the stockholders in the form of a dividend. A *dividend* is similar to the interest you earn from a savings account at a bank—except that bank interest is guaranteed and a stock dividend depends on the company making a profit. Stockholders purchase stock with the expectation that the stock will increase in value or that dividends will be earned. A corporation pays taxes on its profits, and the stockholders pay taxes on the portion of the profits that they receive. IBM, General Motors, and ExxonMobil are all corporations, but corporations are not limited to large companies.

The stockholders control the corporation by selecting the *board of directors,* which operates the company. The board of directors manages the corporation and appoints the officers who run the company. The size of the board of directors varies. Generally, corporations have an annual meeting, where stockholders vote on policy decisions. Each share of stock represents one vote. Stockholders who do not attend the annual meeting are asked to sign a document called a proxy, which gives written authorization for another person to vote on the issues.

There are two types of stock—*common stock* and *preferred stock.* Owners of preferred stock have preference over owners of common stock when a dividend is declared. A company must pay the owners of preferred stock their dividends before the owners of common stock receive their dividends. Owners of preferred stock usually receive a fixed rate of dividends, while owners of common stock do not receive dividends at a fixed rate. If a company does not have enough income to pay dividends to the owners of both preferred and common stock, the owners of common stock will not receive a dividend.

Cooperative

A *cooperative* is a business that is owned by its members. The members are not liable for the debts of the business, but the profits are returned to the members. The cooperative is managed by a board of directors elected by members of the cooperative. An example of a cooperative is a food cooperative, which provides low-cost food to its members.

Bonds and Treasury Securities

Corporations raise money by selling shares of stock which represent ownership in the companies and which include the potential of sharing in the future profits of the corporations. Private corporations—as well as the federal, state, and local governments—often borrow money by selling bonds to investors. *Bonds* are loans made by individuals or financial institutions and do not represent ownership or a potential share in future profits. Repayment of a bond is the first obligation of a corporation, and bond payments must be made before any dividends or profits are distributed to shareholders.

Bonds are issued with a maturity date, which may be one year, ten years, or even thirty years in the future. The bondholder (person who purchased the bond) receives interest payments each year until the bond maturity date. Most bonds pay a fixed rate of interest. At the *maturity date,* the company pays back (redeems) the amount of the loan, which is the face value (principal) of the bond certificate. For example, a person may purchase a bond with a face value of $1,000, paying 5 percent, and with a maturity date ten years in the future. Each year for the next ten years, the bondholder will receive a check for $50 as interest from the company. At the end of the ten-year period, the company will redeem the bond and the bondholder receives a check for $1,000.

Bonds can be bought or sold at any time before the maturity date without the approval of the company. Older bonds can often be purchased for costs either above or below the face value. If a bond is paying an interest rate higher than that which can be obtained through the purchase of a new bond, people are willing to pay a higher price, a *premium*, to obtain the higher income. However, if the bond is paying an interest rate less than that which can be obtained through the purchase of a new bond, the bond will sell at a *discount* of the face value. Bonds selling at a discount will be redeemed at full face value if held to maturity.

Corporate bonds are certificates issued by corporations, and they are usually issued in $1,000 denominations. Investment bankers and security agencies sell these bonds to their clients. Bonds represent a company's promise to pay interest to the bondholder. The stronger the financial condition of the company, the better chance the bondholder has of receiving repayment of the money. The financial strength of many companies is rated by independent companies, such as Moody's or Standard and Poor's.

When a city, state, or local government issues a bond, it is called a *municipal bond*. Interest income from municipal bonds is normally not taxed by the federal government or by the government of the state in which the bond is issued. People in high tax brackets have an incentive to purchase municipal bonds, since the interest income is free of most income taxes.

One way the U.S. government meets its financial needs is through the sale of government securities. Treasury securities may be purchased by individuals or businesses directly from the twelve Federal Reserve banks, the Bureau of Public Debt in Washington, commercial banks, or other financial institutions or via the Internet. Purchases made through commercial banks and other financial institutions usually include a fee in addition to the cost of the security. Additional information about government securities can be found at the Web site *www.savingsbonds.gov/*.

Treasury securities are very safe investments, since both the bonds and the interest to be paid on government securities are backed by the United States government. There is an active market for previously issued securities, and they are easily purchased or sold on the open market. Interest earned from Treasury securities is exempted from state and local income taxes. Payment of federal income tax on the earning of several of the Treasury notes and bonds can be deferred until the security is redeemed.

Types of government securities

- *Treasury bills* (T-bills) are issued by the U.S. Treasury for thirteen weeks, twenty-six weeks, or one year. Treasury bills are sold at a discount from the face value, and the purchaser receives the face value upon maturity. The minimum amount of purchase has a face value of $1,000 and bills are sold in multiples of $1,000.
- *Treasury notes* are similar to T-bills in that they also require a minimum purchase of $1,000. Treasury notes are issued for two, five, and ten years. Notes are sold near face value and the purchaser receives interest every six months. Two types of notes are available, one that pays a fixed rate of interest and another that is indexed with the rate of inflation.
- *Treasury bonds* are issued for thirty years. Bonds may be redeemed by the government before the maturity date, and they are sold with a minimum purchase of $1,000. The Treasury suspended the sale of new bonds in October 2001 but could resume sales of these securities at any time.

Terminology in the World of Business

As an administrative assistant, you will be expected to be familiar with the following business terminology used in an office. Specialized terminology used in finance, law, real estate, and accounting offices follows these general business terms.

General Business Terms

- An *annual report* is a report issued by a corporation each year that reviews the corporation's business activities and financial statements for the year and discusses its future expectations.
- *Business forecasting* provides projections of a business's future. Business forecasting is used to plan budgets, revenues, and expenses under a variety of conditions. Computers and spreadsheet programs are widely used in business forecasting.
- The *Consumer Price Index (CPI)* is an index calculated monthly by the U.S. government showing the change in the prices of a fixed group of consumer goods and services.
- *Deflation* is a general decrease in the price of goods and services and is the opposite of inflation.
- *Depreciation* is the gradual decrease in the value of an item. The value of office equipment, such as computers, depreciates as the item ages.
- *Depression* is a very low point in a nation's economy when there is high unemployment and a decrease in the purchasing of goods and services. A depression is much worse than a recession.
- A *dot com company* is one of the many companies that have been created specifically to provide services via the Internet. The term *dot com* comes from Internet addresses for commercial organizations which end in ".com." Some of these companies actually have ".com" as part of their name.
- A *fiscal year* is a twelve-month calendar period used for budgeting and planning purposes. For the federal government, a fiscal year begins on October 1 and ends the next September 30. State and local governments usually run on a July 1 to June 30 fiscal year or on an October 1 to September 30 fiscal year. A private business can begin its fiscal year with any month, although most begin with January, April, July, or October. A fiscal year usually is referred to by the year that the cycle ends. For example, the U.S. government's fiscal year 2007 (FY 07) begins October 1, 2006, and ends September 30, 2007. Businesses report their earnings and file their tax returns based on their fiscal year.
- The *Gross National Product (GNP)* is the total value of all goods and services produced by a country in one year. GNP is an index used to compare the size of a country's economy over a period of years or to compare one country's total output with another country's total output.
- *Inflation* is a general increase in the price of goods and services. An example of inflation is a house which cost $50,000 twenty years ago which now sells for $150,000. It is the same house, but it now takes many more dollars to purchase it. If wages have risen at the same inflation rate as houses, then houses remain affordable even if the price is three times what it was twenty years ago.
- *Liquidating* means converting securities (stocks or bonds) to cash.
- A *monopoly* exists when there is only one supplier of a good or service or one supplier is so large that it can control the market. In the United States, monopolies are permitted only where government policy determines that a single provider is in the public interest. Many industries which were formerly monopolies, such as telephone or electric services, have been deregulated by the government and the consumer now has many choices in purchasing these services.
- The *Producer Price Index (PPI)* is an index calculated monthly by the U.S. government showing the change in prices of farm products, processed foods, and industrial products.
- A *quarter* is one of four parts of the business fiscal year. Most businesses review their financial status at the end of each quarter of their fiscal year. Each of the four quarters of the business year contains three months. The first quarter is the first three months of the fiscal year, while the fourth (or last) quarter is the final three months of the fiscal year. Financial activity often increases near the end of a quarter as businesses try to complete transactions for inclusion in their financial reports. At the end of the quarter,

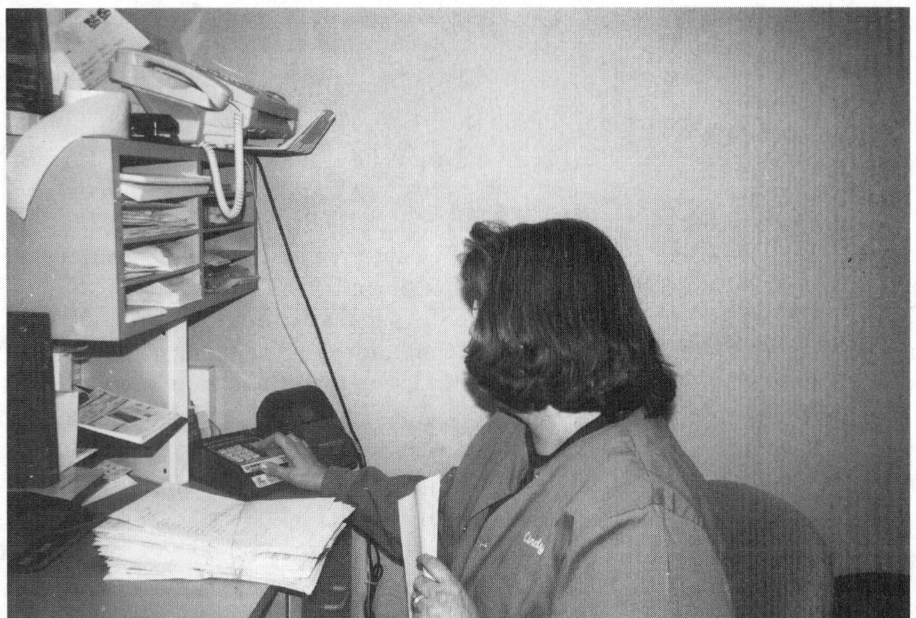

FIGURE 9-1 An employee processing a charge using a credit card approval machine.

corporations may issue quarterly reports to their shareholders which report the business activities during the period.

- A *recession* is a slowdown in economic activity, which is often accompanied by a reduction in sales, profits, and employment.
- *Retained earnings* are the funds remaining after paying taxes and dividends.

Terms Used in Financial Institutions

- A *bear market* is the time period during which the price of stocks decline.
- The *Big Board* is an informal term used to refer to the New York Stock Exchange.
- *Blue-chip* is an informal term for the common stock of a company that is known for long-term, high-quality financial performance. Blue-chip stocks are generally thought of as investments with low risk.
- A *broker* is a person (an agent) who handles the sale or purchase of securities, including stocks, bonds, mutual funds, insurance, or annuities.
- A *bull market* is the time period during which the price of stocks rise.
- A *call provision* is a clause in a bond agreement which allows the bond's issuer to redeem (call) the bond prior to the maturity date by purchasing the bond from its owner.
- A *certificate of deposit (CD)* relates to a specific type of account in a bank or another financial institution. A CD is an investment for a fixed term and pays a higher rate of interest than a regular interest account. Usually the interest is guaranteed during the term of the CD.
- A *commission* is a broker's fee for buying or selling a security for a client. The commission can be a fixed fee or a percentage of the security's purchase or selling price.
- The *Dow Jones Industrial Average* is the most common benchmark used for comparing the price level of common stocks on the New York Stock Exchange. The Dow Jones Company, publisher of *The Wall Street Journal,* calculates the value of a stock portfolio of thirty large companies. Changes in the stocks are compared on a daily basis. The Dow Jones Industrial Average, often referred to as the Dow Jones Average (or the Dow), is only one of many averages used to track the advances and declines of the stock market. Other averages exist for specific areas, such as banking stocks or transportation stocks. There

are also averages calculated for many other types of securities, such as international stocks, bonds, and many other financial securities.

- *Electronic trading* or *online trading* permits a person to establish an account with a broker and then buy and sell stocks, bonds, and other securities using a computer.
- An *individual retirement account (IRA)* is an account permitted by the federal government to encourage people to save money for retirement. There are two types of IRA accounts, and both types allow people to earn income on their investments in the IRA account without paying taxes each year. Money invested in a traditional IRA can be deducted from a person's gross income for income tax purposes, and payment of taxes on income earned in the IRA account is delayed until the person withdraws the money, usually at retirement. In a *Roth IRA,* taxes are paid on the funds which are placed in the Roth IRA, but no taxes are paid on the earnings while they are in the IRA account or when they are withdrawn. An IRA must be established with an approved financial institution and can be invested in a variety of securities, including CDs, stocks, bonds, and mutual funds.
- *Initial public offering (IPO)* refers to a new stock issue. People buy stock in start-up companies in hopes of making great profit. Investing in an IPO is very risky, however, as many new companies fail and investors can lose all of their money.
- *Junk bonds* are bonds that pay a high rate of interest because of a low credit rating that reflects a higher risk of default.
- The *margin* is the amount of money a customer puts down toward the purchase price when buying a security on credit. The broker loans the remainder of the purchase price.
- A *market order* is an order to buy or sell a security (stock or bond) at the best price available when the order reaches the Stock Exchange floor.
- The *market price* is the last price at which a security (stock or bond) was bought or sold.
- The *maturity date* (or *redemption date*) is the date that the bond issuer will pay the principal (face value) of the bond.
- *Mutual funds* are investments in which a financial firm purchases stocks or bonds from many organizations, places the stocks or bonds in a fund, and then sells shares in the fund to the public. The goal of a mutual fund is to diversify investment and, therefore, reduce client risk. Mutual funds often specialize in the types of securities they purchase or in their investment objectives.
- *NASDAQ* is an electronic stock market with over 4,500 companies listed. Many of the companies listed are leaders in the technology or financial service fields.
- An *odd lot* is an order for the purchase of stock in other than 100-share units.
- A *portfolio* is a group of securities owned by a person or a company.
- The *price-earnings ratio (PE)* is the ratio between the market price of a stock and its earnings per share. A stock that sells for $50 a share and earns $2 a share each year has a PE of 25.
- A *prospectus* is a brochure describing securities offered for sale. The Securities and Exchange Commission requires that a purchaser be supplied with a prospectus before a security is purchased.
- A *round lot* is a stock bought or sold in 100-share units.
- The *Securities and Exchange Commission (SEC)* is the agency of the U.S. government that regulates the sale of stocks and bonds. It is the Securities and Exchange Commission's responsibility to ensure that the public is provided truthful information about securities.
- A *speculator* is a person who assumes a large risk in anticipation of receiving a high profit.
- A *stock exchange* is a place where stocks and bonds are traded. Examples of stock exchanges include the New York, American, Philadelphia, Pacific, Tokyo, and Toronto Stock Exchanges. Brokerage firms that are members of a stock exchange are referred to as having a seat on a stock exchange.
- In a *stock split,* a company issues additional shares of stock to its stockholders. For example, a company may double the number of shares (a two-for-one split). Each stockholder

will then own twice as many shares as before the split. Each share, however, will sell for approximately half the previous value. Companies may split the stock in the hope that a stock selling at a lower price will be attractive to more investors. In a reverse split, a company may reduce the number of shares of a stock owned by all stockholders by issuing new stock for each two or three shares previously issued. In a one-for-two reverse split, the new share is worth approximately twice the value of the old share.

- A *stop order* is an order to buy or sell a stock when its price reaches a predetermined level.
- The *yield* is a return on an investment. The yield is usually referred to as a percentage of the purchase price.

There are many sites on the Internet where you can obtain definitions of additional financial terms. Several of these are

www.finance-glossary.com/pages/home.htm
www.forbes.com/tools/glossary/index.jhtml
www.bankrate.com/smm/defhome.asp

How to Read a Stock Listing

Many people own securities, either directly through ownership of stocks and bonds, through the ownership of a mutual fund, or indirectly through participation in a company retirement plan. Following the stock market is easy since most newspapers carry stock quotations. Some newspapers print information on only those stocks of local interest or the ten most active stocks of the day, while other newspapers carry several pages of information about stocks. Stock tables are read beginning with the left column.

52-Week High	The highest price for the stock during the prior 52 weeks
52-Week Low	The lowest price for the stock during the prior 52 weeks
Stock	The name of the stock, which is abbreviated
Sym	A short code assigned to the stock
Div	The amount of the dividend paid by the company for each share stock for the past year
Yld.	The yield on the stock is the dividend expressed as a percentage of the stock price
PE	The price-earnings ratio of the stock is the ratio between the market price of the stock and its earnings per share
Sales	The number of shares sold (in hundreds) during the day
High	The highest price for the stock for that day
Low	The lowest price paid for the stock for that day
Last	The price of the stock when the stock exchange closed for that day
Chg.	The change in price from the prior day's closing price

Prices for stocks are reported to the nearest cent. Newspapers will usually report a stock trade of $45.34 as either 45.34 or 45^{34}.

52-Week							Sales				
High	Low	Stock	Sym	Div	Yld.	PE	100s	High	Low	Last	Chg.
42.34	38	NorW	NXC	4.00	10.3	15	189	39	38.11	39	−.89
117	101	Otell	OWT	4.5	4.5	20	256	112	111	11	+1.34
32.46	19	PlaDa	PRP	2.8	2.8	18	123	31	30.12	31.35	

FIGURE 9-2 A stock table.

Legal Terms

The following legal terms are commonly used in the workplace:

- *Affidavit:* a statement in writing made under oath, usually given before a notary or a judicial officer authorized to administer oaths
- *Appellate court:* a higher court that reviews a lower court's decision
- *Contributory negligence:* failure to do what was wise and reasonable
- *Decree:* an order of the court
- *Defendant:* the person against whom a suit or complaint is brought
- *Felony:* a grave crime punishable by heavy penalties
- *Habeas corpus:* a *writ* (written order) requiring that a person be brought before a judge before being held
- *Injunction:* an order issued by a court requiring someone to do or refrain from doing a particular act
- *Misdemeanor:* a crime less severe than a felony
- *Perjury:* swearing that something is true while knowing it is false
- *Plaintiff:* the person who brings a suit or complaint
- *Tort:* a legal wrong that prompts a civil lawsuit

There are many Internet sites that provide definitions of legal terms. Some sites are sponsored by governments or courts; other sites are sponsored by nonprofit agencies or commercial organizations. Sample sites where you can find further definitions of legal terms are

www.coloradodivorceinfo.com/legalterms.htm
www.courts.state.ny.us/lawlibraries/glossary.shtml
www.jud.state.ct.us/legalterms.htm
www.usdoj.gov/usao/eousa/kidspage/text/glossary.html

Real Estate Terms

The following real estate terms are commonly used in the workplace:

- *Appraisal:* an estimate of the value of an item, a building, or property
- *Assessment:* a charge by the government against real estate to cover improvements such as a sewer; the assessment is usually a percentage of the appraised value of the property
- *Deed:* a written form that transfers property from one owner to a new owner
- *Domicile:* the place where a person has a permanent residence
- *Easement:* one person's right to use or pass through another person's property
- *Encroachment:* property that trespasses on another person's property
- *Escrow:* a deed or money given to a third party to hold until an obligation is fulfilled; an example of escrow is sending the homeowner's insurance payment or real estate taxes to the mortgage company to hold until the payment is due
- *Foreclosure:* the removal of the right to continue paying the mortgage and owning the property
- *Mortgage:* a contract, usually on a house or real estate, specifying that a sum of money will be paid periodically for the repayment of a loan

There are many Internet sites that provide definitions of real estate terms. Sample sites where you can find further definitions of real estate terms are

content.realestateabc.com/glossary
www.real-estate-for-sale.net/glossary

Accounting Terms

The following accounting terms are commonly used in the workplace:

- *Account:* a form that separates business transactions into similar groups
- *Asset:* anything that a business owns; assets include buildings, cash, furniture, and equipment
- *Audit:* a verification of accounting records; an individual not affiliated with the company being audited usually performs an audit
- *Capital:* what the business is worth; capital is found by subtracting liabilities from assets
- *Credit:* an entry on the right side of an account ledger
- *Debit:* an entry on the left side of an account ledger
- *Ledger:* a group of accounts
- *Liability:* anything that a business owes; examples include mortgages, credit card charges, and auto loans
- *Petty cash:* an office cash fund for small expenses
- *Trial Balance:* shows that the debits and credits in the ledger are equal

There are many Internet sites that provide definitions of accounting terms. Sample sites where you can find further definitions of accounting terms are

www.globalbusinessresources.net/business_definitionsA-C.shtml
www.toolkit.cch.com/text/P06_1324.asp
www.your-small-business-accounting-advisor.com/accountingdictionary.html

FINANCIAL STATEMENTS

Income Statement and Balance Sheet

In your role as an office employee, you may be asked to read, interpret, and keyboard an income statement or a balance sheet. An *income statement* is a financial statement that lists the income and expenses of a business over a particular period of time, often a month or year. A *balance sheet* is a financial statement that lists the assets, liabilities, and capital of the business on a specific date.

Budgets

One of your duties may be to help prepare or keyboard a department or office budget. In a large company, departmental budgets may be prepared in addition to company budgets. A budget includes a dollar figure for each anticipated item of income and expense and is usually prepared a year or more in advance. Before budgets are adopted, top management must approve them. When developing a new budget, a company usually considers last year's expenses, any new initiatives that may be undertaken, and an increase in anticipated income and expenses. The development of computer spreadsheet packages have made budget preparations and revisions an easier task and permit budget forecasting many years in advance. The use of computer spreadsheets in the preparation of budgets was discussed in Chapter 5, Computers in the Office.

TAX FORMS

Taxes are a fact of life in every business. Most businesses must be responsible for both the collection of taxes from their customers and the payment of various taxes to federal and local governments. Businesses often collect sales and use taxes from customers and are responsible for

B & W Manufacturing **Balance Sheet** **December 31, XXXX**		
	Assets	
Cash	200,000	
Office Equipment	56,000	
Building	350,000	
Total Assets		$606,000
	Liabilities	
Accounting Receivable	75,000	
Notes Payable	30,000	
Accounts Payable	12,000	
FICA Tax Payable	2,800	
Federal Income Tax Payable	5,000	
Total Liabilities		124,800
	Capital	
B & W Manufacturing Capital		482,200
Total Liabilities and Capital		$606,000

FIGURE 9-3 A balance sheet.

L & K Manufacturing **Income Statement** **For Year Ended December 31, XXXX**		
Revenue		
Professional Fees Income		$150,780
Expenses		
Rent Expense	12,000	
Salary Expense	52,000	
Travel Expense	8,000	
Office Supplies	2,000	
Office Equipment	8,000	
Telephone Expense	1,000	
Electricity Expense	1,200	
Gasoline Expense	900	
Maintenance Expense	2,500	
Total Expenses		87,600
Net Income		$63,180

FIGURE 9-4 An income statement.

forwarding these funds to a government agency. Businesses also pay a variety of taxes based on their payroll and income. Business taxes are very complicated and the office employees should be aware of any tax collection or reporting within their area of responsibility. The federal government and many state governments encourage the submission of taxes electronically via the Internet.

Purchasing Department
Budget for XXXX

Projected Income (Budget Allocation)	
Base Operating Support	$800,000
Special Funds to Support Expansion Project	93,400
Total Projected Income	$893,400
Projected Expenses	
Rent	$ 5,600
Utilities	1,000
Telephone	1,200
Travel	15,000
Insurance	600
Salary	600,000
Taxes and Benefits	220,000
Office Supplies	10,000
Office Equipment	40,000
Total Projected Expenses	$893,400

FIGURE 9-5 A department budget.

a Control number 22222 Void ☐ **For Official Use Only ▶** **OMB No. 1545-0008**

b Employer identification number	1 Wages, tips, other compensation	2 Federal income tax withheld
c Employer's name, address, and ZIP code	3 Social security wages	4 Social security tax withheld
	5 Medicare wages and tips	6 Medicare tax withheld
	7 Social security tips	8 Allocated tips
d Employee's social security number	9 Advance EIC payment	10 Dependent care benefits
e Employee's first name and initial / Last name	11 Nonqualified plans	12a See instructions for box 12 Code
	13 Statutory employee ☐ Retirement plan ☐ Third-party sick pay ☐	12b Code
	14 Other	12c Code
f Employee's address and ZIP code		12d Code

15 State Employer's state ID number	16 State wages, tips, etc.	17 State income tax	18 Local wages, tips, etc.	19 Local income tax	20 Locality name

Form **W-2** **Wage and Tax Statement** 2004 Department of the Treasury—Internal Revenue Service

Copy A For Social Security Administration — Send this entire page with Form W-3 to the Social Security Administration; photocopies are **not** acceptable.

Cat. No. 10134D

For Privacy Act and Paperwork Reduction Act Notice, see back of Copy D.

Do Not Cut, Fold, or Staple Forms on This Page — Do Not Cut, Fold, or Staple Forms on This Page

FIGURE 9-6 A W-2 tax form.

Common tax forms

941	The federal quarterly tax return prepared by businesses
1040	The personal income tax return, not used by businesses
1099	A tax form that lists interest earned at banks, savings institutions, and brokerage firms and is sent at the end of the year to each client

Form W-4 (2004)

Purpose. Complete Form W-4 so that your employer can withhold the correct Federal income tax from your pay. Because your tax situation may change, you may want to refigure your withholding each year.

Exemption from withholding. If you are exempt, complete only lines 1, 2, 3, 4, and 7 and sign the form to validate it. Your exemption for 2004 expires February 16, 2005. See **Pub. 505,** Tax Withholding and Estimated Tax.

Note: *You cannot claim exemption from withholding if: **(a)** your income exceeds $800 and includes more than $250 of unearned income (e.g., interest and dividends) and **(b)** another person can claim you as a dependent on their tax return.*

Basic instructions. If you are not exempt, complete the **Personal Allowances Worksheet** below. The worksheets on page 2 adjust your withholding allowances based on itemized deductions, certain credits, adjustments to income, or two-earner/two-job situations. Complete all worksheets that apply. **However, you may claim fewer (or zero) allowances.**

Head of household. Generally, you may claim head of household filing status on your tax return only if you are unmarried and pay more than 50% of the costs of keeping up a home for yourself and your dependent(s) or other qualifying individuals. See line **E** below.

Tax credits. You can take projected tax credits into account in figuring your allowable number of withholding allowances. Credits for child or dependent care expenses and the child tax credit may be claimed using the **Personal Allowances Worksheet** below. See **Pub. 919,** How Do I Adjust My Tax Withholding? for information on converting your other credits into withholding allowances.

Nonwage income. If you have a large amount of nonwage income, such as interest or dividends, consider making estimated tax payments using **Form 1040-ES,** Estimated Tax for Individuals. Otherwise, you may owe additional tax.

Two earners/two jobs. If you have a working spouse or more than one job, figure the total number of allowances you are entitled to claim on all jobs using worksheets from only one Form W-4. Your withholding usually will be most accurate when all allowances are claimed on the Form W-4 for the highest paying job and zero allowances are claimed on the others.

Nonresident alien. If you are a nonresident alien, see the **Instructions for Form 8233** before completing this Form W-4.

Check your withholding. After your Form W-4 takes effect, use Pub. 919 to see how the dollar amount you are having withheld compares to your projected total tax for 2004. See Pub. 919, especially if your earnings exceed $125,000 (Single) or $175,000 (Married).

Recent name change? If your name on line 1 differs from that shown on your social security card, call 1-800-772-1213 to initiate a name change and obtain a social security card showing your correct name.

Personal Allowances Worksheet (Keep for your records.)

A Enter "1" for **yourself** if no one else can claim you as a dependent . . . . A ______

B Enter "1" if:
- You are single and have only one job; or
- You are married, have only one job, and your spouse does not work; or
- Your wages from a second job or your spouse's wages (or the total of both) are $1,000 or less.

. . B ______

C Enter "1" for your **spouse.** But, you may choose to enter "-0-" if you are married and have either a working spouse or more than one job. (Entering "-0-" may help you avoid having too little tax withheld.) . . . . C ______

D Enter number of **dependents** (other than your spouse or yourself) you will claim on your tax return . . . . D ______

E Enter "1" if you will file as **head of household** on your tax return (see conditions under **Head of household** above) . E ______

F Enter "1" if you have at least $1,500 of **child or dependent care expenses** for which you plan to claim a credit . . F ______

(**Note:** *Do **not** include child support payments. See **Pub. 503,** Child and Dependent Care Expenses, for details.*)

G **Child Tax Credit** (including additional child tax credit):
- If your total income will be less than $52,000 ($77,000 if married), enter "2" for each eligible child.
- If your total income will be between $52,000 and $84,000 ($77,000 and $119,000 if married), enter "1" for each eligible child plus "1" **additional** if you have four or more eligible children.

G ______

H Add lines A through G and enter total here. **Note:** *This may be different from the number of exemptions you claim on your tax return.* ▶ H ______

For accuracy, complete all worksheets that apply.
- If you plan to **itemize or claim adjustments to income** and want to reduce your withholding, see the **Deductions and Adjustments Worksheet** on page 2.
- If you have **more than one job** or are **married and you and your spouse both work** and the combined earnings from all jobs exceed $35,000 ($25,000 if married) see the **Two-Earner/Two-Job Worksheet** on page 2 to avoid having too little tax withheld.
- If **neither** of the above situations applies, **stop here** and enter the number from line H on line 5 of Form W-4 below.

Cut here and give Form W-4 to your employer. Keep the top part for your records.

Form **W-4**

Department of the Treasury
Internal Revenue Service

Employee's Withholding Allowance Certificate

▶ **Your employer must send a copy of this form to the IRS if: (a) you claim more than 10 allowances or (b) you claim "Exempt" and your wages are normally more than $200 per week.**

OMB No. 1545-0010

2004

1 Type or print your first name and middle initial | Last name | 2 Your social security number

Home address (number and street or rural route)

3 ☐ Single ☐ Married ☐ Married, but withhold at higher Single rate.
Note: *If married, but legally separated, or spouse is a nonresident alien, check the "Single" box.*

City or town, state, and ZIP code

4 **If your last name differs from that shown on your social security card, check here. You must call 1-800-772-1213 for a new card.** ▶ ☐

5 Total number of allowances you are claiming (from line **H** above **or** from the applicable worksheet on page 2) | 5 |

6 Additional amount, if any, you want withheld from each paycheck . . . . | 6 | $

7 I claim exemption from withholding for 2004, and I certify that I meet **both** of the following conditions for exemption:
- Last year I had a right to a refund of **all** Federal income tax withheld because I had **no** tax liability **and**
- This year I expect a refund of **all** Federal income tax withheld because I expect to have **no** tax liability.

If you meet both conditions, write "Exempt" here . . . . ▶ | 7 |

Under penalties of perjury, I certify that I am entitled to the number of withholding allowances claimed on this certificate, or I am entitled to claim exempt status.

Employee's signature
(Form is not valid unless you sign it.) ▶ **Date** ▶

8 Employer's name and address (Employer: Complete lines 8 and 10 only if sending to the IRS.) | 9 Office code (optional) | 10 Employer identification number (EIN)

For Privacy Act and Paperwork Reduction Act Notice, see page 2. Cat. No. 10220Q Form **W-4** (2004)

FIGURE 9-7 A W-4 tax form.

Common tax forms (continued)

W-2	The federal tax form provided to employees listing wages earned and taxes withheld
W-4	The federal tax form used by employees to notify the company regarding the employee's income tax withholding; this form is completed by the employee and is used by the employer to determine the amount of federal tax to be withheld

CHAPTER REVIEW

1. Explain the term *economics.*
2. Explain the term *freedom of choice* as it refers to business.
3. Explain the term *marketing.*
4. Explain the term *entrepreneur.*
5. List the four types of business ownership and explain each.
6. List three types of government securities.
7. List five general business terms and explain each.
8. List five terms used in a financial institution and explain each.
9. List five legal terms and explain each.
10. List five real estate terms and explain each.
11. List five accounting terms and explain each.
12. List three tax forms and explain the purpose of each.
13. Explain the following stock quote:

52-Week							Sales				
High	Low	Stock	Sym	Div	Yld.	PE	100s	High	Low	Last	Chg.
12	7	Hargo	HRX	.25	1.7	7	35	8.34	8.12	8.12	–.22

ACTIVITIES

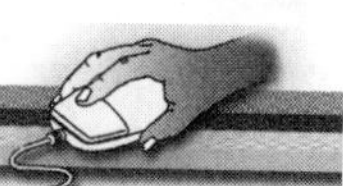

1. Visit a stock brokerage firm, and prepare a written report describing what you saw.
2. Follow five stocks for three weeks, and prepare written and oral reports summarizing the progress of the stocks. You may use the Internet for research for this activity.
3. Select three business publications and summarize one article from each. Also, present one summary orally to your class.
4. Read two articles about current economic forecasts and summarize each.
5. For a two-week period, read your local newspaper and clip all the investment advertisements you find.
6. Watch a financial television program and write a summary of it.
7. Talk with employees of two different types of businesses. Ask what business terms are used in their particular business. Then write a report about the types of companies, the terms used, and the advantages of working in each type of business.
8. Watch three television news shows, and prepare oral and written summaries of the business and economic news discussed.
9. Search the Web for financial information about three companies. Write a report about your findings.

PROJECTS

Project 17

Key in the following letter. Change the style to modified block.

> Joyce C. Kaplan
> Purchasing Agent
> R & W Manufacturing Company
> 2735 Franklin Lane
> Charleston, WV 25311
>
> Dear Ms. Kaplan:
>
> As we have discussed, we are interested in saving your company money. Our office developed a new organization software package last June, and we have installed it in 25 companies in your city. We would like your company to be number 26.
>
> The organization package will allow your company to save over 80 staff hours a week. As you can see, this package will save you the salary of two full-time employees.
>
> Learning to use this package is simple. We will train your staff to use this package in our free one-day seminar, which is offered at your office immediately after purchasing the package.
>
> I will call you next week so we can arrange a demonstration for you.
>
> S. C. Rosen
> Regional Sales Manager

Project 18

Send the following memo to the staff and supply any additional necessary information. The memo is from Rhonda S. Brown, Chairperson, Company Innovation Development Team.

> Please accept my congratulations for a job well completed. The Company Innovation Development Team has done an outstanding job, and every team member deserves our praise. We believe that the report the team created will be a guide to assist us in charting our future. The recommendations will be discussed at the monthly Company Forum next week.
>
> Attached is your copy of the final report. Please review the document prior to the forum, so you will be ready to address any issues of concern.
>
> In addition to the printed copy, an electronic version of this report is available on the network in the Innovation Directory.
>
> I look forward to seeing you at the next Forum.

HUMAN RELATIONS SKILL DEVELOPMENT

HR 9-1 Extra Hours

Working extra hours can be a daily occurrence or just a peak-time problem. Some employees enjoy working extra hours because of the extra money, prestige, or chance for advancement. Other employees prefer not to work extra hours. Additional hours may cause personal problems because of schedule conflicts or childcare responsibilities.

- How would you tell your manager that you do not mind working extra hours occasionally but that you do not wish to do so on a regular basis?
- How would you help a manager who frequently does not give advance notice of overtime understand that you need advance notice in order to make arrangements for the care of an elderly relative?
- What would you do if you were asked to work overtime on a Saturday and you had already planned to go away for the weekend?

HR 9-2 Another Job

Sometimes one job does not pay enough money to meet all of your financial requirements. While moonlighting at a second job may be an option to meet your financial needs, the stress of two jobs can become overwhelming. Persons working a second job can become irritable, argumentative, overwrought, and nonproductive. Exhaustion can turn an excellent employee into a mediocre employee at both jobs. Since some companies prohibit moonlighting, always review company policies prior to beginning a second job.

- As a supervisor, what would you say to an employee who you know is moonlighting and whose production in the office has declined?

SITUATIONS

How would you handle each of the following situations?

- **S 9-1** As a supervisor, you have noticed that Mark, Wilma, and Barry are extending the lunch break, so they can watch the conclusion of a television show.
- **S 9-2** Today you received the sixth call this week from Harry Whitlock. Harry would like to talk with Tim Kendrick, your supervisor, but Tim refuses to talk with Harry.
- **S 9-3** Harriet Peckman always arrives at the office by 8:15 A.M. and it is now 9:30 A.M. Dinora Pazimo has a 9 A.M. appointment with Harriet, and she is still waiting. You know that Harriet's husband works until 2 A.M., and he does not like to be disturbed early in the morning when he is sleeping.
- **S 9-4** Your supervisor asked you to complete a project, but you do not understand the meaning of the business terms that your supervisor used when explaining the project to you.

PUNCTUATION REVIEW

Punctuate each of the following sentences.

1. As the meeting concluded she contacted the director and arranged another meeting
2. Jack who is retiring in June is going to England France and Germany
3. You will I think like the new line of appointment calendars
4. I do not have in my personal library the book you cited but it should be available from the department library county library or university library

5. However the meeting was rescheduled for next month
6. Before she left for her vacation she completed all of the jobs in the basket
7. Ted who recently became assistant director has been with the company for over twenty years
8. When she called I was in conference with Mr Epstein and Ms Chen
9. I am meeting Henry Rosen Junior on Monday and Tuesday I am meeting Henry Rosen Senior
10. The guest speaker is Elliott Jameson III and his topic is Business in the New Century
11. If your total payments to the IRS fall short of your estimate pay the revised estimate by January 15 which is the deadline for the December payment
12. In order to capitalize on the enormous demand for publication 205 Office Environments the price was raised from $15 to $20
13. I bought my Personal Digital Assistant (PDA) and new computer software at Chips Inc which is located at 7th Avenue
14. The brokers offered advice but the stockholders didnt listen
15. While Joseph was manager he wrote a policy and procedures manual for his department

CD ASSIGNMENTS

CD Assignment 9-1

Open the file CD9-1_IT1 on your Student CD and follow the instructions to complete the job.

CD Assignment 9-2

Open the file CD9-1_IT2 on your Student CD and follow the instructions to complete the job.

CD Assignment 9-3

Open the file CD9-1_IT3 on your Student CD and follow the instructions to complete the job.

CD Assignment 9-4

Open the file CD9-1_IT4 on your Student CD and follow the instructions to complete the job.

CD Assignment 9-5

Open the file CD9-1_IT5 on your Student CD and follow the instructions to complete the job.

The Office Environment and Design

10

Objectives

After studying this chapter, you should be able to

1. Handle situations involving the office landlord.
2. Explain security techniques used in an office.
3. Describe a favorable office environment.
4. Explain the important aspects of office design and layout.
5. Describe methods of purchasing office supplies.
6. Explain methods of inventory and their purposes.
7. Prepare a deposit slip and endorse checks.

Introduction

Working in an office can be challenging. While preparing for your profession, it is easy to overlook some activities which are vital to the successful operation of an office but are so common they are often invisible. This chapter deals with activities related to the office and the office environment. The mastery of these operational activities will keep an office running smoothly on a daily basis.

Landlord and Building Staff

Dealing with Your Landlord

Most offices have a landlord. If your office is part of a large organization, the business may lease a floor of a large office building or may even occupy its own building. In these situations, the business will have a professional staff to deal with landlord-tenant relationships or with the responsibilities of building ownership.

If the business is small, you or your supervisor may work directly with the landlord regarding the lease of space. A *lease* is a document which establishes a business's relationship with the landlord and specifies the amount of office space the business will occupy, the rental rate, and the services the landlord will provide. Landlord-supplied services may include heating, lighting, security, provisions for parking, office cleaning, and building maintenance. The lease will also explain the conditions under which the business may occupy the leased space. The lease may include restrictions about the type of businesses, hours of operation, use of machinery, noise, and number of people allowed in an office. If you work in a small office and must work with the landlord, you should become familiar with the terms of your business's office lease.

Building Staff and Maintenance Staff

While most employees do not deal directly with their landlord, every employee should have an interest in the building where they work. The maintenance of the building and of the individual offices will affect the health, safety, and attitude of the people working in it. The *building staff* supervise the building and act as the landlord's representative. They may or may not have an office in the building. The *maintenance staff* are responsible for the daily functioning of the building and its infrastructure, including heating, plumbing, and electricity. It is always best to develop a good relationship with the building and maintenance staff, and it is important to treat them with respect. Some offices even remember the members of the maintenance staff with small gifts at holidays. Keep in mind that people are much more helpful if you are pleasant and ask for assistance rather than order them around and demand service. By developing a friendly, respectful relationship with members of the building and maintenance staff, you will get better service.

Office Security and Workplace Violence

Building Security

Building security has become more visible since the terrorist attacks of 9/11. Many building owners have taken measures to increase building security. These measures include restricting public access to buildings by closing some of the entrances and constructing physical barriers to keep cars and trucks away from the outside of buildings. Parking may be limited in underground garages or in areas adjacent to the building.

> **HINT**
> For your safety, follow your company's security procedures.

Office guards control access to many buildings and permit only authorized personnel to enter. Members of the staff may be required to display photo identification badges. Visitors may have to show identification and sign registers before entry to a building and/or be escorted by employees. In addition, visitors and staff may be required to open purses and briefcases for inspection or even pass through airport-style metal detectors.

FIGURE 10-1 A security guard at a building entrance.

No business wants a visitor wandering alone through an office where that visitor could disturb employees, "accidentally" see confidential information, steal documents or equipment, or even have an accident for which the company is liable. To increase security, many offices are replacing doors opened by traditional keys with new security technologies. Smart cards, often called swipe cards, are plastic cards the size of credit cards which are encoded with door-locking codes. They provide increased security in the office and can easily be recoded to provide entry or deny entry to specific individuals. They can also keep track of which individuals lock or unlock a door.

New technologies are being used to strengthen many areas of office security. Companies now include smart card technology on identification passes or use bar codes similar to those used to maintain inventory of office furniture and equipment as building entrance passes. Technology is advancing in the security field with the use of *biometrics,* which is the study of recognizing individuals through unchangeable physical characteristics. Human characteristics such as voice recognition, fingerprints, and facial contours can be used to verify employee identity prior to his or her entering a building or an office. The biometric authentication software can be built into devices, eliminating the need for passwords, PINs, and keys. Many offices are using fingerprint sensors instead of passwords for building entry or to log into computer systems. Another biometrics security system used to verify a person's identity is a system that scans a person's eyes, using an iris identification system. Since a person's biometric characteristics are practically impossible to replicate, these technologies will become more widespread and will increase security for offices, employees, and computer systems.

Some of these security measures were in place before 9/11 and were intended to protect confidential commercial information and sensitive government documents. As more companies become concerned about safety, the use of these technologies will continue to increase.

FIGURE 10-2 A smart card for an office entrance.

Fire Safety and Emergency Evacuation

One of the major functions of an office building is to provide a safe and secure environment for a business and its employees. Modern building codes and zoning regulations in many communities address the basic safety requirements of office buildings. These regulations address such items as emergency exits, electric and water requirements, the type of business, and the number of people who can safely work in a specific type of building.

Fire safety is a major workplace concern, and many localities mandate fire alarms and fire sprinkler systems. Fire alarms are regularly tested, and often you are notified of the test date. If you hear a fire alarm while working, evacuate the building for your own safety. Sprinkler systems generally have a sprinkler head located in individual offices or spaced at regular intervals in large areas. If a fire occurs, the individual sprinkler heads are automatically activated as needed.

As an employee, it is your personal responsibility to know where the emergency exits are and to ensure that those exits are never blocked in any way. If you see anything unsafe taking place in your building or in your office, immediately call the situation to your supervisor's attention.

Familiarize yourself with your company's emergency evacuation plan so you will be able to respond to a life-threatening situation.

Workplace Violence

In the last several years, there has been an increase in violence in the workplace. Today workplace violence can be directed toward any occupation, not only law enforcement which was traditionally considered a dangerous occupation. Violence, whether physical abuse or verbal threats, can be found in every workplace. All employees should protect their own personal safety by maintaining a keen awareness of their physical surroundings and the people they encounter.

Statistics indicate that workplace violence is often committed by disgruntled employees. Although an individual may appear to be a "model employee," there may be underlying signs of conditions that lead to violence, such as drug abuse, alcohol dependence, depression, financial difficulties, mental unrest, loss of employment, or destructive behavior. Companies can prevent workplace violence by providing employee assistance programs, having procedures to deal with employee grievances, enforcing policies against harassment, and offering personal counseling.

Some violent actions may be prevented by increasing workplace security. Installing a security guard or gate to control entrance to the workplace, using glass partitions to separate employees from visitors, and using security alarms at designated locations all may deter violent confrontations. Additional prevention methods include educating the employees concerning unacceptable behavior and providing bright security lighting, video surveillance equipment, identification badges, and electronic or password-protected entrance access. Information about workplace violence can be obtained from the U.S. Department of Labor, Occupational Safety and Health Administration at 1-800-321-6742 or *www.osha.gov.*

HINT

Workplace violence can be directed at anyone.

Monitoring Employees

Many businesses monitor employees and the workplace to improve security. Employees may be observed, sometimes without their knowledge, by small, concealed video cameras placed in hallways or offices. When companies use surveillance equipment, a safer and more secure workplace is provided to the employee, because cameras can quickly alert security personnel to serious safety problems. However, while electronic monitoring may be a security safeguard for the employee, many employees feel that monitoring violates their personal rights and is an invasion of privacy.

Companies may also monitor employees to increase productivity or reduce theft. Companies that monitor employees experience reduction in theft and an increase in productivity from employees who would have slacked off on the job. In addition to personnel monitoring, companies may monitor employee communications, such as email, telephone, and computer usage. Increasingly, companies are monitoring employee Web traffic to determine if it is used for personal Web surfing.

While it may be legal for a company to monitor its employees, the company should specifically notify employees of policies regarding the use of company equipment and of its employee monitoring activities.

HINT

Many companies monitor employees use of computers.

THE OFFICE FACILITY

Physical Environment

Your office will be the single place where you spend most of your waking hours. Your office, therefore, should provide comfort and meet your needs as well as those of your employer.

With changes in office technology and design, it has become less common for each employee to have a private office. In addition, as companies reduce overhead costs, there is often a reduction in the amount of office space per employee. In some offices, employees may be asked to share office space, where in the past they had separate offices. A work environment may be a large room divided into many individual workstations. These workstations may be grouped or divided by partitions, shelves, or acoustic panels.

Many office workstations are designed using modular furniture systems, which are based on a family of interchangeable parts. Desks and storage units connect directly to freestanding walls and can be reconfigured to meet the changing needs of the office.

Office furniture designers have developed mobile file cabinets that roll out for usage and store under desks when other workers use the space; storage boxes mounted on a pole; adjustable storage towers with multiple directional access for usage by adjacent employees; and cubicle walls with grooves for shelves, binders, boxes, and desktop accessories. To further control employee space, some companies are using storage units instead of movable walls to divide offices.

FIGURE 10-3 An employee in a modular furniture office.

Many people working in a open office environment experience noise pollution. Reducing the level of noise caused by equipment, telephones, conversations, and traffic in an open office is a challenge. Acoustic tiles, partitions, carpeting, and draperies are often used to reduce the level of noise.

The quality of lighting in an office is important, especially for employees who spend much of their day working at a computer. Too much light is as visually disturbing as too little light. Lighting, sun-related lighting problems, and glare on a page or a computer terminal can cause eye strain. In addition overhead lighting, task lighting, and desktop finishes may all produce a glare. Offices should use fluorescent lights and adjust windows and drapes to provide sufficient light and reduce glare. Glossy finishes on desks and countertops reflect more light and provide more glare than surfaces with matte finishes. Eye strain may be reduced by taking breaks from the computer, using eye drops, and using nonglare computer shields.

Indoor air pollution has become a problem in some offices because of improperly designed buildings or poorly ventilated air systems. Another source of indoor pollution is office equipment that produces ozone (electrically charged air), which is inhaled into the body. Employees need to be aware of potential indoor pollution problems and alert the supervisor if they feel sick or lightheaded or if they experience a work-related illness.

Cleaning the Office

In some offices, a professional cleaning staff go through the offices at night when the offices are vacant. In other offices, the cleaning staff clean the offices during normal working hours. In either circumstance, be pleasant to the cleaning staff and know what you should do to help them in their work. Cleaning staffs are instructed about how to clean offices and under what circumstances not to clean offices. If you make cleaning your office difficult, you will probably not be pleased with the way it looks.

Heat and Air Conditioning

Both office electronic equipment and employees are sensitive to temperature, humidity, air quality, and cigarette smoke. In order to control the climate within the office and maintain the health of both the staff and the equipment, modern office buildings are usually constructed as closed, controlled environments with sealed windows. Heating and air conditioning may be controlled for the entire building by the building maintenance staff. Some buildings may have temperature controls for specific floors, zones, or offices, but temperature control for individual office areas often is not available. In addition, heat and air conditioning may not be available after traditional business hours or on weekends or holidays, when the building is not normally used. Heating and cooling should be set at a comfortable temperature of 68 to 75 degrees in winter and 73 to 79 degrees in summer. An uncomfortable employee is not a productive employee. However, a temperature that is comfortable for one employee may be too hot or cold for another. Unfortunately, employees who work in controlled environment buildings must often cope when the office temperature is beyond their immediate control or the individual's comfort level.

- Be aware of the general temperature of your office in relation to other offices. Because of their placement in the building, some offices may be warmer than other offices. Some offices will be comfortable in winter but not in summer, while others will be comfortable only in summer.
- If your office is consistently uncomfortable, there may be a problem with the heating/air-conditioning unit in your area. The building staff may be able to adjust the unit to provide a comfortable temperature.
- The temperature in offices that have windows can be adjusted to some extent by using the window blinds. Opening the blinds on a sunny day will bring in heat as well as light, while closing the blinds will reduce solar heat that warms the office.
- Some employees use small electric fans to cool their offices in the summer and electric heaters to warm their offices in the winter. When using electric appliances, be careful

not to overload electrical circuits. Electric heaters can get very hot and should be used with caution. Also be careful about placing electrical cords for fans or heaters so they are not in a traffic area.

- Many employees dress for the temperature they expect to find in their office. A sweater or suit jacket can be worn or removed as the office temperature changes. Employees often keep a solid-color sweater in the office for the days when the office is cold.

Plants

Plants are used in an office to bring the warmth of the outdoors inside, and they help soothe an office environment by making it seem less harsh. The color that plants bring to the office can enliven a dull decorating scheme. Another function of interior landscaping is to separate work areas and create privacy. In addition, specific types of plants purify the office air and reduce indoor air contaminants. Even silk plants may be used to create a pleasant environment, but most people prefer living plants. Because plants need frequent maintenance, they should be placed at an easily accessible level. Most plants prefer temperatures of 65 to 75 degrees, so it is important to consider room temperature and the location of blowing heating and cooling air when selecting plants. A lack of water or sun will cause plants to die, ruining the attractiveness of the office. Plant specialists can make recommendations regarding the type of plants suitable for a particular office, suggest where to place the plants for maximum enjoyment, and maintain the plants. The philodendron, corn plant, schefflera, ivy, and spider plant require little light and minimum maintenance, so they are frequently used in the office to bring the texture and experience of the outdoors inside. In addition, studies have shown that several types of plants, including bamboo palm, dracaena, English ivy, and gerbera daisy, may be used to clean office air.

Safety

Every employee should be on the alert for unsafe conditions in the office. Items placed in or near walk areas are a major cause of accidents. People walking through an office may not be familiar with the specific location of all office furniture, or they may be thinking about their work and not watching every step. To prevent accidents, electrical wires and cords should be enclosed in tubes, taped to the floor, buried, or placed where people will not trip over them. Trash cans should be placed along walls or next to furniture away from where people walk. In addition, when chairs are not in use, they should be placed close to the desk. If a desk or file cabinet has a pull-out shelf, it should be pushed in when not in use.

File cabinets can be a primary source of injuries. When not in use, the drawers of vertical file cabinets should be closed, not left open. If a file drawer is open, a person walking by could stumble or bump into the drawer. As another safety precaution, only one drawer of a vertical file cabinet should be opened at a time. When several drawers are opened, the weight of the cabinet shifts; thus, the cabinet may become top-heavy and tip over.

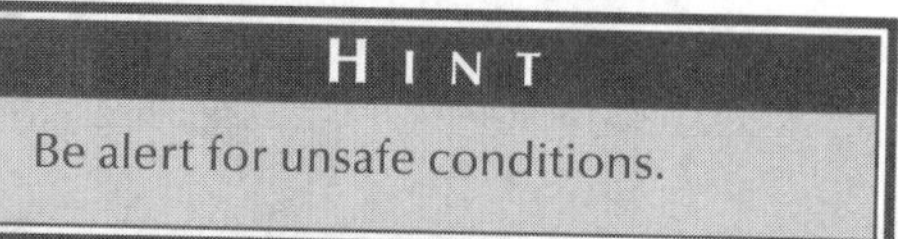

FILE AND COMPUTER SECURITY

File Security

Always be aware of the security requirements of your office and be responsible for the security of your area. When computers were first introduced, some people thought the electronic transfer of data would lead to the paperless office. Unfortunately, the ease and speed of information exchange using computers, word processors, photocopy machines, and facsimile machines have led to more paper in most offices, not less paper. Much of the information that is processed and stored on paper is confidential. To protect the privacy of individuals and the confidential nature of many business transactions, care must be taken to safeguard files and the information they contain.

Many offices require that file cabinets and drawers be locked when not in use. While this may appear inconvenient, it is essential that employees follow the company policy regarding security. Some organizations will conduct surprise inspections to check the security of offices and files. Keys to locks should not be left out, where they can easily be found. People often write down a lock's combination in case they forget it, and then they place the written combination in their desk drawer, where it is easily found. While this may be convenient for the employee, it decreases the security of the files. If other persons know where the lock combination is located, the files are not really secure. If you have been given the combination of the office safe, do not divulge it to anyone. If you are working on sensitive material and you leave your office—even for a few minutes—secure the documents before leaving.

After confidential documents are no longer needed, they are often destroyed before they are thrown out. A *paper shredder* is used to cut the paper into very thin strips or to shred it to the size of confetti. Shredders are categorized according to the size of the shredded sheet, entrance sheet capacity, speed, and waste capacity. Shredders that cut paper into very small pieces provide a high degree of confidentially. Most office-quality shredders can cut papers containing staples and paper clips. After the paper is shredded, it falls into a receptacle, which keeps the documents confidential until proper disposal. For destruction of the most sensitive documents, the shredded paper may be placed in special bags and burned. While working at home, telecommuters who work with confidential documents should also shred and properly destroy materials.

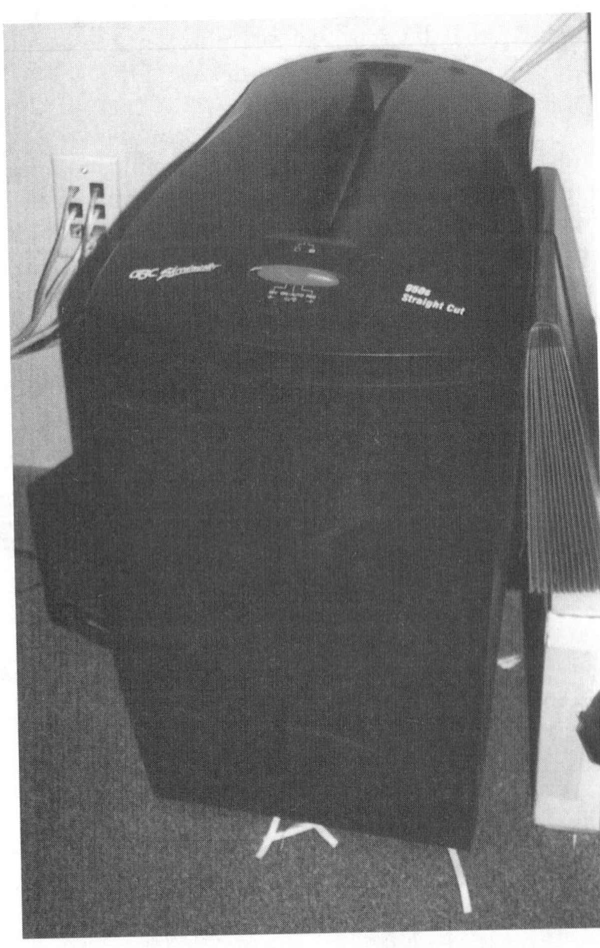

FIGURE 10-4 A paper shredder.

Computer Security

Computer security is a major concern for a company and it may have procedures addressing the security of computer equipment, limitations on access to computer files, and the safeguarding of computer data. The loss of computer information would be a disaster for most offices, so be knowledgeable of and follow the computer security procedures in your office.

Computer systems are vulnerable to *hackers,* people who make unauthorized entry into computers and who may steal, disrupt, or destroy computer data. Hackers are usually people unknown to the company who enter computer systems via the Internet, but they may also be disgruntled present or former employees. The more information unauthorized people have about the company's computer system, the easier it is for them to break into the system and steal or destroy data. Office computer systems frequently require the user to have a login code and a password to gain access to the system. Remember that your password is confidential; so do not disclose it to others. To safeguard your computer system, do not write down your computer password and leave it where others may see it. Passwords should be changed every three to six months. Furthermore, do not tell anyone outside your office how your office computer system operates.

Computer systems are also vulnerable to storms, which can cause electrical surges, destroying computers, computer data, printers, and other electrical equipment. *Surge protectors* are devices that protect computer equipment from damage by smoothing over sudden changes in the electric current. Always be sure that the surge protectors in your office are in use and operating properly.

Theft of computer hardware is a common occurrence. Many computers are attached to their desks with locked chains. Security hardware may be inconvenient, but the loss of a computer and its data can be very damaging to an office. Notebook and handheld computers are designed to be carried out of the office. In some offices, an employee must show written authorization before taking computer equipment out of the office. If you are authorized to take computer equipment out of the office, the equipment has been placed in your care, and you will be held accountable for its return.

All offices should have a plan for recovery in the event that a disaster strikes the office or its computer system. The most common recovery plan involves storing data off-site. If the original files and all backups are kept at the same facility and the facility experiences a catastrophe (fire, water damage, explosion, etc.) all backups will also be destroyed. Off-site storage should be done on a regular basis, at least once a week. With the advances in technology, some companies send electronic backups to a Web server at an off-site location.

Securing computers against viruses is also an important part of a computer security plan. As discussed in Chapter 5, Computers in the Office, scanning for a computer virus is essential to prevent damage to the office computer system. Viruses caused by infectious emails have increased, so virus protection is vital for the safety of your computer.

Office Furniture and Equipment

Before new equipment is purchased, the decision of where to place it and on what to place it must be made. Frequently equipment is purchased and only later is consideration given about where to place it. Without prior planning, equipment is often simply placed where it fits, without consideration of proper lighting, the height of the table on which is it placed, or employee comfort during its use.

An assistant's desk should be large enough to accommodate all of the work and papers used each day. The desk should be placed for easy accessibility to the supervisor. It should be situated so that the assistant can greet clients and not be surprised by an unexpected visitor. In addition, the desk must be away from office traffic, so work can be completed without being hindered by noise, conversations, or persons walking by.

A computer should be placed on a stand or desk which is the correct height for keyboarding documents. To save space and reduce wrist pain, many computer desks have pull-out shelves for keyboards. In addition, a stand or desk area must be available for the printer.

FIGURE 10-5 Today's workplace.

Employees working in a multiperson office should have some personal space. Plants or filing cabinets can be used to create private areas. A multiperson office should be designed to accommodate the traffic caused by a large number of employees entering and leaving.

Studies have shown that office decor and color have an effect on an employee's moods. Color can be used to create enthusiasm and increase productivity. Generally, blue and green are calming and relaxing colors, while red and orange are exciting and stimulating colors. In addition, color can be used to alter the perceived size of a room. Light colors create the appearance of a larger room, while dark colors make a room seem smaller. Creating an office that is comfortable includes the arrangement of furniture, personal belongings, and decor.

Ergonomic Furniture

Ergonomics is the study of the human body in relation to its work environment—that is, the study of how the physical environment affects employees. Employees come in different sizes—short, tall, thin, and not so thin. All employees do not fit comfortably at the same-size chair or desk. To meet the changing needs of the office environment, office furniture has been developed to make employees more comfortable. Prior to purchasing office furniture, look at each employee and determine the best furniture fit for that person. Sitting incorrectly, having an office chair that does not support your back, and having a desk that is not at the correct height can cause back pain. Back pain is one of the major causes of employee absenteeism and can impact the employee's ability to work efficiently.

> **HINT**
>
> Ergonomics is the study of the human body in relation to its work setting.

To accommodate people's differing heights, an office can purchase adjustable chairs, tables, and printer stands. A comfortable employee completes a task more accurately, more quickly, and more efficiently; and an employee who is comfortable is happier. A desk for computer use (keyboarding) should be about 27 inches high, while a desk for writing purposes may be 29 inches high. To accommodate leg movement under the desk, there should be about 27 inches of space. When purchasing a chair, be sure it has an adjustable seat and a backrest. The height of the chair should adjust, so the person's arms are high enough for the desk and the person's feet rest on the floor. For comfort, short people may require a footrest with a nonslip surface. The chair backrest should include a firm cushion to support the lower back. Chair

FIGURE 10-6 Ergonomically designed chair.

legs should have wheels, so employees can easily move their chairs. The seat span should be about 18 inches, but this dimension may change, depending on the size of the individual.

The placement of furniture can also affect an employee's comfort and productivity. Avoid placing equipment at a location that requires the employee to twist around in the office chair to reach the equipment. Twisting in a chair can cause a neck or back injury or can cause the employee to fall from the chair. Preventing injuries is less expensive than the high medical costs and loss of personnel hours resulting from not purchasing ergonomically designed furniture and improperly placing the furniture.

A health problem common in offices and often associated with computers is *carpal tunnel syndrome.* This injury, which is often caused by repetitive motions used in keyboarding documents, results in pain in the hands, wrists, or arms. Carpal tunnel syndrome can be reduced by taking breaks to rest your hands, using correct hand placement on the keyboards, using ergonomic keyboards, or using wrist supports when keyboarding.

Back and neck pain is often caused by incorrectly lifting items or by not properly supporting the back while seated. To avoid back injuries, always use safe lifting techniques, such as lifting from a kneeling position instead of lifting by bending at the waist. It is better to use appropriate lifting techniques and prevent an injury than to treat an injured back.

Equipment Repairs

Office equipment does break and will require repairs. One employee should be responsible for overseeing repair of the equipment. Detailed repair records should be kept, because it may be important to know how often and what types of problems occurred on a specific piece of equipment.

Type of Equipment		
Serial Number		
Model Number		
Purchase Date		
Vendor	Vendor Address	Vendor Telephone No.
Repair		
Date Repair Requested	Date Repaired	Serviced By
Cost	Warranty	
Comments		

FIGURE 10-7 A repair record form.

Some companies lease equipment instead of purchasing the equipment. A lease contract may or may not include maintenance of the equipment, so you should know the terms of the lease agreement before you repair equipment.

Before a repair is requested, the payment of the repair should be considered. Is the equipment under warranty? Is there a maintenance agreement on the equipment? A *maintenance agreement* is a contract for repair of the equipment, and usually a set fee is paid on an annual basis for the repairs. You should have a file of equipment covered by maintenance contracts. Repair for equipment under warranty, for equipment under lease, or when a maintenance agreement is in place will be handled by calling the appropriate vendor. When calling about a repair, indicate the nature of the problem and how often the problem occurs. It may take several telephone calls to have an item repaired. After the repair is completed, you will usually be asked to sign a receipt indicating that the work was completed.

If an office has no agreements regarding the repair of equipment, you must identify a source for repairs. You could contact the company from which the equipment was purchased, the manufacturer, or an authorized dealer or search the Internet for a repair facility. Many areas have independent shops that can repair office equipment. Listings of possible repair facilities can be found in the yellow pages of the telephone directory. When contacting a company about the repair of equipment, you will need to determine whether they are qualified to do the repair, how your company will be billed for the service, all costs, and the length of the warranty for the repair.

Photocopiers

Digital technology has transformed the standard office photocopier into a flexible piece of equipment that can perform many functions. Older, nondigital photocopy machines did one task very well—copying correspondence, reports, and other documents for daily use in the office. A nondigital copier copies one page at a time and can make single or multiple copies of a document. Today most copy machines make copies on at least two sizes of paper—regular-size 8.5″ × 11″ and legal-size 8.5″ × 14″ paper. Larger copy machines can reduce or enlarge the size of the copy, collate and staple multiple copies, copy on both sides of the paper, automatically feed a stack of originals, allow interruption of copying at any time, reset the number of copies after the first set has been run, and diagnose and describe machine problems.

A digital copier scans a page and then stores the page in memory, as a computer does. Original documents are scanned once and then multiple copies can be printed. Since the originals move through the machine only once, copies can be completed quicker and with less paper movement than in a nondigital machine, resulting in greatly increased machine reliability and lower maintenance cost. Since pages are stored in memory, they can be handled like many other documents. Some digital copy machines can enlarge the text or reduce it. By reducing the text, four or more pages can fit onto a single sheet of paper. The digital copier can be connected to a computer network and can then serve as a network printer. The quality of the printing is better than using a standard copier because all the copies are original printed pages, not photocopies of originals. Sophisticated feeders, staplers, and folders are available as attachments to copiers. Some copiers can print paper 11″ × 17″, so a user can create and print a full 8.5″ × 11″ stapled booklet directly from a computer. (A piece of paper 11″ × 17″ folded in half results in a standard 8.5″ × 11″ booklet.) Depending on the software available with the machine, sections of pages can be edited, deleted from the final copy, or centered. Scanning a page into a digital photocopier is identical to using a scanner on a computer, except it is faster, because copiers have large-capacity feeders and operate at high speeds. Images can be scanned and files stored to computers on a local area network. When used with OCR (optical character recognition) software, the images can be brought into a word processor or other software and edited. Finally, a digital copier can be connected to a telephone line and serve as a fax machine, since it both scans and prints images. A digital copier can combine the functions of a photocopier, printer, scanner, and fax machine into one unit, which can be connected to an office computer network and to other computers via

FIGURE 10-8 An employee using a photocopier.

phone lines or via the Internet. In addition to having black-and-white copiers in the office, color copiers are becoming more prevalent because of the increased usage of colored graphics, pictures, and images.

The operating instructions for most copy machines are attached to the machine and are easy to learn. In addition to the general operating instructions, you will need to learn how to replace paper in the machine. Efficient operators should also know how to clear a paper jam in the machine and how to add *toner*—the chemical used to print the text.

An *auditron* is used to count the number of copies made. A company could have an individual auditron for each department, so each department would be charged correctly for its use of the copy machine. Operators need to control the number of copies made, because the annual costs for photocopying can be significant.

Copying and Shipping Centers

Need an odd-sized packaged shipped? Want to photocopy a newsletter in red ink? Your office may not have the materials, equipment, or know-how to handle these and many other unusual requests, but there are many businesses that may be able to help in an emergency or to do that "once-a-year" type of job. If a copy job cannot be completed at your office location because of limited facilities, limited time, or broken equipment, it can be taken to a quick copy store. Copying and shipping centers provide a wide variety of services, but the objective of most of these businesses is to provide quick service at a reasonable cost. The office employee should be familiar with the services offered by copy centers that are convenient to the office.

Copying centers may contain a variety of specialized photocopying equipment and supplies not found in many offices. They usually have high-speed machines, which can photocopy at high volumes, do color photocopying, or use colored inks. They will often do specialized printing—for example, printing on heavy paper for report covers—and will have machines for binding thick documents. Copy centers can be lifesavers when your regular office photocopier is down and you must finish a critical job. Some copy centers are open twenty-four hours a day, so those last-minute jobs can be completed.

Businesses that specialize in shipping have mailing materials, such as boxes, wrappings, and packaging for fragile items. You can buy these specialized supplies, or the shipping center can package the item and have it picked up by an overnight carrier service, such as UPS, FedEx, or DHL. Many shipping centers have photocopying capability, and some rent mailboxes to businesses as an "address of convenience."

Recycling

As society has become more concerned about the environment and the dilemma of disposing of materials, many offices have become involved in recycling. Workplaces often have bins to recycle used paper, and many offices purchase recycled paper for copiers, printers, and folders. In addition, food facilities purchase napkins and cups made from recycled paper and, offices have bins to collect beverage cans and bottles for recycling. Workplace dependency on computers and electronic equipment has created eCycling, which provides opportunities to recycle electronics. Recycling opportunities exist for computers, printers, printer cartridges, circuit boards, monitors, traditional and cell phones, batteries, and so on. These items may contain lead and mercury, which are hazardous materials. Frequent technological changes make computers and other electronics quickly obsolete so recycling resources is a prudent management and environmental choice. For additional recycling information, visit

> **HINT**
>
> Do not waste resources. Participate in your company's recycling plan.

www.eiae.org
www.iaer.org/search
www.plugintorecycling.org

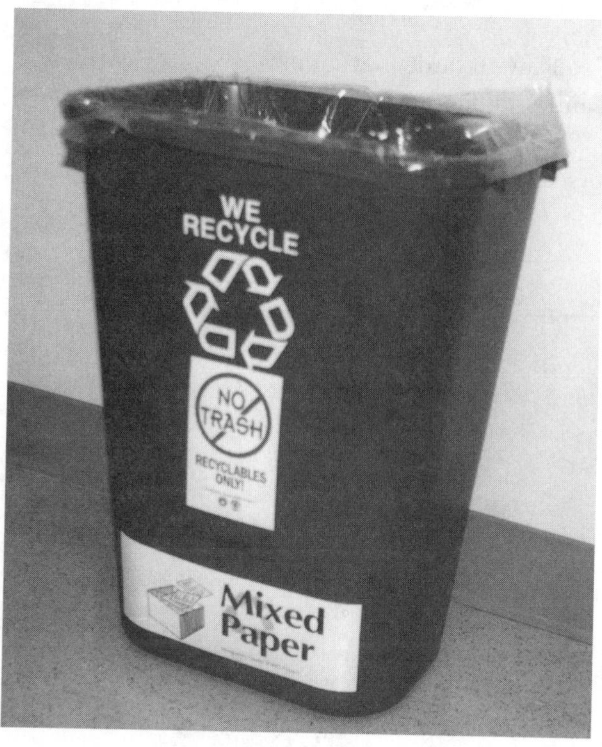

FIGURE 10-9 Recycle trash can.

Office Supplies

The variety and quality of office supplies and equipment have expanded as a result of the introduction of new technology in the office. Supplies and equipment can be purchased from local vendors, from out-of-town distributors, or via the Internet.

Sample supplies and equipment used in a modern office

- A selection of rubber stamps with the following imprints:
  "As per your request"
  Company's return address
  "Completed"
  "Confidential"
  Current date and time
  "Faxed"
  "File copy"
  "Final notice"
  "For deposit only"
  "For your information"
  "Paid"
  "Received"
  "Rush"
  "Urgent"
- Binder clips in several sizes
- Bookends
- Business card stationery

- Business card holders
- Card file boxes—3″ × 5″, 4″ × 6″, or 5″ × 8″, with built-in dividers
- Cartridges for printers, fax machines, and photocopiers
- Coil pens with stand
- Color-coded labels in a variety of colors, shapes, and sizes
- Color-indexed protector sheets
- Colored markers
- Columnar pads
- Computer data storage
  Discs: CD-R, CD-RW, DVD+R, DVD−R
- Computer disk mailers
- Copy holders
- Daily reminders and planners
- Desk and wall calendars
- Desk rack systems for hanging binders and folders
- Electric hole punches
- Expanding accordion file boxes
- Flipcharts and markers
- Get-acquainted badges
- Invitation stationery
- Locator boards to indicate if an employee is in or out of the office
- Magazine and literature storage systems
- Mailing boxes with bubble wrap or plastic peanuts for packing
- Mailing tubes
- Message boards
- Paper clips (regular-size, jumbo-size, and nonskid)
- Paper for printers, fax machines, and photocopiers
- Paper trimmers to cut paper to a desired size
- Platform footrests for computer users
- Portfolios
- Postal scales
- Rubber chair mats—mats placed on top of carpets permitting chairs to slide easily
- Scheduling boards
- Staplers, staples, and staple removers
- Stationery trays
- Stick-on notes and flags
- Wall- or desk-mounted cordless electric pencil sharpeners
- Wall- or door-mounted file folder holders

Storing Supplies

Large offices often maintain a *storeroom* or *stock room* where supplies are kept. Small offices often have a supply cabinet or drawer where commonly used supplies are kept. In some businesses, employees must use a form to request supplies stocked in the company storeroom. In other organizations, employees can pick up supplies as needed.

Inventory

A well-run office will include an individual who is responsible for ordering and distributing supplies. Since essential supplies should always be available, it is important to frequently check the supply inventory. Some offices keep a perpetual inventory, in which every item purchased or removed from the supply room is recorded. The advantage of a perpetual inventory is that it is easy to determine how many of an item are still on the shelf. Therefore, a perpetual inventory system diminishes the chance of running out of an item. If a supply is needed quickly, it can be purchased from a local store, but last-minute purchases should be kept to a minimum. It is helpful to maintain a file of local office supply catalogs and to bookmark favorite office supply Web sites. These catalogs and Web sites will be useful when you need to buy supplies.

PURCHASES AND PAYMENTS

Offices must purchase supplies and equipment to support the operation of the business. Large companies may have a department of several people who purchase supplies for the entire company. In smaller companies, the purchasing of supplies often is the responsibility of an administrative assistant.

Purchasing

Each office has its own specific procedures and forms to be used for the purchase of supplies, services, and equipment. These procedures are often outlined in a purchasing handbook. Study the office purchasing handbook to learn your company's purchasing policies and requirements. In some organizations, purchasing requirements depend on the type of product or service requested or the amount of the purchase. For example, purchases under a set amount (such as \$500, \$1,000, or \$2,000) may be made with a company credit card and minimal documentation. In these cases, however, the person using the credit card may undergo special training to ensure that he or she is aware of and responsible for following company policies.

The purchasing procedures in most offices have two goals. The first is to ensure that the purchase is made at the best price for the quality of the item required for the job. The second goal is to have well-documented records to support the purchase and to prevent fraud. Companies often require multiple copies of all purchasing documents, so each step in the purchase and payment process can be recorded for possible review by the company's auditor.

Requisition

When the company needs an item, a *purchase requisition* is completed and sent to the supervisor or to the company's purchasing department. The purchase requisition lists the item required and the reason for the purchase. If the purchase is unusual or the cost is above a preset dollar limit, a detailed justification may be required.

For the purchase of small items, a listing of several vendors and the price of each item required often accompany the purchase requisition. Price quotations may be obtained by looking through catalogs, by making telephone calls to vendors, or by viewing office supply Web sites. For an online or telephone quote, the source of the price quote and the name, date, and title of the person providing the quote should be recorded. Each company will have its own policy regarding the dollar limit of purchases that can be made using telephone quotations.

Price information for larger purchases may be requested by telephone, but often the vendor must provide a *written quotation* regarding the price and terms of the sale. For the largest purchases, vendors are customarily mailed detailed specifications of the items required, and they must return their *bids* by a specific date and time. The use of specifications and bids is a very formal process and is generally supervised by a company's purchasing department.

Purchase Requisition

L & M Hardware
1556 Lindberg Avenue
Jefferson City, MO 67443-9890

Deliver to:	Joseph Walker	Requisition No.:	672890
Location:	Purchasing	Date:	June 15, XXXX
Job No.:	12424	Date Required:	July 25, XXXX

Quantity	Description
1	Adjustable posture chair
1	Executive desk

Justification: to set up office for new assistant director of the purchasing department

See attached quotations:	Eastman	$1,125
	Miami Equipment	$1,400
	Levy Supplies	$1,750

FIGURE 10-10 A purchase requisition.

Purchase Order

After a purchase has been approved, a *purchase order* is prepared and is sent to the vendor to order the item.

Payment Terms

In reviewing price quotations, be aware of the vendor's return and payment policies. Some vendors have a no-return policy; others have a return policy that requires payment of a percentage of the purchase price for reshelving the items; and others issue a full refund.

PURCHASE ORDER

L & M HARDWARE
1556 Lindberg Avenue
Jefferson City, MO 67443-9890

EASTMAN CORPORATION
3500 Jefferson Drive
St. Louis, MO 67234-7880

PURCHASE ORDER # 91-3434

Date: July 25, XXXX

Deliver to: Joseph Walker

Delivery Required by: Aug. 25, XXXX

Quantity	**Item**	**Description**	**Cost**
1	CH345-A	Adjustable posture chair	275
1	DK8C	Executive desk	850
			Total $1,125

FIGURE 10-11 A purchase order.

The vendor's policy regarding the receipt of payment can be the source of a hidden savings, or it can result in an extra charge. Vendors use the following payment plans:

- Cash on delivery (COD). When an item is delivered, the purchase is paid by cash, company check, or cashier's check. A COD purchase may include a service fee.
- Cash discount. If the item is paid for by a specific date, a discount is applied. The terms of the purchase might be listed as "2/10,n/30." The "2/10" means that a 2 percent discount is applied to the purchase price if the item is paid for within 10 days of the date of the invoice. The "n/30" means that the total purchase price must be paid within 30 days of the invoice date.
- Total payment due at the end of the month.
- Total payment due upon receipt of the invoice (bill).
- Total payment due a specific number of days after the date of the invoice.
- Payment due a specific number of days after the date of the invoice, with a finance charge applied if the total is not paid by the due date.

You should learn how long it takes to process payments in your office to determine whether you can take advantage of cash discounts offered for quick payment.

Managing Money in the Office

As an office employee, your duties may include making bank deposits, endorsing checks, and writing checks for payment of bills.

Bank Deposits and Check Writing

When making a bank deposit, a *deposit slip* must be completed. Deposits can be made in person, by mail, at an automatic teller machine (ATM), and at a night deposit facility. Deposits that include cash should not be made by mail, and coins should not be included in ATM deposits.

Computer software packages are available that write checks and reconcile a bank account. Using computer software is a quick and accurate way of writing checks. The computer prints the checks and records the payment for accounting purposes. Accounting statements and bank reconciliations are then prepared from the information entered on the check payments. The use of computer-prepared checks has simplified the bookkeeping in many offices.

Endorsing a Check

Prior to depositing a check, it must be signed by the payee or *endorsed.* The payee is the name of the person or company to whom payment is made. There are specific rules governing the location of the endorsement of a check. The endorsement should be written on the back of the check, not more than 1.5 inches from the top edge of the check.

The three common endorsements used are restrictive endorsement, endorsement in full, and blank endorsement. A *restrictive endorsement* uses the words "for deposit only" and indicates that the check can only be deposited to an account. An *endorsement in full* uses the words "pay to the order of *payee.*" After writing "for deposit only" or "pay to the order of (payee)," the check is signed by the person to whom the check is made out. Many offices use rubber stamps to speed the endorsement of checks. Rubber stamps are ordered with the company name, bank account number, and "For Deposit Only." The third type of endorsement is a *blank endorsement,* which contains only the signature of the payee. This endorsement is risky, because anyone who finds a check with a blank endorsement can cash it.

Paying Bills by Computer

Using a desktop computer, a business can pay bills electronically without writing checks. After setting up an account with a financial institution, the company enters a list of vendors to be paid through the electronic bill-paying system. When payments are made, the company connects

Voucher Number	________________
Date	________________
Paid to	________________
Purpose	________________
Account Title	________________
Amount	________________
Approved by	________________
Signature of Recipient	________________

FIGURE 10-12 A petty cash voucher form.

to the bank's electronic bill-paying system. Some systems are connected to the Internet, while others require a direct call to the bank's computer. Security is extremely important when paying bills by computer. Passwords and identification numbers are a key to the company's bank account. They should never be left where unauthorized staff or the public can see them.

Electronic Funds Transfer

Electronic funds transfer (EFT) has been a common practice for many years. Many organizations directly deposit salaries to their employees' checking or saving accounts and electronically send withheld taxes to the federal and state governments. The United States federal government uses electronic fund transfers for almost all payments to employees, vendors, and grant recipients.

Electronic fund transfers can be set up between banks that are members of the National Automated Clearing House Association (NACHA). (Almost all banks in the United States are NACHA members.) To set up an EFT account, an organization must authorize the electronic transfer of funds from its bank account. The organization will have to complete an EFT authorization form for each organization that will receive funds electronically. Electronic funds transfer payments are often authorized for reoccurring expenses, such as taxes, rent, utilities, and salaries, but are also used for payment to vendors. Businesses can use EFT to accept payments from the public, and charities can use EFT to receive donations.

Organizations use EFT because the system reduces the time and expense of processing paper checks, funds are available sooner, and there is less chance of fraud or paper checks being lost. If your organization uses EFT, you may be required to prepare EFT payments or review EFT reports to check their accuracy.

Petty Cash

A *petty cash fund* is used to pay for small expenses that occur in the office. Offices usually set a maximum amount for withdrawals from the fund. Depending on the office, the limit can be for purchases below $25, $50, or $100. When an expense is incurred, the purchase receipt is given to the petty cash officer. After signing a petty cash voucher, the employee is reimbursed for the expense, and the receipt is attached to the petty cash voucher. Typical expenses include emergency supply purchases, taxi fares, and inexpensive office purchases.

CHAPTER REVIEW

1. How can the noise in an office be reduced?
2. List three suggestions to improve office safety.
3. Why are plants used in an office?
4. Define *ergonomics* and explain how it is used in the office.

5. Explain the procedure for purchasing items in an office.
6. Define a *restrictive endorsement,* an *endorsement in full,* and a *blank endorsement.*
7. Explain how a petty cash system is used in an office.

ACTIVITIES

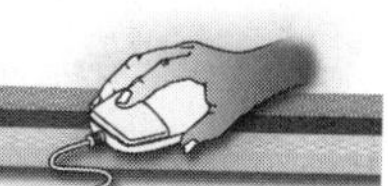

1. Visit an office supply store and write a report describing 10 office supplies or pieces of equipment that you were not aware of prior to your visit. Include in your report how each item is used.
2. Visit two offices and prepare a written report describing the office layout, use of color, use of plants, sunlight, and placement of equipment. Be prepared to give an oral summary of your report to the class.

PROJECTS

Project 19

Send the following letter to Mr. A. J. Lockreim, 1142 Madison Heights, Albuquerque, NM 87109. Use the modified block style with open punctuation. Make a file copy and send a copy to Diane Percy, Associate Director. Set the columns up as a table. Spell in full all the abbreviations. Use an appropriate closing and sign it from Katie L. Barrington, Manager. Use proper formatting and make the document attractive.

We received your Oct. order and have attempted to fill it immediately. Unfortunately, some of the items are out of stock, but they will be sent by the end of the month.

The following items will be sent immediately:

Item	Stock Number	Quantity
Chairs	357NM02	6
Desks	982SRC2	10
Lamps	7243KR1	2

The following items are back ordered:

Items	Stock Number	Quantity
Stands	432158JM	2
Charts	21256CC5	5
Fans	41694PS4	8

We appreciate the opportunity to serve you.

Project 20

Send the following memo from Julie R. Stuart, Budget Director, to all department heads.

I have considered the expenditures that you submitted in September. After careful consideration, the budget team and I have developed a projected expense budget for the next several years. The projections are listed below.

Current Year	Projected Year 1 ($)	Projected Year 2 ($)	Projected Year 3 ($)
Rent	8,400	10,500	12,000
Utilities	1,800	2,200	2,500
Travel Expense	12,400	15,000	18,000
Administration	40,000	45,000	49,000
Temporary Assistance	5,000	7,500	9,000

HUMAN RELATIONS SKILL DEVELOPMENT

HR 10-1 Worker Who Has Too Much to Do

Keeping up with all job responsibilities can be difficult. Improving organizational skills, becoming more knowledgeable about the job, increasing efficiency, and eliminating wasted time all enhance the ability to complete more work in less time. Unfortunately, it may be impossible to complete all of the work to be done because the workload is too heavy for the amount of time in the workday. If this is the case, review your workload with your supervisor. Before discussing the problem, view the situation from the supervisor's viewpoint and prepare a detailed list of all of your duties. Several questions to consider are (1) can some job duties be dropped because they are no longer necessary? (2) can some job assignments be delayed? (3) can job duties be assigned to another employee? and (4) can a new employee be hired?

- What criteria would you use to determine if you have too many job responsibilities?
- You approached your manager and discussed the overload in your work. Your manager said your job responsibilities are not too heavy, but you waste too much time. What would you say to the manager?

HR 10-2 Do Not Underestimate Your Supervisor

Appearances can be deceiving, so it is easy to underestimate the importance of your supervisor. It is possible to have a preconceived idea of the "important" supervisor. Do not permit your conceptions to rule your thoughts. Remind yourself that in your job as a new employee you are not in a position to judge your supervisor's power and influence.

- Describe what you believe to be the appearance of the "important" supervisor. Include a description of the supervisor's office.
- Have you met an influential businessperson who did not meet your idea of the influential businessperson? Describe the appearance of this person.
- From the company's viewpoint, list three criteria that would demonstrate the effectiveness of a supervisor.

SITUATIONS

How would you handle the following situations?

- **S 10-1** Several times you have requested that an electrical cord be removed because of a potential safety problem. Today a client tripped and fell because of the electrical cord.
- **S 10-2** You have an assigned parking slot at your office. Mark, a co-worker, frequently parks in your slot, and you have difficulty finding a place to park.
- **S 10-3** As you walked past the petty cash drawer, you saw Daniel take money and not sign a petty cash form.

GRAMMAR REVIEW

Select the correct word from the words in parentheses.

1. Alexis (is, are) the director of the new project.
2. Bob and Malcolm (is, are) attending the seminar at Georgetown University.
3. Audrey (was, were) late for the staff meeting.
4. Ms. Moore and Mr. Wong (was, were) qualified for the new position.
5. Alan and Allison (is, are) members of the Boston Business Association.
6. The bus (was, were) late arriving downtown.
7. All of the managers at the meeting (was, were) from the Southeast region.
8. Everybody (was, were) satisfied with the results of the research.
9. What (is, are) the result of the advertising campaign?
10. Either Herbert or Carlos (was, were) a management trainee at the bank.
11. Both of the managers (was, were) ready to go to the airport.
12. Chan (write, writes) a newspaper article each week.
13. Hung and Jennifer (donate, donates) to the office flower fund.
14. Vicky and Mary (represent, represents) the department at the annual meeting.
15. Each of the employees (is, are) responsible for a segment of the budget.

CD ASSIGNMENTS

CD Assignment 10-1

Open the file CD10-1_*RPS* on your Student CD and follow the instructions to complete the job. You will also need the file *Repair Record,* which is on your Student CD.

CD Assignment 10-2

Open the file CD10-2_*RP* on your Student CD and follow the instructions to complete the job. You will also need the file *Repair Record,* which is on your Student CD.

CD Assignment 10-3

Open the file CD10-3_IOS on your Student CD and follow the instructions to complete the job.

CD Assignment 10-4

Open the file CD10-4_IOF on your Student CD and follow the instructions to complete the job.

Seeking Employment 11

Objectives

After studying this chapter, you should be able to

1. Conduct a job search.
2. Use the Internet to assist in a job search.
3. Write a letter of application.
4. Write your résumé.
5. Complete a job application.
6. Conduct yourself in a professional manner during an interview.
7. Write a thank-you letter after an interview.
8. Explain the types of health insurance discussed in this chapter.
9. Explain *EAP.*
10. Explain a *stock option.*
11. Be familiar with government employment regulations.

Getting Started

Your employment attitude and mind-set are very important to finding employment. Before you begin your job search, it is very important that you understand the job selection process from the employer's viewpoint. The company's objective is to sell a product or provide a service and, in order to meet this objective, the company must hire employees. Most organizations would prefer to spend the least amount of time and money advertising, interviewing, and training applicants. Interviewers are looking for an employee who will contribute to their organization. Throughout your job search, you should focus on the skills, ideas, and qualifications you can bring to a prospective employer. Your objective is to let a business know what you can do for it, not what you would like it to do for you. Employers want to hire smart and energetic employees who have strong social skills. Conduct your job search and the interview so the employer knows that you are the best person for the job.

Planning for Your Career

The First Step

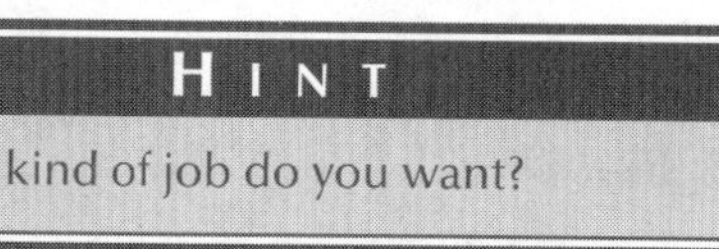
HINT

What kind of job do you want?

The first step in seeking employment is to determine what kind of a job you would like. If you do not carefully think through this question, you may not find a job that will suit your needs. The correct answer to the question "What kind of job would I like?" is not "Any job that pays well."

Before beginning your job search, ask yourself the following questions.

- Am I interested in part-time or full-time employment?
- What are my career goals?

- Do I have personal interests that I would like to incorporate into my job (for example, interests in music, art, finance, politics, journalism, or photography)?
- Do I want to work in a specific type of office, such as a legal, medical, insurance, advertising, or real estate office?
- Do I want to work for a large, medium, or small company? Is the size of the company important to me?
- Do I want a job with many responsibilities?
- Do I want a job with a defined path for advancement?
- Can I work under pressure? Which jobs would have more pressure?
- Do I want a job near my home?
- Am I willing to commute farther for a higher salary?
- Am I willing to move to another city? If so, where?
- Am I willing to travel overnight on business? Am I willing to be away from my family for several days at a time?
- Do I want to work overtime?
- Am I willing to work overtime occasionally to complete a project?
- Do I need advance notice of overtime because of personal commitments?
- Can I work on an established time schedule or, because of personal requirements, must I have flexible hours?
- Can I work equally well with a male or a female supervisor?
- Do I have difficulty working with certain personality types? If yes, what personality types create problems for me?
- What salary do I expect? What is the least salary that I would be willing to accept? (This is an important issue that must be carefully thought through.)
- What benefits are important to me?
- Is medical insurance coverage especially important? Do I or does someone in my family have a medical problem that must be covered by insurance?
- Are investment benefits important?
- Is the type of retirement plan important?
- What amount of sick leave or vacation time would I expect?
- Is the availability of educational assistance important for my future goals?
- Is the availability of recreational or exercise facilities at the office important to me?

Take the time now to accurately answer each of these questions. Then review your answers. Your answers should provide guidance in selecting the job that will satisfy your needs.

Job Satisfaction

A career choice is not an easy decision to make. Your decision should be based on whether the career can bring you both personal and economic satisfaction. In addition to salary, your profession must satisfy your personal goals. Does your job make you happy? Do you leave at the end of the day and want to return to work the next day? We do not live in a perfect world. There is no perfect employer and no perfect job, but your job should make you happy and create an environment where you enjoy the hours you spend working.

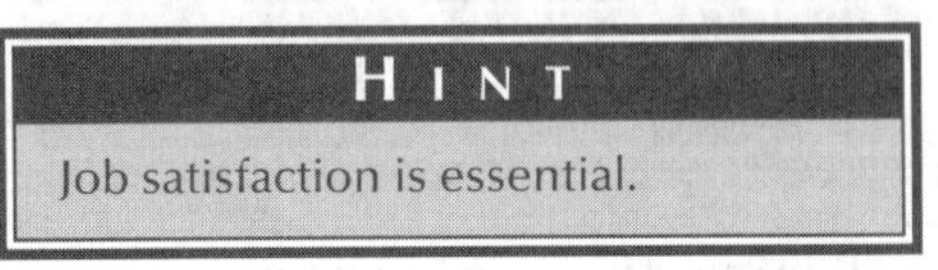
HINT

Job satisfaction is essential.

How an organization treats its staff influences the happiness and fulfillment a worker receives from a job. Employee satisfaction is vital to employee and company success and it is one of the criteria you use when seeking a job. Many organizations survey employees regarding their job satisfaction and publish the results. *Fortune* magazine's annual list of the "100 Best Companies to Work For" can be found on the Internet at *www.fortune.com*. For information on family-friendly employers, visit *Working Mother*'s Web site at *www.workingmother.com*.

Types of Office Positions Available

A variety of positions are available for the office assistant, and they all require superior office skills, good grammar and punctuation skills, attention to detail, and excellent human relations skills. There are positions in accounting, education, government, law, medicine, real estate, retailing, science, technology, and many other fields. Also, careers are available in small businesses, such as auto repair, construction, and lawn service. Each community has a variety of businesses which reflect the economy of that area. Your goal in finding a job will be to match your interests and skills with an employer's needs. Finding the "perfect" job may require you to reevaluate your goals and to accept a position that is "almost perfect." Do not be afraid to take a chance on a position. It may be your path to success.

Jobs are obtainable in most fields because every company, regardless of size, needs to manage its operations. While a good background in office procedures is essential for getting the job you want, it is also helpful if you know the terminology used in that business and, better yet, have some experience in the field. As you search for the types of companies where you would like to work, learn some of the terminology used in those fields. Suggestions on how to become familiar with terms used in various fields and examples of some business terms were discussed in Chapter 9, Terminology of Business and E-Commerce. For example, an assistant in a law office must be knowledgeable of legal terminology, while an assistant in a medical office must know medical terminology. Displaying knowledge of the business where you are applying for a job will help you during job interviews and will increase your chances for getting the job you want.

One way to gain a background in a particular field is through working for a temporary employment agency. Working for a temporary employment agency also gives an employee the flexibility to determine when, where, and how long to work. A job as a temporary worker may last from one day to six months or more. A temporary employee also has the opportunity of working for a variety of companies. This can be an opportunity to gain valuable experience in a particular field, it can be a method of deciding what kind of a job you want, and it can be an opportunity to meet people in your field. A temporary worker must be adaptable and knowledgeable. Studies have indicated that jobs for temporary workers will grow, because companies are using more temporary workers to meet their peak-time staffing requirements. Many employment agencies provide temporary workers with benefit packages and other opportunities that in the past were only associated with full-time employment.

How to Find Employers

No single method is the "best" way to find an employer. There is some truth in the adage that a successful applicant must be at the right place at the right time. You must, therefore, expand your job search to contact the largest number of potential employers. When seeking employment, find companies that are hiring. Look in the local newspapers for companies that are "hot" or "growth companies." Read the local business pages to see which companies are expanding. Using a variety of job-seeking methods will help you find a job that meets your goals.

When seeking employment, it is wise to work for a company with a stable future. Before accepting a position at a company that has recently experienced restructuring or downsizing, try to determine the business climate for that company and the morale of its employees. Does the company have a future and do the employees enjoy working there? If the business will soon merge with another organization, you might be reassigned to another position or even might be laid off.

Friends and Networks

Because some jobs are never advertised, contacts through friends are good ways to hear about available positions. Tell everyone you know that you are looking for a job. When you tell people that you are looking for a job, also tell them about your skills and training. Ask people to pass your name on to others.

Many people believe finding a job through your network or friends is the best way to obtain a job. In response to online job searching, networking sites have appeared which build professional relationships between employees and job seekers. Networking sites allow the user to create a profile, which is a background summary, and then search for associates with similar career interests. When a match is made, an email relationship can begin. Networking contacts may provide the connection you need to obtain a job. Prior to applying for a position, search your network for persons employed at the company. Then, when you apply for a position via the company Web site or by traditional mail, include a referral from the company employee. This referral may be the extra push you need to get the job.

> **HINT**
>
> Networking is a terrific technique for finding a job.

College Placement Offices

Most educational institutions have a placement office to assist their students in job hunting, and many colleges have on-campus recruitment or job fairs. When you talk with recruiters, have a copy of your résumé with you. (A résumé is a brief summary of your background, education and experience; preparation of a résumé is discussed in detail later in this chapter.) A meeting with an on-campus recruiter should be treated the same as an interview at a company, and you should wear your interview outfit for this meeting. Job fairs are usually more informal, but you should also dress in office attire.

Employment Agencies (Free and Fee-Paid)

The purpose of an employment agency is to bring together a job seeker and an employer. Most employment agencies screen applicants before referring them to employers. Employers do not want to waste their time talking with unqualified applicants. In some of the larger cities, the best jobs may be handled only through an employment agency. If the employment agency is not a government-sponsored agency, either you or the employer will pay the agency's fee. Many jobs are listed as *fee-paid*, which means that the employer pays the fee. If the job is not listed as fee-paid, you, the job applicant, must pay the fee.

Read an employment agency contract carefully before you sign it. While you should talk with the employment counselor in great detail before you sign anything, remember that only what is in the written contract is binding. Be sure to ask in advance if the jobs are fee-paid by the employer or if you will pay the fee. If the fee is paid by the applicant, the fee is normally a percentage of the first year's salary. If you decide to use an employment agency, ask employers and friends to recommend reputable employment agencies.

Temporary Employment Agencies

Employment agencies can specialize in permanent or temporary employee placement or both types of placement. As mentioned earlier, a temporary employment agency can provide opportunities that may not be available with a full-time employment agency. Because the temporary agency is the employer, it is responsible for paying the employee and withholding the appropriate taxes. Many temporary agencies provide benefits, such as vacation, holiday, and sick leave. Some positions are considered temp-to-hire, which means that, if the supervisor is satisfied with the employee's work performance, the employee is later hired as a full-time employee of the company and ceases to be an employee of the temporary employment agency.

Newspaper Advertisements

The classified ad sections of city and local newspapers can provide the job seeker with information about a wide selection of jobs. Carefully read the qualifications printed for each position. Often telephone numbers are included in the ad, so that you can quickly arrange an interview. Since the employer may use the call as a screening device to eliminate applicants, prepare in advance what you are going to say during the telephone call. If the newspaper advertisement requests a résumé, you should send it immediately, because your procrastination could result in another applicant being hired. You should always include a cover letter with the résumé. Newspaper advertisements often ask that a response be sent to a post office box to keep the name of the company confidential and to allow the company to screen applicants. Today, many employers request that the résumé be faxed or emailed to them. If you do not have a fax machine, copy centers offer faxing at a nominal fee.

Job Searches through the Internet

Another way to search for a job is through the Internet. Jobs can be located on the Internet in several ways. Many newspapers list job openings in their community and professional organizations often list job openings in their field. As these postings can change daily and can be accessed by many job seekers, check Web sites often if you are seriously interested in finding a job.

Businesses and governments have discovered that the Web can facilitate and promote the search for potential employees. Various organizations will post job openings on their Web pages. If you think you are interested in working for a specific company, go to its Web page and view any job openings listed. While at the Web site, carefully review its other pages to obtain background information about the organization and its products or services. Many companies believe they hire more employees through their own Web site than through general résumé posting and bulletin boards.

As technology advances, companies increasingly are accepting applications and résumés over the Internet. Many companies believe online recruitment has made job vacancy fulfillment less expensive and more efficient. The Web has eliminated the paper delay associated with a job hunt and has decreased the time needed for the job search. The Web-based job opening may include a link to the company Web site, where the company mission statement, office locations, benefit packages, and additional employee information is shown.

The technology has made Web-based automated hiring practices common. Many companies now require that applications be submitted electronically, and these application forms are often called e-forms. To complete an e-form, you may need to copy and paste information from your résumé into the form and keyboard answers to any additional questions. After completing an application, print a copy of it for your records. Some systems will ask you to send a short email message with two attachments, a cover letter and a résumé. The résumé can be sent as a Word document attachment or sent as a plain text attachment. If you have a choice, send the résumé as a Word attachment so that it will retain the original formatting. If the résumé is sent as a plain text attachment, it could lose some of its formatting and will not look as attractive as the original.

Since security may be an issue when job seeking on the Web, be careful about sending personal information over the Internet, even if you think you know the company. Depending on the circumstances, it may be wiser to send a well-written résumé and cover letter through the mail than to submit an application via the Internet. In some circumstances, it may be appropriate to send an electronic résumé and cover letter and then follow up with a paper résumé and cover letter sent by traditional mail.

There are also many Internet sites that specialize in jobs and several are listed at the end of this section. Some sites post job openings, while other sites are set up so job seekers post résumés to an online job board where employers can view their qualifications. If you post your résumé, you must be comfortable with others viewing your skills, previous employers, home address, telephone number, and email address. Furthermore, some online job sites share personal data, so your privacy may be in jeopardy. If confidentiality is a concern, you can (1) list only your skills and job experiences without listing employer names, (2) use a rented mailbox as your address, or (3) use a new email address designated for your job search.

To preserve your privacy whenever you seek a job using the Internet, do not give out your social security number until you have accepted a job and never provide credit card numbers. In addition, set your Internet browser to nullify cookies, so advertisers cannot follow you with advertisements. Remember to remove your résumé from all sites upon acceptance of a job and cancel any job email address accounts you may have created for your job search.

Before you use the Internet to search for a job, create your résumé, cover letters, and thank-you letters in a word processing package. This will allow you to organize and prepare your materials in advance, to format your documents, and to use spell checking features so the documnts look polished. These documents can often be stored on job-seeking Web sites and emailed to prospective employers when you find an opening that interests you. Then, when you find a position of interest, customize the cover letter and send it to the hiring manager.

The following are employment-related Web sites

Employment sites

www.americasjobbank.com
www.acinet.org/acinet
www.ajb.dni.us
www.careerbuilder.com
www.cityjobs.com
www.monster.com
www.hotjobs.com
www.jobs.com
www.salary.com

Federal government jobs

www.fedworld.gov
www.usajobs.opm.gov

Hoover's Business Dictionary, company information in the Career Development section

www.hoovers.com

National Partnership for Women and Families

www.nationalpartnership.org

Newspapers and Magazine articles from company newsletters

www.elibrary.com

9to5, National Association of Working Women

www.9to5.org

Labor issues from the Department of Labor Web site

www.dol.gov

Occupational Outlook Handbook, U.S. Bureau of Labor Statistics, careers information

www.stats.bls.gov/oco/home.htm

Salary information

www.jobstar.org
www.salary.com

Work and family life information

www.familiesandwork.org

HINT

New jobs can be posted on the Internet at anytime. Check job Web sites daily.

Other Employment Options

Many professional organizations assist in matching employees and employers through job announcements in a monthly publication, sponsoring job fairs at a conference, posting job openings on a Web site, and providing contacts about jobs from the members of the organization.

Professional journals list positions that are available locally or nationally, and these publications can be found at the library or through professional organizations. Entry-level positions are not usually found through professional journals, but these journals may provide information on companies that are expanding and may be helpful when seeking career advancement.

Many communities have a chamber of commerce, which maintains a membership list of its business organizations. You could call or send letters of application to members of the chamber of commerce. Since unsolicited applications are considered a *cold call* on a business, the response rate may be low. On the other hand, you may find the one company that is interested in you.

If you are interested in working for a particular type of business, the telephone book yellow pages provide lists of businesses by the type of service or product they offer.

If you know you want to work for a specific company, research the company, complete your résumé, and then contact the company and request an interview.

LETTER OF APPLICATION

When a résumé is sent, a letter of application must accompany it. A letter of application, which is also called a cover letter, should be sent with résumés that are mailed or faxed to perspective employers. The letter of application should *never* be sent on the letterhead stationery of your current employer. Since you probably do not have printed personal letterhead stationery, you must include your address at the top of the letter. Because your name should be contained in the complimentary close at the bottom of the letter, your name should not be included with your address at the top of the letter.

A letter of application should include the following information.

- The position for which you are applying
- Where you heard about the job
- Why you think you are qualified for the job
- A *brief* description of your qualifications
- A request for an interview

A letter of application should be short and to the point. It should encourage the reader to read your résumé and contact you to arrange an interview. Give enough details in the letter to create interest, but save information for the résumé and for an interview.

If possible, address the letter to a specific person at the company where you are applying. If you do not have a specific name, call the company and ask for the name of the person who will receive the application. When writing the letter of application, verify the spelling of all names, because misspelling the company or interviewer's name may immediately disqualify you from the position.

The letter of application must sell your skills and abilities, and it must focus special attention on your résumé. Emphasize what you can do for the company, not what you want the company to do for you. Remember that the company is interested in the service it performs or in the product it sells. The company is not interested in what it can do for you. Customize the letter to spotlight the skills you have that the potential employer is seeking.

When writing your cover letter, be specific about your accomplishments, but be brief. Details can be included in your résumé or they can be discussed at the interview. Do not overstate your skills, because discrepancies on your application will place your credibility in doubt—always be honest.

The letter of application should look attractive, and it should be one page in length. A page crammed with type, with long paragraphs, and with small margins will not make a good impression on the reader. In addition, proofread the letter for spelling, grammar, and punctuation. Always keep a copy of everything you submit to a prospective employer—including a copy of the letter of application.

Your letter of application should include your email address and your telephone number, so the employer can contact you to arrange an interview. If you are employed, you should include your home phone number, not the number where you are employed. Since you may not be home when the employer calls, it would be best to have a telephone answering system take your messages. The first contact an employer may have with you may be your phone answering message system, so create a professional greeting for your messages.

You do not want your current employer to be aware of your job search, so include a sentence in your letter of application stating that you are submitting the résumé in confidence. The perspective employer should respect your request.

After you submit your letter of application and résumé, the next step is one of the most frustrating stages in searching for a job, waiting to hear from a prospective employer. The time lag between submitting the application and receiving a response from the company can range from a few days to months. Unfortunately, many applicants never receive a response to their letter of application. Some employers never acknowledge receiving an application, whether it was sent by email or by traditional mail.

Your Street Address
Your City, State, ZIP Code
Today's Date

Name of Person Receiving Applications
Company Name
Address
City, State, ZIP Code

Dear :

Please consider me an applicant for the position of office assistant as advertised in the May 2 edition of *The Cincinnati Enquirer.*

While pursuing office technology studies at Midwest College, I have worked part-time in an insurance office. In that position, I processed claims, performed general office duties, and keyboarded letters and reports. I am also familiar with computer spreadsheet and database application software. Next week I will receive an Associate of Arts Degree in Administration Technology.

I feel that my job experience and my education have prepared me for an office assistant position with your company, and I look forward to showing you how my computer skills will benefit your company. I have enclosed my résumé for your review.

Please call me to arrange an interview, so that I can discuss my qualifications with you personally. I can be reached after 2 P.M. at 513-297-5222.

Very truly yours,

Your Name

Enclosure

FIGURE 11-1 A letter of application.

REFERENCES

Selecting references is very important, because the comments made about you by your references can help or hinder your ability to obtain a job. When you select a reference, choose someone who knows your work ability. Do not ask your minister, friends, or next-door neighbor unless these people are familiar with your work, job skills, or business accomplishments. Instead, you should seek references from teachers, co-workers, or people you have worked with in a volunteer organization. Former supervisors are usually listed on a job application, so they should not be used as references.

Talk with your references and obtain permission before you use their names. It could be very embarrassing to you if a prospective employer contacts a reference who does not remember you. If a person whom you want to use as a reference is not familiar with all of your accomplishments, send the person a copy of your résumé. The better informed your references are, the better chance you have to get the job. You should select references who will make positive comments about your abilities. A poor reference could destroy a potential job offer. If your references are not listed on your résumé, take a printed sheet to the interview with their names, addresses, and telephone numbers.

RÉSUMÉ

> **HINT**
> Your résumé describes your education, jobs, duties, and accomplishments.

A résumé is a summary of your background, education, work experience, accomplishments, and interests. The terms *résumé* and *data sheet* are used interchangeably. Most résumés for entry-level jobs are limited to one page, but a person who has been employed for many years may have a two-page résumé.

Since your résumé is the major initial contact a prospective employer has with you, it must convince the employer that you are the right person for the job. Most job listings receive many responses, so companies use résumés to screen out less qualified applicants. Research the company prior to sending them a résumé, because your knowledge of the company can influence and alter the writing of your letter of application and résumé. Review the job listing to determine what specific qualifications and skills the employer is seeking and emphasize those items in your résumé. It is important that your résumé be included in those that are considered for the position, not those that are eliminated.

Companies which post job openings on the Internet often request that the applicant apply via the Internet. With this procedure, the applicant completes an application form directly on the Web. The responses are evaluated and those candidates who are highly ranked are considered for an interview. This process eliminates sending a letter of application and résumé. The résumé is provided at the interview.

Formatting the Résumé

There are computer software packages and word processing templates that assist in the creation of a résumé. Do not, however, just fill in the blanks in these programs. The key to creating a successful résumé is analyzing your strengths and deciding what information to include.

Today, many companies electronically scan résumés to reduce time and the costs of the job-hiring process. In general, computer scanning of résumés relies on the computer's recognition of keywords which relate to the required and desired skills included in the job opening announcement. The software is written to filter, which means that it seeks specific keywords. The computer performs a keyword search based on artificial intelligence to select qualified candidates. The applicants who have high rankings are then considered for the position.

Prior to submitting your résumé, ask if it will be scanned by computer. In order for a résumé to be properly scanned into the computer, it must be prepared in a scannable format. Guidelines for preparing résumés for scanning may be found on a company's Web site or included with its application. Your résumé must contain enough detail of your skills and background and the keywords appropriate for the position you are seeking. It is also essential to use only the abbreviations used in the announcement. Scannable résumés may require that skills and education be described in only a few words, not complete sentences, so they can be recognized by the computer software. When preparing a résumé that is to be scanned, use a common, nondecorative font and short phrases, such as "wrote manual," "designed system," "planned meetings," and so on. Do not use bullets and columns. In addition, if the résumé is to be scanned, educational degrees should be written as A.A., not as Associate of Arts degree. The résumé should be mailed in a flat envelope, not folded, because folding may result in the scanner being unable to read the résumé.

Suggestions for formatting a résumé

- Place the résumé on standard 8.5" × 11" white bond paper.
- Print the résumé on one side.
- Limit the résumé to one or two pages.
- Use a good printer.
- Use plain type fonts, such as Helvetica, Arial, Courier, or Times New Roman.
- Avoid using italics, underlining, lines, shadows, or graphics if the résumé is to be scanned.
- Make the appearance attractive.
- Make the résumé easy to read.
- Proofread—*never* send a résumé with misspelled words or grammatical errors.
- Use action verbs, such as the following:

administered	generated
analyzed	improved
arranged	increased
completed	instructed
conducted	organized
coordinated	performed
created	presented
developed	processed
enlarged	promoted
established	represented
evaluated	researched
examined	sponsored
expanded	unified
formulated	wrote

What to Include in Your Résumé

The standard résumé usually consists of seven parts, each of which is discussed in this section. Since a person's résumé reflects that person's background, the type of information included on a résumé will vary widely from one individual to another. Your résumé should be tailored to demonstrate your life experiences to a prospective employer. Carefully read the job description and focus on your talents and experiences that apply to the position. A résumé prepared by someone who has had many years of work experience or by someone who is returning to the workplace after not working for many years may look very different from the résumé of someone who has recently graduated.

It is important to market only the skills you want to use. Persons who have been employed for many years have a variety of skills, some of which may not pertain to the job they are seeking. Target the job you want, and develop realistic employment goals that are applicable in today's high-technology world. Women who have been out of the workplace for several years raising children often have gaps in their employment experience. To avoid emphasizing that the last year of employment was, for example, ten years ago, do not list dates on the résumé. Instead, list years of experience and job duties with the specific employer.

In this chapter, you will find several very different résumés. Design your résumé to capture the employer's attention, so you will be called for an interview. Each item included or omitted from the résumé tells the company something about the person. As you review the sections of the résumé, consider how you are going to use the résumé to present yourself to prospective employers.

> **HINT**
>
> Your résumé includes
>
> Personal Data
> Objective
> Education
> Skills
> Work Experience
> Personal Interests and/or Accomplishments
> References

Personal Data

This section includes your name, street address, city, state, ZIP Code, email address, and telephone number. The personal data section is usually centered at the top of the page, but it can be keyed at the left margin. You should *not* include your marital status, sex, height, weight, or age.

Objective

Write an objective that will show the employer the type of job you are seeking, but the focus of the objective should not be too limiting or you may be eliminated from consideration for a position. The objective should be customized for the specific job. Therefore, it may be necessary to revise your résumé and adapt the objective to meet the criteria of each job.

Sample job objectives

An administrative assistant's position with growth potential and the opportunity to use office technology skills

An office assistant's position with a large legal firm where my legal and office administration skills would be used

An assistant position with a high-tech company where I could use my computer skills to perform the functions of running an office while developing and monitoring the company Web site

Education

Include any information pertinent to the job. List schools with the most recent experience first.

College — **Include the following for each college attended:**
- Name of college, date of graduation or dates of attendance
- Course of study (also list specific classes pertinent to the job)
- Degrees or diplomas received

High school — **Include the following:**
- Name of high school, community, date of graduation
- Course of study (list specific classes pertinent to the job)
- Degrees or diplomas received
- (The high school section is included only by recent high school graduates.)
- If you attended college, it is logical to assume you attended high school. Therefore, do not include high school on your résumé.

Other — **List any other relevant educational experiences, such as**
- Seminars
- Short courses
- Evening classes
- Courses sponsored by software companies and professional organizations

Skills

Include specific information, such as

- Keyboarding speed
- Knowledge of specific software programs
- Any unusual skills that may be of interest to an employer
- Foreign language fluency

Work Experience

List your work experience and dates of employment, with the most recent experience first. If most of your experience is not full-time, include part-time experience and indicate that it is part-time. Employers are interested in the job duties you performed, so explain the duties of each job that you list. Volunteer jobs may also be included in a résumé if they are relevant to the type of job you are seeking or if you have minimal paid work experience. Volunteer experience is looked upon favorably by many companies, because they appreciate employees who "give back to the community."

Personal Interests and/or Accomplishments

Some people feel that listing your interests is a waste of time, while others feel that your personal interests describe you to an employer. Whether or not to list your interests is your decision. If you decide to list your interests, include activities that show that you are able to work productively both alone and as a member of a team. For example, volleyball is a team activity and reading is a solo activity, so listing both on a résumé demonstrates that you function well as a member of a team as well as in individual activities. Any awards or recognitions that you have received should be listed under accomplishments. Examples of accomplishments include dean's list, scholarship awards, and honor societies.

References

If you have space on your résumé, include information regarding three references. If space is not available, indicate "References Available upon Request."

Application for Employment

Companies request that all candidates whom they are seriously considering for employment complete the company's standard application form. Some companies require applications to be submitted online, while other organizations use the traditional paper application form. If you are asked to complete an application for employment prior to the interview, make a copy of the application before you begin keyboarding or writing on it. Practice keyboarding or writing on the copy to determine how many words fit on a line. Your practice will indicate if you must omit something or abbreviate words.

When you have completed keyboarding or writing the entire practice application, complete the original application and proofread it carefully. Before submitting the application, make a copy for your files.

The Art of Interviewing

Planning for the Interview

Most interviews are scheduled by telephone, and some companies conduct a telephone interview prior to an in-person interview. Be calm and polite when making the appointment,

Patrick J. Fishman
7802 E. Jefferson Drive
Cincinnati, OH 45077
513-422-6807
pjfishman@worldtoday.com

Objective

To obtain an assistant position in a company that stresses professional responsibilities in the workplace

Relevant Experience

Administrative Responsibilities

- Responded to multiple telephone calls in high-traffic office
- Maintained calendars for ten managers
- Greeted clients
- Developed a new office filing system
- Maintained office supply inventory
- Planned meetings
- Trained new employees
- Planned travel for ten managers
- Completed travel expenditure forms

Work History

- Cosmo and Sons 2004–present
- L & L Enterprises 2002–2004
- Joseph Accountants, Inc. 1999–2002

Personal Skills

- Proficient in Microsoft Word, Excel, Access, and PowerPoint
- Excellent oral and written communications skills
- Strong work ethic
- Well organized
- Detail-oriented
- Team player

Education

Central Community College, Columbus, Ohio

- Associate of Applied Science (A.A.S.) 2000, in Computer Applications
- Certificate 1999, in Office Skills

Seminars

- Workplace Skills 2004
- Human Relations in Office 2003
- Responding to the Demands of Technology 2003
- Web Designing 2003

References Available upon Request

FIGURE 11-2 A résumé emphasizing experiences.

and be sure to obtain clear directions to the business's location. If you are invited to an interview and have not completed the company's application form, request that an application be sent to you or ask if it may be downloaded from the company Web site. You will then have the opportunity to prepare your application form in advance of the interview, as discussed in the section Application for Employment.

Maria S. Williams
8725 Churchill Drive
Gatlinburg, TN 37738
931-820-4522
mwilliams@mailmy.com

OBJECTIVE: To obtain an office assistant position in an organization where my office and computer application skills can be utilized

EDUCATION: Associate of Arts degree, 2004
Western Community College
Major—Computer Applications
Courses:

Computer Applications	Computer Literacy
Computer Presentations	Web Design
Keyboarding	Word Processing
Office Procedures	Accounting
Management	Psychology
Communication Skills	Business Statistics

Seminar 2003, Changes in Office Computers
Seminar 2004, Global Technology

SKILLS: Keyboarding 80 wpm
Knowledge of
Word, Excel, Access, PowerPoint, DreamWeaver, HTML
Fluent in Spanish

EXPERIENCES: 2004–Present — Memorial Community Hospital
Assistant to Vice-President;
Duties—planning conferences, writing and editing reports, and general office jobs. Wrote a desk manual for the new computer application software.

2003–2004 — Lawrence Health Center
Part-time position while in college;
Duties—greeting clients, answering telephones, keyboarding, and filing.

INTERESTS: Tennis, jogging, and classical music

REFERENCES: Available upon request

FIGURE 11-3 A résumé emphasizing education.

Prepare a file folder for each interview and place the following information in your interview file:

- Name of the interviewer
- Name of the company
- Date and time of the interview
- Location of the company, including its street address

Wilma F. Shadow
812 Century Lane
Missoula, MT 59801
406-555-9807 (Home) or 406-555-9662 (Cell)
wfshadow@mailmy.com

Objective: An administrative assistant position using my soft skills and computer application knowledge in an office environment

Profile

- Willing and eager to learn
- Mature and dependable; can work without supervision
- Professional work ethic
- Conscientious
- Knowledge of grammar and punctuation rules
- Knowledge of Word, Excel, Access, PowerPoint, Publisher, and HTML

Work Experience

- Administrative Assistant, Michael Communications
  Duties: answered telephone, processed mail, prepared payroll, conducted marketing research
- Administrative Assistant, Maverick and Associates
  Duties: greeted clients, prepared travel documents, ordered supplies, managed petty cash fund
- Administrative Assistant, Great Mountain Enterprises
  Duties: answered telephone, managed fax machine, processed mail, keyboarded letters and memos

Additional Experiences

- Manager of charity ball for six years
- Treasurer of homeowners association
- Hospital volunteer

References available upon request

FIGURE 11-4 A functional résumé emphasizing skills and experiences for a person returning to the workplace.

- Building and room number of the interview
- Directions to the company
- Directions to the building if it is in a large office complex

HINT

Research the company prior to the interview.

Before you go to an interview, learn about the company. Never walk into an interview without knowing something about the employer. Doing research on the company will not only give you background for the interview but also demonstrate to the interviewer your initiative and interest in the business. Understanding the organization and its products, services, and goals will help you during the interview to relate and match your experiences to the company's needs.

The same sources used in researching the position can be used to obtain information about the company. Many companies have Web sites, which are excellent resources for current information about the company's products, services, staff, and goals. Also, search the

Barry J. Clifton
20 Silver Lane
Houston, TX 77582
281-244-8896
barryjc@theworld.net

Objective

To obtain a position in a mortgage company where I can effectively use my accounting, event planning, and communication skills to support the director

Qualifications

- Diligent team player
- Committed to detail
- Strong work ethic
- Shows initiative
- Decision maker
- Self-directed
- Professional business demeanor
- Excellent interpersonal skills
- Excellent oral and written communication skills
- Proficient in Microsoft Office Suite

Experience

- Windy River Industries
  Prepared monthly and quarterly accounting reports
  Liaison with board of directors
  Scheduled meetings
  Handled multiple projects

- M & T Research
  Prepared accounting reports
  Planned special events
  Supervised staff of ten
  Wrote and keyboarded documents

- B & C Service Center
  Maintained payroll records
  Answered telephones
  Tracked report status
  Dispatched repair personnel

Education

- B.S. Central University
  Double major in Accounting and Business

- Seminars
  Tax Law Changes
  Event Planning for the Executives
  Program Coordinator Projects
  Supporting Multiple Directors
  Accounting for Professionals

FIGURE 11-5 A résumé for a person who has worked for many years.

Internet for other information about the company. If the prospective employer is a national company, information about the company may be found in reference books contained in the reference department of your local library. The chamber of commerce may have information about local businesses. Newspapers are also a good source of information about local businesses through both articles and advertisements. Also, ask friends who work at the company for information. As a last resort, call the company's main telephone number and ask about the company's business and obtain its Web address.

Use a folder, portfolio, or small briefcase to carry your résumé and your list of references. Several copies of the résumé should be taken to the interview. The résumés *should not* be folded.

Go *alone* to the interview. Do not make plans to meet friends after the interview, because you do not know how long the interview will last. You may be asked to complete an application, take a test, or tour the company's facilities as part of the interview process. If you have a friend waiting for you after the interview, you may hurry through the interview and you may not make a good impression.

Preparing for the Interview

The interview is your opportunity to sell yourself to the company, and you must sell yourself quickly, because most hiring decisions are made during the *first few seconds* of the interview. Since the first impression you make is very important, appear confident, smile, be enthusiastic, stand or sit straight, use positive body language, use eye contact, and use a reasonably firm handshake.

During the interview, emphasize what you can do for the employer, not what the employer can do for you. Your experiences may have landed you the opportunity for an interview, but the interview is the time to discuss your potential with the employer. Do not dwell on your past experiences; concentrate on the future.

In the last several years, technology companies have created an upheaval in office clothing. In the past, conservative business attire, such as a suit, was appropriate for the interview. Today, in many of the high-tech companies, casual attire is the norm. Therefore, a job applicant dressed in a suit would be inappropriately dressed. Overdressing for a casually attired company is as much of a problem as underdressing for a professionally attired company. Because of uncertainty in today's business dress code, call the company prior to the interview and inquire about its clothing style or visit the company parking lot to see what the employees are wearing. You want to be appropriately dressed for the interview, because your attire may influence the hiring decision. If you decide it is appropriate to wear the traditional interview clothing of a suit, a man can enliven the outfit with a brightly colored tie, or a woman can wear a snappy-colored blouse.

Personal appearance for the interview

- Your hair should be clean and combed.
- Your clothing should be pressed.
- You should wear interview-appropriate clothing, which may be a suit, depending on the company's dress code.
- You should appear rested, so get a good night's sleep the night before the interview.

Prior to the interview, do a practice session in front of the mirror or ask friends or family members to do a mock interview with you, so you will have the opportunity to rehearse answering interview questions. Rehearsing your answers should improve your interviewing skills. Dress as you would dress for the interview and look at yourself in the mirror—at your clothing, facial expressions, and *body language.* Body language demonstrates your feelings and attitudes by gestures and posture. For example, sitting forward demonstrates interest and attention, while folding your arms across your chest demonstrates a defensive attitude.

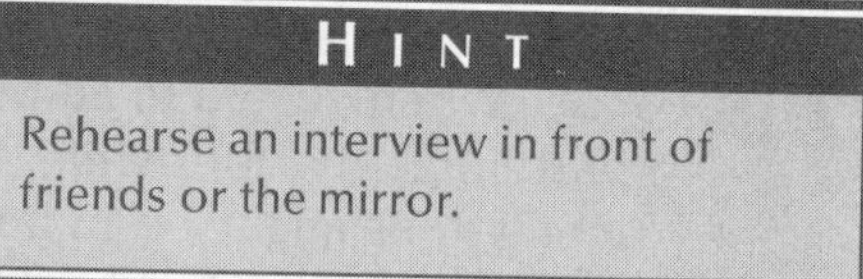

HINT
Rehearse an interview in front of friends or the mirror.

FIGURE 11-6 Dressed for an interview.

Later in this chapter, you will find a list of possible questions that an interviewer may ask. Practice answering questions that you think the interviewer may ask you. Also, review your résumé and determine what questions it may prompt.

If you hope to work for a specific company, do not interview with that company first. You will be less nervous when you interview with your targeted company if you have already practiced and honed your skills by interviewing with other companies. By talking with other companies first, you will also have a better perspective regarding your favored company. You may decide that your preferred company is not the company for you.

Arrive at the interview fifteen minutes early. If you arrive too ahead of schedule, walk around outside or sit in your car. You do not want to be too early, but *never* arrive late for an interview. A day or two before the interview, make a trial run to locate the building and determine how long it will take you to travel to the company during typical business-hour traffic. When you arrive at the building, locate a rest room and straighten your hair and clothing.

> **HINT**
>
> Create a portfolio and take it to the interview.

When you go to an interview, take a sample portfolio. The following are examples of documents that might be included in your portfolio: letters and memoranda you have written, reports you have created, surveys you have conducted, and other business documents you have written. To maintain confidentiality, it is acceptable to block out names and sensitive information in documents in your sample portfolio. Since students may not have work-related documents, they may substitute copies of assignments. After you have selected your portfolio documents, attractively arrange them in a binder with an appropriate cover sheet. By creating a portfolio of work samples, you demonstrate to prospective employers the quality of work they can expect from you.

Take the following items to the interview:

- Pen
- Small notebook
- Résumé
- List of references
- Copy of grades
- Proof of citizenship or work permit
- Sample portfolio

The Interview Experience

HINT

The interview is the opportunity to sell yourself to the employer.

You want to make a positive first impression, so put a smile on your face and look confident. Do not carry any more to the interview than you absolutely need. Leave as much as possible in the car. If you are nervous (most applicants are nervous), you might drop everything, which would be extremely embarrassing. It is better for female applicants not to carry purses. Put your résumé and personal essentials in a small briefcase or portfolio. If possible, leave your coat in the reception office, and never put your personal items on the interviewer's desk.

Always be pleasant to the receptionist and everyone you meet, because you do not know who will be asked to evaluate your job suitability. Consequently, never ask indiscreet questions of, or gossip with, other employees.

If possible, complete an application form at home prior to the interview. If you must complete an application form by hand at the time of the interview, use a pen and print your answers carefully, so the application can be easily read. Interviewers are becoming concerned about handwriting legibility, and some interviewers believe that handwriting reflects a person's personality.

Interviews may be conducted by one person or a team and may last a few minutes or all day. In addition to basic interview questions, some interviewers will present a scenario, and the applicant is then judged on the ability to quickly respond to a hypothetical office-related case study. Some recruiters use behavior interviewing, which concentrates on instances of past behavior as a predictor of future efforts. You may be asked to describe in detail an incident you experienced in the workplace. To prepare for this type of interview question, you should review how you have resolved various problems in your office and how you would address the types of problems presented in the Human Relations sections at the end of each chapter in this book.

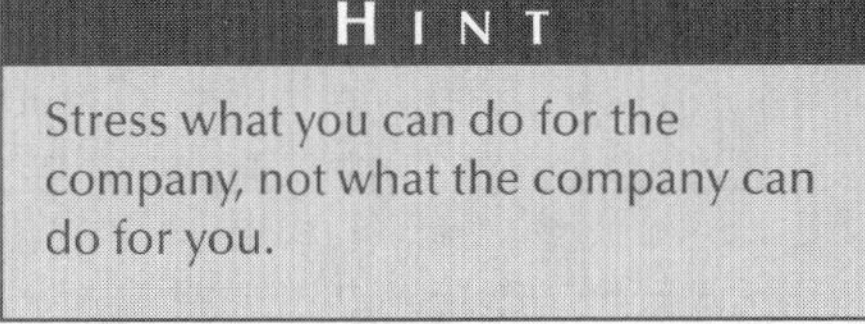
HINT

Stress what you can do for the company, not what the company can do for you.

Some companies have interview screening rounds. If you make the first screening cut, you go to the first interview; if you make the second screening cut, you go to the second interview; and so on. If you do not make one of the screening cuts, you can always write a letter reinforcing your qualifications for the position.

If an employer does not have an opening that fits your qualifications, ask if the employer knows of another department within the company or another company which might have a job for someone with your qualifications and talents.

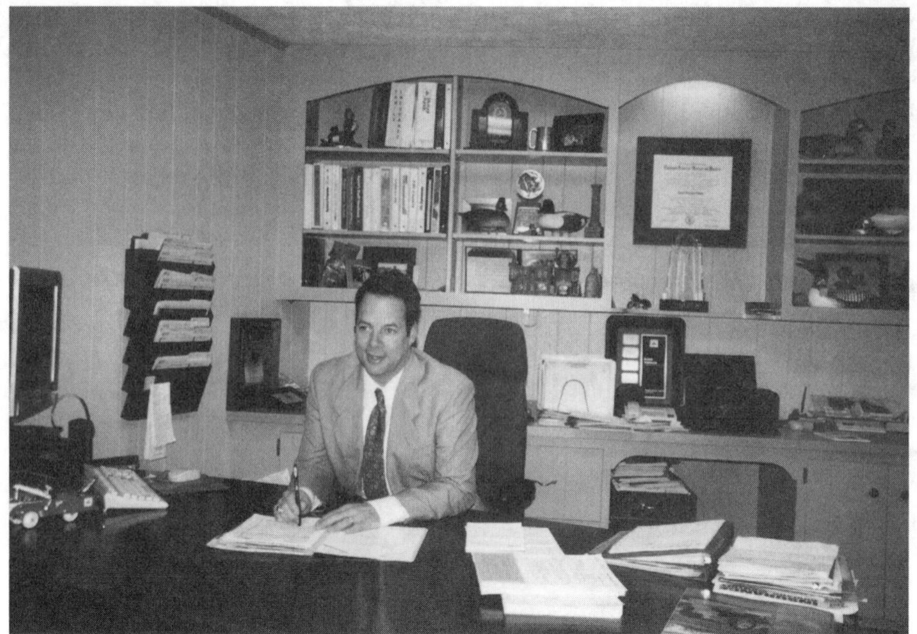

FIGURE 11-7 Employer conducting an interview.

Many businesses now require drug testing of prospective and current employees, because persons using drugs or abusing alcohol perform below expected work levels and may cause harm to other employees. You may be asked to take a drug test as part of the interview process.

During the interview,

- Do not sit until asked to sit.
- Smile.
- Be pleasant.
- Do not smoke or chew gum.
- Do not wear heavy perfume.
- Look the interviewer in the eye.
- Listen carefully to the interviewer.
- Do not allow nervous gestures to show.
- Do not giggle—this is a sign of nervousness.
- Do not slouch in the chair.
- It is better not to accept coffee or a soft drink—you could spill it.
- Use positive, not negative, body language.
- Do not interrupt the interviewer.
- At the end of the interview, ask specific questions about the job or the company. (Do not ask questions about benefits, sick time, vacation, pay, and so on. These questions should be saved until a *specific job offer* is made, because they indicate a personal, not company, concern.)
- When the interview is over, leave immediately.
- If the interviewer wishes to shake hands, do so with a firm handshake.

Some people who conduct interviews know the techniques of interviewing, while others are not aware of them. As discussed later in this chapter, civil rights legislation prohibits discrimination in employment based on the applicant's race, sex, age, or disabilities. Most employers today are familiar with antidiscrimination laws and ask only job-related questions. If you are asked questions on the following topics, you will have to decide how to respond. You could say that the question is illegal or that you would rather not answer it.

Questions on the following topics are *not* usually relevant to the position and, therefore, may be illegal:

- Age
- Skin color
- Religion
- Limitations because of gender
- Marital status
- Number of children
- Race
- Ethnic background
- Credit rating
- Employment of spouse

Most interviewers have techniques that they use to encourage you to answer their questions. Some will be very pleasant and make you relax, so that you do not realize how much you are telling about yourself. Other interviewers are very rude. Rude behavior may be used to determine how you react in a stressful situation. When you go to an interview, accentuate your positive skills and talents.

Questions That May Be Asked by the Interviewer

HINT
Answer each question truthfully.

The following questions are often asked during interviews. How would you respond?

- Tell me about yourself.
- What are your personal goals?
- Why should I hire you?
- What can you do for me?
- Why did you choose this company?
- Where do you plan to be five years from today?
- Why did you select this field?
- What was wrong with your last job?
- Why did you leave your last job?
- Did you get along with your supervisor and co-workers?
- Are you punctual?
- What personal characteristics are necessary for success in your field?
- What were your favorite subjects in school?
- What were your least favorite subjects in school?
- How do you spend your leisure time?
- What are your strengths?
- What are your weaknesses?
- How do you rank yourself as an employee?
- What gives you the greatest satisfaction?
- What do human relations skills in the workplace mean to you?
- What was the last book that you read?
- What do you know about my company?
- What are your future plans?
- What have you learned from other jobs?

- What personal characteristics do you have that will help you in this position?
- What have you done that shows initiative?
- How did you learn about this job?
- What salary do you expect?
- Do you like to work?
- Are you more comfortable working alone or in a group?
- Why do you job hop?
- Will you fit in here?
- What does being a team member mean to you?
- How do you use common sense in the workplace?
- How do you manage stress?

Answer all questions honestly. Try to emphasize your positive, not negative, characteristics.

Questions an Applicant Might Ask

During the interview, you should be given an opportunity to ask questions regarding the position. The questions you ask should reflect your interest in the job and the company.

Questions to ask

- Who would be my supervisor?
- How would my work be evaluated?
- How often would my work be evaluated?
- What are the opportunities for advancement?
- Are there educational opportunities?
- Was my predecessor promoted?
- What would my duties be?
- Describe a typical day.
- How would I be trained for the job?
- What duties are most important for the position?
- How would I receive job feedback?
- If hired, would I fill a newly created position or would I replace someone?
- What is the next step in the interview process?
- Is this department team-oriented?

Questions to be deferred until after the job is offered

- What is the salary for the position?
- What are the hours?
- Is there overtime?
- What are the medical benefits?
- What are vacation and sick-leave policies?
- What other benefits are there?

Reasons Applicants Are Not Hired

The following are reasons that applicants for jobs are not hired. How would you measure up during your interview?

- Insincere
- Too interested in money

- Too interested in what the company can do for them
- Poor appearance
- Inability to speak clearly
- No interest in working
- No enthusiasm for the job
- Spoke badly of past employer
- Lack of skills
- Late for interview
- No job goals
- Too aggressive
- Failure to look at the interviewer
- Lazy
- Poor responses to questions
- Too nervous
- Did not smile
- History of job hopping
- No experience

The interview is the time to emphasize your strengths and downplay your weak points. You will be compared with other candidates, and you must demonstrate that you are the best employee for the job.

HINT

The interview is the opportunity to highlight your strengths and downplay your weaknesses.

AFTER THE INTERVIEW

Interview Review

You should not take notes during an interview. Shortly after arriving home you should record your impressions of the interview. It will be easier for you if you develop an interview review sheet.

Thank-You Letter

Within a couple of days after each interview, you should write a thank-you letter to the interviewer. Since few applicants write a thank-you letter after an interview, thank-you letters impress employers; this letter may be the slight push you need to obtain the job. A thank-you letter also is your opportunity to express interest in the job and to emphasize any qualifications that are pertinent to it. Stress a qualification to which the interviewer seemed particularly responsive. It is also an opportunity to mention anything you forgot to express at the interview and to emphasize your written communication skills. Do not wait too long to write the letter, because an employment decision could be made quickly. In today's technology-driven world, some applicants will immediately send a short email thank you and then send a traditional thank-you letter. If a hiring decision will be made quickly and time is of the essence, it may be acceptable to fax the thank-you letter. If the letter is faxed, mention in the letter your reason for faxing it.

HINT
Always write a thank-you letter.

Call Back

At the end of the interview, most interviewers say they will call you. If you have not heard from the interviewer in a couple of weeks, you could call and ask if a decision has been made. (*Caution:* Some interviewers indicate that *frequent* telephone calls are overly aggressive.)

Name of company ____________________
Address ____________________
Phone ____________________
Name of interviewer ____________________
Title of interviewer ____________________
Duties of job ____________________
Beginning date ____________________
Salary ____________________
Benefits ____________________
Atmosphere of company ____________________
Transportation/parking ____________________
Positive aspects of job ____________________
Negative aspects of job ____________________
Would I like to work there? ____________________
Do I think the position would be offered to me? ____________________
Date of the interview ____________________
Date I sent thank-you letter ____________________
Personal evaluation ____________________
Was I nervous? ____________________
Did I answer all of the questions effectively? ____________________
Did I look the interviewer in the eye? ____________________
Did I sell myself? ____________________
Was I courteous? ____________________
What did I do right? ____________________
What did I do wrong? ____________________
What could I have done better? ____________________
Did I ask questions? ____________________

FIGURE 11-8 An interview review sheet.

Job Offer

If you are offered a job, you must make the decision whether or not to accept it. If you have interviewed with several companies, you may be offered a job that is not your first choice. Within a day or two of being offered the job, you may have to make a decision about accepting the offer. Carefully choose your job. Do not rush and accept an offer if you are uncertain about it. You do have the option of thinking about the job offer before you accept it. Ask yourself if the offer fits your criteria. When you are offered a new job, ask to receive a written and signed employment offer that details the starting salary and company employment policies.

Of course, if you did not receive a job offer that you hoped to receive, your ego can suffer a blow. Ask yourself why you did not receive the offer. If you did not receive the offer because of your limited qualifications or negative personal characteristics, take appropriate action to improve. Remember, finding the perfect job and employer takes time and effort. The stress of job hunting can cause you to feel frustrated, angry, depressed, and discouraged. Always boost your deflated ego with positive comments and reduce your stress level with the suggestions discussed in Chapter 13, Tips of the Trade.

Questions to ask yourself before accepting or declining a job offer

- Is this job right for me?
- Do I have the knowledge and skills to perform the duties of the position?
- Does the job fulfill my needs?

Your Street Address
Your City, State, ZIP Code
Today's Date

Interviewer
Company Name
Address
City, State, ZIP Code

Dear :

Thank you very much for the opportunity to interview for the administrative assistant position you have available. I believe my education and job experiences have prepared me for the responsibilities of your administrative assistant position, and I am eager to become a member of your team.

As I mentioned at the interview, I feel my recent experience in writing the manual for the computer applications software at my company demonstrates my ability to use many computer software programs. I would like the opportunity to use office skills and my computer software knowledge for your company.

If I can provide you with additional information, please call me at 513-297-5222. I hope that you will consider me for the position of administrative assistant in the marketing department, and I look forward to hearing from you soon.

Sincerely,

Your Name

FIGURE 11-9 A thank-you letter.

- Would I be happy with this job?
- Would I be happy with this company?
- Do I think that I can work with the supervisor and the other employees?
- Am I satisfied with the salary offer?
- Is the company financially stable?

HINT

Before accepting a job, consider all of the positive and negative aspects.

FRINGE BENEFITS

Whether you are seeking your first employment or considering a job change, there are many factors other than salary that should be considered before making your final decision. In addition to the starting salary, you should review such factors as opportunities for promotion, working hours, commuting time, quality of the working conditions, and your interest in the job.

While these issues are important, you should also consider the other benefits that a job has to offer, such as medical and life insurance, retirement plans, annual and sick-leave policies, and opportunities for further training. These benefits are often referred to as fringe benefits and are usually offered to all employees of the business. Some benefits, such as the amount of annual and sick leave, may be standard for all employees, although the amount of annual leave may increase the longer the employee works with the organization. Employees may have the option of participating in other benefits, such as medical insurance or retirement plans.

Even if these benefits are not an important consideration in accepting a job offer, you should carefully review the benefits material that is usually given to new employees. As a new employee, you may be asked to make a decision about benefits that cannot be easily changed while you work for that organization. Changes may be permitted only during limited times during the year or when the employee undergoes a life-changing event, such as a marriage, divorce, or birth of a child.

HINT

What fringe benefits are important to you?

Medical Insurance

The major benefit frequently provided to employees is *medical insurance*. The employer often contributes a portion of the cost of a medical insurance plan, with the employee paying the balance. Some companies have a single health plan, while other companies give employees the option of selecting from a number of medical insurance plans. Plans may include health maintenance organizations (HMOs), preferred provider organizations (PPOs), and direct-pay plans. While the differences among the three plans are complex, in general the choice is between direct cost to the employee and the flexibility the employee has in choosing a doctor. Those enrolled in an *HMO* plan, usually the least expensive plan, must go to doctors who are members of the HMO. The insurance premium employees pay for a PPO is usually more than the premium for an HMO. Those enrolled in a *PPO* plan can pick any doctor, but employees receive less insurance coverage when the employee uses a doctor who is not a preferred provider. Employees will pay the highest premiums in a *direct-pay plan* but can choose any medical provider. You usually will be given the option of selecting medical insurance for yourself (single plan) or to include members of your family (family plan).

Some companies offer dental insurance as a fringe benefit. This insurance provides additional dental coverage, since the dental coverage under most general medical insurance plans is not very comprehensive.

As a cost reduction measure, some companies are reducing their contribution for family health insurance and, in some cases, are not insuring a working spouse but are requiring the working spouse to obtain health insurance from his or her employer.

The costs and types of medical coverage vary widely. You may be given only thirty or sixty days in which to make a choice, so this is something that you should promptly consider when given the opportunity.

Flexible Spending Accounts

Some employers offer *flexible spending accounts (FSAs),* in which you can have money taken from your salary and placed in a special FSA for either *health care* or *dependent care.* These deductions are taken before taxes, which means that the deductions will reduce your salary for income tax purposes. Funds in the FSA will be used to cover out-of-pocket expenses that are not covered by your insurance. Sample expenses covered under a health care FSA are as follows: medical insurance co-pays and deductibles, eyeglasses, contact lenses, medical and hearing aids, and prescription drugs. However, in most instances, you must use the amount deducted within the calendar year. If you deduct $500 for childcare expenses and do not use the $500 within the year, you lose the balance. If you know you are going to have certain types of expenses, these plans are a good way of putting money aside for the expense; in addition, they reduce your taxes.

Retirement Plans

An important benefit of most jobs is being able to participate in a *retirement plan.* You were just hired; why worry about retirement? You will not have to worry about how you will live during retirement if you regularly save money through a retirement plan. Although it's best to start saving money while you are young, it's never too late to put money into a retirement fund. Someone who won't retire for thirty or forty years can benefit from the miracle of *compounding.* If you can save $1,000 and invest it at only 5 percent for forty years, it will grow to become $7,000. If the $1,000 is invested at 7 percent, it grows to become $14,000.

Many employers will put money into a retirement plan in addition to paying your salary. Money in the retirement plan will earn tax-free income until it is taken out, though there may be a penalty to withdraw the money before you retire. In some organizations, the employer will also match contributions made to the retirement plan by the employee. Some companies run their own pension plans, while others offer plans in conjunction with banks, mutual funds, or other financial institutions. Perhaps the best type of retirement plan is known as a *401(k) plan,* which refers to a section of the Internal Revenue Service law. Under a 401(k) plan, you can ask your employer to make a deduction from your salary for a contribution to the 401(k) plan. The deduction reduces your salary for tax purposes, so, if you invest $500 in a 401(k) plan, not only does your money earn tax-free income over the years, but you also save the income taxes you would have paid on the $500 for that year. In addition, you may be eligible to invest in an *Individual Retirement Account (IRA),* which was discussed in Chapter 9.

Other Fringe Benefits

The range of other fringe benefits is broad. Some employers provide *low-cost life insurance.* You can purchase life insurance, usually in multiples of your salary, and frequently without having to undergo a physical exam. In some instances, you can also purchase life insurance for your spouse.

As companies increasingly realize the importance of happy and well employees, *employee assistance programs* (EAPs) are becoming popular. These programs offer counseling (personal or business), day care, elder care, health benefits, and wellness programs, including exercise facilities. In addition to health-related activities, companies frequently provide work-related training opportunities as a component of employee assistance programs. Educational opportunities help update employee skills and teach employees new skills applicable to other jobs within the company, thus retaining good employees. Furthermore, under the Employee Assistant Program, some employers provide free parking or provide funds, tax-free, to underwrite commuting costs using mass transportation, such as the bus, train, or subway.

Some companies have added *bereavement leave* to their employee benefits. In today's mobile society, employees often live thousands of miles away from the rest of their family. Because of the travel distance, a bereavement trip may require several days of leave, so this may be a very important benefit.

Employee Stock Options

A *stock option* is an increasingly available benefit which gives an employee the right to buy company stock at less than the market price. The employee is given the right to purchase the stock at a fixed price at a future date. When using, or *exercising,* the stock option, the employee purchases the stock for the set price and then can keep the stock or sell the stock on the open market, hopefully for a higher price. Stock options permit employees to share in the success of the company. The more successful the business, the higher the stock price and the greater the profit the employee can make on selling the stock.

Cafeteria Benefits

Some employers offer a variety of employee options, which are called *cafeteria benefits.* Cafeteria-style benefits allow the employee to select specific benefits the employee wishes to receive from a predefined group. For example, an employer may offer an employee $1,000 in benefits and let the employee choose to use the money to purchase a more expensive medical plan, pay childcare expenses, purchase stock options, or invest in a retirement plan. With this type of plan, the employee can tailor the benefits to best fit his or her requirements.

Anti-Discrimination and Family Leave Legislation

Several federal laws protect employees and applicants for employment from discrimination and harassment in the workplace. Most of these antidiscrimination laws are part of the Civil Rights Act of 1964.

Race/Color Discrimination

Title VII of the Civil Rights Act of 1964 protects employees and applicants for employment against discrimination because of race or color with regard to hiring, termination, promotion, and any condition of employment. Job policies that disproportionately exclude minorities and policies that are not job-related are also prohibited by Title VII. Title VII also prohibits harassment on the basis of color or race that creates intimidating, hostile, or offensive working conditions.

National Origin Discrimination

Title VII of the Civil Rights Act of 1964 protects employees and applicants for employment against discrimination because of national origin with regard to hiring, termination, promotion, and any condition of employment. National origin includes an individual's birthplace, ancestry, culture, or linguistic characteristics. In addition, a workplace rule requiring employees to speak only English on the job may violate Title VII unless the employer shows that it is necessary for the conduct of business. Employers should maintain a workplace free of national origin harassment.

Religious Discrimination

Another function of Title VII of the Civil Rights Act of 1964 is to protect employees and applicants for employment against discrimination because of their religion with regard to hiring, termination, promotion, and any condition of employment. Employers must also make reasonable accommodation for the religious practices of employees unless the accommodations would cause an undue hardship on the employer.

Gender Discrimination

Title VII of the Civil Rights Act of 1964 protects employees and applicants for employment against discrimination because of their gender with regard to hiring, termination, promotion, and any condition of employment.

Sexual harassment is also prohibited by Title VII. Sexual harassment is defined by a federal government agency, the Equal Employment Opportunity Commission, as unwelcome sexual advances, requests for sexual favors, and other verbal or physical conduct of a sexual nature. Hostile or intimidating work environments can be created by sexual comments or jokes. The harasser can be a man or woman and can be the same gender as the victim. Sexual harassment can occur between co-workers as well as between employees and supervisors. Both forms are against the law.

Sexual harassment occurs when:

- Submission to such conduct is made either explicitly or implicitly a term or condition of a person's employment.

- Submission to or rejection of such conduct by a person is used as the basis for employment decisions affecting that person.
- Such conduct has the purpose or effect of unreasonably interfering with a person's work performance or creating an intimidating, hostile, or offensive working environment.

The law requires all employers to provide their employees with a workplace that is free from sexual harassment. The law also requires employers to give prompt attention to sexual harassment complaints.

Pregnancy Discrimination

The Pregnancy Discrimination Act is an amendment to Title VII of the Civil Rights Act of 1964 and protects employees and applicants for employment from discrimination on the basis of pregnancy or childbirth. An employer cannot refuse to hire a woman because of her pregnancy and must treat a woman who cannot perform her job because of her pregnancy as any employee temporarily disabled.

Age Discrimination

The Age Discrimination in Employment Act of 1967 (ADEA) protects employees and applicants for employment over age forty against discrimination based on age. The Older Workers Benefit Protection Act of 1990 amended the ADEA to prohibit employers from denying benefits to older workers.

Disability Discrimination

The Americans with Disabilities Act of 1990 protects qualified individuals with disabilities from discrimination in hiring, termination, promotion, and any condition of employment. Disabilities are defined as mental or physical impairments that substantially limit one or more major life activities. Employers must make reasonable accommodations for workers who are disabled unless accommodations would impose undue hardships on the operation of the employer's business.

Equal Pay and Compensation Discrimination

The Equal Pay Act of 1963 requires that men and women be given equal pay for work when jobs require substantially equal skill, effort, and responsibility under similar work conditions in the same establishment. Jobs must be substantially equal but do not need to be identical. Differences in pay are permitted due to seniority, quality or quantity of work, merit, or factors other than the employee's sex.

The Equal Employment Opportunities Commission (EEOC)

The EEOC is the federal agency that enforces the antidiscrimination laws. Many states also have state agencies that provide protection to employees and applicants for employment from discrimination.

Information about the EEOC and discrimination protection for employees can be found at the EEOC Web site at *www.eeoc.gov*. This site also provides information on how to file complaints with the EEOC.

Family and Medical Leave Act (FMLA)

The Family and Medical Leave Act of 1993 does not refer to discrimination but permits employees to take unpaid leave up to twelve weeks for family- and health-related circumstances without losing their jobs. Information about the Family and Medical Leave Act can be found on the Department of Labor Internet site at *www.dol.gov/esa/whd/flma*.

CHAPTER REVIEW

1. Name three fields in which office assistants are employed.
2. Name four methods for finding a job.
3. What should be included in a letter of application?
4. List five of the suggestions given in this chapter for preparing a résumé.
5. List the types of information that should be included in your résumé.
6. What items should you take to the interview?
7. What types of questions are illegal for an interviewer to ask?
8. What types of questions might an applicant want to ask during an interview?
9. List five reasons applicants may be rejected for a job.
10. Discuss medical insurance as explained in this chapter.
11. Discuss three types of antidiscrimination protection in the workplace.

ACTIVITIES

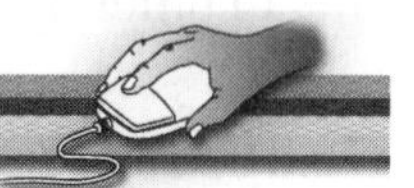

1. Find a partner and practice a firm handshake. A weak handshake often indicates that you have no interest in the person.
2. At home, practice your interview in front of a mirror. Watch your body movements, gestures, and facial expressions.
3. Listen to an audiotape of your voice. If your voice is whiny or high-pitched, it may be necessary to lower the pitch of your voice. Notice words that you continually repeat, such as "ah," "huh," and "OK."
4. Videotape a mock interview, and then critique it either privately or in class. Use a partner and trade being the interviewee and being the interviewer. Prepare a list of questions that you will ask when you interview the other person.
5. Practice sitting. Are you sitting in a graceful, professional way? Is your body slouched? Is your body language demonstrating positive or negative attitudes?
6. Practice smiling. Remember, a friendly employee is valued.
7. Practice walking in an assured manner. Keep your head high.
8. Talk with a member of your class and look the person in the eye.
9. Make a list of the questions you plan to ask a potential employer.
10. Ask a friend in business to do a mock interview with you and then critique it. Write a summary of the interview and the critique.
11. Invite a wardrobe consultant to talk with your class.
12. Go to two stores and look at appropriate clothing for an interview. Select two interview outfits and determine their cost. Talk with a sales representative about building an appropriate work wardrobe for yourself and determine the cost of this new wardrobe. Decide which purchases you would make immediately and which would be deferred to a later date. You are not actually purchasing the clothing. You are researching clothing availability, price, and style.

13. If you have responsibility for the care of a child or an elderly parent, decide how you will handle last-minute illnesses or problems. Locate a backup person if your regular care provider is not available.
14. Even if you plan to drive to work, investigate the potential of using mass transportation. Your car may not always be operable.
15. Research the local newspapers for jobs for which you are qualified. Write a summary of the qualifications, types of jobs, benefits, salary, and locations.
16. Select a job from the newspaper or from an online source and prepare the following for that job.
    a. Letter of application
    b. Résumé
    c. Thank-you letter
17. Ask a company about the accommodations it has made for persons with disabilities.
18. Ask a company how it handles family medical leave requests.

PROJECTS

Project 21

Prepare the following letter and make all decisions concerning the letter style. Supply any additional information required to complete the letter.

Send this letter to Thomas O'Malley, Attorney at Law, 710 Cherry Hill Court, Denver, CO 80204. The letter is from Robert Rosenblot.

> Dear Tom:
>
> How is life in Denver? As you know, we enjoyed seeing you while we vacationed there last year.
>
> I have a favor to ask. My friend's daughter is moving to Denver, and I thought you might be able to help her. I have known Terri Tabber and her family for years. Terri's father and I attended college together and have continued our friendship all of these years. Terri is getting married in April and is moving to Denver after the wedding.
>
> She graduated from college with a degree in business and a 3.4 average. Terri's experience has been during the summer working for temporary agencies. In addition, she is intelligent, willing to work, and creative.
>
> I think she would be a benefit to your company, because she has the ability to grow and learn with you. I hope you will call her and arrange an interview. Her phone number is 716-555-8924.
>
> Tina and I send regards to you and Suzanne. We should plan to get together again soon.

Project 22

Send this letter to Tanya Troll, Office Manager, Sade & Uriz, Inc., 5207 Colony Lane, Nashville, TN 37901. The letter is from Emanuel W. Giegerick, Plant Director. Use block style with mixed punctuation.

Are you aware of the health benefits of plants in your office? Plants remove harmful pollutants from the air and make our office a healthier environment. Now that we are an environmentally conscious society, we are aware of the pollutants that grow in our offices.

Our plant service will plant, arrange, water, and maintain your plants. All you have to do is enjoy the plants.

We base the charge for our service on the number of plants in the office. If you have more than twelve plants, we have a special plan. Below is a sample of our costs.

Number of Plants	Costs per Visit
1–3	$10
4–7	$12
8–12	$26

We have contracts with many businesses in your area and would like you to join our family of customers. Please call us at 615-555-7844 to make arrangements for a free consultation. We hope to hear from you soon.

HUMAN RELATIONS SKILL DEVELOPMENT

HR 11-1 Bragging Workers

An office environment where one individual is constantly bragging about something can become uncomfortable for others. Learning to tolerate a person who boasts is easier than attempting to change the other person's personality. Sometimes people brag in order to gain attention. Agreeing with and listening to a person is a passive way to tolerate the situation. Also, changing the subject, but allowing the other person to speak, may solve the problem.

- What would you say to co-workers who constantly tell you how brilliant their children are?
- What would you say to a co-worker who brags about job successes?
- What would you say to a supervisor who wastes time telling you about job successes?

HR 11-2 Increasing Your Self-Confidence

Increasing your self-confidence is important for your professional growth. A low opinion of yourself can be transmitted to others, and they can adopt the same opinion of you. To increase your self-confidence, make a list of your attributes, review past evaluations, review your letters of recommendation, and review favorable comments that you have received from employers and peers.

- Name three people who believe that you are a success.
- Do you have confidence in your abilities?
- List five of your successes.

SITUATIONS

How would you handle the following situations?

- **S 11-1** Next week the office is having a retirement party at 3 P.M. for Bart, and everyone wants to attend. Your supervisor has said that the office must be staffed. Because you are the receptionist, you will be the person staying at the office. What options do you have?
- **S 11-2** Ms. Kathryn Leadman, the director, has asked you to plan the annual picnic again this year. You are very busy with your high-priority assignments, and you feel that you do not have enough time to do everything.
- **S 11-3** It is 12:30 P.M. and everyone is at lunch. Your supervisor's 1 P.M. appointment has arrived, and the client only speaks a language that you do not understand.

PUNCTUATION REVIEW

Punctuate each of the following sentences.

1. Linda Meyers president of Golds Inc was my mentor
2. Dr Levitt cannot see you at 12 however she can see you at 1 PM
3. At Mollys Gallery we pride ourselves on offering the best quality art and customer service to our family of clients.
4. Charleston West Virginia Columbus Ohio and Harrisburg Pennsylvania are all capitals of states
5. His finances are in poor condition however he is not concerned
6. The cost of living is increasing and interest rates are rising
7. There are many jobs available in the computer industry therefore Bill decided to attend several seminars
8. The new telephone system was installed however there are problems with two office telephones
9. We recently completed a five year study examining the effects of employee training programs and have published the report on our Web site
10. If you own $20,000 worth of stock with an average dividend yield of 5 percent you can now save $475 after federal taxes
11. I just met Mr Hoover who is the assistant
12. In effect you will build market share and increase your profits by expanding your sales force
13. Would you rather meet at 10 AM or would you rather meet at 12 noon
14. Most savings and loan institutions are solvent but a few fail each year
15. Jennifer Minks the lawyer questioned the witness then she requested a delay in the trial

CD Assignment 11-1

Open the file CD11-1_EAF on your Student CD and follow the instructions to complete the job. You will also need the file CDEAI, which is on your Student CD.

CD Assignment 11-2

Open the file CD11-2_IGS on your Student CD and follow the instructions to complete the job.

CD Assignment 11-3

Open the file CD11-3_MSV on your Student CD and follow the instructions to complete the job.

Career Advancement 12

Objectives

After studying this chapter, you should be able to

1. Understand downsizing and outsourcing.
2. Obtain a promotion.
3. Understand the procedures of changing jobs.
4. Negotiate a raise.
5. Work with a new supervisor.
6. Define and use the term *networking*.
7. Describe the duties of a manager.
8. List suggestions for becoming an effective supervisor.

CHANGES IN YOUR COMPANY

> **HINT**
> Today it is unusual to spend an entire career with only one employer.

It is rare today for an employee to spend a lifetime of work with only one company. Even if you intend to work with a firm for many years, changes in your personal life may result in the need to change jobs. Organizations also experience change, and, while some companies grow financially stronger over the years, others weaken. A company that was financially secure a few years ago may experience financial problems due to increasing competition, a slowdown in the economy, or other changes in the business climate. Companies restructure and *downsize,* or lay off employees, in order to reduce their costs and remain competitive with other companies in their industry. Restructuring of a company may create an uncomfortable working environment for the employees who remain after a downsizing, since they often must perform the work of departed workers. In addition, the morale at the companies that have experienced restructuring may be very low.

As a way to reduce operating costs, some firms will hire independent contractors who are not paid full benefits. A company may also engage in *outsourcing* job duties. Outsourcing is a method of shifting an office function from regular staff to an outside company. Usually the intent is to reduce costs and sometimes to increase the level of service. For example, a small office may shift its payroll function from its own clerk to a business that specializes in processing payrolls. Because it specializes in preparing payrolls for many organizations, the outsource organization may be very experienced and proficient and, therefore, may charge less than the original company would have to pay to complete its own payroll. Outsourcing often results in loss of jobs for the company's employees, though employees may be given the opportunity to join the organization which received the outsource contract. Job losses may also occur because in today's economic atmosphere there is a trend to move jobs to other countries where labor and operating costs are lower. This movement of jobs outside of the country is called *offshoring.*

> **HINT**
> Outsourcing moves a job duty to an outside company.

In a rapidly changing business environment, no employee is guaranteed a job. Always be aware of your options for growth, training, advancement, and change. Keep your opportunities open and plan for your future.

Growing in Your Profession

With the passage of time, your career goals or job duties may change. You may decide that the first job you accepted was perfect at the time but, as you grew in job knowledge and proficiency, it no longer met your expectations. Moving to a new job can be a lateral or vertical career change. A *lateral change* is a change in duties but with the same level of responsibility as the current job, while a *vertical change* is the acceptance of a position with more responsibilities than your present job. Both lateral and vertical career changes can result in an increase in salary.

Your education should not stop because you have a job. Employees must continually upgrade their skills. Some employers encourage their staff to take courses, while others require that a specific number of courses be taken each year and many even pay for retraining. There are numerous avenues available for retraining or updating your knowledge. They include college courses, seminars, workshops, CDs, Internet courses, and audio- and videotapes. Being successful in the workplace depends on a lifetime of learning.

Perhaps you have continued to grow in your profession by taking courses or attending seminars. It is reasonable that you now want to use the knowledge that you have recently acquired. You may have to inform your employer about your new skills and your desire to use them in the office. If you cannot use these new skills in your current position, you may have to obtain another position, either with your current employer or at another company. The following is a framework for planning your career.

HINT

Create a career map for yourself. Develop your career goals and objectives.

Develop your own career plan

- Identify new duties that you would like to perform.
- List courses that you have taken.
- Summarize knowledge that you have gained.
- Search for courses that you should take to advance your career.
- Determine the knowledge that you must obtain through on-the-job training.
- Set your future goals.

This is not a once-a-year project, but a continuous process that you should conduct throughout your professional career. When you have reached your goals or when you have become bored with your job, it is time to seek a change. A job without a challenge can be monotonous and dull. If you are not challenged, you will not produce to the best of your ability. It is important to remember that you do not want to become stagnant in your job. The potential for advancement is up to you. You must show initiative and desire in order to be promoted to a new and challenging job.

The opportunity for professional advancement is only one reason for you to seek a new assignment. You may have taken your present job knowing that it was not the career of your dreams, but you had to accept it for financial reasons. There may be a personality conflict between you and your supervisor or between you and a co-worker. Your present job may not be giving you enough responsibility or you may be disenchanted with the duties. Your personal situation may require that you have a position with a higher salary. Any of these reasons may be motivation for your desire for advancement.

Before you talk with your employer, decide what kind of a change you desire. Do you want new responsibilities with your current firm or do you want to move to a new company? By analyzing your career plan, you will be able to intelligently discuss your concerns with your supervisor.

Demonstrate Your Excellence

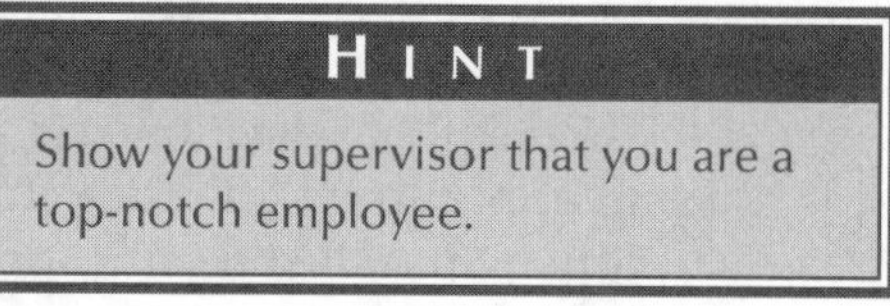

Not everyone deserves a promotion. In today's business climate, you must prove that you deserve any promotion, job change, or raise. In order to obtain the change you desire, you must demonstrate outstanding performance in two critical areas—initiative and excellence of work. Demonstrate that you are a top-level person who is valuable to the company and earns the salary you are being paid.

To establish a reputation for initiative and excellence of work,

- Read and comprehend the information you work with on your job. This is a good way to learn about the company and its projects.
- Offer to draft reports for your supervisor. Also offer to edit reports written by other employees.
- Be financially responsible and develop money-saving techniques that increase efficiency.
- Do not be a clock watcher. Be willing to arrive early or stay late if it is necessary in order to complete an important project on time.
- Be courteous to the clients and to all employees, regardless of their job status.
- Take advantage of company training programs to learn new skills. Also, update your present skills as technology changes.
- Learn about something that no one wants to learn. After you become an expert, you can train the other employees.
- Learn new software packages and offer to train other employees in their use.
- Let your supervisor know that you are active in professional activities.
- Always be professional in the way you dress and act.
- Complete each project accurately and promptly. Always meet every deadline.
- Read professional journals, so you are aware of developments in your field.
- Be consistent with your excellent performance. Do not allow yourself to slip, even for one day.
- Tell your supervisor that you are ready for a new and challenging project. Then develop the project and obtain the desired results.

As you establish a reputation for initiative and excellent work, make yourself more visible to management by letting others know about your accomplishments. When you meet a goal or successfully complete a project, diplomatically let your co-workers know about it. Management usually hears news through the grapevine. If your company has a staff newsletter, send a note to the editor, listing your recent achievements.

Indicate that you are planning to stay with the company for a long time. Diplomatically inform your supervisor that you have no desire to find a new job, because you enjoy your current and anticipated responsibilities. In addition, talk with your supervisor about your desire for advancement and your willingness to try other challenging assignments. Present your supervisor with a detailed plan for your advancement, and include in your plan projects on which you would like to work so you can grow in your job responsibilities.

Carefully analyze your present job description and work with your supervisor to redesign your current position into the career you want. Then rewrite the job description including the new tasks you plan to complete, but omit the tasks that you feel are no longer important. Prepare a justification that supports your recommendation that those tasks be omitted entirely or reassigned to another colleague.

Certification of Competency

One way to demonstrate your excellence is to pass national tests that document your office skills. There are several organizations that will certify your office skills. Passing the tests developed by these organizations is solid evidence of your competency in these areas.

Microsoft Office Specialist Certification

Microsoft has developed many software packages that are used in businesses and has created an opportunity for office employees to validate their desktop computer skills. The Microsoft Office Specialist certification is a comprehensive testing program designed to test Microsoft Office skills. The examinations are given in many languages and at sites throughout the world. There are two testing levels, Core and Expert. Tests are given for Word, Excel, Outlook, PowerPoint, Access, and Project. Employers use Microsoft Office Specialist certification as a screening device to validate a job candidate's knowledge and to promote employees to new positions. Additional information can be obtained from Microsoft at *www.microsoft.com/learning/mcp/officespecialist/*.

International Association of Administrative Professionals

One avenue for advancement in your career is to become a Certified Professional Secretary (CPS) or a Certified Administrative Professional (CAP). The CPS and CAP are professional titles granted only to those individuals who meet the educational and work-experience requirements developed by the International Association of Administrative Professionals.

Employers may look for CPS or CAP certification as verification of your knowledge and skills and may recognize this achievement with an increase in salary. Many colleges offer credit for passing the CPS and CAP exams.

The CPS exam is a full day exam and covers the following areas:

- Office Systems and Technology
- Office Administration
- Management

To become a *Certified Administrative Professional,* you must pass a one-and-a-half-day exam, which includes the three sections of the CPS exam as well as a section on Advanced Organizational Planning.

The CPS and CAP exams are given twice a year in May and November. Prior to taking the exam, it would be wise to take a CPS or CAP review course and to study the CPS and CAP Review Modules.

Information about qualifying for the CPS exam and other information about the exam is available from the International Association of Administrative Professionals at *www.iaap-hq.org/*.

Asking for a Raise

A *raise* is an increase in salary, and a *promotion* brings changes such as better benefits, a preferable job assignment, a more desirable office, a new title, or improved working conditions. A promotion may occur either with or without a salary increase.

Before you ask for a raise, research the job market to determine the accepted salary range for the duties you perform. As you research salary ranges for the type of job you have, remember that salary ranges can vary considerably from one geographic area to another. Also, survey the job market to determine what types of jobs are available for people with your qualifications. Maintain a file of your accomplishments and positive comments from colleagues and supervisors. Review this file prior to your performance evaluation. Prepare a detailed list of your achievements, including problems that you solved as well as projects you organized, developed, and completed. Hand your list of achievements to the supervisor when you discuss the potential for a raise.

Before you make the decision to negotiate a raise, consider all of your options first. Do not go into your supervisor's office and ask for a raise without considering the fact that you may not get the raise you want. The following are issues to think about prior to requesting a raise.

- If you do not get the raise you want, how would you feel?
- Would not receiving the salary increase cause a strained relationship between you and your supervisor?

- Would an improvement in benefits, a better office, or improved working conditions be an acceptable alternative to you?
- Would the promise of a raise in a few months be acceptable to you?
- What amount is acceptable to you in terms of a raise and what is not acceptable?
- What other alternatives would you consider? Would you consider resigning from the position?

If you do not receive the salary increase you requested, do not resign immediately. There are many considerations to be made before resigning from a job.

Considering a Job Change

HINT

Carefully weigh your decision to seek a new job.

Is It Time to Change Employers?

If you are thinking of resigning from your job, do not make a hasty decision to leave. Everyone has bad days and thinks of quitting. Make a list of the positive and negative aspects of the job. Which list is longer? Which list contains the most important items? Weigh the decision to leave very carefully.

Before changing a job, ask yourself the following questions.

- What do I expect from a new position?
- Am I satisfied with my present job? Why not?
- What changes would I like to make?
- What do I like about my supervisor?
- What do I dislike about my supervisor?
- What characteristics would I like to see in a supervisor?
- Is my present salary reasonable?
- What should my salary be?
- What types of projects do I like doing?
- What types of projects do I dislike doing?
- What opportunities are there for advancement in my present job?
- Which companies have better opportunities for me?
- Whom do I know who works for a company that might provide opportunities for me?
- Am I satisfied with my job location?
- Would a better job location be important enough to cause me to change jobs?
- Am I willing to commute longer for a better job?
- If I have a personality conflict with my supervisor or with a co-worker, is it serious enough to cause me to seek another job?
- Am I better off staying with this job a little while longer or looking for a new job?

Thoroughly research other positions in the same company and decide if there are openings for which you might qualify. If the reason you are leaving your job is for more money, discuss this with your supervisor, because you may be offered a higher salary. If you are leaving because of a problem with a co-worker, job responsibilities, or working conditions, discuss the problem with your supervisor, who may be able to resolve the problem so a job change is not required.

If you do decide to leave, wait before you notify anyone, because you may change your mind. Quitting immediately will not solve all of your problems; you will then have the "job search issue" to resolve. After you announce your decision to leave, stick with the decision. You will appear ambivalent if you constantly change your mind about leaving and will weaken your credibility if you stay.

HINT

Compare salaries for similar positions in comparably sized companies. Compare apples with apples, not apples with oranges.

When you decide to change jobs, assess your skills. Examine all of the opportunities available without limiting yourself to your current type of position. Most employees have skills which are common to all jobs and, therefore, can be transferred to a position in another field. These transferable skills include management, human relations, training, organization, computer skills, teamwork, oral and written communications, and public speaking. When seeking a new position, do not limit yourself to your current job type. By using your transferable skills, you are able to explore all options regardless of job category.

Looking for a New Job While You Are Employed

After you have made the decision to seek other employment, you must decide whether to give immediate notice of your resignation or to begin your job search while you are still employed. Most people simply cannot go without a salary for a long period of time between jobs and must begin their search for a new position while continuing with their current job.

If you will continue in your old job while searching for a new one, you must handle your job search with discretion. You should not tell co-workers you are looking for other employment, work on your résumé at the office, or use the office telephone to set up interviews. Job-seeking phone calls can be made during your lunch break from your cell phone or a pay phone outside your office complex. Once your decision to seek other employment is known by your supervisor, you may not receive choice assignments. People will think you are no longer interested in your present job, and your supervisor's attitude toward you may change. Therefore, keep the news of your job search away from your co-workers as long as possible, because it may take an extended period of time to find a new position.

Your job search should include the techniques discussed in Chapter 11, Seeking Employment. Talk with others in your field and let your contacts know that you are ready for a new challenge. You should also use the two techniques, which are discussed later in this chapter, using networking skills and becoming active with professional organizations.

The Trailing Spouse

In a two-career family, a problem occurs when one person's career requires relocation to another city. The remaining spouse may be perfectly content with the current job but will usually want to move to be with the spouse. Large companies that often relocate employees may provide job assistance to the trailing spouse. Even if the relocation is not because of a transfer but is to accept a position with a new employer, that employer may offer assistance to place the trailing spouse in a suitable position.

LEAVING THE OLD JOB

Letter of Resignation

Since considerable time and money is spent training employees, most employers would like you to stay in your job forever. That is not a realistic situation in our mobile society. Although employers frown upon job hopping, it is acceptable to change a job after two years. In large metropolitan cities, it may be acceptable to stay in a job for only one year. However, a record of constant job hopping may jeopardize your chances of future employment.

If you do decide to change employers, do it courteously and graciously. When you leave a job, do not voice all of your grievances and past problems with the office and your co-workers. Leaving on a negative note will influence how people remember you. They will remember the negative comments, not the terrific job skills you had. You may need help from your co-workers or supervisors as future references, or they could eventually be employed at the same company where you work, so their thoughts about you are important. Your reputation is valuable; do not tarnish it.

HINT

Inform your supervisor of your new job prior to telling your colleagues.

September 10, XXXX

Mr. Jerry Edens, Director
Watson, Inc.
3000 Running Brook
Forest Grove, OR 97116

Dear Mr. Edens:

I have enjoyed the three years that I have been employed by Watson, Inc., but the time has come for me to accept another position. I have been offered a position too promising for me to decline, so my last day of employment at Watson, Inc, will be September 27.

I realize how important it is to have continuity for my projects; therefore, I will complete all current projects prior to my last day here at Waston. In addition, I will be glad to train my replacement, so all ongoing projects will continue in a satisfactory manner.

Because of the many opportunities I have experienced here, I have grown a great deal in my field. I know that I will miss everyone at Watson. Thank you for your help and consideration during the last three years.

Sincerely,

Alicia Webster

FIGURE 12-1 A letter of resignation.

Tell your supervisor about your decision before you tell your friends and co-workers that you are quitting to accept a new job. It would be embarrassing for you if your supervisor heard from another source of your decision to leave the company. Select the right time and atmosphere in which to tell your supervisor of your new job. Indicate that you have enjoyed working with the supervisor and the company, but you have received an employment offer that you cannot refuse. Since your leaving may present a problem for the supervisor, be prepared for the possibility that your supervisor may not be happy with your decision to leave.

It is customary to give at least two weeks' notice before leaving a position. To demonstrate your professionalism, always offer to train your replacement and complete any projects in progress. A letter of resignation should be given to your supervisor when you resign. The letter should express your satisfaction with the company, demonstrate your professionalism, and indicate the date you intend to leave. You do not need to include the name of your new company or when you will begin working at the new job.

Leaving a job is not easy—whether you enjoyed the job or hated it. Because of emotional attachments at your current organization, you probably have a feeling of belonging to the company, pride in your job, and camaraderie with your colleagues. Leaving a job and moving to a new endeavor can create stress and a sense of uncertainty, but you will also be able to look forward to a new future and a stimulating new job.

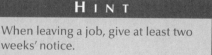

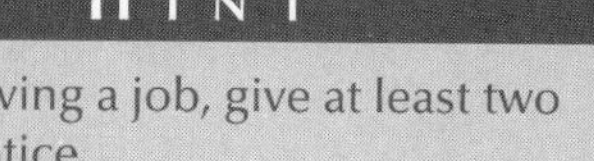

HINT
When leaving a job, give at least two weeks' notice.

Job Dismissal

In today's complex business world, people are released from a job for a variety of reasons. The traditional reasons for being fired are poor work habits and personality conflicts, but a company reorganization plan may result in a change of duties and dismissals. Furthermore, as budgets are reduced, company cost-saving initiatives may trigger layoffs. It is important to remember that losing a job does not mean you are incompetent.

If you are released from your job, assess why you lost the job. If the situation occurred because of circumstances that you could not control, such as companywide layoffs, accept the situation and seek another position.

If you were fired because of problems you could change, you should evaluate the situation carefully and alter your behavior. For example, if you lost your job because you were rude to someone, make an effort to improve your personality. Do not carry the same problems to a new job. If a prospective employer asks why you were fired, be honest. State the reason for the dismissal and then state how you have corrected the problem.

The loss of a job, even if it was not your fault, is still a blow to your ego and self-esteem. Always try to leave the company on a positive note, even if you have negative feelings about the job or you were dismissed. After you have recovered from the initial shock of the job dismissal, spend time building your self-confidence and doing something you enjoy. Spend time with your family and friends, and relax a little to gain a positive and optimistic attitude. Then accept the challenge of a job search and go on with your life. Take a positive outlook on your job search and notify business associates, friends, and everyone else you know that you are now career transitioning.

> **HINT**
>
> Do not let a job loss destroy your self-confidence.

Continuation of Health Insurance under COBRA

For many people, the second greatest impact of the loss of a job (the first being loss of salary) is the loss of health insurance. In 1986 Congress passed the Consolidated Omnibus Budget Reconciliation Act, often identified as COBRA, which gives some former employees, retirees, spouses, and dependent children the ability to continue their employee group health coverage after they lose their jobs. While the entire COBRA continuation insurance premium is paid by the employee (without employer co-payment), the premium is at a group rate and, therefore, is less expensive than purchasing coverage at an individual policy rate. Health insurance under COBRA is generally available for eighteen months, but the period may be extended for persons with disabilities. Further information about COBRA continuation insurance can be found on the Internet at *www.dol.gov/dol/topic/health-plans/cobra.htm.*

> **HINT**
>
> COBRA allows workers to maintain health insurance benefits after a job dismissal.

WORKING WITH A NEW SUPERVISOR

Employee turnover at all levels is very common in modern offices. At some time in your career, it is likely that your supervisor will change jobs while you remain in the same position. A new supervisor will have different ideas about how to manage situations. You will have to relate to the new supervisor's operating style and personality, so give yourself time to adapt to the restructured office environment.

Suggestions for success with a new supervisor

- Do not indicate that the way the former supervisor did a job was the only correct approach. Accept the fact that two managers do not have the same work style or ideas. You should realize that there are many ways to reach the same goal.
- Do not gossip with co-workers about the new supervisor. Accept the change and decide that you will profit and learn from the new situation.
- As soon as possible, make an appointment to talk with the new supervisor about your job responsibilities. Have a copy of your job description with you. You and your supervisor can compare your current job description with the new supervisor's expectations.

> **HINT**
>
> Give yourself time to get to know the supervisor before you form an opinion.

- Let your supervisor know that you are ready and willing to work as part of the team.
- Offer to answer any questions you can to acquaint the supervisor with ongoing projects.
- Do not relay stories about your impressions of the new supervisor to other co-workers. Always be courteous and pleasant.
- Give the new supervisor time to meet the challenges of the job. If you are unhappy with the new supervisor's attitude or performance, wait. It may take a few months for the supervisor to adjust to his or her new responsibilities. If you have a new supervisor and you are dissatisfied with the management style, it is a good idea to wait at least six months before you consider looking for another job.

Obtaining Support to Grow in Your Field

Networking

Growing in your chosen career includes meeting other professionals. One of the terms used today for meeting and forming your own group of professional contacts is *networking.* A network is an informal association of business associates who can provide assistance to each other. A group of business associates meeting and sharing ideas at a business meeting, at home, or at a party can be a network. A network is not a formal organization and may consist of only one or two other people, who, in turn, know a few other people. When you attend business or social meetings and parties, talk with other professionals and exchange business cards. Then arrange to meet for lunch or after work. When you or another member of your network needs business assistance, you have friends, or friends of friends, to contact who can make helpful suggestions and recommendations. A network would be advantageous to you if you were looking for a job, because people in your network could recommend companies and employers to you.

Professional Organizations

A professional organization can help you grow in your field. Professional organizations expose their members to new and changing ideas, provide discussions on and solutions to important problems, and provide a means of meeting other professionals in your field. There are professional organizations for persons interested in many fields, and attending meetings of professional organizations is an excellent opportunity to network.

Becoming a Manager or Supervisor

HINT
Do you have management potential?

If you are in an entry-level position, your goal may be to advance to the position of manager or supervisor. The two terms are often used interchangeably. Both terms refer to people who direct or administer the activities of a business. Some businesses have many layers of management, with each level of management responsible for increasingly larger divisions of the organization. But whether a person manages a division or just a single project with no employees to supervise, managers at all levels must deal with many of the same concerns—motivating and guiding.

As you advance to a position of supervision, your perspective, your duties, and your responsibilities will change. Many of the techniques discussed earlier, in the section Demonstrate Your Excellence, will help you build the experience, reputation for excellence, and initiative you will need to move into management.

A manager's duties

- Managing the office includes overseeing the daily activities of the office and planning for the future.

- Planning office work schedules so that all work is completed by the due date requires knowledge of the project and the ability to realistically determine the amount of time necessary to complete a project.
- Motivating subordinates is a human relations technique that encourages employees to work to the peak of their abilities.
- Establishing and enforcing office rules requires foresight into problems and situations and a tactful individual to mediate office problems.
- Delegating work requires established work procedures and the equitable division of the workload. A team approach is necessary when dividing the workload.
- Disciplining subordinates is a difficult job requiring diplomacy and objectivity. It is easy to become involved in the personal life of an employee and overlook negative work situations.
- Purchasing supplies and equipment is necessary for the efficient operation of your office.
- Maintaining safety is a constant concern in the office. One lapse in safety could result in personal injury, as well as financial loss for the company.
- Supporting the company's mission and philosophy is critical in achieving the business's goals.
- Knowing the company's written and unwritten polices will help ensure that they are properly followed.
- Designing and implementing a budget may be the responsibility of the supervisor. This includes coping with unanticipated as well as expected expenses. Operating within a framework of a budget is a fact of business life.
- Hiring and evaluating employees requires selecting the best person for the job. Selecting the best person for the job includes knowing the objectives and skills necessary for the position. After a person is hired, a periodic review is used to determine if the employee is meeting the objectives of the position. Employee evaluation may require the development of objective forms and a personal conference with the employee.
- Making decisions after weighing the positive and negative aspects of a problem is a manager's major responsibility.

FIGURE 12-2 A professionally dressed businessman.

- Planning and supervising training for employees in a fast-changing, technological world is important.
- Leading employees during normal daily business activities and through periods of chaos is an important duty of every manager. Employees want someone to help them solve problems in their daily work, but most people like to be led gently and not forced in a harsh way to reach a goal. Therefore, diplomacy is important.
- Using effective human relations skills is very important for success in the office. A good supervisor should have the ability to solve problems that interfere with the employees' ability to complete their work. These problems include experiencing personality conflicts, being unqualified to complete some jobs, having negative feelings about the office, and allowing personal problems to affect the employee's ability to effectively produce on the job. Depending on the problem, it may be necessary for the supervisor to refer the employee to a counselor or physician.
- Listening to employees' suggestions and accepting the best ideas and rejecting less favorable recommendations without damaging employee morale is essential.
- Reviewing assignments with employees before the completion date of a project reduces the chance of a last-minute crisis. By monitoring the progress of a project, you will have time to take corrective actions if the project is not progressing toward its planned goals, if the employee needs assistance, or if the job requires additional staff.
- Guiding will be one of your major objectives. As a supervisor, you will guide your employees as they make decisions and complete their projects.

Problem-Solving Techniques

An important skill for office supervisors is the ability to understand and apply problem-solving techniques. A manager who cannot solve problems is ineffective.

Suggestions for solving problems

1. Define the problem.
2. Develop several possible solutions.
3. Write the positive and negative points of each possible solution.
4. Analyze and consider each point.
5. Study the ramifications of each possible solution.
6. Make a list of the people who will be affected by the decision.
7. Consider how this type of problem was solved in the past.
8. Consider whether the solution being considered may set a precedent.

Suggestions for the Supervisor

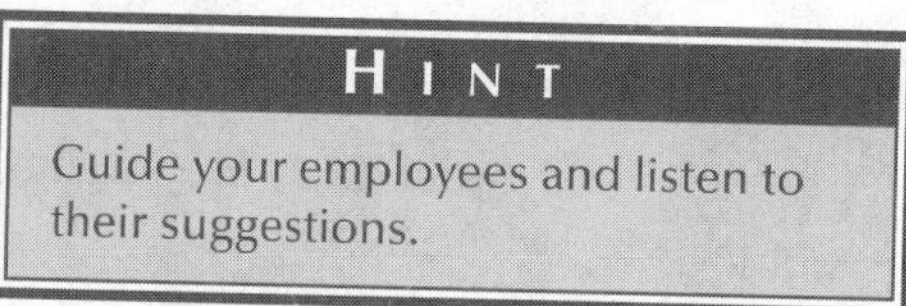

HINT
Guide your employees and listen to their suggestions.

A good manager knows how to lead and help employees improve themselves. Although employees want to improve, they often need leadership and direction to reach their goals. Supervisors must led employees so they will achieve the company goals. Supervisors guide employees to produce desired results.

The supervisor should encourage each employee to become more knowledgeable of company policies and to grow within the company. Competent employees can be "acting supervisors" while the supervisor takes a vacation or travels on business. It is in the supervisor's best interest to prepare employees to accept the responsibilities associated with higher-level jobs and become potential supervisors.

As a supervisor, you must decide when to reprimand an employee or make remarks that criticize his or her performance. The decision should be based on the receptiveness of the employee. If the employee is busy, agitated, or angry, then this is not the best time for this type of discussion. If you have a job performance discussion when a person is in a positive mood and not preoccupied, there is a greater chance that the comments will be accepted. In addition to the mood of the employee, the location for providing criticism is an important consideration. Criticism should usually be delivered in private in the supervisor's office. Sometimes a meeting outside of the office for lunch or coffee can provide a neutral site for a work-related discussion. Always end a conversation with a positive comment, such as "I know that you have the ability to make the appropriate changes, and I am confident that you will strive to improve."

When praise is used properly, it can be a motivational tool. Praise is a reward that the supervisor gives the employee, but the supervisor must be comfortable commending the employee for it to be beneficial. If the supervisor is uncomfortable praising an employee, the supervisor's attitude will be apparent to the employee. In addition, the supervisor's feelings and attitudes will be evident in gestures and other nonverbal messages. The motivational advantage of the recognition will be worthless if the praise is not given in a positive manner.

Employees should be recognized and rewarded as often as possible. A thank you from the supervisor for a job well done can occur daily. Recognition is not something that should be given once a year during the performance evaluation process. Praising an employee reinforces positive conduct and encourages the employee to succeed. Recognition should be given in private and before peers. Supervisors should praise all employees, not only the best or favorite employee. Sometimes it is difficult to find something positive to say about the mediocre employee, but the supervisor who does find something positive to say may raise the employee's personal esteem and encourage the employee to become a better worker.

Hints to make you an effective supervisor

- Be a leader and a visionary for the future.
- Stop what you are doing when someone talks with you.
- Do not believe employees will ask for assistance. People are reluctant to request help.
- Recognize that employees may have personal/family problems, which may occasionally interfere with their work.
- Encourage the employees to trust you.
- Discuss your plans and goals for the company with the employees. Make them aware of any changes you anticipate.
- Involve the employees in the planning stages of any changes you propose.
- Involve the employees in the operation of the business.
- Be objective, not critical, when an employee discusses a concern with you.
- Do not betray employee confidences.
- Motivate the employees to reach their personal aspirations and objectives.
- Encourage the employees to communicate with you. Always have an open-door policy.
- Encourage the employees to retrain and update their skills.
- Encourage the employees to become stars. Star employees reflect well on the entire department and company.
- Understand the strengths and weaknesses of each employee and take advantage of the strengths.
- Be an advocate for your employees.
- Give your staff as much responsibility as they can handle.
- Do not show favoritism to any employee.
- Do not ignore a problem, because dismissing it may encourage the problem to grow.
- Treat each employee with dignity and courtesy.
- Understand the duties and skills involved in all of the projects that you assign to your employees.
- Make the job fun.
- Ask your employees what would make them happy at work.

- Accept innovation; do not reject it.
- Empower your employees to make decisions; that is, give power to your employees to make decisions without consulting you.
- Ask employees what you, as the supervisor, can do to make the work experience more positive.
- If a conflict arises, listen to each employee's comments before making a decision.
- Meet employee resistance to ideas or projects without displaying antagonism. It is better to solve employee resistance with positive ideas than to build barriers that create more resistance.
- As a new supervisor, do not simply change a procedure for the sake of changing it. Employees are comfortable with familiarity. When employees see that a change is not justified, they often ignore all changes, including those that are warranted.

Distance Managing

In today's technology-driven workplace, employees often work and are managed from a distance. Administrators who telecommute or manage employees who telecommute have special issues with which to contend. The success of the employee or manager will depend on the ability to create a working environment without the traditional walls, office chats, and workplace friendships. Employees who work outside the traditional office need to be part of the office community, and creating a productive distance office community is the responsibility of the manager in conjunction with the employee.

Suggestions for managing a telecommuting staff

- Employees who telecommute must be kept informed, but not overloaded with nonessential information.
- Telecommuting employees should not be overloaded with email.
- Employees who work off site need immediate feedback on all projects. Without accurate and worthwhile feedback, employees cannot fulfill the company's objectives.

Motivational Incentives

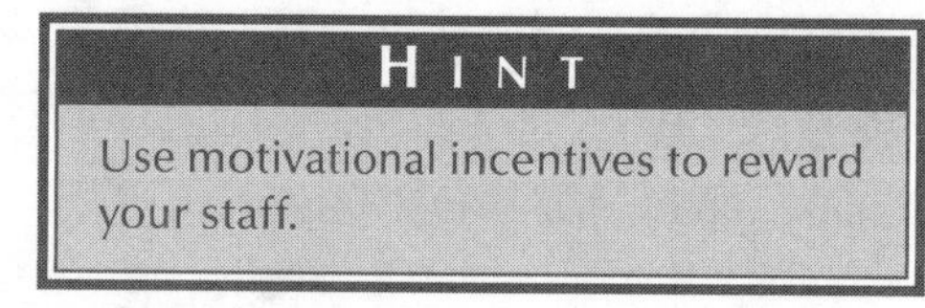

HINT
Use motivational incentives to reward your staff.

Recognition motivates employees to achieve success, improves employee morale, and creates an employee-oriented work environment. Companies who reward their people gain employee respect and gratitude. The following is a list of employee morale boosters that can be used if permitted by company policy. Some of these morale boosters require small outlays of money; some do not.

- Permission to leave a few hours early before a holiday
- Morning or afternoon off after completing an important project
- Company-provided weekend getaway packages
- Frequent-flyer miles
- Special parking space
- Employee-of-the-month award
- Stars of the department, with pictures of employees
- "Great Employee" certificates or trophies
- Company T-shirts, hats, or mugs
- Lunch delivered to the office
- Pizza, ice cream, or popcorn party

- Gifts of candy, cake, cookies, fruit, turkey, ham, and the like
- Gifts of flowers and plants
- Snacks of cookies, pastries, or bagels
- Private employee and supervisor lunch
- Holiday parties (Halloween, Thanksgiving, Valentine's Day, Groundhog Day, and so on)
- Individual or monthly birthday celebrations
- Gift certificate for lunch, dinner, movies, video store, shopping mall, and so on
- Inexpensive gift from a business trip
- Letter of recognition for the employee's file
- Email thank you to the employee, with a copy to co-workers
- Thank you in the company newsletter
- Casual clothing for a week
- Calendar with employees' pictures
- Company-provided home computers
- DVD or CD gift
- Day at a spa
- On-site neck and back massage
- Monetary reward of $25, $50, or $100

Welcoming a New Employee

One of the responsibilities of the supervisor is to welcome new employees and introduce them to their new workplace and co-workers. The following are suggestions to help you orient new employees.

- Provide a tour of the department.
- Introduce the employee to department members.
- Assign a mentor from the department.
- Explain the daily work routine.
- Explain when and where breaks and lunch are taken.
- Explain the department's objectives.
- Explain how the employee's job relates to other jobs in the department and in the company.
- Explain the company organization chart.
- Explain building fire and safety procedures.

HINT

Make a new employee feel comfortable and quickly become a member of the team.

Evaluation

One of the duties of the supervisor is the evaluation of employees. Evaluations should be based on realistic criteria, not on subjective thoughts. Positive and negative comments should be documented and kept in the employee's file to be reviewed prior to the evaluation. Review the sample evaluation form, and revise it to meet the specific objectives of your office. The specific duties of each employee as listed on the job description are placed on that employee's evaluation form. The performance evaluation should rate how well employees are performing the job duties contained in their job descriptions. Prior to completing an employee's evaluation, the supervisor should review past performance evaluations and compare past evaluations with current performance. The supervisor also should review whether there are changes in the employee's duties or changes in the workplace that could impact employee performance. While company policy determines how often a review is conducted, standard times for reviews are three months, six months, and yearly.

Name
Job Title
Date
Supervisor

Complete the following for each duty in the job description.
1 = Unsatisfactory 2 = Marginal 3 = Acceptable
4 = Commendable 5 = Outstanding

Duty Rating: 1 2 3 4 5
Comments:

Duty Rating: 1 2 3 4 5
Comments:

Duty Rating: 1 2 3 4 5
Comments:

Duty Rating: 1 2 3 4 5
Comments:

Duty Rating: 1 2 3 4 5
Comments:

Work Habits Rating: 1 2 3 4 5
Comments:

Cooperativeness Rating: 1 2 3 4 5
Comments:

Flexibility Rating: 1 2 3 4 5
Comments:

Initiative Rating: 1 2 3 4 5
Comments:

Overall Rating Rating: 1 2 3 4 5
Comments:

FIGURE 12-3 An employee evaluation form.

CHAPTER REVIEW

1. List three suggestions for obtaining a promotion.
2. List five questions that employees should ask of themselves before changing jobs.
3. Define the term *networking*.
4. Describe two reasons employees are dismissed from jobs.
5. List five duties of a supervisor.
6. List five suggestions, as discussed in this chapter, for a supervisor.
7. List two suggestions for managing a telecommuting staff.
8. List three motivational incentives.
9. List two suggestions for welcoming a new employee.

ACTIVITIES

1. Review local newspapers for meetings of professional organizations. The chamber of commerce and library may have a list of professional organizations in your area. Contact three organizations that interest you and ask for information concerning the scope of the organization, frequency of meetings, location of meetings, cost of membership, and requirements for membership.
2. List ten people who are members of your network. Indicate how you have helped them and how they have helped you. Also, indicate the future assistance you expect to receive from them and how you expect to help them.
3. Describe the type of office environment in which you would like to be a supervisor. Include the number of employees, type of business, description of the office, and duties of the supervisor.
4. Observe an office environment and write a report describing either how time was used efficiently or how time was wasted.
5. Videotape a role-playing situation in which you request a raise in salary. Include the following situations: the raise is given; it is denied; it is denied, but a job-title change is offered with the promise of a raise later.
6. Prepare a videotape of a role-playing situation in which you notify your supervisor that you have accepted another job.
7. Write a letter of resignation for a position you have held for three years.
8. Ask two companies to describe motivational incentives they use.

PROJECTS

Project 23

Write a memorandum to the staff requesting the completion, by the end of the month, of the following survey form. The memo is from you, and your title is Benefits Officer. Create a survey form which provides space for responses to the questions. If possible, insert an appropriate graphic on your survey form.

Do You Need Childcare or Elder Care?

Name
Home address
Home telephone number
Department
Department telephone number
How many children need care?
Ages of children
How are children cared for now?
What arrangements have you made if the child is ill?
Is your spouse employed?
Does your spouse's employment offer child-elder care?
Do you need elder care?
Age of adult
Comments

Project 24

Send the following letter to Danielle Levine. It is from Maxine R. Woodman, Director of Employee Development. Provide any information necessary to complete the letter and use a modified block style with open punctuation.

> Developing your management skills is essential to your professional and personal growth. We are offering several seminars to help you reach your potential and grow professionally.
>
> Listed below are the titles and dates of the seminars.
>
> | | |
> |---|---|
> | Assertiveness Training | Sept. 2, 3, 4 |
> | Decision Making | Sept. 18, 19, 20 |
> | New Computer Techniques | Oct. 2, 3, 4 |
> | Review of Basic Skills | Oct. 10, 11, 12 |
> | Writing for the Future | Nov. 6, 7, 8 |
>
> Contact Sharon McKinley at 800-286-5175 to reserve your place at the seminar.

HUMAN RELATIONS SKILL DEVELOPMENT

HR 12-1 Anger in the Office

The ability to control anger is an important skill to develop. There are many office-related situations which can cause the most even-tempered person to become angry. A temper tantrum, however, is not professional behavior for an office. Removing the frustrations a person feels can be a healthy release for the body; internalizing anger can cause problems, including physical illness. Outlets for anger include tearing up paper, engaging in physical exercise, talking with a friend, writing a nasty note and destroying it, performing an activity that you enjoy, and deciding that the anger is not worth the bother. In the workplace, do not allow others to see your anger. If you are furious about something, go for a walk, get a drink of water, or close your door and rest for a few moments. Understanding and responding appropriately to your own anger and the anger of clients, supervisors, co-workers, and others will help you create a better working environment.

- Do you lose your temper easily?
- What causes you to lose your temper?
- In the office, how are you going to manage your anger?
- You are the manager, and an employee approaches you in a fit of anger. How are you going to handle the situation?
- Describe an incident in which a co-worker showed great anger.

HR 12-2 Emotions in the Office

Some people are very sensitive and become hurt easily. They may have difficulty accepting criticism—either justified or unjustified. A negative comment about a project may be taken personally, although the comment was meant to be constructive criticism. A nasty remark from a co-worker may make a person feel worthless. All of these situations can cause a person to cry. Telling someone to control his or her emotions is easy, but it may be difficult for the person do so. If you feel your emotions are out of control and if you feel you are going to cry, walk quickly to the rest room. This should give you the privacy you need to regain your composure. If the rest room does not give you privacy, walk to another floor, walk outside, or sit in your car. Most supervisors do not like to deal with tears and do not know how to handle them.

- How would you handle the situation if your supervisor screamed at you in front of a client?
- How would you handle the situation if your supervisor has personal problems at home and takes the frustration out on you by telling you that everything you do is wrong?
- How would you handle the problem of an employee crying as you discussed the employee's poor performance?

SITUATIONS

As the supervisor of the department, how would you handle the following situations?

- **S 12-1** Katie used to be a good team worker and would do her share of the work. For the last three months, she has not been doing her share of the work, and other employees have begun to complain to you.
- **S 12-2** Daniel is habitually late for work. During the last seven days he has been late four times. When he arrives, he always has an excuse.
- **S 12-3** Marsha has a negative attitude and she constantly exhibits it by being rude and snapping at clients and co-workers.

PUNCTUATION REVIEW

Punctuate each of the following sentences.

1. Did the computers arrive Mary asked
2. Yes Ms Cheung we can repair the copying machine before 2 PM on Friday January 16 so you can print the report by your due date
3. Ms Patterson the realtor works most weekends but she enjoys her job
4. After work we are going to a professional meeting
5. Our efficient easy to learn computer software base package will take only eight hours to learn and you do not need prior computer experience to understand it
6. My vacation time has been changed from August to September
7. According to an industry survey JoLib was ranked No. 1 in client service among mid-size accounting firms
8. Mr Ford said I had approval to take my vacation in July
9. If you study the Martin Report carefully you will see the error on page 12 therefore you will understand the problems we are now experiencing
10. When the computer crashed I lost the document I was creating
11. Dr Mason cannot see you on Wednesday but Dr Johnson is available then

12. The top two floors of the Champagne Office Complex which is located at 7th Avenue have been renovated
13. Todays staff meeting is canceled but we will reschedule it for tomorrow
14. When I travel on business I usually fly northern airlines
15. Because of the court decision the company changed its name

CD ASSIGNMENTS

CD Assignment 12-1

Open the file CD12-1_EE on your Student CD and follow the instructions to complete the job. You will also need the file Employee Evaluation Form, which is on your Student CD.

CD Assignment 12-2

Open the file CD12-2_EIC on your Student CD and follow the instructions to complete the job.

Tips of the Trade

13

Objectives

After studying this chapter, you should be able to

1. Improve your office efficiency.
2. Handle office stress.
3. Dress appropriately for the office.
4. Improve your map-reading skills.
5. Handle work-related problems.

INTRODUCTION

This final chapter is different from the other chapters in this book. Rather than discussing another specific area of office procedures, this chapter will concentrate on *you* and how you can improve your office efficiency and handle work-related problems. This chapter is filled with hints and techniques that usually come only with years of on-the-job experience. Many of the techniques discussed in this chapter are as applicable to your personal life as they are to your professional career. Mastery of these skills, therefore, will aid in your personal as well as your professional growth.

PERSONAL HINTS

- Be a productive member of the team.
- Be a catalyst for innovation.
- Build a consensus for implementing your ideas.
- Use feedback from co-workers to fine-tune your projects.
- Anticipate problems, so you are ready to solve them.
- Prioritize your jobs and constantly review your priorities.
- Keep yourself focused on your objectives.
- Look for projects that will spotlight your talents.
- Avoid statements that trigger a negative response.
- Repair damaged professional relationships before it is too late.
- Use a smile to help you win the support you need for an idea.
- Redirect anger in a positive way.
- Change your mind-set to see obstacles as opportunities to succeed.
- Always be nonjudgmental.
- Always have a positive attitude.

- Inspire creative thinking and inspire employees.
- Understand that learning is an ongoing process. Do not limit yourself to what you know today. Learn for the future. Realize that your skills are quickly outmoded and need to be updated frequently.
- Expect interruptions but do not allow them to irritate you. Interruptions are a daily occurrence in the life of an office employee. Do not allow interruptions to sabotage your productivity.
- In your role of office assistant, people will think you have answers for everything. They may expect you to be able to answer questions that are not pertinent to your job. Never be rude to anyone. Always answer questions in a courteous manner and to the best of your ability. If you do not know the answer to a question, indicate that you will try to locate the requested information.
- Read the newspaper daily to be informed about the political and business environment in your area. The business world changes frequently, and it is essential that you read articles in professional journals. Read about your competitors to learn as much about them as you can. Learn what they are planning, their goals, their image, who their clients are, and their financial position.
- Use sick leave when it is appropriate. Do not expose your colleagues to germs, but do not use sick leave because you want a day free from work.
- Join professional organizations, so your name will become familiar to business associates inside and outside your company. By increasing your visibility, you may reap the benefits professionally.

Separating Your Personal and Office Lives

Leave your personal life and problems at home, and leave your office life and problems at the office. Make a conscious effort to separate the two phases of your life. Taking your office problems home every day will interfere with the enjoyment of your personal life. The relaxation and stimulation you receive from your personal life will enhance your ability to handle office problems. Separating office problems and home problems is not easy, but with practice it can work.

Pick Yourself Up

Everyone has days when nothing seems to go right. To boost your morale, remember your strong points and the positive comments you have received. Also, remind yourself that there will be good days again.

Do not become upset or become defensive after receiving constructive criticism; accept it and learn from it. Consider the validity of the comments and modify your behavior accordingly.

Compliments

If someone gives you a compliment, accept it and say "thank you." Some people respond with a denial of the compliment. For example, if you receive a compliment on your presentation, do not say, "I did not think that I made a good presentation."

Recognition

Employee recognition is motivating and uplifting. People like to know that their contributions to the workplace are valued, and they like to feel that they are important and appreciated. Offices often remember employees on Bosses' Day, during the second full week in October, and Administrative Professionals Week, during the last full week (Sunday to Saturday) in April.

Rumors

Use rumors to your advantage. For example, if you hear that your department or company will be restructuring, talk with your supervisor about accepting responsibility for a new project that will allow you to improve your skills and demonstrate your capabilities. Then, when a new opportunity arises, you will have the required knowledge to step into the job.

Mentors

A mentor is a person who advises and guides. Frequently, a mentor is a person who has obtained a position higher than yours and who is willing to provide advice. A mentor can make your career advance more quickly and can steer you in the proper direction when a career choice must be made. The selection of a mentor is an informal process, and the relationship often is not directly stated between the parties. Rather, the mentoring relationship gradually develops through mutual understanding and trust. Sometimes mentoring is more formal, and some organizations establish mentoring programs for new employees, in which the new hire is guided by a senior employee.

Thank-You Notes

Write thank-you letters to people, such as teachers, mentors, and supervisors, who have helped you. Also write to colleagues and employees who have positions at a higher level than yours. People enjoy knowing that their help is appreciated.

Office Clothing

Let your voice, appearance, and personal characteristics create the stage for your professional image. A professional is aware of the importance the business community attaches to appearance. When first entering the working world, you may have to adjust your wardrobe from that of a college student to clothing appropriate for a working person. It is wise not to completely change your wardrobe at one time. Buy a few things and decide if they are appropriate. Look at how the others in your office dress, and give special attention to the wardrobes of people who have jobs to which you would like to advance. Do the men wear ties, suits, or sport coats? Do the women wear suits, dresses, blazers, or separates—slacks, skirts, and sweaters? Then try to dress like those who have the job you would like in the future, rather than dressing for your present job. Executives may see that you are a candidate for advancement if your professional appearance supports your professional work.

In some traditional offices, jackets must be worn by men and women. The jacket may be removed while working but should be worn when a client comes into the office. When wearing jewelry, keep it classic; if you can hear it, too much is being worn.

In the last few years, the clothing worn in the workplace has become more casual. In some offices where the employees daily dress in traditional business attire, employees dress casually on Fridays. On Fridays, the employees wear *business casual,* casual clothing with a professional appearance—not jeans or sweat outfits. Dress-down days have become more popular, particularly in the summer months. Offices that have a casual Friday policy may have a provision that states that, if there is a meeting with clients on a Friday, traditional business attire is appropriate instead of casual attire. In some offices, dress-down Fridays have evolved into business casual every day. Workers in many high-tech and dot com companies daily wear casual clothing instead of business professional attire.

Some employers feel that the clothing worn today is too casual and inappropriate for the office. In most offices jeans are not acceptable, and T-shirts with ludicrous remarks are unsuitable. For women, skirts that are too short or blouses that are cut too low are not appropriate office attire.

Always dress appropriately for the office. The one day that you dress in a nonbusiness manner will unexpectedly be the day that it will be important for you to look professional.

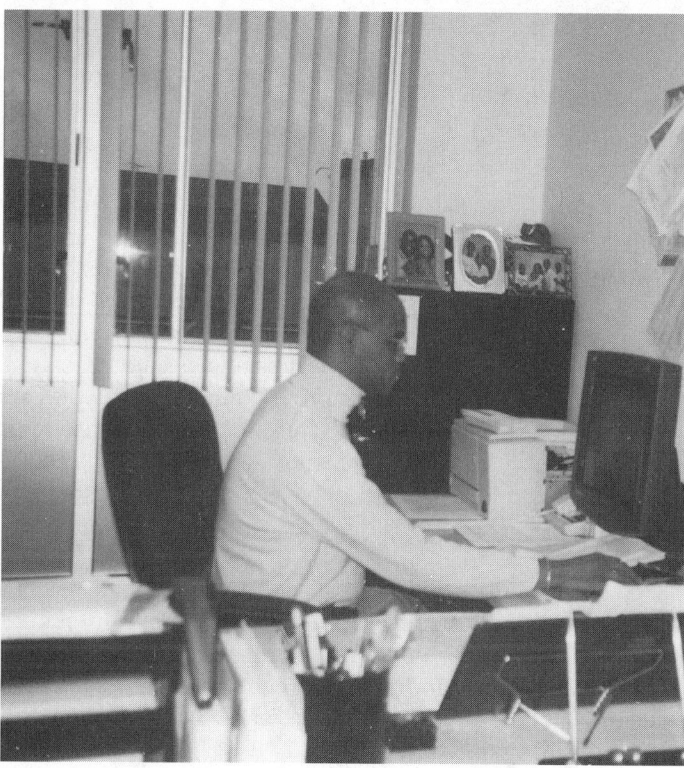

FIGURE 13-1 An employee dressed in business casual clothing.

In bad weather, some people dress in a sloppy manner. Do not embarrass yourself by dressing in a messy and unprofessional style.

Plan your outfit the night before, so you do not waste precious morning hours selecting an outfit. To save time, organize your closet, so that it is easy to coordinate outfits.

Buy good-quality clothing that will last, rather than fad items that quickly go out of style. Update your wardrobe each season with a few fashionable purchases.

HINT
What is the proper attire for your workplace?

An important aspect of appearance is a rested body. Always allow sufficient time for rest and sleep because you cannot function properly in the office if you are drowsy and exhausted.

Humor in the Workplace

As adults, we have learned to control our humor and often do not allow it to enter the workplace. Today the trend is changing. Humor has a respectable place in the world of work. Humor encourages people to see fun and laughter in difficult or tiresome situations, and it can help dissipate an angry confrontation. In addition, humor can help relieve stress, put people at ease, improve morale, and boost your ability to focus on the issue at hand. However, do not laugh at or exploit the plight or background of others.

Is humor a part of your lifestyle?

- Do you often see the humor in a situation?
- Do you laugh at jokes?
- Do you tell jokes?
- Do you sparkle when you hear a funny story?
- Do you share humorous situations or stories with others?
- Would your friends and colleagues say you have a sense of humor?

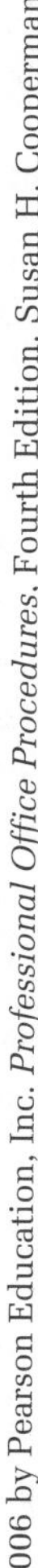

- Would your supervisor say you have a sense of humor?
- Do you take yourself too seriously?

Hints for Your Office

Write It Down

One of the most important hints for the office is *read, watch, listen, and take notes on everything.* Pay particular attention to details. Handheld computer organizers are very helpful for note taking and personal organization, because they are easily accessible. If you do not take notes, you will not remember how to do something the next time the same situation occurs. Write yourself notes about a project and, most importantly, organize your notes so you can find them later. To organize your notes, use a 3" × 5" card file box, a notebook with dividers, file folders, or a computer software package. A year later, you may have a question about something you did. If you cannot find your notes, it is as if they were never made.

Know Your Office Location

Be able to give directions to your office from public transportation, main roads, and interstate highways. Be able to explain to others the location of your office by describing the distinctive features and color of your building, as well as the landmarks, street intersections, restaurants, and stores near it. Can you describe where a visitor should park, how to enter the building, or how to walk through a large building to find your office?

Employee Notification

An emergency situation or weather-related problem could occur, requiring the unexpected closing of the office before employees leave home for work in the morning. There are several ways an office can create an employee at-home emergency notification system. Information about the closing can be posted on a company's public Web site or on a site available only to employees. If the office has employees' home email addresses (for those employees with home email), you can send a group email regarding the office closure. You might place a voice mail message on a phone number employees are instructed to call in case of emergency or inclement weather. In addition, employees could call their voice mailbox and retrieve a message distributed to all employees. Another alternative is to establish a telephone tree. In a telephone tree, each employee is given the home phone numbers of several other employees. For example, the first person calls four people, and then each of the four people call four additional people, and so on. Telephone trees may not be reliable, because, if one person is not contacted, many people further down the tree will be affected.

Employee Suggestion Box

Create an employee suggestion box. Read the suggestions and discuss them with your supervisor. Of course, never ridicule any suggestions.

Leaving the Office

Do not be the first person to leave the office each day or the first to leave office-related functions, such as holiday parties or luncheons. You may appear disinterested in your work or dismissive of your colleagues.

Elevators

An elevator conversation can be overheard by everyone riding in the elevator. If your conversation can be overhead by others, discuss only casual, nonsensitive subjects. Conversely, if you are with only one other person in the elevator, it may be the perfect opportunity to discuss a project or reinforce an idea.

The Lost Supervisor

Be able to locate your supervisor at all times. If the supervisor is going to be out of the office, know when the supervisor is expected to return.

Where Is It?

It is important to remember where you put things. If you cannot remember where everything is located, keep a "where-is-it book."

Food at Your Desk

Avoid eating at your desk. If a client walks in, food scattered across your desk looks messy and may even have a strong aroma. Also, you might spill food on important papers or on your computer. If you must eat at your desk, keep food in a desk drawer and remove a bite at a time. Keep all food out of sight.

Unknown Title

Sometimes it can be difficult to determine if a name is male or female. If you are unsure of a person's gender when writing a letter, call the person's office and ask. Also, if you are unsure of a person's title, verify your information. Some people are offended if an incorrect title is used.

Check the Desk

Because of illness or unanticipated problems, an employee may not come to work. The absence of an employee should not be an excuse for delay in a project. The absent employee's desk, in-basket, and out-basket should be checked to determine if there is a project that must be handled or a telephone call that must be made. Many offices have a policy that co-workers check the desk of an absent employee. If there is no policy, you should ask your supervisor whether you should check the co-worker's desk. The courtesy of checking a desk is important.

Clean-Up Day

Designate a clean-up or an organize day. Employees dress casually and spend the day cleaning offices by organizing, filing, or throwing out office clutter. A designated clean-up day may inspire everyone to organize their offices.

List of Employees

A list of all employees should be available to all persons answering the telephones. Use the list, so you do not have to ask important company officials what their titles are or how to spell their names. Also, be able to correctly pronounce the names of all employees.

Commitments

When you say you will do something, do it. Make a commitment and adhere to it. Be responsible.

Assistance

When you receive a telephone call or someone approaches you with a question, say, "Hello. How can I help you?" After someone thanks you for your help, respond with "my pleasure."

Remembering People

Prepare a card file or use computer software to record the names and addresses of all clients, business associates, and co-workers. Include important information about these people, such as descriptions of the people (so you will recognize them the next time they come to the office), important dates in their lives, their preferences about restaurants and foods, and their spouses' and children's names. Do not pry for this information, but, if they mention these items, you can enter it into your file. People like to feel important. Review the information prior to the person's next visit at your office.

Employees like to be remembered, and computers have made remembering easier. One way to show interest is to develop an employee birthday list and add it to your calendar. Then send computer-designed or store-purchased cards to each person on the appropriate date. Offices often celebrate birthdays with parties for each person or a party for all persons with a birthday in that month. In some companies, the birthday person provides the food for the celebration.

Addressing Clients by Name

When clients call on the telephone or visit the office, call them by name. Say, "Good morning, Ms. Sanchez. It is nice to see you."

Meeting People

If you meet people at a party and you do not feel it is an appropriate location and time to discuss business or the possibility of a new job, tell them that you would like to arrange at their convenience to talk with them about a job, business, and so on.

Contact List

Always keep a file of people you meet, and put everyone you meet in your file. These contacts can be very helpful if you have a problem. A last-minute crisis may be solved by a person on your contact list. This list can be kept in your computer software contact list, computer or written address book, business card file, 3" × 5" card index system, or database file. The list should include telephone numbers and email addresses.

Smoking in the Office

Because of concerns about indoor air pollution and health risks, many organizations now restrict smoking in offices. In some areas of the country, it is illegal to smoke in public buildings. Many companies restrict smoking to designated areas outside the building, usually away from the main entrance. Be aware of your company's policy regarding smoking. Knowledge of this policy is important if you smoke or if you have clients who smoke.

Serial Numbers

Maintain a list of serial numbers and model numbers for equipment in your office, as well as computer software. You may have to supply a serial number to receive authorization for repair of equipment which is under warranty. To upgrade software, the serial number of the current version is frequently required.

Desk Organization

Organize your desk for easy accessibility. Always be able to quickly locate supplies and working materials, such as project files. Use desk organizers and dividers to arrange supplies in your desk. Place dictionaries and frequently used reference materials on the top of your desk or in another easy-to-reach area. Dictionaries and reference manuals should not be hidden in the bottom desk drawer. You may not be motivated to use these reference materials if they are not easily accessible.

Work Area

Keep your work area neat. Some people believe that a neat workplace means a neat and efficient person. Do not allow your desk to accumulate stacks of papers and folders. Use a desk file drawer as a temporary location for folders frequently used. If your office becomes cluttered with papers and files while you are working on a crucial project and you do not have time to file the documents, find another desk or an unoccupied space where you can work. Some people become agitated when working in a cluttered environment. It is very easy to misplace a paper when your work surface is covered with papers and file folders.

Place only a couple of personal items on your desk. These items should reflect your personal taste but continue to demonstrate your professional image. Your office and desk are good display areas for certificates or awards you have received.

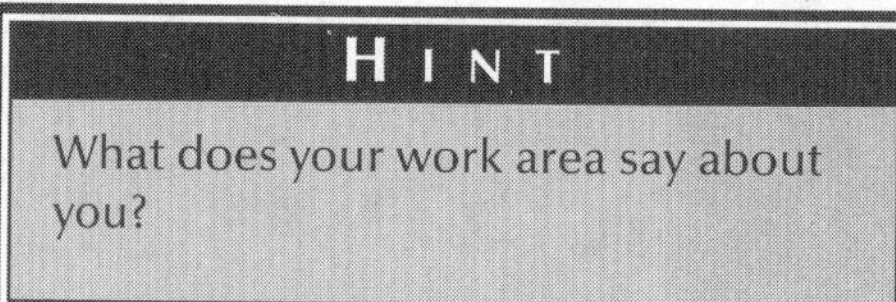

HINT
What does your work area say about you?

Proofread

Proofread everything—even if you use a computerized spelling or grammar package. The spell check built into your word processing software will only check to see if the word you keyed is in its dictionary, not if it is the correct word. It is very difficult to proofread a document you have keyed. Because you are already familiar with the document, your eyes will read words that are not even there. The secret to proofreading is to read every document three times. First, read the document in the normal order. Then read the document backwards—from the bottom right of the page to the top left of the page. It is easier to spot an error if the words are not in their proper context. Proofread the third time in the proper sequence. Since it is easy to overlook an error, it is helpful to proofread the document again another day or to exchange proofreading duties with a co-worker.

Reviewing a Draft Document

It is important to read an entire document before making comments on it. Do not make handwritten notes to yourself on the document. The last paragraph may change your original thoughts. If you feel compelled to write notes immediately, write your comments on a sticky note, which can easily be removed.

Envelopes

Remember that all correspondence needs an envelope. Because teachers do not always require an envelope for each assignment, students sometimes forget that envelopes are required for mailing documents. When keyboarding a document, prepare the envelope for it.

Pinch Hit

In any office, but particularly a small office, be prepared to do any job. If someone is absent or if there is a rush job, be willing to help complete a project. Be a team player and work together with others. Getting along with people in the office and advancing in your position may mean doing any job that is necessary.

Company Policy on Personal Use

Be aware of your company's policies on personal use of the office email, telephone, voice mail, and Internet. Many companies have increased their surveillance of employee usage. If you are uncertain about "allowed use," do not do it.

Charitable Activities

Many companies participate in communitywide charitable fundraising activities, such as the United Way, and may match employee contributions with company funds. Many companies sponsor volunteer activities, so employees may contribute to their community. Office-sponsored activities include adopting local families in need, visiting sick children or elderly persons, working with schools, rehabilitating old houses, participating in community clean-up days, working in homeless shelters, and so on. Some organizations allow employees to perform community outreach projects on company time. While involvement in these charitable activities is usually voluntary, you may receive subtle peer pressure from your co-workers or from your supervisor. Carefully consider whether you wish to contribute funds to these organizations or to participate in these activities. Participating in these extra activities may result in your being a part of the team and advancing in an organization.

YOUR DAY

Organize Yourself the Night Before

Home responsibilities can make mornings hectic. To reduce stress, use the following suggestions to organize yourself the night before.

- Check the weather forecast.
- If you need an umbrella, locate one.
- If it is winter, gather your coat, scarf, hat, and gloves.
- Select your clothing and accessories.
- Have alternative clothing cleaned and pressed, in the event you decide that you cannot wear your original outfit.
- Put money in your wallet.
- Put everything that you need into your briefcase.
- If you must make personal telephone calls during the day, place the telephone numbers in your briefcase.
- If you take your lunch, make it the night before.
- If you take nonperishable food, put it in your briefcase at night.
- Set the breakfast table, place coffee in the filter, place cereal bowls on the table, and place the pans you need on the stove.
- Buy a coffeemaker with a timer.
- Use paper plates to speed clean-up from breakfast.
- Put gas in the car on your way home from work, rather than on the way to work.
- If you are going to run errands after work, put everything that you need for the errands in your car before you go to sleep.
- If you have children, verify that they have everything that they need.
- If you ride mass transportation, purchase weekly or monthly bus or subway passes. Purchase several passes at one time.

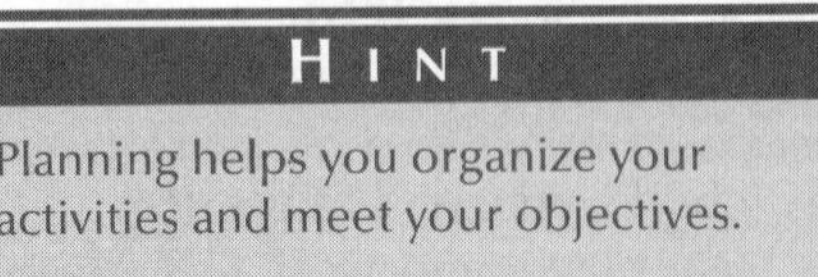

HINT
Planning helps you organize your activities and meet your objectives.

Plan Each Day

You should always have a *to-do list* or *task list* which includes major as well as minor projects. Computer software can be used to create task lists, and computer calendars can be used to plan your day. Computer organization software helps you list and prioritize your projects and can be used on handheld or desktop computers.

Prepare a schedule of your work each day, listing the projects you will work on, and set realistic time lines for each item. It is often wise to add time to each task as a contingency for office interruptions and unscheduled events. Review the schedule during the day and revise it as needed. At the end of each day, prepare a work schedule for the next day.

Learn to juggle your regular job responsibilities while completing major projects. People often do not get to the major projects because they become involved in minor projects, and their day disappears. If you have a major project, plan to work on a portion of it every day. Set a specific time each day for the major project and adhere to the schedule.

Efficiency

Always prioritize your work assignments. If necessary, ask your supervisor to help you prioritize your work. Review and update the list at least once a day.

If possible, arrange appointments or meetings for specific times or specific days. This method eliminates wasted time and moves people quickly from one appointment to another. For example, schedule appointments and meetings only on Tuesday and Thursday afternoons. This scheduling technique can be used when arranging appointments and meetings for your supervisor or for yourself.

When the projects are too numerous, decide if a project could be eliminated or if a project could be completed by another staff member. Do not continue to do a job just because it was always done. Question the need to do the job if it appears unnecessary. Jobs that cannot be eliminated can often be streamlined. Once you have analyzed the project and prepared an alternative, discuss the recommendation with your supervisor.

Deadlines

Keep your supervisor informed of all deadlines. Set preliminary checkpoints to measure progress. When the due date arrives, it is too late to make adjustments. If you are not going to be able to meet a deadline, inform your supervisor early, not at the last minute. This gives both you and the supervisor time to revise the deadline or add resources to meet the deadline.

To avoid a last-minute dilemma for yourself, ask co-workers to submit projects a couple of days before they are actually due. Then you will have time to review the projects before they are sent out of the office.

Pending Folder

Prepare a *pending folder* for all items for which you are waiting for an answer. Check your pending folder daily. If possible, decide on a specific time each day to check the folder. The best time to review the pending folder is at the end of the day when you make up the next day's to-do list.

Bring-Up Folder

Meet with the employer once a day to discuss problems and review your assignments. If possible, establish a specific time each day for the meeting and adhere to it. Go to the meeting with a prepared list of items to be discussed. Use a *bring-up folder* to store your problems and questions until the next meeting. This meeting is also a good time to compare your version of the employer's calendar with the employer's version of the calendar.

Carry Disk

If you telecommute and work at home, create a "carry disk" with the files you are currently using. Always make two copies of the carry disk in case one is defective. These disks always travel to the office and home with you. It may also be helpful to email files to yourself at home or work.

Myrtle P. Silver
Communications Manager
Globe S. Communications
2788 Roosevelt Drive
Albany, NY 12186

Globe Communications

FAX 518-886-0769
Email MSilver@GlobeC.com

Phone 518-886-2276
Cell 518-877-2449

FIGURE 13-2 A business card.

Business Cards

An administrative assistant and the executive should have business cards printed. The cards should be placed in a business card holder on the top of the desk, so they are easily accessible when a client visits the office. Also, each person should have a business card carrying case which will fit in a pocket or purse.

Business cards include the following:

- Company name and logo
- Person's name
- Title
- Address
- City, state, ZIP Code
- Telephone number
- Cell phone number
- Pager number
- Fax number
- Person's email address
- Business's Web address

Carry your business cards when attending meetings outside the office, so they can be exchanged with other colleagues. People often collect business cards at meetings but later cannot remember where they met. On the back of the card, write where and when you met the person. Some people file business cards by category instead of alphabetically. Business cards can also be entered into contact management software programs that organize the information. In addition, if two people have similar Personal Information Managers (PIMs) or handheld computers, they may be able to transfer their business cards electronically. It is very important after you have exchanged business cards to contact the person periodically to continue the relationship. The contact may be a quick email to say hello, a telephone call, lunch, dinner, or a drink after work.

HINT
Always carry your business card.

If you are mailing a document to someone outside the office, clip your business card to the document. You may also write a short note on the back of the card.

Business Lunches

Business lunches are part of the working day and an integral aspect of your professional life, so do not feel that a business lunch infringes on your personal time. Use the opportunity of a business lunch to your advantage. Meet co-workers and supervisors in a nonoffice environment and demonstrate your knowledge and skills. Attending a business lunch may also be an opportunity to show that you are an individual who has interests outside the office. Mention a book you recently read or a play you attended. You want your office colleagues to know that you are a well informed and social person. Business lunches are also an important opportunity to network.

Do not order the same food as your supervisor unless it is something that you really enjoy. Use some originality when you select your food and remember to eat slowly. Nervousness may make you eat too fast, and then you will have nothing to do while the others are still eating. Always order something you can easily eat, not a messy food. It may be better to order a sparkling water instead of a beer or wine, because you do not want to be the only person drinking an alcoholic beverage. You also do not want to drink too much and appear lightheaded or drunk. Do not be the only person to order dessert, because everyone will watch you eat. If it is a small group, speak with everyone at the table, not just the people seated near you.

It is not appropriate to comb your hair, apply lipstick, remove a contact lens, or insert eye drops in the presence of others. All personal toiletries should be done in the rest room.

Rest Breaks

Employers are becoming aware of the effects that illness, sleep deprivation, and exhaustion have on work performance. Some employers provide sofas and chairs in rest rooms or company break rooms, where employees who need to rest can do so in a quiet area. Some employers may even permit employees who are ill or exhausted to take a short nap, so they can improve their productivity, increase their alertness, improve their morale, and reduce accidents. Never nap or put your head down on your desk, because it may appear that you are ignoring your duties. If you feel ill, inform you supervisor. Depending on company policy, you may be directed to go to a company health unit, where you may be treated by medical staff, permitted to rest, or allowed to go home.

Security

If you must arrive early, work late, or work alone, you should be aware of your personal safety. Lock your office and car doors. Always have your keys in your hands when you walk to your car. If there are security guards, inform them of your schedule. If you must go to a dark parking lot, try to walk with someone, have a flashlight easily accessible, and always be alert to any danger. In some companies, a security officer is available to walk you to your car.

Strains Caused by Computers

If you use a computer terminal for several hours each day, frequently take breaks. Every fifteen minutes, look away from the terminal for a few seconds, and every couple of hours take a ten-minute break from the terminal. Periodically take a walk around the hallway and get a drink of water. Neck and back muscles also need a break from working at the computer terminal. If your muscles are tired or ache, loosen tight muscles by rubbing them or doing some stretching exercises.

Your Job

The New Job

During the first week of any new job, you should carry a pad of paper and a pen with you at all times. Try to make notes constantly since you will not remember everything. Write notes to yourself, so you can remember names, faces, and instructions that you are given. Review your notes each night, so each day you will feel more comfortable with your new job.

Be friendly with everyone, but do not form intense friendships too quickly. In a new environment, introduce yourself and be pleasant to everyone. Give yourself time to become acquainted with all the workers in your office. Quickly establishing close friendships with some co-workers may be seen as excluding others or attaching yourself to a group. Later, it may be difficult to withdraw from the group.

Employees should not gossip. Not only is gossip impolite and unprofessional, but it can be dangerous for the new employee who does not know the relationships of the people involved or the sensitivity of the information being discussed.

The new employee wants to be accepted as a credible, professional member of the staff, so demonstrate that you consider your job important. Arrive early and do not rush out the minute the workday is over. If you have nothing to do, at least look busy. Look through the files and become familiar with the company or read professional publications that are in the office. As soon as you complete one project, ask for another job. Do not wait for the supervisor to discover that you are ready for another assignment.

If you do not know how to do something, ask questions, so you will be able to complete the project correctly. Always appear interested in learning all of your new duties, even if you think that they are boring and inefficient.

Changing Jobs

When seeking a new job, changing jobs, or changing fields, ask friends to introduce you to people who might be able to help you. If you want an entry-level job, do not just ask to meet the head of the organization. Ask to meet supervisors, because people at this level might be better able to help you meet your job goals.

Accessing Your Personnel Information

Many companies permit their employees to access their benefits program directly through the company's computer system or the Internet. Computer-based benefits systems allow employees to use their office or home computer to access their personnel records. These computer systems often permit an employee to make changes in the number of their payroll deductions, revise their retirement withholdings, select different insurance carriers, update the record of their marital status, change their home address, and so on. Some employers use telephone-based systems, which permit the employees to make the same types of changes to their personnel file as the computer-based systems. Using the telephone keypad, employees can access company information about their benefits and personnel files, respond to computer-based options, and make simple revisions in data. Telephone systems are often used to obtain internal job vacancy information. With many companies reducing staff in their personnel office, these self-service capabilities benefit employees, because systems are always available and can complete the employees' changes with little delay.

Clipping Service

Begin a clipping service for your supervisor. Read the daily newspaper, out-of-town newspapers, and professional publications. Then clip and mark articles of importance for your supervisor or company. Also, read online articles from newspapers and Web sites. Then print the important articles for your supervisor.

Dealing with the News Media

Always have approval from your supervisor prior to speaking to reporters from newspapers, broadcast stations, Web sites, or other news media.

Know Which People Have Power in Your Company

To improve your effectiveness, you should know what group of people in your company establishes the company's goals, who sets the agenda, and who are favored by the company's top management.

Make Your Supervisor Look Good

Always make your supervisor look good in the eyes of clients and other company personnel. If your supervisor is held in high regard, you may also be held in high esteem.

Communicate Efficiently

Office personnel are always busy. When you are asked to prepare brief explanations of projects for your supervisor, limit your comments to one page. If additional information is required later, you can supply it at that time. Supervisors want brief, not lengthy, comments.

Chain of Command

In the business world, the term *chain of command* can have many meanings. One use of the term refers to a series of people who report to each other as shown on the company's organization chart. Another chain of command may relate to a particular project, where several people are involved in approving an action. Follow the chain of command instead of bypassing a person or bypassing required procedure. You may not understand the reasons for the procedures, and you may ignore an important step. Bypassing personnel may cause more problems for you, because you have ignored or disregarded a person. People often have a long memory when they feel they are bypassed in the chain of command. To foster good relations with people whom you will have to deal with in the future, always follow the chain of command.

Names

The office environment will determine what you should call your supervisor. In many offices, the supervisor is addressed by first name. Depending on the environment, it may be preferable to address your supervisor with the title "Ms." or "Mr." while in the presence of clients.

Relationships

The most important working relationship in your office is between you and your supervisor, so nurture the relationship.

Sharing Ideas

"I would like to share this information with you" is a tactful way to tell an individual something.

Expressing Understanding

Feedback is very important in a conversation. When you are being told something by a client, supervisor, or co-workers, indicate that you understand what he or she is saying. You can nod your head; make a noncommittal sound, such as "uh huh"; or change your facial expression. By indicating that you understand, you will encourage the speaker to continue the discussion. However, do not leave the speaker with the misimpression that you understand what he or she is saying if you do not. If you do not understand what he or she is saying, ask the person to clarify the comments, perhaps by giving you examples or more details.

Buddy System

Create a buddy system for your department or company. When employees have office-related problems or questions, they will have a buddy to consult. An official buddy system can be more helpful than asking a friend for help, because an official system includes company-approved time for assistance.

Cross-Training

Employees should be encouraged to learn as much as possible about each department and the duties of the employees. Knowledge of other jobs, whether in your department or in other departments, will help you grow professionally and may lead to a promotion. You will also be better able to answer questions for clients. It is very frustrating to both you and clients when you must say, "I do not know the answer. Jane is the only person who knows, and she is out of town."

Making a Group Decision Stick

Before you leave a meeting, verify that everyone is satisfied with the decision. Reinforce the decision with both an oral and a written summary of the meeting.

Death in the Family

It may be your responsibility to notify the staff of the death of an employee or of a family member of an employee. Notification can be made by sending an email or posting a notice. It is customary to send a gift of flowers or a tray of food to the family or to make a charitable donation in memory of the deceased. Money for these purposes may be collected from the staff or may be taken from an office fund. It is always proper to send a letter of condolence to the family. Also, it may be necessary to notify clients of the death of an employee and indicate who will assist the clients in the future.

Delegate

If possible, assign work to other employees. Do not feel that you are the only person who can do a job correctly or who should be able to do a specific job, even if you can do the job faster than another worker. You should train other staff members, so you will have time for more challenging projects.

Negotiate with Your Supervisor

Understand your supervisor's personality, and know when it is the best time to approach your supervisor to discuss an important issue. Some people are more responsive in the morning, others in the afternoon. Perhaps the best time to approach your supervisor is after the supervisor has had coffee or read the mail. Timing could be the key factor in receiving the response you want.

Begin a negotiation with a compliment. The compliment sets the mood for the discussion, and it is more difficult to turn down a request that is begun with a compliment. Always be honest and realistic with your compliment—for example,

> I have always enjoyed working for this company because of the help and guidance you have given me.

Be flexible, know what can be negotiated, and know what the options are. Present the benefits the company will receive by granting your request—for example,

> By allowing me to begin my day an hour later, I will be at work an hour later. Therefore, after everyone else leaves, I will still be here to help clients.

Discuss one point at a time. Do not overwhelm the supervisor by requesting too much at one time. You have a greater chance of success if you make only a single request.

Dealing with Problems

When you are given a project, analyze it carefully. Outline the project, list possible problems and solutions, and develop a timetable for completion. Try to anticipate problems that might occur and allow extra time for unanticipated problems.

Do not run to your supervisor each time you have a problem; try to solve it yourself, instead. If you cannot solve a problem, review your project and list possible solutions before you talk with your supervisor. This preparation will organize your thoughts and prepare you to answer your supervisor's questions.

There are some problems for which there are no easy answers. Accept the fact that you cannot solve them. If a problem does not have a deadline, try to let the problem solve itself. Put the problem in a pending file, but do not forget about it. Monitor the situation periodically.

An Indecisive Supervisor

If your supervisor or co-worker will not make decisions, you will have to assist in the decision-making process. When you present the person with a problem, also present a solution. If the person says, "I will get back to you later," write a note to yourself and put a reminder on your calendar. To assist the supervisor in reaching a decision, ask if you can gather any information about the subject. If you have not received a decision, diplomatically jog your supervisor's memory. You may need to gently remind the person that a decision must be made for the project to continue.

Crisis Management

Some offices seem to operate by *crisis management.* That means that management seems to respond only to a crisis and often runs from one crisis to another in a panic. While it is fine for an office to solve problems immediately, it is better to use careful planning to prevent problems before they occur. Unfortunately, not all situations can be anticipated.

Job Competition

Competition in the office between co-workers is a natural occurrence. Competition may occur for a promotion or for a special project. While everyone hopes to be selected for the promotion or to be given the favored assignment, learning to deal with disappointment is also a part of professional growth. If someone has received the promotion you wanted, congratulate the individual and work with the person in a professional manner.

The Unwanted Project

You may be given a project to complete that you do not want to do. You may find the project uninteresting or distasteful, or you simply may not have the time to do it. You should never flatly refuse to do a project, but the following suggestions may be helpful.

- Explain to your supervisor that you are too busy, because you are involved in other projects.
- Explain that you have already had the opportunity to learn this duty, so someone else should have the same opportunity.
- Explain that it would be beneficial to have another person know how to do this job, and offer to assist the other colleague.
- Ask for help from other co-workers to complete the project.

Mistakes

Everyone is human and makes mistakes. If you made a mistake, talk with your supervisor, acknowledge the mistake, and apologize. Do not hide the mistake or try to blame someone else. In addition, tell the supervisor what action you will take to ensure that this mistake is avoided in the future.

Responding to a Nasty Memo

At one time or another, everyone will receive a memo or an email that is negative in tone and that may even be rude. Do not write a nasty memo in response. It is better not to write anything. Instead, arrange a meeting, so the problem can be discussed. If the memo writer is still angry at the time of the meeting, let the writer talk until the anger is released. Then attempt to solve the problem. You may not agree with the writer's position, but you should try to maintain a good working relationship with the person.

Responding to a Bad Idea

Your supervisor approaches you with an idea, and you think the idea is terrible. Before you respond in a negative manner, ask questions about the idea. Perhaps you did not understand the idea and how it could be implemented. If you still think that it is a bad idea, diplomatically make suggestions to improve the idea.

Common Business Acronyms

There are many acronyms that are often used in informal communications, such as email messages and internal memos. A few of these are

ASAP	As soon as possible
BTW	By the way
CFV	Call for votes
COB	Close of business
CEO	Chief executive officer
COO	Chief operating officer
CFO	Chief financial officer
FAQ	Frequently asked question
FYI	For your information
FWIW	For what it is worth
IMHO	In my humble opinion
IT	Information technology
POS	Point of sale
TIA	Thanks in advance
Q&A	Questions and answers

Stress Management

Unfortunately, stress can be a part of your everyday work life, so learning to handle it is important to your physical and emotional well-being. The biggest causes of stress usually are other people and their actions which impact on you. Of course, you cannot eliminate your contact with other people, but you can learn to manage the people you come in contact with so you can reduce stress. You must learn how to deal effectively with your supervisor, your co-workers, and the public when they are under a great deal of stress. Other factors that cause stress in the office are interruptions, too much to do and too little time to do it, lack of advancement opportunities, little input into decisions, lack of communication from supervisors, conflicting assignments from several supervisors, and constant interruptions caused by the telephone.

HINT
Be familiar with business acronyms.

To keep problems in the proper perspective, remember that today's problem will probably be forgotten and unimportant by next month or next year.

Symptoms of stress

- Upset stomach
- Rapid breathing
- Rapidly pounding heart
- Heavy perspiration
- Tense muscles, often in the neck, back, arms, or legs
- Exhaustion
- Inability to sleep
- Irritability
- Lack of appetite
- Weight gain or loss
- Nausea
- Sweaty palms
- Crying
- Fears
- Lack of attention to details
- Perfectionism
- Feelings of worthlessness

HINT

Manage stress before it controls you.

There are many techniques that you can use to reduce or deal with stress before you go to a professional for medication or psychological assistance. Using these techniques are quicker, cheaper, and healthier than taking medicine to cope with stress.

Techniques to reduce stress

- Recognize stress before it is too late.
- Stop and tell yourself to relax when you feel stress.
- Make a list of when you feel stress.
- Attack stress at its source.
- Do not create stress by procrastinating on a project.
- Do not try to do everything at the office. Delegate responsibility and permit other employees to work on projects.
- Eat a well-balanced diet.
- Create a balance between work and home.
- See the humor in a situation. Tell yourself to laugh about the problem that is causing your anxiety.
- Find something you enjoy and then do it.
- Make a list of the small pleasures in your life; when stressed, remind yourself of them.
- Tell yourself that a stressful situation or problem is only for a short time and then it will be over.
- Tell yourself that the stressful problem is just not worth the aggravation.
- Ask yourself why you are upset. Then alter or accept the situation that causes the stress.
- Ask yourself why you are hurrying.
- Ask yourself if what you are doing is really essential.
- Stop and ask yourself if the problem is really worth all of the trouble it is causing you. If the problem is not worth the trouble, modify the situation or ignore it.
- Exercise—swim, walk, run, dance, bike, do aerobics, or do any exercise that relieves tension.

- Develop a hobby that captures your attention and relaxes you.
- Squeeze a stress-reducer ball.
- Visualize an activity that provides pleasure.
- Remind yourself that today's problems will probably be unimportant next week.

To avoid job burnout,

- Become involved in a new office project or personal activity.
- Rearrange or paint your office.
- Adjust your office hours or lunchtime.
- If you take your lunch, take something new. If you buy your lunch, try a new restaurant.
- At lunch, take a walk, read a book, go shopping, or attend a concert.
- Take a new route to work.
- Mentor a new employee.
- Remind yourself of the reasons you originally accepted your job.

BUSINESS ETIQUETTE

Social and personal relations skills are important to your ability to manage any situation in the workplace. Knowing the right time and the proper way to do something may mean the difference between success and failure. Proper business etiquette improves your professional image and may help your career advancement. Your professional image reflects your thoughts, your knowledge, and your skills.

HINT

Knowing business etiquette is essential.

The following are typical workplace circumstances when you will have to display your social and business etiquette:

- How to express your condolences to someone who has experienced the loss of a family member
- How to express congratulations to a supervisor or co-worker on receiving an award, on a recent engagement, on marriage, or on the birth of a child or grandchild
- What to say to the newly separated or divorced co-worker
- Who pays the restaurant bill
- How to pay the restaurant bill
- When and how much to tip
- How to respect or acknowledge the religious customs of clients and co-workers
- Use of proper table manners
- Proper conduct during an office party
- Attending a business banquet
- Purchasing appropriate business gifts
- Writing thank-you letters for gifts and meals

If you are uncomfortable handling any of the situations mentioned, review etiquette books at bookstores and libraries or visit etiquette Web sites.

Sample etiquette Web sites

www.lettgroup.com
www.gradview.com/careers/etiquette.html
www.everyrule.com/etiquette.html

Working with People from Foreign Cultures

> **HINT**
>
> Employees today work in a culturally diverse environment.

The globalization of products and services brings people and business from various cultures into contact with each other. Companies should recognize the potential for conflicts with foreign business cultures and should create a cultural diversity plan to encourage a working relationship with international clients or partners. Employees who have international business skills, or have knowledge of the cultures or the economic systems of other countries, therefore, are assets to an organization.

Not understanding a culture can create barriers to communications. Cultural differences exist in oral and written communications, and one untactful remark can destroy a relationship that took many months to establish. Even when an employee of your company speaks the language of another country, cultural differences may alter the interpretation or meaning of what is said. Earning the trust and respect of members of all cultures can be vital to a business's success. Learning to share and enjoy the cultures of the world can be a personally rewarding experience for you and a bonus for your company.

Employees who work in a global company must adapt to new customs and economic practices, so they will be able to execute their job responsibilities successfully. In order to create a good impression with foreign business associates and let them know that you are interested in them and their company, learn a few words of their language. Learning simple words such as "hello," "good morning," and "thank you" is not difficult and demonstrates your interest in working with international clients.

Prior to traveling to another country or working with foreign businesses, research the customs of the country. Become knowledgeable of the proper behavior and protocol of the country. In some countries, shaking hands is not acceptable, while in other countries it is expected. Also, taking business gifts when visiting one culture may be expected, but in other societies it may be inappropriate. Although a slang expression may be common to you, it should not be used, because it may not be understood by persons from other cultures. Remember that a joke that you find very funny may offend a person from another culture.

HINT
Show respect for all cultures.

You can find information on foreign cultures by consulting cultural relations books or searching the Web. The U.S. State Department has a Web site (*travel.state.gov/links/html*) that links to U.S. embassies around the world and which contains cultural information about many countries. There are several Internet sites which discuss proper business etiquette in foreign countries. One of these sites is *www.executiveplanet.com.*

The following are suggestions for working with international clients in the United States or in foreign countries.

- Always show respect for and interest in the culture of others.
- Be aware of religious and national holidays and their customs.
- Be aware that some businesses in foreign nations close for a few hours during the afternoon, so that employees and customers can rest.
- Be aware of business attire in foreign countries. In some countries, professional business attire is expected, but in others casual clothes are appropriate. Some countries dress very elegantly. Casual attire, such as shorts, may be inappropriate. Adapt your clothing so you do not look out of place.
- Translate your business cards into the language of the foreign country. Some business travelers print their card in English on one side and in the local language on the other side.
- Know when it is appropriate to discuss business. In some foreign countries, business matters are discussed only while entertaining and dining.
- Know the etiquette of gifts. Gift giving may be an important ritual in the foreign country.

- Know when to shake hands, hug, or kiss. Cultures differ on how to greet people.
- Be aware of where to stand. In some countries, people stand very closely to each other, so do not move back automatically if a person is close to you.
- Know the etiquette of time. In some countries, being late is accepted and expected. It may be inappropriate to be on time. In other countries, people are very punctual.
- Know when to toast the host at a meal. In some cultures, toasting is a form of respect.
- Always take a gift if you visit someone's home.
- Do not criticize the country or the people.
- Know that in some countries, if you avoid eye contact, you may be perceived as being dishonest.
- In some countries, a business referral or introduction may be very important and may be the only means of meeting someone.
- Business moves very slowly in some countries, so do not expect to rush meetings or business conversations.
- Seating at a dining table may be arranged according to the highest-ranking person.
- Do not whisper to one person, because others may think you are talking about them.
- Know that it may be inappropriate to eat food with your fingers. Conversely, be aware that in some cultures eating with only your fingers is appropriate.
- Know when it is the proper time to eat. Some countries eat a late lunch or late dinner. A late dinner may start at 10 P.M.
- Be aware of hand gestures in the particular country. It is easy to offend someone with an inappropriate hand gesture.
- Always ask permission prior to taking a picture.
- Be aware of how the culture addresses people. While Americans prefer informal business discussions and often like to be called by their first names, persons from some countries prefer a formal business discussion and prefer to be addressed by a title such as Mr., Dr., or Professor.
- Be aware of cultural differences regarding the human body. In some cultures, touching another person is inappropriate.
- Always be aware of the etiquette used in the foreign country.

Map Reading

The ability to read a map is a skill valuable to every traveler. It can be intimidating to travel alone to a strange city. The fear of the unknown can be eased by having a good map and being able to read it. Try, if possible, to get a map of the city or area you will be traveling to *before* you leave on your trip.

In addition, have a map of your area. Even if you are not traveling, you may be asked to drive to an unknown location in your city or to give directions to a client.

Sources of maps

- Road atlases are sold in most bookstores. These atlases may have a small map of the city you will visit which displays major streets, area landmarks, and items of interest.
- Your auto club may have detailed city maps that will be helpful.
- If you have enough time, you can call the chamber of commerce of the city you will visit and request that it send you a map.
- Maps of many cities can be found on and printed from the Internet.

If you have a map, review it before your trip. Look at how the city lies in relationship to major geographical features, such as mountains, rivers, or the ocean. Try to locate the airport, train station, or highway you will use in arriving. Locate the interstates, numbered routes, and major local roads, which are usually shown in thick lines.

Maps can also be obtained from several sources after you arrive in the city:

- *Auto rental agencies.* If you rent a car, the rental agency usually has a map of the area. Be sure to ask for the map if it is not offered.
- *Hotels/motels.* These places usually have a map of the immediate area, so ask for a map at the front desk when you check into a hotel or motel.
- *Information centers.* Many communities have tourist information centers with maps and brochures of the area. These centers may be located with the chamber of commerce or at the airport. Also, information centers are usually located on interstate highways soon after the highway enters a new state.
- *Gas stations.* Many gas stations sell maps for a few dollars.

BUSINESS STRATEGIES

Conflict Resolution

Conflict resolution is a term often used to describe a process used for solving conflicts. For supervisors, solving conflicts may be a daily occurrence. Even if you are not a supervisor, you will often be placed in situations in which you will have to resolve conflicts between employees or between clients and employees. Petty disagreements may evolve into long-term conflicts if they are not diplomatically resolved quickly. As an office employee, it is important to become an expert at conflict resolution and to learn to use a nonaccusatory and constructive approach to resolving problems. Always remember that a cooperative workplace is a more productive workplace, and the ability to solve conflicts can be a step toward your advancement.

Conflicts between people can erupt for numerous reasons. Sometimes people bring their personal problems and attitudes to the office and create an environment which results in conflicts with co-workers. Many arguments begin without malicious intent but continue to grow and create a destructive climate. One person can be insulted or feel taken advantage of, while the other person is oblivious to the situation. All employees should understand the reasons conflicts occur, so they can reconcile them immediately. The following are circumstances that may cause conflict.

- Needs are ignored.
- Needs are incompatible.
- Misperceptions exist.
- Guidelines have not been established.
- People do not listen to what others say.
- People have different ideas.
- People have differences in values and principles.

To resolve an argument, it is essential to understand the origin of the disagreement and to recognize that conflicts are part of an overall relationship. Prior to solving the problem, there must be a clarification of ideas and an identification of hidden conflicts or thoughts. Without this component, the dilemma may never be resolved. The workplace atmosphere, timing, and comments from involved parties all join together to resolve or ignite a conflict. To be successful, conflict resolution must address each party's underlying concerns, improve their relationship, and provide mutual benefits to both parties. In addition, it is important to learn from past experience and realize what can and what cannot be accomplished.

Conflict resolution suggestions

- Be objective.
- Identify the issue.
- Identify the results each person wants.
- Do not become emotionally involved in the issue.
- Offer suggestions to solve the problem.

Your Personal Conflict Resolution Style

It is important that you understand and, if necessary, modify your own behavior prior to attempting to resolve problems in your office. Critically answer each of the following questions and evaluate your personality style. Then review your answers and devise a plan to improve your temperament.

- Do you know when not to express your opinion?
- Do you sometimes not express your opinions as a method of avoiding conflict?
- Do you shout when you are angry?
- Do you overreact to situations?
- Do you like to antagonize others?
- Do you make sarcastic comments?
- Can you control your emotions?
- Do you enjoy arguments?
- When angry, do you make negative comments unrelated to the real issues?
- Do you allow irritation to hinder important business relationships?
- Do you blame your colleagues for your problems?
- Do you have a negative personality?

If you are aware of your conflict resolution style, you can make changes to improve it, so you will be more successful when working with others.

Critical Thinking

Critical thinking is a thought process often used to solve problems. In critical thinking, the first step is to define the issue and then to design a creative, preliminary solution to the problem. One of the goals of conflict resolution is to create an accurate statement of the problem. This is very important, because, if the problem is not correctly defined, the solution cannot solve the problem and will fail. It is often difficult to reach an agreement on how to define a problem because not all employees may see the problem the same way.

After the problem is defined, the next step is to develop a solution. Critical thinking uses an unlimited imagination to create inventive alternatives to problem solving, rather than being limited to the obvious solution to a problem.

Mission Statement

Companies write mission statements to describe the reason the company is in business. The following example is a bicycle store's mission statement.

> Our company was organized to provide our customers with the highest-quality bicycles at the lowest price. We believe that customer service is an integral aspect of our business, and we demonstrate this belief in every encounter with our patrons.

It is important to reexamine the mission statement periodically, because the corporate objectives and policies may have changed.

CHAPTER REVIEW

1. List ten hints that you can use in the office.
2. Define the word *mentor* and explain how a mentor may be helpful to you.

ACTIVITIES

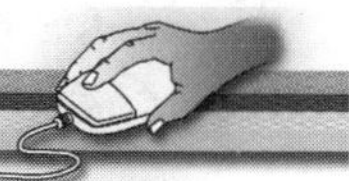

1. Plan your schoolday or workday for the next five days. Include your assignments, classes, meetings, future projects, employment, and personal responsibilities.
2. Write exact directions to your
   a. School
   b. Home
   c. Favorite shopping center
3. Find a partner and have each person give oral directions to a building in your area. Take notes as the oral directions are given. Can you now locate the building?
4. Write a description of the physical appearance of each of the three locations used in Activity 2.
5. Select three friends. Prepare a 3" × 5" information card on each and include the following information:
   a. Name
   b. Favorite restaurant
   c. Birthday
   d. Information about family—names, likes, dislikes, and so on
6. Read your daily newspaper or a magazine. Clip articles of interest to office employees. Circulate the articles by sending them to four members of your class.
7. List four occasions when you felt stress. Describe how you felt. Explain how you should have managed the stress.
8. For the next week, select your clothes in advance. Write a description of your weekly selections.
9. Look at your state map and write directions from your school to the state capital.
10. Role-play how you would handle the following situations:
    a. Your supervisor's mother passed away.
    b. A co-worker has become engaged.
    c. You are meeting the president of your company at an office party.
    d. A co-worker has received a promotion and will leave the department.
    e. A client from another part of the world has just walked into your office.
    f. You are meeting your supervisor's spouse for the first time.
11. Select a person who you think would be a good mentor and explain why.
12. What changes would you make in your work wardrobe and why?
13. Name four stores in your area that carry clothing appropriate for your career image.

PROJECTS

Project 25

Create the following itinerary.

The supervisor will be attending the meeting Communications Changes and Updates, which will be held in the Ballroom at the Marriott at the Capitol in Austin, Texas, September 2, 3, and 4. Travel will be from Washington Dulles Airport on American Airlines flight #399, leaving at 12:36 P.M. Change planes in Dallas to flight #872, leaving at 3:44 P.M. to arrive at 4:39. The hotel confirmation number is 920342WS. The phone number for the Marriott is 512-478-1111. Return flight #1054 leaves Austin at 3:38 P.M., connecting to flight #622 in Dallas, leaving at 5:32 P.M. and arriving in Washington at 9:32 P.M. Add any additional information you feel necessary.

Project 26

Set this up in an attractive format.

Next Year's Travel Plans

Name	Department	Destination	Month
Louis Parker	1621	Harrisburg, PA	January
Samuel Snyder	1617	Tampa, FL	February
Mike Lezcano	1620	Louisville, KY	April
Ferando Grasso	1620	Baton Rouge, LA	May
Ruth Eden	1621	Corpus Christi, TX	May
Janet Weinberg	1618	Miami, FL	July
Brian Lerner	1618	Dallas, TX	August
Laura Smyth	1621	Richmond, VA	August
Rodney Newton	1620	St. Paul, MN	September
Wanda McGee	1620	Des Moines, IA	September

HUMAN RELATIONS SKILL DEVELOPMENT

HR 13-1 Irritating Habits

Personal habits can be irritating to others. Co-workers may irritate their colleagues by drumming fingers on the desk, chewing gum and popping it, or cracking their knuckles. If a co-worker's habits annoy you, the best solution is to ignore the habits; however, if that has become impossible, diplomatically request that the person discontinue his or her actions. The person with the habits may not even be aware that they are irritating to others.

- What personal habits irritate you?
- Which of your personal habits could irritate your co-workers?
- What would you say to a co-worker whose gum chewing disturbs you?

HR 13-2 Social Behavior in the Office

Social etiquette is important for your success in the business world. Congratulating supervisors or co-workers on happy occasions and expressing sympathy on sad occasions are part of daily life in the office. Your colleagues will expect you to be able to express your feelings appropriately. Business events may occur outside the office building. You may meet colleagues at a company dinner, at a co-worker's wedding, or at a funeral for a member of a co-worker's family. Away from the office environment, a hug may be a better expression of your feelings than a handshake. However, before you make an outward gesture, always think about how the recipient of the gesture is likely to react.

- Are you knowledgeable about current rules of business and social etiquette?
- At a business dinner, would you know which piece of silverware to use, which plate is your butter plate, and which glass is yours?
- What would you say when introduced to your supervisor's spouse at a company dinner?
- How would you express your joy when your manager became engaged?
- How would you express your sorrow at the death of a co-worker's mother?

SITUATIONS

How would you handle each of the following situations?

- **S 13-1** You have been promoted to supervisor of your department, and you are having problems with your former co-workers, who are now your subordinates. They ignore your orders and decisions.
- **S 13-2** Your supervisor has informed you that next month your office will be hosting a delegation from a foreign country.
- **S 13-3** On your business flight to Denver, you placed your briefcase in the overhead compartment. When leaving the plane, you noticed that your briefcase was gone. A similar briefcase was found in another compartment. What suggestions do you have to avoid the problem in the future?

PUNCTUATION REVIEW

Punctuate each of the following sentences.

1. The local government sponsored a job fair investigated childcare facilities and developed automobile educational courses
2. The office clean up day is set for September 20 and all employees are expected to participate
3. Registration will be Friday and orientation will be Monday Tuesday and Wednesday
4. Participants gain an overview of computers graphic packages and fax machines
5. Upon successful completion of the program you will receive a certificate
6. Enclosed is a list of our clients which should be helpful to you
7. During a two month period our sales rose 25 percent but our profits fell 10 percent
8. As you may recall from my memorandum of February 12 effective March 31 our office will be implementing a Health Care Reimbursement Account Plan
9. Designed for todays mobile workforce 401(k) plans allow employees to change jobs and encourage employees to continue building on their retirement savings
10. We are happy you have joined our club but we must remind you to pay your dues
11. Under the present tax law the amount by which you may reduce your salary is limited to 14 percent of your gross income
12. West Virginia the mountain state is near Washington DC
13. Our best friend an authority on business ethics is speaking Friday September 1
14. We are constructing a new office complex at 1400 Executive Drive Omaha Nebraska
15. When I read a book I become absorbed in it

CD ASSIGNMENTS

CD Assignment 13-1

Open the file CD13-1_OA on your Student CD and follow the instructions to complete the job.

CD Assignment 13-2

Open the file CD13-2_SM on your Student CD and follow the instructions to complete the job.

CD Assignment 13-3

Open the file CD13-3_PR3 on your Student CD and follow the instructions to complete the job.

CD Assignment 13-4

Open the file CD13-4_PR4 on your Student CD and follow the instructions to complete the job.

Software Applications

Word Processing Applications

Spreadsheet Applications

Database Applications

Leader Practice

Word Processing Application

Problem 1

- Key in the document shown at the bottom.
- Right align the room numbers.
- Change the heading to font size 18.
- Change the heading font to a font of your choice.
- Use leaders between the columns.
- Visually adjust the tab settings so the information appears to be centered.
- Save As SAS1-1.
- Print.

Problem 2

- Use SAS1-1 and revise it as shown below.
- Insert the following below Newsletter Discussion
    - Communications Review, Room 303
- Insert the following below Web Site Ideas
    - Teleconference Plans, Room 319
- Save As SAS1-2.
- Print.

Meeting Schedule

L & J Report .... Room 100
Newsletter Discussion .... Room 103
Future Plans .... Room 105
Web Site Ideas .... Room 101A
Budget Forecast .... Room 107B
Satellite Communications .... Room 104C
Board of Directions .... Room 109
Computer Security .... Room 204
Legal Issues .... Room 210

Williams Corporation

Database Application

1. Create a database and name it SAS2.
2. Create the table shown below. Save it and name it Presenter. Let the software create the AutoNumber.
3. Create a query. List Project, Presenter, and Number Attending. Save as Query 1.
4. Create a query. List AutoNumber, Project, Presenter, and City. Save as Query 2.
5. Create a query. List Project, Presenter, and Date. Save as Query 3.
6. Create a query. List Project, Presenter, and Cost_per_Person. Save as Query 4.
7. Create a query. List Project, Presenter, and City for City equal to Rochester. Save as Query 5.
8. Create a query. List Project and Presenter for Presenter equal to Joseph. Save as Query 6.
9. Create a query. List Project, Presenter, and Date for Date equal to June 20. Save as Query 7.
10. Create a query. List Project, Presenter, and City for City equal to Annapolis. Save as Query 8.
11. Create a query. List Project, Presenter, and Cost_per_Person for Cost_per_Person equal to or greater than 700. Save as Query 9.
12. Create a Form based on the Presenter Table. Include all fields. Save as Form 1.
13. Create a Form based on the Presenter Table. Include AutoNumber, Project, and Presenter fields. Save as Form 2.
14. Create a Form based on Query 1. Include all fields. Save as Form 3.
15. Create a Form based on Query 2. Include all fields. Save as Form 4.
16. Create a Form based on Query 3. Include all fields. Save as Form 5.

Project	Presenter	City	Date	Number_ Attending	Cost_per_ Person
1001	Nguyen	Rochester	June 1	225	500
1004	Joseph	Albany	October 15	300	600
1020	Robertson	Annapolis	November 12	250	700
1004	Joseph	Jefferson City	January 15	145	600
1004	Nguyen	Miami	June 20	250	600
1020	Joseph	Rochester	November 12	300	700
1025	Robertson	Jefferson City	October 15	445	800
1001	Nguyen	Annapolis	June 20	300	500
1004	Joseph	Rochester	February 20	200	600
1020	Robertson	Jefferson City	June 20	175	700
1001	Nguyen	Annapolis	October 15	200	500

Agenda

Word Processing Application

- Create an agenda similar to the example. Place the budget on a separate page. Save the file as SAS3. Print.

Monthly Staff Meeting

June 1, XXXX

Agenda

2:00 Call to Order
2:05 Approval of Minutes of May 1, XXXX
2:15 Whitcomb Report
2:45 Committee Reports
3:15 Research Survey
4:00 Stress Management Workshop Plans
4:10 Budget
4:30 Adjournment

Attachment
Budget

Budget XXXX

Expenses	Quarter 1	Quarter 2	Quarter 3	Quarter 4
Salary	100,000	102,000	106,000	112,000
Benefits	22,000	22,000	24,000	24,000
Computer hardware	3,000	3,000	3,000	3,000
Computer software	1,000	1,000	1,000	1,000
Consultants	5,000	5,000	9,000	9,000
Entertainment	500	500	500	500
Honorariums	300	300	300	300
Postage	500	500	800	800
Rent	7,500	7,500	7,500	7,500
Supplies	1,500	1,500	2,500	2,500
Telephone	2,000	2,000	2,000	2,000
Travel	5,000	5,000	8,000	10,000
Total	148,300	150,300	164,600	172,600

Snow Project

Worksheet Application

- Create the following worksheet.

First Snow	Tons Salt Used First Snow	Tons Sand Used First Snow	Number Hours	Cost per Hour
January 15	1200	1200	10	350
December 1	1500	1500	22	380
November 5	1700	1700	15	440
November 12	2200	2200	14	310
October 31	800	800	26	350
December 3	600	600	28	370
November 23	1400	1400	17	280

- Bold and center the column headings.
- When necessary, wrap the column headings.
- Add a header with your name.
- Format the dates with the style of your choice.
- Change the font color for First Snow to blue.
- Change the fill color for Cost per Hour to yellow.
- Calculate the total salt used.
- Calculate the average salt used.
- Calculate the total sand used.
- Calculate the average sand used.
- Title a new column Total Cost. Multiple the Number Hours by the Cost per Hour. Format this column for currency.
- Title a new column Projected Hours. Multiply the Number Hours by 3.
- Where appropriate, format all values for currency.
- Set the worksheet for gridlines and landscape with fit to page.
- Save the File as SAS4.
- Print.

Beach Rental

Worksheet Application

- Create the following worksheet.
- Bold and center the headings.
- Total all columns.
- Average all columns.
- Create a new column and title it Total Chair Rentals for July. Use Total Chair Rentals for June. Calculate a 15 percent increase. (Show the June amount plus the 15 percent increase.)
- Create a new column and title it Chair Rental Price. Enter $10 for Piers 1–4 and $12 for Piers 5–7.
- Create a new column and title it Chair Income June. Multiple the Chair Rental Price by the Total Chair Rentals for June per Site.
- Title a column Average Number of Chairs Rented Each Day. Divide the Total Chair Rental for June Per Site by the number of days in June. (Hint: how many days are there in June?)
- Create a new column and use the If Function. If the number of Umbrellas rented in June is greater than 250, the answer is yes.
- Create a new column and use the If Function. If the number of Boats in June is less than 20, the answer is yes.
- Create a new column and use the If Function. If the Average Number Chairs Rented Each Day is greater than 40, the answer is yes.
- Format for currency where appropriate.
- Format the cells for color to enhance the worksheet.
- Print the worksheet in landscape with fit to page.
- Save the File as SAS5.

Location	Total Chair Rentals for June Per Site	Umbrellas Rented June	Surf Boards Rented June	Rafts Rented June	Boats Rented June
Pier 1	1300	275	25	50	25
Pier 2	1250	325	27	36	26
Pier 3	1400	275	32	47	18
Pier 4	1100	212	21	52	22
Pier 5	1000	253	27	48	29
Pier 6	1900	208	19	39	25
Pier 7	1875	248	17	52	27

Julie's Ice Cream Parlor

Worksheet Application

- Create the following worksheet. Your worksheet may not look exactly like the sample shown below.
- Bold all headings.
- Wrap column headings.
- Change the font color for Cost per Item to blue.
- Calculate the total sales for each week. Put a border around the total.
- Calculate the average sales for each week.
- Create a new column and title it Gross Income Week 1. Then multiply the Sales Price by the No. Sales Week 1.
- Create a new column and title it Gross Income Week 2. Then multiply the Sales Price by the No. Sales Week 2.
- Create a new column and title it Cost per Item Increase. Then multiply the Cost Per Item by 25 percent. Show only the amount of the increase.
- Center the company name, Julie's Ice Cream Parlor, over the worksheet. Apply a light color fill to the title.
- Format the worksheet for currency where appropriate.
- Print the worksheet in landscape with fit to one page.
- Save the file as SAS6.

Flavors	**Cost Per Item**	**Sales Price**	**No. Sales Week 1**	**No. Sales Week 2**	**No. Sales Week 3**	**No. Sales Week 4**
Chocolate Chewy	1.25	2.50	500	620	540	500
Apple Spice	.99	2.00	575	785	600	475
Chocolate Fudge	1.20	2.50	496	506	522	498
Absolute Vanilla	.97	2.00	388	388	388	402
Strawberry Delight	1.04	2.25	472	472	400	489
Chocolate Nutty	1.20	2.50	605	605	627	645
Peppermint Surprise	1.00	2.25	377	378	366	399

Music

Database Application

- Create a database titled SAS7.
- Create a table titled Name 1.
- Let the software create the AutoNumber.
- Enter the information in the table as shown.
- Modify the design and add a Year field.
- In the Year field enter 1994 for Ross, Lewis, Lawson, and Stevens.
- In the Year field enter 1996 for Wong, Kim, Nguyen, and Smithy.
- In the Year field enter 1999 for Wallace, Gleason, Summit, and Baum.
- Create a query. List Last_Name and City. Save as Query 1.
- Create a query. List Last_Name and Music. Save as Query 2.
- Create a query. List Last_Name, First_Name, and City. Save as Query 3.
- Create a query. List Last_Name, Music, and Month. Save as Query 4.
- Create a query. List Last_Name and Month. Save as Query 5.
- Create a query. List Last_Name, First_Name, and Amount. Save as Query 6.
- Create a query. List Last_Name, City, Month, and Amount. Save as Query 7.
- Delete Annie Lewis from the database.
- Add yourself to the database, and complete the row with the following: Music is Blues, Month is September, and Amount is 400. Enter the Current Year in the Year Field.

First_Name	Last_Name	City	Music	Month	Amount
Clifton	Ross	Ft. Wayne	Blues	June	900
Annie	Lewis	Toledo	Classical	August	500
Barbara	Lawson	Chicago	Jazz	November	700
Jane	Stevens	Houston	Rock	December	450
Amy	Wong	Chicago	Classical	August	600
Louise	Kim	Ft. Wayne	Jazz	June	500
Julie	Nguyen	Chicago	Classical	December	745
Mollie	Smithy	Ft. Wayne	Blues	August	800
Ted	Wallace	Toledo	Jazz	June	900
Jeff	Gleason	Ft. Wayne	Blues	August	580
Roger	Summit	Toledo	Classical	June	900
Bart	Baum	Toledo	Blues	December	900

Clifton Travel

Word Processing Application

Part 1 Instructions

- Key in the document exactly as shown.
- Save as SAS8-1.
- Print the document.

Clifton Travel Company

Now is the time to have fun and take a vacation. When you join our cruise family, you will have the opportunity to meet new friends and visit exciting places.

The best way to see the world and have your dreams come true is to cruise Europe with us. On our trips, you will feel the history, enjoy the areas, and meet people all from the veranda outside of your spacious suite.

A European adventure will bring you close to the people and their lives. You will feel and experience the European atmosphere. In addition, you will see crafts people, historical sites, cobblestone streets, villages, well-known works of art, and magnificent sunrises. Also, you will meet and talk with the people who live in the countries and learn to appreciate their culture and understand their lives.

Your ship will be your home while on this memorable trip and will dock in the romantic cities of Europe, such as Amsterdam, Venice, London, and Paris. Naturally, you will want to bring your camera and lots of film to capture your memories. Our activities include guided tours, many meals, free time, and optional tours to meet each traveler's personal taste.

Clifton Travel, which has been in business for over fifty years, promises you a lifetime of fun-filled memories. Ask your friends about their favorite travel agent, and they will give you the name Clifton Travel. We are a family-operated business with dedicated family members.

Call us at 888-555-1234 and talk with one of the family, and he or she can help you arrange the trip of your dreams.

Agent (insert your name)

Part 2 Instructions

- Open the file SAS8-1.
- Save the file as SAS8-2.
- Set all paragraphs for justify.
- Begin each paragraph with a tab.
- Change the line spacing to double. Delete blank lines between paragraphs.
- Make the following changes to the heading Clifton Travel Company.
  - Center.
  - Bold.
  - Change font to Arial.
  - Change font size to 20.
- Underline "Now is the time to have fun and take a vacation."

- Change Amsterdam to size 14 and italicize it. Using the format painter, apply the same formatting to the other cities.
- Using the symbol feature, insert two symbols into the document, and write a paragraph which would be appropriate for the symbols. Place this new paragraph before the last paragraph.
- Place a border around the last paragraph.
- Print the document.
- Save the File as SAS8-2.

Part 3 Instructions

- Open the file SAS8-1.
- Save the file as SAS8-3.
- Delete the second paragraph.
- Change the side margins to 2 inches.
- Change the top and bottom margins to 2 inches.
- Write a paragraph about a location you would like to visit. Place this paragraph before the last paragraph.
- Print the document.
- Save the File as SAS8-3.

Toys

Database Application

1. Create a database and name it SAS9.
2. Create the table shown below. Name it Toy Table. Let the software create the Auto-Number.
3. Create a query. Sort on Toy. List Toy, Recipient, and Reason. Save as Query 1.
4. Create a query. Sort on Toy. List Toy, Recipient, and Price. Save as Query 2.
5. Create a query. Sort on Toy. List Toy, Recipient, and Price for Price greater than $35.00. Save as Query 3.
6. Create a query. List Toy, Recipient, and Price for Price less than $25.00. Save as Query 4.
7. Create a query. List Toy, Recipient, and Reason for Reason equal to Birthday. Save as Query 5.
8. Create a query. List Toy, Recipient, and Reason for Reason equal to Valentine's Day. Save as Query 6.
9. Create a query. List Toy, Recipient, Purchase_Month, and Reason for Purchase_Month equal to September or for Reason equal to New Year's Day. Save as Query 7.
10. Create a query. List Toy, Recipient for Recipient equal to Julie. Save as Query 8.
11. Create a query. List Toy, Recipient for Recipient equal to Penelope. Save as Query 9.

Toy	Recipient	Purchase_ Month	Reason	Price
Doll	Julie	September	Birthday	$29.99
Stove	Hope	February	Valentine's Day	$59.99
CD	Patrick	September	New Year's Day	$17.99
Doll	Penelope	June	Birthday	$49.99
Dog	Ted	April	Spring	$25.00
Doll	Mollie	September	Birthday	$39.99
Talking-book	Penelope	February	Valentine's Day	$12.00
Giraffe	Hope	November	Thanksgiving	$24.99
Doll	Penelope	July	Birthday	$19.99
Video game	Hope	January	New Year's Day	$17.99
Truck set	Patrick	June	Birthday	$27.00
Video game	Julie	January	New Year's Day	$22.99

Bullet Practice Word

Word Processing Application

Problem 1: Key in the exercise shown below. Save the file as SAS10-1.

Fall Classes

- Computer Applications
  - Introduction to Computers
  - Word Processing
  - Spreadsheets
  - Database
- Literature
  - American Studies
  - English Literature
- History
  - Government Theory
  - United States History I
  - United States History II
- Foreign Languages
  - French
  - Spanish
  - Russian

Problem 2: Change the bullet style to the snowflake style. Save as SAS10-2.

Problem 3: Change the bullet style to the numbered style. Save as SAS10-3.

Jennie's Gift Gallery

Worksheet Application

- Create the following worksheet.
- Bold and wrap the column headings.
- Save the file as SAS11-1.
- Name sheet 1 January.
- Copy the January worksheet to a new worksheet, which you rename February.
- Copy the February worksheet to a new worksheet, which you rename March.
- Group all three sheets.
- Calculate the total for each item. Verify that the total is shown in all three worksheets.
- Calculate the average per column. Format the average to a whole number. Verify that the average is shown in all three worksheets.
- Ungroup the worksheets.
- Save the file as SAS11-2.
- Calculate the maximum sold per store. (Hint: use row.)
- Calculate the minimum sold per store. (Hint: use row.)
- Calculate the average sold per store. (Hint: use row.)
- Save the file as SAS11-3.

Store Number	Manager	Porcelain Figurine No. Sold	Glass Figurine No. Sold	Gift Wrap No. Sold	Collector Bears No. Sold	Photo Frames No. Sold	Tea Set No. Sold
500	Lewis	200	75	120	200	114	74
501	Wong	175	84	148	245	158	63
502	Harper	193	96	126	278	136	45
503	Garcia	224	74	145	266	147	72
504	Fulton	218	88	135	233	185	74
505	Carlton	195	73	139	224	200	93

Museum Project

Worksheet Application

- Create the worksheet at the bottom.
- Bold column headings.
- Wrap text in column headings where it is needed.
- Bold the Museums, which are in column A.
- Total the monthly attendance per museum. (Calculate across the row.)
- Average the monthly attendance per museum. (Calculate across the row.)
- Total attendance per month. (Calculate down the column.)
- Per Museum, calculate the minimum attendance. (Calculate across the row.)
- Per Museum, calculate the maximum attendance. (Calculate across the row.)
- For July, increase June's attendance as follows. (Write a formula for the calculation.)
  - American History 12 percent
  - Natural Science 8 percent
  - Space Ideas 9 percent
  - Science & Studies 5 percent
  - Arts and Life 7.5 percent
  - Great Mountains 6 percent
  - South Gallery 6.2 percent
- For August, increase May's attendance by the number shown. (Write a formula to add the increase shown below to the May values.)
  - American History 300
  - Natural Science 700
  - Space Ideas 800
  - Science & Studies 275
  - Arts and Life 300
  - Great Mountains 400
  - South Gallery 600
- Save the file as SAS12.
- Print the worksheet in landscape with fit to 1 page.

Museums	Jan Attend	Feb Attend	March Attend	April Attend	May Attend	June Attend
American History	6602	7415	8802	8772	8802	9815
Natural Science	8405	7926	9405	9460	9405	10501
Space Ideas	7523	7728	9800	8823	9823	11050
Science & Studies	4908	6025	6754	5688	6008	8040
Arts and Life	7891	8203	7903	8355	8891	9607
Great Mountains	3608	3607	2509	3689	4008	6007
South Gallery	3502	4663	3892	4533	4792	5007

Arnold Corporation

Worksheet Application

- Create a worksheet using the information shown below.
- Widen the columns as needed.
- Add a new column titled Income 1. Multiply the Selling Price by the Number of Units.
- Add a new column titled 5% Increase. Multiply the Selling Price by 5%. The answer should show the original price plus the increase.
- Add a new column titled 7% Increase. Multiply the Selling Price by 7%. The answer should show the original price plus the increase.
- Add a new column titled 12% Increase. Multiply the Selling Price by 12%. The answer should show the original price plus the increase.
- Total the Selling Price column.
- Total the 5% Increase column.
- Total the 7% Increase column.
- Total the 12% Increase column.
- Add the header, Arnold Corporation.
- Set the Selling Price, Income 1, 5% Increase, 7% Increase, 12% Increase for currency.
- Set the file for landscape.
- Save the file as SAS13-1.
- Make any enhancements you desire.
- Save the file as SAS13-2.
- Print.

Vendor	Selling Price	Number Units
Beckman	300	120
B. W. Supplies	100	35
Sugar Limited	207	55
Cosmo Supplies	250	95
D and D Services	407	135
P & J Enterprises	250	340
Calvin's	125	150
Phu & Phu Corporation	89	135
Patrick Family Industries	95	175

Appendix
Review of Grammar, Punctuation, and Spelling

As a member of today's technology-driven workforce, it will be important for you to use correct grammar and punctuation in all of your oral and written communications. These skills are used when you speak to clients and colleagues; answer the telephone; record telephone messages; write notes to your supervisor; write and keyboard letters, memos, and reports; proofread documents; send emails; and create Web pages.

This appendix reviews grammar, punctuation, and spelling. The objective is for you to apply knowledge, not memorize rules. A list of frequently misspelled words and a list of cities are provided, so you can improve your spelling skills. Although spell check software is available as a component of many computer packages, the ability to spell correctly is still an important asset to your future. A list of similar-sounding words is also provided to help you increase your knowledge of word usage.

Grammar

Capitalization

- Capitalize the first word of every sentence.

  The final draft of the report is on my desk.

- Always capitalize the pronoun *I*.

  Matthew and I are attending the convention.

- Capitalize the days of the week, months of the year, and holidays.

  We are speaking at the meeting on Monday, May 30, which is Memorial Day.

- Capitalize proper nouns and proper adjectives.

  They videotaped the Pittsburgh Business Association Conference.
  We have IBM, Xerox, Kodak, and Sharp equipment.
  The French report was translated into English, German, and Spanish.
  This year we have representatives from North Carolina, Minnesota, New Mexico, and Maine.

Subject and Verb

- The *subject* is the name of a person, place, or thing and the subject tells who performed the action. The *verb* is the action in the sentence, and it tells what was done.

  She pointed to the director.

she	(subject)
pointed	(verb)

Management donated the equipment.
management (subject)
donated (verb)

Subject and Verb Agreement

- The verb must agree with the subject in number and person. If the subject is singular, the verb must be singular. If the subject is plural, the verb must be plural.

Louise writes three reports a week.
Louise (singular subject)
writes (singular verb)

Juan and Teki write three reports a week.
Juan and Teki (plural subject)
write (plural verb)

- *Helping verbs* help the main verb.

The following are examples of singular helping verbs:

is, am, was, has, have

The following are examples of plural helping verbs:

are, were, have

The report was read by everyone in the department.
was (singular helping verb)
read (main verb)

Richard and Bob were delighted with the results of the sale.
were (plural helping verb)
delighted (main verb)

The following are examples of *singular* pronouns:

he, she, it, you, another, anybody, anyone, each, either, everybody, everyone, neither, one, somebody, someone

Everyone in the department was late for work because of the snow.
Everyone (singular pronoun)
was (singular verb)

The following are examples of *plural* pronouns:

they, we, you, both, few, many, others, several

Several were late for work because of the snow.
Several (plural pronoun)
were (plural verb)

Phrase

- A *phrase* is a group of related words not containing a subject and verb.
black box (phrase does not contain a verb)

Clause

- A *clause* is a group of words that contains a subject and a verb.

An *independent clause* is a complete thought and can stand alone.
Julie has meetings at all three locations.

- A *dependent clause* does not make sense by itself and cannot stand alone.

  If you complete the project by June, you will receive an outstanding evaluation.
  If you complete the project (dependent clause)

PUNCTUATION

Period

- A period is used at the end of a sentence that makes a statement or issues a command.

  She attended every department meeting.

Question Mark

- A question mark is the ending punctuation for each sentence that asks a question.

  When will we have the report completed?

Exclamation Mark

- An exclamation mark is used after words or sentences to express a strong emotion.

  Our department won the contest!

Comma

- A comma is used to separate items in a series. A series must contain at least three items.

  Ed completed the survey, evaluation, and revisions yesterday.

  Yesterday I saw demonstrations of printers, scanners, and network systems.

- A comma is used in apposition. An appositive explains the noun or pronoun that it follows.

  Ms. Halley, the director, is an enthusiastic speaker.
  Ms. Halley (noun)
  the director (appositive)

- A comma is placed before and after nonrestrictive clauses and phrases. Nonrestrictive clauses and phrases are words that can be removed from the sentence while keeping the clarity of the sentence. Although words have been removed, the sentence still makes sense.

  The training facility, which offers computer courses, is located at 966 Rose Tree Lane.
  which offers computer courses (nonrestrictive clause)

- A comma is used in a direct address. Direct address indicates to whom you are speaking.

  Jane, please finish the report by 5:00 on Friday.
  Jane (direct address to Jane)

- A comma is used in introductory expressions. An introductory expression introduces the remaining part of the sentence.

  When Larry returns from the Boston meeting, he will write a report summarizing the meeting.
  When Larry returns from the Boston meeting (introductory clause)

  If I am late for the meeting, do not wait for me.
  If I am late for the meeting (introductory clause)

- A comma is used to separate a direct quote from the remaining portion of the sentence.

  Ben said, "The guest speaker was fantastic."

- A comma is used to separate clauses in a compound sentence. A compound sentence contains two independent clauses and is joined by a coordinating conjunction—*and, but, for, or, nor,* and *yet.* If the clauses are very short, a comma is not used.

  My office bought the latest computer software, but I do not understand it.
  I like it but she doesn't. (Clause is short.)

  Louise bought a computer, and Matthew bought a printer.

- A comma is used after *yes* and *no* when they begin the sentence.

  Yes, Richard is the reporter.

- A comma is used before and after parenthetical expressions. These are expressions that interrupt the sentence. The following are examples of parenthetical expressions.

fortunately	*however*
as you know	*of course*
perhaps	*I think*
I believe	*in fact*

  Of course, she passed the test.
  Jung, as you know, is the most qualified applicant.

- A comma is used to separate the day of the month from the year.

  The building is scheduled to be completed by January 27, XXXX.

- A comma is used to separate two adjectives describing the same noun.

  Her office was in a large, old mansion.
  The long, difficult project was completed.

- A comma is used to separate contrasting expressions.

  The briefcase is fine leather, not vinyl.
  The meeting began at 10:00, not 9:00.

- A comma is used to separate names from titles and degrees. Numbers in names do not use commas.

  Raymond Soloman, Jr., was the guest speaker.
  We are meeting Dick Madison, Ph.D., at the airport.
  Donald Watkins III is my attorney.

- A comma is used to separate numbers of four or more digits. The comma is not used in house numbers, telephone numbers, or ZIP Codes.

  23,800 tons

Semicolon

- A semicolon is used to separate independent clauses not joined by a conjunction.

  Michelle enjoys classical music; Nancy prefers jazz.
  We stayed at the convention hotel; George stayed at the hotel across the street from the convention hotel.

- A semicolon is used to separate items in a series if at least one of the items in the series contains commas.

  They spent their vacation in Portland, Maine; San Francisco, California; and Orlando, Florida.
  The seminar will be held Friday, June 16; Tuesday, August 25; Thursday, September 28; and Monday, November 5.

- A semicolon is used to separate clauses containing internal punctuation.

  Marsha, my supervisor, is an effective leader; but Arleen motivates employees more quickly.
  The agenda indicated that the meeting is Tuesday, October 15, XXXX; but we would like to change the meeting date to Friday, October 18, XXXX.

Colon

- A colon is used to introduce a list.

  I purchased the following items: fifteen legal pads, ten computer disks, and twenty-five boxes of computer paper.

Dash

- A dash is used to indicate an abrupt change in thought.

  Kathy, my mentor, is my best friend—at least I hope she is.

Parentheses

- Parentheses are used to set off words or phrases that are not essential to the sentence.

  The chairperson of the committee (the woman from Tulsa) is receiving her doctorate this year.

Apostrophe

- An apostrophe is used to show the omission of letters in contractions.

  Walter can't attend the meeting. (contraction of *cannot*)

- An apostrophe is used when a noun is possessive.

  Sara's office is small.

Hyphen

- A hyphen is used to divide syllables of words.

  scis-sors

Quotation Marks

- Quotation marks are used to enclose exactly what was said or written. Periods and commas go inside the quotation mark. Question marks are placed inside the quotation mark if only the quotation is a question. Question marks are placed outside the quotation mark if the entire sentence is a question.

  He asked, "Is the report collated?" (Only the quotation is a question.)
  Did he ask, "Is the report collated"? (The entire sentence is a question.)
  Tu said, "The report is completed."

SIMILAR-SOUNDING WORDS

The following words are similar in pronunciation but have different meanings. Become familiar with the words, so you can spell and use them properly.

accede	to give consent
exceed	too much; go beyond
accept	to take
except	everything but
adapt	to fit for new use
adept	proficient
adopt	to take as a member of a family; to accept (to adopt a policy)
addition	an increase
edition	form in which a literary work is published
advice	suggestion (noun)
advise	to inform; to notify (verb)
affect	to influence (verb)
effect	end result (noun)
all ready	all prepared
already	before
all together	all in one place
altogether	completely
ascent	going up
assent	agreeing to
bear	an animal
bare	without covering
by	near
buy	to purchase something
canvas	coarse fabric
canvass	to ask or solicit
capital	money; seat of government of a state or country
capitol	building where the legislature meets
carat	unit of weight
caret	mark indicating that something is to be inserted
carrot	vegetable
cash	money
cache	place where supplies are hidden; temporary computer memory
cereal	food made of grain
serial	published in intervals
cite	to quote an authority
sight	something seen
site	location

consul	government official living in a foreign country
council	government body
counsel	to give advice
course	method of doing something
coarse	rough
die	to cease living
dye	to change the color
eminent	high esteem
imminent	going to happen
envelop	to surround
envelope	container for a letter
farther	additional physical distance
further	additional nonphysical distance
flour	ingredient used in baking
flower	blossom in a garden
grate	to make into small pieces, a harsh sound, a metal frame
great	wonderful
hangar	shelter for an airplane
hanger	device to hang garments on
hour	time
our	possessive of *we*
immoral	contrary to commonly accepted morals
immortal	living forever
interstate	between states
intrastate	within one state
new	recently received
knew	had knowledge of something; was certain
no	negative
know	to have knowledge of something; to be certain of
one	singular number
won	victorious
pair	two of the same type
pear	type of fruit
passed	met the goal; die
past	former time; ended; beyond
peace	tranquility
piece	part of something
personal	concerning a particular person
personnel	employees in a business
precede	to go before
proceed	to continue

principal	head of something; most important
principle	theory
right	correct
rite	ceremonial act
write	communication that is recorded; to inscribe
rode	past tense of *ride*
road	way for public or private passage
role	part that an actor takes in a play
roll	to move by turning; list of names; food
steal	to take illegally
steel	metal
stake	support for a fence; interest in a project
steak	food
stationary	not moving
stationery	paper to write on
their	possessive noun
there	place
to	preposition meaning direction
too	in addition
two	number
vary	to change
very	complete, as in *very happy*
wait	to stay in one place; inactive
weight	unit of measure
waive	to give up claim
wave	to move back and forth
ware	manufactured item
wear	to have on as a garment
where	in or at a place
weather	atmospheric conditions
whether	if that is the situation

Frequently Misspelled Words

The following are lists of frequently misspelled words.

List 1

accidentally
acquittal
admissible
alphabetize
ambivalent
believable
beginning
bicycle
constituent
contagious
disbursement
delegation
description
eliminate
etiquette
facsimile
government
haphazard
interrupting
innovation
jewelry

knowledgeable
license
library
maintenance

List 2

assistance
bequeath
bulletin
calendar
carte blanche
chronicle
despondent
disappointment
entrepreneur
expense
independent
influence
management
municipal
ninth
noticeable
official
opponent
optimism
ostensible
peculiar
punctual
questionnaire
rationalize
reminisce

List 3

accountability
accreditation
additional
belligerent
beneficiary
conscious
conservation
deceive
defendant
dessert
disappear
economize
electronic
foreign
forty
genuine
guarantee
height
inevitable
occurred
outfitted
particular
perception
realization
reciprocate

List 4

adherence
advertisement
benevolence
bizarre
cancellation
capitalize
ceremony
decision
deficiency
disseminate
embarrass
endurance
flamboyant
flexible
gratuitous
guidance
habitually
movable
oblivious
observance
perpetual
personality
persuasion
rendezvous
renovate

List 5

ambiguous
antagonize
appreciation
bankruptcy
benefitted
bureaucracy
deliverance
demonstrate
embassy
embezzle
emphasize
identical
impatient
judgment
liquidate
litigation
occurrence
ordinarily
residence
reversible
sabbatical
satellite
satisfied
saturate
severance

List 6

apprehension
arbitration
architect
depreciation
despicable
encumbrance
ethical
exaggerate
friendship
frivolous
grammar
grievous
ledger
leisure
manuscript
mysterious
recommendation
reconcile
reimbursement
representative
similar
simultaneous
technical
telecommunications
utility

List 7

believe
boulevard
clientele
commence
compensation
competitive
destructible
development
dilemma
exception
extravagance
familiar
feasibility
harmonious
hindrance
lieutenant
likelihood
nineteenth
ninety
numerical
requisition
restaurant
tangible
transmittal
vicinity

List 8

absenteeism
arrogant
attorney
autonomous
brochure
compliant
congratulate
conscientious
continuity
correspondent
deceitful
deference
discretionary
enthusiastic
environment
facilitate
fascinating
friend
guardian
humorous
hypocrisy
regrettable
relevant
replaceable
zealous

List 9

abandoned
accelerated
accessible
accommodation
acquaintance
affidavit
affluent
equipped
extraordinary
improbable
insolvency
itinerary
jeopardize
justifiable
obvious
occasionally
perquisite
proprietor
prosecution
rescind
ridiculous
sincerity
sophisticate
specialize
transferred

List 10

amateur
character
eighth
eliminate
execute
illegible
immediately
inventory
malicious
mediocre
merger
necessary
neighbor
nuisance
perseverance
prosperous
psychology
statistical
strategy
subpoena
substantial
useful
vacillate
weird
Xerox

List 11

abdicated
abeyance
abhorrent
analysis
annoyance
applicable
approximately
endorsement
erroneous
February
interfered
interrupt
irrevocable
minimize
miscellaneous
mischievous
misdemeanor
negation
pamphlet
precede
predominance
souvenir
successor
sufficient
suspicious

List 12

absence
advantage
advise
agenda
arbitrary
argument
assignment
barricade
council
counsel
credibility
criticism
monopolize
mortgage
occurring
omitted
organize
remembrance
secretary
seize
separate
stationery
subsidy
sympathy
synonymous

List 13

anecdote
autumn
cafeteria
camouflage
changeable
collateral
congratulate
contribution
controlling
generation
geographic
germane
glossary
gorgeous
gubernatorial
legislation
lethargic
liaison
logistics
longevity
sympathize
transparent
tremendous
triplicate
waiver

Cities and States

Cities in the United States

Akron, Ohio
Albuquerque, New Mexico
Amarillo, Texas
Anaheim, California
Anchorage, Alaska
Atlanta, Georgia
Baltimore, Maryland
Baton Rouge, Louisiana
Birmingham, Alabama
Boston, Massachusetts
Buffalo, New York
Charlotte, North Carolina
Chattanooga, Tennessee
Chicago, Illinois
Cincinnati, Ohio
Cleveland, Ohio
Columbus, Ohio
Corpus Christi, Texas
Dallas, Texas
Denver, Colorado
Detroit, Michigan
El Paso, Texas
Honolulu, Hawaii
Houston, Texas
Indianapolis, Indiana
Jacksonville, Florida
Kansas City, Missouri
Knoxville, Tennessee
Lexington, Kentucky
Los Angeles, California
Louisville, Kentucky
Madison, Wisconsin
Memphis, Tennessee
Miami, Florida
Milwaukee, Wisconsin
Minneapolis, Minnesota
Nashville, Tennessee
New Orleans, Louisiana
Newark, New Jersey
Norfolk, Virginia
Oklahoma City, Oklahoma
Omaha, Nebraska
Philadelphia, Pennsylvania
Phoenix, Arizona
Pittsburgh, Pennsylvania
Portland, Oregon
Raleigh, North Carolina
Rochester, New York
Sacramento, California
San Antonio, Texas
San Diego, California
San Francisco, California
San Jose, California
Seattle, Washington
Shreveport, Louisiana
Spokane, Washington
St. Louis, Missouri
St. Petersburg, Florida
Syracuse, New York
Tampa, Florida
Toledo, Ohio
Tucson, Arizona
Tulsa, Oklahoma
Wichita, Kansas

Cities in Canada

Calgary, Alberta
Edmonton, Alberta
Halifax, Nova Scotia
Montreal, Quebec
Toronto, Ontario
Vancouver, British Columbia
Windsor, Ontario
Winnipeg, Manitoba

Index

C

D

E

F

G

H

I

J

K

L

M

N

O

P

Q

R

S

T

U

V

W

Y

Z